REGAINING PARADISE

REGAINING PARADISE

Milton and the eighteenth century

DUSTIN GRIFFIN

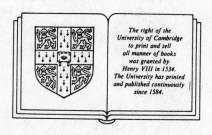

The right of the
University of Cambridge
to print and sell
all manner of books
was granted by
Henry VIII in 1534.
The University has printed
and published continuously
since 1584.

CAMBRIDGE UNIVERSITY PRESS

Cambridge

New York   New Rochelle   Melbourne   Sydney

Published by the Press Syndicate of the University of Cambridge
The Pitt Building, Trumpington Street, Cambridge CB2 1RP
32 East 57th Street, New York, NY 10022, USA
10 Stamford Road, Oakleigh, Melbourne 3166, Australia

First published 1986
Reprinted 1987

Printed in Great Britain at
the University Press, Cambridge

British Library cataloguing in publication data
Griffin, Dustin
Regaining paradise : Milton and the eighteenth
century.
1. Milton, John, *1608–1674* – Influence
2. English poetry – 18th century – History and
criticism
I. Title
821'.5'09   PR3588

Library of Congress cataloguing in publication data
Griffin, Dustin H.
Regaining paradise.
Bibliography: p.
Includes index.
1. Milton, John, 1608–1674 – Influence. 2. English
literature – 18th century – History and criticism.
3. Influence (Literary, artistic, etc.) I. Title.
PR3588.G75   1986   821'.4   85-17103

ISBN 0 521 30913 1

WS

For Jenny and Matt

Publication of this book has been aided by a grant from the Abraham and Rebecca Stein Faculty Publications Fund of New York University, Department of English.

CONTENTS

CONTENTS

PREFACE

A number of studies have been written since the early part of this century on Milton's reception, reputation, and influence. Many readers will come to this book with some knowledge of R. D. Havens' *The Influence of Milton on English Poetry* (1922), if not of the work by George Sherburn, J. W. Good, Ants Oras, W. R. Parker, and others. I should alert such readers at the outset that my aim in this book is not simply to update the work of my predecessors. First, I offer not an exhaustive survey of Milton's influence on eighteenth-century English literature, but some selected perspectives on those points at which Milton's influence is creative, or contributes to significant changes in outlook or sensibility. Second, my emphasis lies, properly speaking, not so much on Milton's *influence*, or in cataloging *imitations* and *debts*, as it does on eighteenth-century responses to Milton as a resource to be drawn on, re-created, transformed. Third, I do not focus on Milton's prosody and diction (Havens' primary interest), but on some deeper features and above all his myth of a lost garden.

The older kind of "influence" study, now dated and even discredited, was naively empirical. In the last fifteen years, beginning with W. J. Bate and Harold Bloom, critics and literary historians have reconsidered the ideas of "influence" and a writer's relationship to his predecessors. I am concerned to meet and oppose their arguments that Milton stifled or oppressed the writers that came after him. The record of the eighteenth century's attitudes toward Milton and its own literary achievement suggests, on the contrary, that Milton helped to stimulate some of the best poetry of the century. The picture of the eighteenth century that I draw is one of literary opportunity and freedom to draw eclectically and idiosyncratically upon received tradition. Though it may seem attractive to us to imagine that every writer's life is filled with literary anxiety, and that his relationships with his predecessors are intense, charged, and highly conflicted, I do not find this to be true of writers in the ages of Dryden, Pope, and Johnson. Indeed, I find instead a sense of detachment, friendly rivalry, and literary possibility. I attempt to re-create the shape of the literary world as it presented itself to poets during the century after Milton's death. This requires some attention to literary issues – such as the epic – that seemed important in the eighteenth century. It also involves attention to some currently underrated writers – Dennis, Watts, Akenside, John Philips, Dyer – who worked variously with Miltonic materials. The age, I suggest, was a consciously "post-Miltonic" one. But the term need not imply loss of potency or of amplitude. It may stand as a temporal marker, and as a sign of the differences between themselves and Milton that most writers in the age would have heartily insisted on.

Because I am finally concerned with major achievements, I concentrate (in Part III) on the major poets from Dryden to Cowper. Dryden, Pope, and Thomson were obvious choices. Johnson and Cowper illustrate the powerful responses, in critical biography and poetry, to Milton's personality and his theology. Although I largely limit myself to poetry and biography, I briefly consider the novel in chapters six and seven. Some readers will be disappointed not to find a discussion of Blake. I exclude him on grounds that the response of Blake to Milton is itself a very large and complex subject; that it has recently received a good deal of helpful critical attention; and that it opens up a new era – Romantic responses to Milton – that lies outside my chosen subject.

Other readers may be surprised not to find a chapter on Satan. My reading suggests that Satan was after all not very interesting to the eighteenth century, except as a polemical image in political satire, and (as in Cowper) as a figure for the damned and lost soul. On the whole Satan is not problematic for the eighteenth century – and thus not attractive. Johnson, untroubled, says simply that Satan speaks and acts as you would expect the devil to act. Some critics such as Dryden claimed Satan to be the hero of the poem, but only in the technical sense that, in the short run, he triumphs. Mid-century critics found Satan sublime, but primarily arousing terror, not admiration.

It is a pleasure to record here my own debts (and hope they may be thought of as creative responses). Thanks go first to Thomas Edwards, Jean Hagstrum, J. Paul Hunter, Maynard Mack, and Earl Miner, who encouraged and supported my work at an early stage. I thank Robert Hume, William McClung, John Richetti, Gardner Stout, and especially Paula Backscheider for generously responding to inquiries. I thank Douglas Canfield, Stephen Fix, J. Paul Hunter, Anthony Low, Gordon Pradl, John Shawcross, John Sitter, and James Winn for their attentive readings of and comments on draft chapters. I am grateful to the staffs of the Bobst Library of New York University, the Butler Library at Columbia University, the New York Public Library, the Firestone Library at Princeton University, the British Library, and the Sterling and Beinecke Libraries at Yale University for their cooperation.

I am grateful to the American Council of Learned Societies for the fellowship and to New York University for the sabbatical leave in 1982–83 that largely freed me from other duties and permitted me to complete a draft of this book.

I also thank editors and publishers for permission to use or reprint materials previously published elsewhere. Milton's poems have been quoted from the edition by Merritt Hughes (New York, 1957), his prose, where possible, from the Yale edition (*Complete Prose Works*), and where necessary from the Columbia edition of the *Works*, 18 vols. (New York, 1931–38). For convenience of reference I have cited much eighteenth-century reaction to Milton from John Shawcross's *Milton: The Critical Heritage*, 2 vols. (London, 1970, 1972). Dryden's poems, plays, and prose are quoted where possible from the California edition; I have occasionally had to cite his prose from George Watson's *Of Dramatic Poesy and other Critical Essays*, 2 vols. (London, 1962). Pope is quoted from the Twickenham edition, Thomson from *The Seasons*, ed. James Sambrook (Oxford, 1981). Passages from Johnson are taken from the Yale edition. Cowper is quoted, where possible, from the recent Oxford English Texts editions by James King and Charles Ryskamp (1979), and John Baird and Charles Ryskamp (1980), and Collins from the Oxford English Texts edition by Richard Wendorf and Charles Ryskamp (1979).

Portions of this book have appeared earlier in different forms. One section of chapter four appeared, in different form, as "Milton and the Decline of Epic in the 18th Century," *New Literary History*, 14 (1982), 143–54. Parts of chapters six and seven are based on "The Bard of Cyder-Land: John Philips and Miltonic Imitation," *Studies in English Literature*, Summer 1984. A large part of chapter twelve first appeared as "Cowper, Milton, and the Recovery of Paradise," *Essays in Criticism*, 31 (1981), 15–26.

INTRODUCTION

Most twentieth-century accounts of Milton's influence on the eighteenth century suggest that it was on the whole a baleful one. Harold Bloom's dramatic and colorful hyperbole is but one recent rendering of the conventional wisdom: "Milton is the great Inhibitor, the Sphinx who strangles even strong imaginations in their cradles." He is the "central problem in any theory and history of poetic influence in English."[1] Bloom's theory of the influence of "strong" poets like Milton has provoked much controversy, though he was perhaps in part only elaborating what a few hostile critics had been saying of Milton for fifty years. As early as 1926, in a study of Keats, Middleton Murry asserted that

To be influenced beyond a certain point by Milton's art...dammed the creative flow of the English genius in and through itself. To pass under the spell of Milton is to be condemned to imitate him. It is quite different with Shakespeare. Shakespeare baffles and liberates; Milton is perspicuous and constricts.[2]

And though T. S. Eliot took issue with the severity of Murry's statement, he accepted the substance of it. Eliot himself had once deplored the "Chinese Wall of Milton's blank verse" which allegedly descended on English poets of the eighteenth century, and in a 1936 essay darkly observed that "there is more of Milton's influence in the badness of the verse of the eighteenth century than of anybody else's."[3] By 1947 Eliot tempered his view, though he still declared that Milton had inhibited aspiring poets: "Milton made a great epic impossible for succeeding generations."[4] *Comus*, he had pronounced earlier, is "the death of the masque."[5] Great poets must remain silent because they do not wish to imitate; only the second-rate continue to produce faint echoes of Milton's manner. Like Eliot, Leavis too dismisses "the conventional poetizing of the meditative – melancholic line of versifiers who drew their inspiration so largely from the minor poems of Milton."[6]

The most comprehensive argument for Milton's bad influence is found, ironically, in R. D. Havens' *The Influence of Milton on English Poetry* (1922), the pioneering work that firmly established that eighteenth-century writers knew, admired, and imitated Milton almost continuously. Openly unsympathetic to what he calls the regularity and narrowness of "neo-classicism," Havens finds Milton a force for liberation, especially in diction and prosody. Yet unhappily, in Havens'

1

view, Milton's diction proved to be "a dangerous model for mediocre bards who were dealing with prosaic themes." The freedom offered by blank verse was likewise "fatal to mediocrity."[7] The influence of *Paradise Lost*, he laments, "was unquestionably away from simple directness and towards the high-sounding and the elaborate" (p. 67). For Havens, eighteenth-century writers show little of the "complexity and subtlety of influence" (p. 88) that characterize the Romantic poets, his own literary heroes.[8]

Modern judgments about Milton's bad influence then are in part the consequence of a generally low estimate of much eighteenth-century verse common in the first half of this century. In the light of the upward revaluation of eighteenth-century poetry during the last thirty years, we are in a position to see that Milton may in fact have contributed positively to the special character of eighteenth-century literature. We now need to re-examine freshly what eighteenth-century writers *said* about the challenge of past greatness and what they *did* with Milton's work. My argument, most broadly, is that Milton offered to the eighteenth century a wide range of literary possibilities. While, admittedly, second-rate writers seized on superficial or merely technical features of Milton's works, his blank verse prosody or octosyllabic measure, his Latinate diction or his inverted syntax, greater writers saw deeper and found inspiration in Milton's great myth of a lost garden of innocence, in his recurrent and related themes of freedom, choice, and responsibility, his celebration of marriage, his defiant stance against his detractors. Without much exaggeration one might even say that Milton as it were set the poetic agenda for the century. Thus contrary to Havens, Eliot, and Bloom, we must conclude that ultimately Milton's influence on the major English writers from Dryden to Johnson and Cowper was a creative one. Much of the best work in the period was in several senses a *response* to Milton. The eighteenth-century literary landscape would look very different – and, I would argue, a good deal poorer – without him.

Why should Milton have provoked such a powerful response? For any writer born after Pope (b. 1688) it was in fact not possible to ignore Milton, not possible to proceed as if he had not written. As a formidable presence in recent English history and in English culture, Milton no less than Newton *demanded* the muse. By 1700 he had become part of the English writer's tradition, part of the very literary air he breathed, and the language in which he had to write. To use an old term recently given fresh currency, he possessed authority. The source of that authority, in the eyes of eighteenth-century writers, was not what Milton thought it was – scriptural grounding and the inspiration (quite literally) of a "heavenly muse."[9] It lay rather in Milton's mastery of the highest literary forms, and in his comprehensive and compelling synthesis of disparate traditions, native and European, Christian and classical, Reformation Protestant and medieval Catholic. Though his materials were traditional – the ancient themes of temptation, of proud rebellion, the narrative pattern of innocence, fall, and recovery – it was Milton who gave them paradigmatic form. For the eighteenth century he became a modern classic, and England's national poet.

Unlike earlier classics and national poets, Milton for the eighteenth century was a giant of the *recent* past. He was not so separated by time and by cultural change as were the ancients in the eyes of Dante and Petrarch, or even as was Chaucer, two hundred years after his death, in the eyes of Spenser and the Renaissance.[10] A little more than three-quarters of a century separated the births of Milton and Pope. Milton was to Pope, as Spenser was to Milton, and Ariosto to Spenser, a past master in a living tradition. This status created special pressures as well as opportunities: as a near-contemporary, Milton presented a sharper challenge to emulators and rivals than, say, Homer did to Pope. But Milton's nearness also meant that a poet need not laboriously recover and reconstruct the Miltonic heritage, as Dante had to recover Virgil. Though accessible, Milton was also sufficiently remote to a writer born after 1700 that he was seen as a representative of an earlier "age," born "before the Flood" of the English Civil War and its attendant cultural change. He was sufficiently alien in his republican political principles, his almost unworldly moral character, and his links to a lost literary world of Renaissance fabling, that he in some ways had to be "translated" in order to be used in the eighteenth century. Indeed, the best literary uses of Milton in the period were those that acknowledged both his greatness and his difference, his pastness.

Acknowledging Milton's greatness, however, seems not to have induced in eighteenth-century writers any distress or anxiety. Nor do their acknowledgements – indeed, their assertions – of his difference spring from an Oedipal need to define themselves as distinct from a father. Viewed historically, as a writer of an earlier age, Milton inhabited a world that was unlike the social and political world they inhabited, and that they by and large chose to describe. Viewed ahistorically, as a fellow writer, Milton's rich literary harvest hardly prevented other poets from laboring in another part of the same vineyard. His achievement did not lessen their opportunities. Indeed, in some ways it increased them, for his work was now available, through imitation and allusion, for their use.

Imitation and allusion are two of the main means by which a poet records, and a reader registers, Milton's presence. It is worthwhile to be clear, at the outset, about what these terms mean, and to note that their use need not be the mark of a derivative poetry. As we are recently more aware, allusion and imitation, familiar concepts in modern literary history and criticism, are complex terms covering a range of different literary responses. It has long been commonplace to say that Renaissance and neo-classical writers set out to imitate their classical predecessors, in part because they represented the best models, in part because Homer and nature were the same. But recent scholars have distinguished several imitative strategies in Renaissance writers, from the merely "reproductive" or reiterative to those which advertise both their derivation and their distance from a subtext, or even offer criticism or rivalry.[11] In the eighteenth century it is only the third-rate writers who are content to reproduce Milton by imitating the superficial features of his style or by working in the same genres without rethinking generic conventions. The greater writers typically recognize their differences from Milton, and turn those differences to advantage.

"Allusion," likewise, has been widely used, at least since Reuben Brower's *Alexander Pope: The Poetry of Allusion*, to designate a mode of invoking a classical past or a wider European context. But allusion needs to be defined carefully, as a conscious and deliberate process of reference or memory, intended to be recognized by the literate reader. It should be distinguished from at least two related phenomena, what has been called echo, and what might plainly be called theft. The eighteenth-century poet who makes seemingly unconscious use of Milton's language, meter, or materials, may be said to *echo* Milton. For my purposes, this phenomenon is perhaps an interesting aspect of psycho-aesthetics. It says something about the ways in which Milton has pervaded the literary culture and the generative imagination of a given writer. Such echoes, however, will have little *critical* significance, and do not register as more than unacknowledged responses to Milton. Theft, by contrast, implies that the poet is aware of his Miltonic source, but that he conceals it from his reader, and seeks to prevent Milton from entering the reader's mind. Only in allusion proper, with which I am most concerned, does the poet acknowledge both to himself and to his reader his use of Miltonic materials. For it is only if imitation is acknowledged that the poet can be said to respond deliberately and publicly to his predecessor.[12]

Miltonic allusion, in its proper sense, can furthermore have different purposes. As critics and editors have long noted, allusions to an Edenic past can provide a standard by which to measure a fallen present, just as allusions to Horace's Sabine villa can suggest a kind of civilization toward which a poet aspires. Allusions to Satan can endow a villain with mythical resonance. Allusion may be systematic, invoking substantial parts of a predecessor text (though I think it rarely is, apart from poems like Pope's *Imitations of Horace*) or local, suggesting a single analogy, or merely providing a sophisticated kind of literary pleasure for well-read readers. More recently we have focused attention on the way in which allusion may enact a poet's tribute to a predecessor, or may acknowledge kinship, or claim a place in a tradition.[13]

For my purposes the most interesting allusions to Milton are those in which a poet appropriates a Miltonic text in order at once to declare affinity and distance. The most obvious examples are the well-known eighteenth-century mock-epics and other Miltonic parodies. Though I will comment on *Absalom and Achitophel*, *The Splendid Shilling*, *The Rape of the Lock*, and *The Dunciad*, I am more concerned to direct attention to the ways in which this allusive or imitative strategy operates widely in various eighteenth-century poetic genres, enabling writers to acknowledge Milton as a master and to make creative use of his work.

An account of eighteenth-century literary responses to Milton appropriately begins with Milton the man. In his 1947 essay on Milton, Eliot wrote that "of no other poet is it so difficult to consider the poetry simply as poetry, without our theological and political dispositions, conscious and unconscious, inherited or acquired, making an unlawful entry."[14] Given his critical principles, Eliot clearly would find intrusions from a poet's history and opinions "unlawful," and would seek to keep man and poet separate. But readers in the eighteenth century thought otherwise. Milton influenced eighteenth-century literary culture as much through the force of his personality, his opinions and actions in public life, and the shape of his career, as through his published poems. To an extent that we have perhaps not properly recognized, eighteenth-century readers were accustomed to read poetry biographically. Johnson, who loved above all else "the biographical part of literature," was representative of those many critics, editors, and literary biographers in his age who, in considering the "various merits" of the English poets, turned naturally to examine "the niceties of their characters, and the events of their progress through the world."[15] This seems to have been especially true of Milton, perhaps because so much more was known about his life (as opposed to Shakespeare, for example, or even Dryden), perhaps because his life was inwoven with the public life of the nation like that of no English poet before him. Nowadays we tend to follow Eliot's lead in separating man and poet, and too often assume, without looking carefully, that the history of Milton criticism in the eighteenth century shows that Johnson and his contemporaries did the same. It is true that some eighteenth-century admirers of Milton's poetry deplored his politics, morals, or theology, but they thought such matters were relevant. They tended to keep all of the man in view, and to notice links we now tend to dismiss between the historical figure and his works.

Milton clearly thought such links worth remarking, and is perhaps himself in part responsible for the habit of reading his poems in the context of his personal and political life. He published forthright apologetic accounts of himself in the *Defense of the English People* and other tracts, works widely known and extensively quoted by Milton's eighteenth-century biographers from Toland to Hayley. He published sonnets in which he dramatized his own struggles during the Civil War period, and commented proudly on the role he had played in the defense of freedom. And the blind poet expressed himself feelingly and personally in the famous proems to Books I, III, VII, and IX of *Paradise Lost*, lines that eighteenth-century commentators did not hesitate to read biographically.[16] These proems were among the century's favorite Miltonic lines. As Johnson wrote, "perhaps no passages are more frequently or more attentively read than those extrinsick paragraphs."[17]

Other factors too would have contributed to a biographical reading. Eighteenth-century editions of Milton's works regularly included a biography by the editor, from Edward Phillips in 1694 and Elijah Fenton in 1725 to Johnson in 1780. Popular "Lives" such as Toland's (1698) and Newton's (1749), which originally appeared with Milton's works, were frequently reprinted in later editions by other editors. Throughout the century Milton's editor-biographers quoted, corrected, and supplemented their predecessors, and kept a composite image of Milton before the reader's eye. To construct that image editors referred indiscriminately to life and to art.

Milton's poems were used to illustrate his life, but his life – more than has been noticed – was also used to gloss the poems. Editors throughout the century regularly found reflections of Milton's life in the major poems. One common example is Eve's apology to Adam in Book X of *Paradise Lost*:

> [she] with tears that ceased not flowing,
> And tresses all disordered, at his feet
> Fell humble, and embracing them, besought
> His peace.   (X. 910–13)

Jonathan Richardson is the first of several commentators to see in these lines a "copy" of the pathetic scene in which Milton's first wife suddenly returned to beg his forgiveness.[18] Thomas Newton prints Thyer's note to the description of Adam and Eve's spontaneous devotions (*Paradise Lost*, IV. 736): "Here Milton expresses his own favorite notions of devotion, which, it is well known, were very much against any thing ceremonial."[19] William Hayley suggests that the recollection of having been deluded by Cromwell "inspired the poet with his admirable apology for Uriel deceived by Satan."[20]

Not surprisingly, *Samson Agonistes* was often read as a thinly disguised reflection of Milton's own life. Thyer notes that "it is suppos'd, with probability enough, that Milton chose Samson for his subject, because he was a fellow sufferer with him in the loss of his eyes."[21] When Samson laments his blindness, Newton remarks that "Here Milton in the person of Samson describes exactly his own case. He could not have written so well but from his own feelings and experience."[22] Hayley found that "the lot of Milton had a marvellous coincidence with that of his hero" with respect both to his marriage and his great change of fortune.[23] Biographical readings of particular passages are increasingly common in the latter part of the eighteenth century in the notes of Hayley, Dunster, and Thomas Warton, but they begin with the earlier commentators, Richardson, Upton, Heylin, Warburton, and Newton.[24]

A final factor from the critical climate which may have encouraged eighteenth-century readers to conflate the man and the poet is the popularity of Longinus, and of the Longinian conception of the sublime poet as a "noble soul." The first and most important source of the sublime, Longinus says in chapter nine of his treatise, is greatness of mind, and a capacity for "Elevation of Thought": "The Sublime is an Image reflected from the inward Greatness of the Soul."[25] Milton was of course the great example to the century of the sublime poet, and as Hayley put it, "although sublimity is the predominant characteristic of Milton's poem, his own personal character is still more sublime." Milton's poetry, he asserts, "may be regarded both as the offspring and the witness of his virtues." Thus distinctions between the man and the poet are arbitrary: "there is a striking resemblance between the poetical and moral character of Milton."[26]

Again, it is Milton himself who encouraged an integrative view. In the *Second Defense*, surveying his early career, in words often quoted by eighteenth-century editors and biographers,[27] Milton wrote of his devotion to liberty and to its "three species" which are "essential to the happiness of social life" – religious, domestic, and civil freedom – and of the works he had written "to the promotion of real and substantial liberty." Eighteenth-century commentators implicitly build on Milton's own foundation when they describe him as the defender – and poet – of freedom in all its forms, religious, domestic, civil, and literary. For Toland, *Paradise Lost* is essentially a political statement: "to display the different Effects of Liberty and Tyranny" is the "chief design" of the poem.[28] For Henry Felton and numerous others, Milton is "the Assertor of Poetic Liberty, and would have freed us from the Bondage of Rhyme."[29]

To recover the eighteenth century's picture of Milton, then, we will have to ignore Eliot's implicit caution. We cannot otherwise understand the powerful responses in the period to Milton's life and art. For some few, it is true, Milton was simply a great poet and a bad man. But for most, including the great writers of the century, Milton's devotion to "liberty," his public righteousness, and his profound Christian faith helped shape their responses to the great poems.

PART I

England's Milton

Greece, sound thy Homer's, Rome, thy Virgil's name,
But England's Milton equals both in fame.

> Selvaggi's 1645 distich, translated by William
> Cowper, *Latin and Italian Poems of Milton*,
> ed. William Hayley (London, 1808), p. 3

1 · MILTON'S POLITICS

Because he played a highly visible role as apologist for the Puritan Revolution and for Cromwell's government, because he was polemical and outspoken, and because he appealed to the highest principles, Milton's politics, like his poetry, demanded an eighteenth-century response. Most modern readers have mistakenly assumed that the century's response was essentially hostile, and that Johnson's *Life of Milton*, the most influential eighteenth-century account of Milton's politics, accurately represents the age's suspicions and resentments. A few modern scholars have gone to the opposite extreme and claimed that Milton was an eighteenth-century Whig and "Commonwealthsman" hero.[1] Misled by these minority and extremist reactions, modern readers have heard almost nothing about the broad middle range of eighteenth-century opinion; most eighteenth-century readers found it difficult simply to dismiss or to embrace Milton's politics. Some called for toleration of an honest difference of opinion; some attempted to make Milton a founding father of modern constitutional government; some assigned him the special (and limited) role of visionary.

What is common to the whole range of responses, from hostility to idealization, is the sense that the political Milton is both near to and distant from their world. Near, because his political principles remained very much alive, provocative, challenging. Distant, not only because Milton lived in an earlier age, but also because he seemed to stand apart and judge the world of everyday politics. Distant and near, Milton helped the post-Miltonic world to define itself politically.

One prominent and enduring tradition defined itself by wholly rejecting Milton and denouncing him as "a notorious Traytor" who "most impiously and villainously bely'd that blessed Martyr King Charles the First."[2] This reaction, common before 1700,[3] can be found throughout the eighteenth century. It focuses narrowly on the same themes: king-killer, servant to a usurper. Its characteristic notes are curtness, intemperance, and (up to about 1750) a sentimentalized royalism. One defender of absolute royal sovereignty still thought it necessary in 1703 to denounce the "Prodigious *Subtlety*" of this "Cursed ENEMY of KINGS" and to "Expose" Milton's name "to the *Scorn*, and *Abhorrence* of all *Honest Men*."[4] In 1718 Milton appeared as one of 365 "Hellish Saints" in *The History of King-Killers*, a sensationalized

11

compilation of brief lives "Published for the Consolation of the Sancti-
fied Tribe of Blood-Thirsty Republicans and for the information of true
Christians and sincere Lovers of Monarchy."[5] At mid-century the
Critical Review reveals that bitter feelings remained strong. What the
Review and most other hostile observers cannot forgive is Milton's public
defense of the "murder" of the king, and his service to the "usurper":

> Milton insulted the ashes of his murdered king with calumny and reproach; and,
> with all his professed attachment to the natural rights of mankind, acted as
> secretary to the usurper and tyrant Cromwell, who destroyed the liberties, and
> trampled upon the constitution, of his country.[6]

In the popular *Biographica Britannica* (1760) Milton appears as a
hypocrite. His principles are "guilded [sic] with the specious name of
the love of absolute liberty," and yet he found himself able to support
Cromwell in his dictatorial role as Protector: "This part of our author's
conduct is perhaps the least defensible of any... abjectly crouching to
wear the yoke of slavery, and even licking the hand that put it on. Here
his boasted resolution not to do a mean thing failed him."[7]

At the end of this tradition comes Johnson's famous attack in 1779
on the "acrimonious and surly republican" whose principles were
"founded in an envious hatred of greatness, and a sullen desire of
independence; in petulance impatient of controul, and pride disdainful
of superiority."[8] Johnson's words are more systematic and more
psychologically searching than those of Milton's earlier enemies; and
his hostile analysis of Milton's republicanism is not founded on any
sentimental reverence for Charles the Martyr. By this time, however,
the tradition of denunciation is nearly played out. Outraged reactions
to Johnson's "Life" show that many of his countrymen took a much
less partisan view. It is arguable that Johnson's biography, like so many
of his other critical works, was written not to endorse a traditional view
but to refute popular opinions Johnson thought foolish or dangerous.[9]

Much more common than denunciation, particularly among
Milton's biographers, was the view that Milton, even if misguided, at
least *thought* he was fighting for a good cause. Though one cannot support
Milton's principles, one can at least, in this view, give him credit for
sincerity and disinterestedness. John Aubrey sounds this theme as early
as 1681: "Whatever he wrote against Monarchie was out of no animosity to the King's person, or out of any faction, or Interest, but out
of a pure zeall to the Liberty of Mankind, which he thought would be
greater under a free state than under a Monarchall government."[10]
The so-called Anonymous Biographer in the 1680s likewise declares
Milton acted from "Sincerity" and "higher Principle," without "self
Interest," "Animosity," or "private ends."[11] Another apologist, the

Reverend Elijah Fenton, Pope's collaborator and the author of a brief biography of Milton in 1725, speaks undisguisedly as a defender of an establishment that Milton threatened:

far be it from me to defend, his engaging with a Party combin'd in the destruction of our Church and Monarchy. Yet, leaving the justification of a misguided sincerity to be debated in the Schools, may I presume to observe in his favor, that his Zeal, distemper'd and furious as it was, does not appear to have been inspirited by self-interested Views.[12]

A more partisan biographer, Jonathan Richardson, shares Fenton's principles and asks his reader to indulge or tolerate Milton's mistaken opinion and "Erroneous Conscience," but goes further and urges that Milton be viewed as a self-sacrificing patriot:

Consider *Milton* as a *Briton*, and a *Brave One too*, and One who sacrific'd More than Most of us will Care to do, and Ventur'd Still More in the Cause of Civil and Religious Liberty, as he Thought, though upon Principles, and in a Manner, as You and I are Far from Approving. be [sic] That to God and his Own Conscience.[13]

Some fifteen years later the Reverend Thomas Newton adopted what was becoming a conventional view and conventional rhetorical tactics. He admires the poetry and wishes to avoid condemning (or approving) the politics. To avoid passing judgment he reports what Milton *thought* he was doing. The tactic may have been inspired by early biographers, who often quoted without comment from Milton's own autobiographical defenses.[14] Newton notes that in his controversial writings, "Whatever others of different parties may think, he thought himself an advocate for true liberty."[15]

By a second familiar tactic, Newton, like Richardson before him, approves the cause but implicitly questions the means: "the darling passion of his soul was the love of liberty; this was his constant aim and end, however he might be mistaken in the means."[16] By this tactic Newton, like other defenders of Milton, could apologize for alleged inconsistencies in his political conduct. Thus he suggests that Milton did not serve in the Civil War (detractors suggested hypocrisy as the reason) because he thought he was of more service to his country with the pen than the sword. He served under Cromwell not because he was a mere time-server, but because he thought Cromwell was "the only person who could rescue the nation from the tyranny of the Presbyterians."[17]

By a third tactic Milton is placed among the republicans of Greece and Rome. This ploy at once removes him from an uncomfortable English context and confers honor by associating him with classical heroes: "He was a thorough republican, and in this thought like a Greek or Roman, as he was very conversant with their writings.''[18] Richardson had used the same tactic: '' 'tis Certain he was a Republican: So was *Cato*, So was *Brutus*, So was *Phocion*, *Aristides*. – Such were by Much the Most of the Greatest Names of Roman and Greek Antiquity.''[19] And Toland praised the *Defense of the English People* for "equalling the old *Romans* in…their highest Notions of Liberty.''[20] To be sure, political writers in the seventeenth and eighteenth centuries commonly cited classical republicans as examples or models, but in Milton's case classical precedent serves not to adorn abstract argument about "liberty" or civic virtue but to remove the opprobrium of 1649.

It is clear then that a liberal, tolerant view of Milton's politics was established by 1750. William Hayley, whose sympathetic *Life* (1794; 2nd edn, 1796) has sometimes been thought to presage a new Romantic revaluation of Milton, in fact was relying on popular eighteenth-century views. Milton, he argues, may have mistaken "the mode" of promoting the public good, but we should give him "the credit he deserves for the merit of his intention":

liberal spirits…however they disapprove or oppose the opinions of the sectary and the republican, will render honorable and affectionate justice to the patriotic benevolence, the industry, and the courage, with which Milton endeavoured to promote what he sincerely and fervently regarded as the true interest of his country. (pp. 52, 65)

Newton's edition may be said to mark the culmination of the tolerationist view of Milton's politics. It also marks the beginning of what might be called an assimilationist view: Milton is no threat to our political institutions; indeed, if he were alive today, he would support the monarchy, based as it is on 1688 Revolution principles. "Liberty" in eighteenth-century British politics, though associated with the radical Whig tradition, was seen less and less as a dangerous rallying cry and more as the foundation of the English constitution. Milton of course was the great champion of "Liberty," and his *Areopagitica* was consistently praised throughout the century.[21]

Newton called it "perhaps the best vindication, that has been published at any time or in any language, of that liberty which is the basis and support of all other liberties, the liberty of the press.''[22] In dedicating his edition of *Paradise Lost* to the Earl of Bath, Newton makes clear that Milton's defense of liberty is completely consistent with English constitutional government as practiced in mid-eighteenth-century England. Milton, he says, "would have rejoic'd in [Bath's] long, and glorious struggle in the cause of Liberty, in the cause of Your country…Your acting always upon the true Whig principles, and asserting equally the prerogatives of the crown and the privileges of the people."[23] Milton was no less than a political ancestor and ally of the reigning government.

One clear sign of his status at mid-century was the Milton monument in Westminster Abbey. Although in 1710 the Dean of Westminster had refused to allow Milton's very name to appear on a monument for the Miltonic poet John Philips in Poet's Corner, by 1737 he was respectable enough to have a monument erected in his own honor in that "venerable repository of kings and prelates." Thomas Warton reports that when Milton's bust was installed the Provost of Eton provided a Latin epitaph to "apologize" for the monument's reception. But in his lines we can see too how eighteenth-century Englishmen literally and figuratively made room for Milton in their national shrine: "Both liberty and the sacred inviolable right of the sceptre now come together...Let it be lawful, under Augustus the king, to praise Cato."[24]

At mid-century Milton is also respectable enough that his works may even be dedicated to the king himself. In his popular edition of *Paradise Lost* (1751) John Marchant anticipates an objection from his royal patron: "But perhaps, great Sir, it will be objected that Mr. Milton, the Author of this inimitable Poem, however celebrated for his great Abilities and extensive Learning, was a zealous Republican, and, consequently, a professed Enemy to Regal Government" (p. iv). Marchant grants Milton's republicanism, but argues that allowance be made for "the times he lived in" (the danger of faction, the feared threat to the "rights and liberties of the Subject"). Milton may in the mid-seventeenth century have wanted to see England governed as a republic, but if he had lived under George II, Marchant claimed effusively, he would take pleasure in seeing British rights, liberties, and privileges protected, would have enjoyed full freedom of conscience, and would have been a happy and loyal subject.

Later in the century Thomas Hollis, another defender of Milton, followed the same line. Though attacked by his contemporaries as a republican, Hollis vigorously claimed to be a defender of the Hanoverian monarchy under the Revolutionary settlement.[25] Likewise, Hollis argued that Milton was not really a republican. Rather he was, like Locke, a sort of constitutional monarchist, and a proponent of government by contract. When a king becomes a tyrant (as Charles I and James II did) the compact is broken, and power reverts to the people who may then reconstitute a new government. Milton was thus not an enemy to regal government "as such." His principles and those of the 1688 Revolution were compatible. As Hollis wrote in a 1760 letter to the Reverend Jonathan Mayhew of Boston, "It is to Milton, the divine Milton, and such as he, in the struggles of the civil war, that we are beholden for all the manifold and unexampled blessings which we now

15

everywhere enjoy.''[26] By reading Milton's politics through Lockean spectacles, as it were, Hollis and others could assimilate Milton to mainstream political thinking.

What I have called the assimilationist view was perhaps never as widespread in the period as the tolerationist, but it persisted down to the end of the century. Members of the Revolution Society at their one-hundredth anniversary meeting on November 4, 1788, apparently saw no contradiction in toasting first the liberties of the people, the king, and the royal family, and then "the Memory of Andrew Marvell, Milton, Locke, [and] the late Mr. Hollis.''[27] Hayley in 1796 finds Milton a "resolute enemy to tyrants" but a "sincere friend to such Kings as merited the benediction of their people" (he gives as example Milton's favorable treatment of Alfred in his *History of Britain*). Responding to charges that Milton's political thought is subversive, Hayley sees no cause for fear:

Can any man justly think it has such a tendency, who recollects that no government, similar to that which the Revolution established for England, existed when Milton wrote. His impassioned yet disinterested ardour for reformation was excited by those gross abuses of power, which that new settlement of the state very happily corrected.[28]

And the anonymous editor of the 1790 reprinting of Milton's *Treatise of Civil Power* identified himself as "an Englishman, a lover of liberty, his country, and its original constitution, as most nobly confirmed at the glorious revolution." This makes him, he says, a friend of Milton, who "with consistency and fortitude, maintained those principles which at present enlighten the world" (p. iii).

None of these defenders of Milton, from Richardson and Newton to Hollis and Hayley, can be said to be true republicans, who always remained a tiny minority in English political culture in the century.[29] Though few in number, republicans championed Milton with none of the equivocation or accommodation that we have seen among his more moderate defenders. At the beginning of the century, John Toland celebrated the poet as a great defender of English liberties, and implicitly endorsed Milton's own largest claims for himself: "as he look'd upon true and absolute Freedom to be the greatest Happiness of this Life, whether to Societies or single Persons, so he thought Constraint of any sort to be the utmost Misery.''[30] The edition of the prose, to which Toland's *Life* was prefixed, remained the standard work for forty years. His "Life" of Milton, from which this tribute is taken, provided materials for subsequent biographers, many of whom simply quoted Toland, and was itself republished as late as 1761.[31] This image of the Defender of Freedom was apparently a popular one. It appears, for example, in an article in *The Universal Spectator*, a loose paraphrase of Toland's own words: "Our famous *Milton* was the greatest Example which our Nation has produc'd of a Mind impatient under any Apprehension of *Slavery*; and no one has shew'd himself so zealous a Champion for that Freedom of Our *Being*, which he contended to be so essential to the Dignity of our *Species*."[32]

At mid-century another radical editor probably helped keep vivid the image of Milton as republican hero. In 1753 Richard Baron, a self-styled "lover of liberty," revised Birch's 1738 edition of Milton's prose, and as editor supplemented Birch's defense of Milton's service under Cromwell. Three years later he edited the 1650 version of *Eikonoklastes*. In his editorial preface Baron trumpeted the perennial importance of the tract, "a Work, wherein the principles of tyranny are confuted and overthrown, and all the arts and cunning of a *great Tyrant* and his adherents detected and laid open" (p. iv). Where Newton and Marchant saw themselves as pillars of orthodoxy, Baron was quite self-consciously a man in opposition to the dominant political culture of his day. His adversaries included the "pretended friends of Liberty" (p. iv) – perhaps establishment Whigs? – who apparently failed to carry their professed political principles into practice. In a brief note, he drew a contrast between Milton, who on the eve of the Restoration of the Stuarts did not give up his struggle, and Englishmen of his own day who made no effort to prevent their country's further ruin (pp. 1–2). Milton can now serve, in Baron's view, not as an implicit supporter of constitutional liberties under the Hanoverians, but as an unsullied example of pristine English love of liberty, a reminder of contemporary political decline, and a beacon in dark times, "to be read and studied by all our young Gentlemen as an Oracle."[33]

A generation later Francis Blackburne, the memoirist of Thomas Hollis, remembered Baron as "a most useful man to the cause of liberty, civil and religious,"[34] and thought a knowledge of Milton important "for instruction upon what only foundation the preservation of [our] rights and liberties depend."[35] Distribution of Milton's works could now help, Blackburne thought, "to stem the pernicious current, and apprise the men of England of their danger." He did this part by reprinting, as an appendix to his own *Remarks on Johnson's Life of Milton* (1780), Milton's "Tractate on Education" and his *Areopagitica*.[36] Milton's prose might also help the fires of liberty burn brighter, or prompt a sympathetic view of the French Revolution. Such was the hope, at any rate, of the editor of a 1791 edition of Milton's *Readie and Easie Way to Establish a Commonwealth*, who hoped that Milton might offer a "rational and satisfactory answer to the splendid sophistries of Edmund Burke...If it shall contribute, in the smallest degree, to enlarge the general stock of political information, or kindle a sentiment of liberty in the breast of an individual in the community, [the editor's] wishes will be completely fulfilld'' (pp. iii – iv).[37]

Such claims for Milton during the course of the eighteenth century are really quite rare, and his reputation as a symbol of republican ideals and resistance to tyranny, even in the French Revolutionary period, has probably been overstated.[38] So too are the fears, expressed by a few contemporaries near the end of the century, that it would be dangerous to reprint the works of so subversive a political thinker:

In point of doctrine [wrote Thomas Warton], they are calculated to annihilate the very foundations of our civil and religious establishment, as it now subsists; they are subversive of our legislature, and our species of government. In condemning tyranny [Milton] strikes at the bare existence of kings; in combatting superstition, he decries all public religion.

Milton's works, Warton concluded, present a ''system of politics'' both ''unconstitutional'' and ''Obsolete.''[39] Edward Gibbon, worried about the ''French disease'' of rebellion, likewise urged that Milton's prose works be suppressed, since their publication might be ''productive of public evil.''[40]

The best answer to such expressions of fear comes from Hayley, an admirer, as it happens, of both Warton and Gibbon. In his *Life of Milton*, dedicated to Warton, Hayley suggested that fears of subversion were probably prompted by ''panic'' in England at the Revolution in France, but more seriously that they were based on a misconception of Milton's importance for his contemporaries. Hayley's point is that Milton's fearful enemies (and implicitly his radical friends too) are mistaken in thinking that the opinions of a seventeenth-century republican can be directly applied to late eighteenth-century politics. One can admire Milton's ideals and his motives and yet recognize (perhaps reluctantly) the claims of practical reality. Milton's conduct, he elsewhere says, deserves the name of ''public virtue'' and of ''genuine patriotism,'' and yet ''his sentiments, both on ecclesiastical and civil policy, are such as the majority of our countrymen think it just and wise to reject'' (p. 65). His arguments about divorce have been thought by ''the majority of modern legislators and divines'' to be ''inconsistent with sound morality and true religion,'' and yet they may be admired for their ''pure and benevolent'' intention (p. 84).

Hayley was not the only one of his defenders to admit that Milton's political ideas are impractical.[41] Mrs. Catherine Macaulay, a popular writer whose *History of England* (1768 – 81) rehabilitated the republicans of the mid-seventeenth century, conceded that republican principles are impractical in a country ''whose laws, manners, customs, and prejudices are ill adapted to a republic."[42] And yet she publicly praises Milton, during a debate over copyright laws, for his "attempt of fixing the ideas of good government and true virtue in the minds of a wavering people."[43]

To judge by the words of his editors and biographers, then, Milton's practical impact on the political culture of eighteenth-century England was slight. They frequently regret that Milton's political works are unpopular or even unknown.[44] As Blackburne notes, Milton is "seldom quoted in our present political squabbles."[45] The exception is *Areopagitica*, perhaps the best-known of Milton's political works in the period, reprinted or adapted on several occasions when licensing acts lapsed or were renewed. Even so, it is now thought unlikely that Milton's principled arguments had much effect on the decision to end licensing in 1695.[46]

In 1772 an editor thought that "part of Milton's reasoning may appear obsolete and part unnecessary" in the present day.[47] One finds virtual silence on Milton in quarters where one might expect to hear his name invoked, whether in the Trenchard–Gordon *Cato's Letters* in the 1720s, John Wilkes' writings on English liberty in the 1760s, James Burgh's *Political Disquisitions* (1775), the *Junius Letters* (1769–72),[48] or the extraparliamentary activities of the Wilkesite London Association.[49]

Why, it might be asked, was not Milton the republican cited as often by eighteenth-century political writers as that other seventeenth-century republican, James Harrington, whom J. G. A. Pocock and others have urged us to see as a dominant force behind "Country" ideology in the eighteenth century?[50] Plausible reasons suggest themselves. First, Milton, unlike his contemporary Harrington, was indelibly associated with the still-reviled Puritan party and its particular actions in the Civil War. The eighteenth century did not forget that Milton himself had spoken up to defend the regicide of 1649, and served under Cromwell in the 1650s. Harrington, on the other hand, never played a prominent role in public life, and spoke out against the "saints" who dishonorably pretended to "civil power."[51] Milton's political writings were occasional; they responded to particular events (1649 or 1660), and justified action or proposed temporary expedients which required constitutional change (the need for a Protector under transitional conditions, for a permanent Grand Council of wise men to forestall an election of Stuart sympathizers).[52] In the eighteenth century such arguments sometimes seemed "obsolete." By contrast Harrington's *Oceana* (1656) took the form of a utopia. Though plainly calculated for England, it was in fact detachable from time and place and could be examined as a theoretical political system.[53] Thus, for all its republican purity, it did not carry the same associations as Milton's political tracts for the times. And yet curiously the utopian Harrington may have come to seem more in touch with practical politics than the occasional writer Milton.[54] For Milton political considerations are subordinate or reducible to spiritual ones, and religious liberty is the supreme value and prime end of civil government. Milton was a practical politician only to "parlor republicans" like Thomas Hollis. Unlike Harrington, Milton offered little to those eighteenth-century radicals and country gentlemen concerned with parliamentary reform, the burden of taxation, or the power and cost of the central government.[55]

Ultimately, it is Milton not Harrington who is the real utopian. Not only are Milton's theories "Obsolete" (as Warton realized); to most eighteenth-century observers they are essentially "visions," and not the proposals of a "practical statesman." Hayley compares Milton to Plato, "a writer whom Milton passionately admired, and to whom he bore, I think, in many points, a very striking resemblance."

Perhaps they both possessed too large a portion of fancy and enthusiasm to make good practical statesmen; the visionaries of public virtue have seldom succeeded in the management of dominion, and in politics it has long been a prevailing creed to believe, that government is like gold, and must not be fashioned for extensive use without the alloy of corruption.[56]

What Milton offered above all was the ideal of public virtue. Though absent from the parliamentary arena in the eighteenth century, he was lodged as an exemplary political figure in the minds of thousands of readers. Despite the reassurances of Newton and others that he would have endorsed the status quo *c*. 1750, Milton inhabited another country. As he wrote late in life to Peter Heimbach, "Patria est, ubicunque est bene," which Hayley translates "wherever we prosper in rectitude there is our country."[57] Even if he had little or no influence on particular political issues and contexts in the Age of Walpole or the Age of Pitt, he made nonetheless an extraordinary impression on his countrymen. Just as we cannot measure Milton's influence as a poet simply by compiling parallels, so we cannot measure his political "influence" by numbering republicans. Milton was politically remembered – at any rate by his biographers and editors Toland, Richardson, Newton, Hayley, and their readers – primarily as a man of sincerity, self-sacrificing, willing to put his very life on the line, a lover of liberty, and of his country. "That which you call my political virtue [*virtus politica*]," he wrote in Latin to Heimbach, "I should rather wish you to call my devotion to my country [*pietas in patriam*]."[58] He provided not a practical model upon which a king and parliament might proceed to build, not even an ideal *polis* like Harrington's, but a personal example of individual integrity and purity of motive, divorced from circumstances, and an essentially moral standard by which men might be encouraged to measure their public behavior.

2 · MILTON'S MORAL IDEALISM

As *Paradise Lost* makes unmistakably clear, politics in Milton's view is an essentially moral activity. What provides the basis for man's virtue is his freedom and responsibility to choose. The moral life, then, is made possible only in conditions of liberty. Virtue, in turn, is the only source of "true and internal liberty."[1] If Milton was intimately linked in the minds of the eighteenth century with English liberty, his sympathetic biographers tried to make his presence felt all the more strongly as an exemplar of moral integrity. But they met or anticipated resistance in their readers. Richardson concedes that Milton "was Now, and has long Since shone in the Eyes of the Generality of the World, rather as a Great Poet than as a Good Man."[2] His biography proceeds to attempt to rectify the imbalance. Half a century later Hayley still feels the need to defend Milton's character. He trusts that as Milton's life is examined "with intelligence and candour ... his virtue will become, as it ought to be, the friendly rival of his genius, and receive its due share of admiration and esteem."[3] Johnson complained about the hagiographical tone of some earlier biographies, as if Milton had become a remote icon, above criticism. But we should perhaps see the somewhat idealized portraits of Milton as polemical assertions in a continuing debate: was Milton's self-proclaimed righteousness an inspiration (and an implicit reproach), or was he no better than his fellows (and his readers)?

One biographical tradition vilified Milton's moral character. Writing to Birch in an attempt to influence his biographical presentation, Warburton condemned an earlier biographer for representing "Milton's moral character, as a member of society, to be excellent, which was certainly the most corrupt of any man's of that age."[4] In Warburton's view Milton was a time-server, willing to change his allegiance when the government changed, "without a struggle." Attacking more directly, Aaron Hill, in a letter to Samuel Richardson, wrote of Milton's "malice and wickedness." "[I]n short," Hill later observed, "he is selfish, arrogant, and revengeful; – conceited, sophistical, and odious."[5] Attacks on Milton's politics, whether they accused him of "malevolence," "malignity," "envious hatred of greatness," prostituting his pen, or "virulency" in writing against literary adversaries,[6] were essentially attacks on Milton's moral character. They began as early as the 1650s, when Milton's name was

22

defamed by Salmasius and others, and continue sporadically throughout the eighteenth century,[7] the most sensational being Lauder's charges of plagiarism in 1747 and Johnson's biography in 1779. But such attacks in fact represent a small minority of eighteenth-century opinion and aroused vigorous and outraged defenses of Milton's character.[8]

Those defenses begin with, and largely build on, Milton's own autobiographical writings in his *Defenses of the English People* and his *Defense of Himself* in the early 1650s.[9] In these defenses Milton insists repeatedly that he has "always led a pure and honourable life," and rebuts all charges of immoral conduct or unprincipled acts. His characteristic note is offended righteousness. Milton does not merely claim that he is a good man; he declares that his character is immaculate: "I am incapable of ever disgracing honorable speech by dishonorable conduct." At Cambridge, he says, he passed several years "untouched by any reproach." On his European tour he "lived free and untouched by the slightest sin or reproach."[10] He acted not out of interest, but for the glory of God, the service of virtue, and the "honour and instruction of my country."[11] He spoke sharp words not out of malice but necessity, for he felt the commandment of God to take up the trumpet, to use "those few talents which God at that present had lent me."[12] For his pains (and the loss of his eyesight) he received little or no recompense, except the best kind, "the conscience" to have served in "the noble task" of "liberty's defense" (Sonnet 22, addressed to Cyriack Skinner, lines 10–11).[13]

Milton's defenses of his own character, though written in Latin and published in the heat of rancorous and obscure controversy, were nonetheless widely available to eighteenth-century readers. They were reprinted with his prose works in the editions by Toland (1698) and Birch (1738, 1755). The *First Defense* was also translated into English by Joseph Washington in 1692 and later inserted in the Toland and Birch editions. Part of the *Second Defense* was translated in Peck's *Memoirs of the Life and Actions of Oliver Cromwell* (1740). More important, the defenses were mined by Milton's biographers and quoted at length, in English translation. Indeed, it is common practice among the biographers from Toland to Hayley (with the signal exception of Johnson) to let Milton speak for himself, and to insert extracts from the *First* and *Second Defenses* into the narrative of his life or the discussion of his character. Thus Toland says that "In the Character of Sects and Parties, Books of Opinions, I shall produce his own words, as I find 'em in his Works."[14] Richardson, citing aspersions cast at Milton's character, says that "he shall Answer for Himself. he will be forc'd to say Somthing in his Own Praise."[15]

Though Milton himself had little to say about it, even his domestic conduct – a sore point for admirers in the eighteenth century and our own – prompted thoughtful discussion and apology. As heirs to post-Miltonic ideas about the education of daughters and the status of women generally, we find repugnant the severity of Milton's relations with his family. In the eighteenth century too – when traditional ideas about women were undergoing rapid change – readers like Johnson were disturbed by Milton's "Turkish contempt of females" (*Lives*, I, 157). But biographers from the time of Richardson came to Milton's defense. Milton, as is well known, had taught his daughters to pronounce, though not to understand, several learned languages, so that they might read to him. Even Milton's nephew Edward Phillips finds the daughters must have suffered "a tryal of Patience. almost beyond endurance" (*Early Lives*, p. 77). Richardson, though troubled, asks "Whether 'tis a Fault or no" (*Early Lives*, p. 225). It was, he maintains, "done very Commonly" even in Richardson's own time. And the "Distress" of the father must be considered. Furthermore, the youngest daughter, Deborah, is said to have "Express'd no Uneasiness" about her father, and to have spoken of him "with Great Tenderness" (p. 229). Hayley, following Richardson, found the daughters "disobedient and ungrateful" (*Life*, p. 200), "utterly unworthy of their father" (p. 201). He refutes the claim, made by Newton and Johnson, that Milton did not allow his daughters to learn to write, by citing Aubrey's remark that Deborah was her father's "Amanuensis" (Hayley, p. 198, citing Aubrey, *Early Lives*, p. 2). Recognizing that there must have been pain and difficulty on both sides in this "scene of misery," even Johnson asks whether the daughters or the father "are most to be lamented" (I, 145).

Pictorial evidence too suggests that readers in the late eighteenth century found little offensive in the demands Milton placed on his daughters. Hayley's edition of Milton's *Poetical Works* (1794) includes an engraving of Romney's "Milton and his Two Daughters" (1793). Milton sits deep in thought while one daughter (apparently writing from his dictation) bends over her work and the other (apparently reading to him) raises her head, looking solicitously toward the blind poet. The scene is suffused with nobility and pathos. This is only the first of many subsequent paintings of a subject that easily lent itself to sentimental and idealized treatment.[16]

Although Milton's honesty, "purity and vigour of mind," "Temperance," and "General Love of Vertue" recur in eighteenth-century biographical accounts,[17] he seems particularly to have left his mark on their moral imaginations for two prominent traits. The first is reflected in one of the biographers' favorite and recurring images of Milton – courageous and cheerful even in adversity, or as Edward Young puts it, "nobly smiling in distress."[18] Again the source of this image is Milton himself, who in his *Defenses* and his familiar letters[19] presents himself afflicted by blindness, surrounded by adversaries, and yet encouraged to carry on through his sense of duty. In a letter to Leonard Philaras describing his blindness, for example, Milton concludes:

as under an evil that admits no cure, I regulate and tranquilize my mind... As long as [God] looks forward, and provides for me as he does, and leads me backward and forward by the hand, as it were, through my whole life, shall I not cheerfully bid my eyes keep holiday, since such appears to be his pleasure?[20]

In his later sonnets too, and in the proems to Books III and VII of *Paradise Lost*, Milton reflected on his own condition in words that gave eighteenth-century readers extraordinary pleasure. Hardly any biographer, for example, fails to quote the lines from Book VII:

> More safe I sing with mortal voice, unchang'd
> To hoarse or mute, though fallen on evil days,
> On evil days though fallen, and evil tongues;
> In darkness, and with dangers compassed round,
> And solitude; yet not alone, while thou
> Visit'st my slumbers nightly, or when morn
> Purples the east; still govern thou my song.
> (lines 24 – 30)

Richardson quotes the lines three times, and illustrates them by citing the "Affliction," the "Terror of being Assassinated," and "Melancholy Circumstances" of Milton's later career.[21] He also quotes a long extract from the *Second Defense* to show that Milton, though afflicted, found grounds for comfort and a will to persevere in his duty:

Let them Know that I neither am Sorry for, nor Repent me of my Lot; that I remain Unmov'd and Steddy in my Purpose; That I neither Feel God Almighty Angry nor Is He, but rather in the Greatest things I experience his Clemency and Fatherly Goodness towards Me.[22]

Richardson wonders how Milton had "the Courage to Undertake, and the Resolution to Persist in Such a Work [as *Paradise Lost*] with the Load of Such Difficulties upon his Shoulders! Ill Health, Blindness; Uneasy in his Mind, no doubt, on occasion of the Publick Affairs, and of his Own."[23]

Newton, who remarks that all biographers find Milton to have been "of an equal and chearful temper,"[24] annotates the famous lines from Book VII as a "lively picture" of the poet's "wretched condition":

he was blind...obnoxious to the government, and having a world of enemies among the royal party, and therefore oblig'd to live very much in privacy and alone. And what strength of mind was it, that could not only support him under the weight of these misfortunes, but enable him to soar to such highths [*sic*], as no human genius ever reached before?[25]

That Johnson felt the need to challenge this reading of the passage suggests that by 1780 it had become a commonplace of biographical interpretation. He doubts that Milton was in fact in danger and warmly censures his insolence in daring to complain of "evil tongues."[26] And yet Johnson was unable to dispel the image of Milton cheerful and determined in adversity. Hayley sharply challenges Johnson for his failure of compassion and vindicates Milton from the unjust charge. He poignantly – indeed, somewhat melodramatically – evokes a picture of the poet "concealed in an obscure corner of the city, that resounded with the triumphant roar of his intoxicated enemies" (p. 152). The editor of the 1790 edition of Milton's *Treatise of Civil Power* likewise praises the author, "who, with dangers compassed round, yet undismayed by the terrors of absolute power, the frowns of fortune, and the malignity of the times, never relinquished those principles which at present enlighten the world" (p. iii). Like his own Abdiel (the comparison became a conventional one),[27] Milton in his later years stood single to maintain "Against revolted multitudes the cause / Of truth" (*Paradise Lost*, VI. 31 – 32). This is an image that animates Wordsworth's picture of Milton in the *Prelude*, not a Romantic reinterpretation but the culmination of a century of editors and biographers:

> our blind Poet, who, in his later day,
> Stood almost single, uttering odious truth,
> Darkness before, and danger's voice behind;
> Soul awful!   (III. 284 – 87, 1805 edn)

The power and appeal of this image is that it provides a model for both passive endurance and active resistance, for meek submission and heroic assertion. Perhaps such an image has perennial appeal in western civilization, but it may have had special appeal for the eighteenth century. In a culture still strongly attracted to the pagan moralists who taught the value of mental contentment and equanimity, and still deeply imbued with Christianity which taught submission to the will of God, Milton's cheerful determination had it both ways. With Milton as model, one might serve both God and man, both obey divine will and still defend human liberty, and avoid both the "Stoic's pride" on the one hand, and debilitating religious fears and gloom on the other.

The second prominent moral trait in the eighteenth-century Milton is akin to the first, and helps to account for his cheerfulness in adversity.

A strong sense of the favor and guidance of God may perhaps underlie all else, but next to that was the satisfaction of a good conscience. Again and again Milton's biographers admiringly describe a man of conscious rectitude who took both pleasure and comfort in the purity of his motives and the honesty of his actions. Not surprisingly, Milton's own writings provide the source for this image. "What I have done," Milton wrote in the *Second Defense*, "hath, of it self, given Me a Good Conscience within, a good Esteem amongst the Good, and, with all, this Just and Honest Liberty of Speaking."[28] Elsewhere in the same work Milton declares that he "would not Exchange for any other of [God's] greatest Benefits, the Consciousness of this Action that they Reproach Me with, nor Lay down the Remembrance of it, which is a perpetual Fund to me of Tranquility and Joy."[29] A good conscience and a properly-founded self-esteem is both a pleasure in itself and an incentive to remain pure. After remarking in the *Apology for Smectymnuus* that a good poet must make himself a good poem, Milton observes that "These Reasonings, together with a certain Niceness of Nature, an Honest Haughtyness and Self-Esteem, either of what I Was, or what I Might be, (which let Envy call Pride)...kept me still above those Low Descents of Mind."[30] Despite the charge of pride, the moral man should not only esteem himself; he should revere himself: "He that holds himself in Reverence and due Esteem, both for the Dignity of God's Image upon him, and for the Price of his Redemption, which he thinks is Visibly Markt upon his Forehead, accounts himself both a Fit Person to do the Noblest and Goodliest Deeds."[31]

Virtually every biographer in the eighteenth century is struck with Milton's extraordinary self-esteem and satisfied conscience. Toland notes that Milton found his own reward largely within himself: "he gratuitously lent his Country the aid of his Pen, content with the esteem of good Men, and the internal Satisfaction of having perform'd his Duty." And in his closing account, Toland remarks that Milton "us'd frequently to tell those about him the intire Satisfaction of his Mind, that he had constantly imploy'd his Strength and Faculties in the defence of Liberty, and in a direct Opposition to Slavery."[32] Newton found this statement important enough to paraphrase it closely (without attribution) in his *Life*.[33] Bentley, in the Preface to his edition of *Paradise Lost* (1732), had picked up the same note. Marveling at Milton's ability to "abstract his Thoughts from his own Troubles" and at his "Strength of Spirit," he finds Milton a preeminent example of the animating power of conscious virtue: "*there is that Power in the Human Mind, supported with Innocence and Conscia virtus; that can make it quite shake off all outward Uneasinesses, and involve it self secure and pleas'd in its own Integrity and Entertainment.*"[34]

Richardson elaborates the theme of virtue as its own reward. Milton, he says, "never made Riches or Show his Aim...Whatever Mistaken Notions may be imputed to him, he Appears to have been Rich, and Splendid in a Consciousness of his own Integrity." Although fallen on evil days, "in the Muse was His *Joy and Crown of Rejoycing*, and in the Testimony of a Good Conscience." Milton enjoyed the esteem of good men ("he was Greatly Honour'd by Those whose Approbation is True Glory") but enjoyed the greater pleasure of his own approbation:

Above All, He had Vertue and Piety; not only an Unmolested Conscience, Unpolluted, but a strong Sense of having done his Duty, What He Conceiv'd to be So; the very Utmost the Best of Us Can do, and which Whoever Has, will believe he finds *The Spirit bearing Witness with his Spirit that he is a Child of God*. This was His Rejoycing. Whether he was in the Right or Not, Alters not the Case as to the Approbation and Exultation of his Own Mind.[35]

Once again Richardson shifts attention away from the act (of which one might wish to dispprove) to the moral agent (who glories in his own approbation). Richardson's allusions to Paul make clear that for all the reliance on human virtue Milton still owns himself a "child of God."

Hayley's biography returns again and again to the ideas of conscious integrity, self-esteem, a clear conscience, and a satisfied mind: Milton, he says, displayed "the frankness and fortitude of a noble mind, perfectly conscious of its own integrity" (*Life*, p. 80). His controversial writings confirmed in him "that well-founded and upright self-esteem, to which we are principally indebted for his sublimest productions" (p. 73):

since it was assuredly his constant aim to be the steady disinterested adherent and encomiast of truth and justice, hence we find him continually displaying those internal blessings, which have been happily called, "the clear witnesses of a benign nature," an innocent conscience, and a satisfied understanding.
(p. 158)

That "retrospect" of a life well spent, Hayley suggests elsewhere (p. 73), provided Milton the mental vigor that enabled him to complete his great poems. Self-esteem is then carried over from the moral sphere to the literary. The poet is animated by his own clear conscience to persist in the service of truth and justice. Even Johnson, who is reluctant to praise Milton's moral character, transfers the century's praise of Milton's proper self-esteem to his character as a poet: "It appears in all his writings that he had the usual concomitant of great abilities, a lofty and steady confidence in himself."[36] Largely ignoring the ground of Milton's self-confidence in his moral self-approbation, Johnson imagines Milton's reaction to the slow progress of *Paradise Lost*'s reputation. "I cannot but conceive him calm and confident, little disappointed, not at all dejected, relying on his own merit with steady consciousness, and waiting without impatience the vicissitudes of opinion and the impartiality of a future generation" (I, 144). This is a note we will hear again in Pope's late satires.

Milton's eighteenth-century biographers then clearly seek to establish him as a preeminently virtuous man. Yet one may pause to ask why – apart from the natural tendency to think well of a writer whose works one admires – a Puritan's moral character should have appealed to a broad range of eighteenth-century readers. The popular conception of the irreconcilable differences between the seventeenth-century Puritan and the eighteenth-century rationalist may of course be dismissed. We know now, as did the eighteenth century, that Puritans were not all sour,[37] that they delighted in poetry and music (as did Milton) and the pleasures of friendship and marriage. We know too that the eighteenth century (in England, at any rate) was no simple "Age of Reason," that it was still a traditionally (if not deeply) devout Christian culture. And yet some temperamental differences between the centuries remain that might have made Milton seem an alien figure in 1750. If it is broadly true that eighteenth-century Englishmen were urbane, tolerant, sensible, moderate, good-humored, suspicious of enthusiasm and excess, what might attract them to a man who refused to accommodate or adjust to the way of the world, dogmatic, extreme in his likes and dislikes, rigorous and demanding of himself and of other people, a devout enthusiast?[38] Richardson, though an ardent admirer, speaks of a "Certain Severity" in Milton's mind, a "Mind not Condescending to Little things." He is "a Man that Practises Severity on Himself in an Exact Observation of Vertue's Commands" and exacts "a like Obedience" from others.[39] In a century dominated by the Latitudinarian branch of the church, an era that nurtured the "Man of Feeling," and smiled at heroes with good hearts and lax morals, it is perhaps surprising to find Milton advanced as a moral hero. True, Milton offered an example of rectitude and self-esteem, but what of the biblical warning that one should "Be not righteous over much" (Eccles. 7. 16), on which Joseph Trapp preached a famous sermon in 1739?[40] Or what of the secular equivalent, found in Hume's polite observation that "a genuine and hearty pride or Self-esteem" must be "well-conceal'd" if we are to procure "the esteem and approbation of mankind."[41] Milton relied on his clear conscience as a moral guide and incentive. But Sterne preached a famous sermon on "The Abuses of Conscience" (on the text "For we trust we have a good conscience" – Hebrews 13. 18). "Conscience," as another literary churchman wrote, is like a "Pair of Breeches, which, tho' a Cover for Lewdness as well as Nastiness, is easily slipt down for the Service of both" (A Tale of a Tub, sec. 2).

And yet Milton seems largely to have overcome widespread eighteenth-century skepticism about loud and insistent professions of righteousness. If he did, it was perhaps because he convinced many readers that his claims for himself were justified. Even Johnson concedes that Milton lived up to his reputation. In a *Rambler* essay Johnson notes that "Milton, in a letter to a learned stranger, by whom he had been visited, with great reason congratulates himself upon the consciousness of being found equal to his character, and having preserved in a private and familiar interview that reputation which his works had procured him" (*Rambler* 14). The age that found a culture hero in Cato – Swift thought him "the wisest and best of all the Romans"[42] – might well admire a poet more than once compared to him as patriot, republican, champion of liberty, austere in his private life, an exemplar of conscious rectitude.[43] Perhaps he won other eighteenth-century admirers because his moral convictions were not simply a result of rational conclusions or an acknowledgement of duty. Milton plainly found pleasure in righteousness. Both Richardson and Hayley quote his letter to Diodati in which Milton speaks of his "intense love of moral beauty... Ceres, in the fable, pursued not her daughter with a greater keenness of inquiry, than I, day and night, the idea of perfection."[44] It is an intense pleasure both to follow virtue and to look back, as we have seen him do, on a life well spent. Did Milton's moral pleasure perhaps soften his rigor, make him even amiable? Did his innate love of virtue seem a confirmation of the "moral sense" which Hutcheson, Shaftesbury, and other moralists made the foundation of their moral systems?

There are other points of correspondence which might help explain Milton's appeal. Though they scorned "enthusiasm," Shaftesbury and his contemporaries preserved respect for genuine inspiration: "For Inspiration is a *real* feeling of the Divine Presence, and Enthusiasm a *false* one."[45] Enthusiasm was likewise to be contrasted with "true Righteousness," which William Law vigorously championed in his answer to Trapp's sermon on being "righteous over-much."[46] The manifest "sincerity" of his political, moral, and theological views would have increasingly found sympathetic readers in an age when, as Leon Guilhamet has shown, sincerity was being increasingly valued.[47] Broad church preachers like Tillotson urged their hearers "really to be what we would seem and appear to be."[48] Good actions, wrote Benjamin Hoadly, are not worthy in themselves but because they are "honestly entered into, by the dictates of our conscience."[49] Sincerity, claims a writer in the *Gentleman's Magazine* in 1736, is "the only necessary recommendation to the esteem, friendship, and communion of our fellow Christians."[50] To discover a Puritan to be sincere is also of course to aquit him of that crime of which he is often suspected, the sin of hypocrisy.

Milton's religious principles in other respects would have found favor with liberal churchmen. His insistence that "no man or body of men in these times can be the infallible judges or determiners in matters of religion to any other mens consciences but thir own"[51] corresponds to Dryden's "My Salvation must its doom receive, / Not from what OTHERS but what I believe" (*Religio Laici*, lines 303–04) and to the first principles of the Protestant faith. His insistence on toleration (for all but papists) accords with those Broadchurchmen inclined not to quarrel over points of doctrine, and with an age that embraced the spirit of Locke's *Letters on Toleration* (1689–92). Even his extraordinary self-esteem corresponds to that quality which Hume calls "heroic virtue" or "greatness and elevation of mind," founded on "a steady and well-established pride and self-esteem."[52] Hume's words might almost recall Milton's own Raphael: "oft times nothing profits more / Than self esteem, grounded on just and right / Well managed" (*Paradise Lost*, VIII. 571–73). As a moralist, Milton remained current. His "moral sentiments," wrote Johnson, "excel those of all other poets... Raphael's reproof of Adam's curiosity after the planetary motions, with the answer returned by Adam, may be confidently opposed to any rule of life which any poet has delivered."[53] For some biographers, indeed, Milton could be explicitly offered as a moral model. For Newton Milton is "an example of sobriety and temperance." For Richardson Milton is "within the reach in Some degree, I mean his Piety and Vertue, of our Imitation."[54]

To provide useful moral models was indeed the prime purpose of biography in the eighteenth century.[55] But to be useful a model had to be imitable. "What is nearest us, touches us most." The life of an extraordinary man does not move us; the life of a saint may well discourage us from attempting to imitate his many virtues.[56] Did the eighteenth-century lives of Milton finally provide an imitable model? Despite Richardson's qualified affirmative, one may conclude finally that on the whole Milton's biographers thought not. Milton attended no "visible worship." Though his devoutness is not in question, Johnson worried about the effect of Milton's example on lesser mortals: "To be of no church is dangerous."[57] Likewise, biographers repeatedly honor Milton's sincerity, though they hesitate to approve his principles.[58] Newton found his integrity extraordinary, and described it with language usually reserved for heroes: "he had a soul above dissimulation and disguise; he was neither afraid, nor ashamed to vindicate the truth; and if any man had, he had in him the spirit of an old martyr."[59] Hayley too repeatedly emphasizes Milton's uniqueness:

no man ever maintained, with more steadfastness and resolution, the native dignity of an elevated spirit, no man more sedulously endeavoured to discharge his duty both to earth and heaven. (p. 144)

Milton is the man of our country most eminent for energy of mind, for intenseness of application, and for frankness and intrepidity. (p. 219)

of all men living, the most perfectly blameless in his sentiments of government, morality, and religion. (p. viii)

a poet of the most powerful, and, perhaps, the most independent mind that ever was given to a mere mortal. (p. xvii)

rare abilities, and perhaps the still rarer integrity. (p. 13)

With this praise Milton emerges not as a good man among men, but as a man whose soul, as Wordsworth said, "was like a Star, and dwelt apart."[60]

To praise Milton in this way runs the risk of elevating him beyond the reach of human capacity. Just as Milton's political principles seemed admirable to many, and yet to be obsolete or inappropriate in eighteenth-century England, so his moral principles and conduct commanded respect, even reverence, and yet were not readily transferred to a world of social reality. Like Samuel Richardson's Clarissa, Milton displayed a single-minded purity, a determination to sacrifice everything, if need be, for his principles, and a fundamental conviction that he was doing God's will. Such heroic integrity must serve, in any age, as a reminder of the inevitable compromises of most moral lives.[61]

3 · MILTON AS LITERARY HERO

About what they would have called Milton's political character and his moral character, eighteenth-century readers did not agree. But there was no controversy about his stature as a literary figure: for the eighteenth century Milton was simply "the great English Author,"[1] "the favourite poet of this nation."[2] It was of course this aspect of his character that had the most impact on eighteenth-century culture, and under this aspect that he was most often remembered. Those who disapproved of the man or his politics found it convenient to remember only the poet. But even those who admired Milton's moral character or sympathized with his political principles saw poetry as central to Milton's achievement. For Jonathan Richardson, "no Quality of Mind is More Conspicuous in Him, not even Piety and the Love of Civil and Ecclesiastical Liberty, than his Passionate Fondness for the Muses...He was a Poet Early, and Always in his Soul...He, if ever Man was, was *Smit with the Love of Sacred Song*."[3] In his capacity as the age's ideal poet, Milton served to focus eighteenth-century England's literary self-consciousness, its sense of its relation to the literary past, its own achievements, and its ambitions. No matter how one mapped the literary landscape, Milton was a central and dominating figure, far more than we might suppose from conventional accounts of the eighteenth century as the age of satire and the novel. How the aspiring poet or critic located himself in relation to that figure remained a problem that each had to solve in his own way.

For many Milton simply paralyzed the critical faculty and gave rise to what one might call the idolatrous tradition: "the divine..the immortal...the incomparable Milton." Toland, for example, speaks of Milton's "divine and incomparable Poems, which, equalling the most beautiful Order and Expression of any antient or modern Compositions, are infinitly above them all for Sublimity and Invention."[4] These epithets are found everywhere in eighteenth-century comments on Milton, largely but not exclusively among minor poetasters and critics. Milton is the "British Homer," the "Ornament and Glory of his Country."[5] *Paradise Lost* is "the noblest Poem, next to those of *Homer* and *Virgil*, that ever the wit of man produc'd in any age or nation,"[6] "the prime Poem in the world."[7] A parallel response might be called the sentimental tradition: Milton labored in blindness and adversity, was mistreated by cruel and selfish wives and daughters, and died in relative obscurity. An indifferent and ungrateful nation left his tomb unmarked and ignored his works until Lord Somers' recommendation belatedly led to the elegant *Paradise Lost* folio of 1688.[8] This image, based on half-truths, and a pathetic rendering of them, and fed perhaps by clichés, beloved of writers, about "neglected merit" and "the uncertainty of literary fame," provoked ritual expressions of shame at least until 1780, when Johnson felt the need to refute the case.[9]

But the idolatrous and sentimental reactions to Milton are not without cultural significance. They should be seen as uncritical extensions of an admiration for Milton's achievement that was based on critical reflection. Milton *was* remarkable not only for setting poetry aside while he engaged, with his left hand, in the heat of polemic and controversy, but for publicly announcing, in those early prose works, his literary ambitions, which he considers henceforth as a debt and "cov'nant."[10] Even Johnson is impressed with the "fervid, pious, and rational" promise that led, some twenty-five years later, to *Paradise Lost*.[11] Although Johnson may have had personal reasons to admire the fulfillment of literary promises,[12] he shared that admiration with Milton's other biographers. Richardson quotes the passages from *Reason of Church Government* and marvels that Milton produced a poem that "Intirely and most Remarkably Answers the Description here given of it."[13] Hayley recurrently emphasizes Milton's early literary ambitions, and their later fulfillment:

In a noble consciousness of his powers and intentions, he was not afraid to give, in his early life, a most singular promise to his country of producing such future works as might redound to her glory; and though such personal calamities fell upon him, as might fairly have absolved him from that engagement, yet never was any promise more magnificently filled.   (*Life*, p. 225)

Likewise, the claim that Britain now had a writer to rival the great classical poets was not simply journalistic puffery. It suggests that in the eighteenth century British writers first became conscious largely because of Milton's achievement that their literature had come of age, that it had acquired a distinct character, and that it could match the poetry of any country.[14] Shakespeare, though an acknowledged genius, was not enough to prompt this sense of national accomplishment and identity, perhaps because he was conventionally thought to be an untutored genius, perhaps because even English tragic drama was still considered a popular form, not to be compared with the tragedies of Greece. As Hayley put it, "it is by the epic compositions of Milton alone that England may esteem herself as a rival to antiquity in the highest province of literature" (p. 230). For Cowper, Milton's poems and prose had established the credentials and the power of their native tongue: his works are "proof that no subject, however sublime, can demand greater force or expression, than is within the compass of the English language."[15]

Paradise Lost's "general reputation," wrote Defoe in 1711, is that of "the greatest, best, and most sublime work now in the *English* Tongue."[16] Addison's famous series of *Spectator* papers on *Paradise Lost* (1712), examining the poem "by the Rules of Epic Poetry," confirmed and strengthened its reputation by judging it against classical standards. Recommended by these popular essays, said Thomas Warton, *Paradise Lost* "acquired the distinction of an English classic."[17] In 1741 there appeared a *Verbal Index* to the poem. In 1749 Newton, who reprinted the index, gathered the work of his predecessor editors into his own edition "cum notis variorum."[18] Within a few years William Massey opens his companion commentary by asserting that *Paradise Lost* is "the first *Classic* in the *English* tongue." In the latter part of the century the accolade became a commonplace.[19] The idea of a vernacular or national "classic" was clearly only just establishing itself in the eighteenth century, perhaps as a consequence of the Battle of the Ancients and Moderns. For some, like Richardson, a "classic" was perhaps the kind of work that was good enough to have been written by one of the ancients. "Milton's true Character as a Writer," he says, "is that he is an Ancient, but born Two Thousand Years after his Time."[20] But for Richardson's contemporaries the term "classic" seems to carry a different historical meaning. A classic is not simply a great work of enduring value, but a work that belongs to and stands at the head of a *national literature*.[21]

To have a "classic" among its writers meant that England's literature and culture had matured. Of this any Englishman should be proud. Indeed, Milton came to be regarded in the eighteenth century as a national treasure. When Milton appeared, says the author of "Cibber's" *Lives of the Poets* (1753), "the pride of Greece was humbled, the competition became more equal, and since Paradise Lost is ours, it would, perhaps, be an injury to our national fame to yield the palm to any state, whether ancient or modern."[22]

Such treasures are to be guarded carefully. When Lauder lodged his notorious charge of plagiarism against Milton, a correspondent to the *Gentleman's Magazine* noted that "the question whether Milton borrowed from Masenius, concerns in my opinion the whole nation."[23] Even Johnson recognized that to "lessen the reputation of Milton" would "diminish in some degree the honour of our country."[24] When he undertook to comment on the faults of *Samson Agonistes* in *Rambler* 140, Johnson assured his readers that such criticism could not harm the "everlasting verdure of Milton's laurels…nor can my attempt produce any other effect, than to strengthen their shoots by lopping their luxuriance."[25]

That Milton should have been valued as an especially "English" poet may surprise us if we think primarily of his profound classical learning, his conscious place in a European epic tradition, or Johnson's complaint about his "Babylonish Dialect."[26] But eighteenth-century readers, familiar with Milton's autobiographical writings, would have known that he consciously thought of himself as an English-language poet. In *Reason of Church Government* he aims at "the adorning of my native tongue." (Dryden later commented on the "ancient words Which he had been digging from the mines of Chaucer and Spenser."[27]) Milton's goal is distinctly national, "to be an interpreter and relater of the best and sagest things among mine own citizens throughout this island in the mother dialect."[28] The fame he seeks is likewise local, "not caring to be once named abroad, though, perhaps, I could attain to that, but Content with these British ilands as my world."[29] In his early career, furthermore, Milton had thought of writing a national epic. Eighteenth-century biographers were familiar not only with the early poems (*Epitaphium Damonis, Mansus*) in which he spoke of an epic on a British subject, but also with Milton's Trinity MS, in which he lists numerous subjects for tragedy from his country's past. As Warton noted, Milton "was very fond of the old British history, in which his imagination discovered many fine subjects for poetry."[30] In the end Milton turned, perhaps not without reluctance, from ideas of national epic. Hayley writes that "a passionate attachment to his country made him first think of celebrating its ancient heroes…but…Arthur yielded to Adam, and England to Paradise."[31] Still, Milton did not abandon his literary interest in his native country. Late in his career Milton published his *History of Britain* (1670, but written earlier), a work little regarded now, but often reprinted in the eighteenth century, and frequently cited as a historical authority.[32] Thomson spoke for many contemporaries when he referred to Milton quite simply as "the British Muse" (*Winter*, line 535).

Not only could his country boast a British poet to match the ancients; it could also claim that Milton had surpassed Homer and Virgil because he was a *Christian* poet. For Dennis religion is the source of poetic excellence: "Sacred Subjects are infinitely more susceptible of the greatness of Poetry than profane ones can be."[33] By the same token Milton is superior to Virgil because of the "excellence of his Religion" (I, 274). "Our *Briton*" is as much superior to Homer "as the Angels of the one are more potent than the other's Gods" (II, 223–24). In presenting Milton as the ideal poet ("he Possess'd the Soul of Poetry")

Richardson notes that he had great learning, a knowledge of the classics, "with the Additional Advantages of Later Times; Chiefly of Christianity."[34] The "superior dignity of his subject," according to Warburton, enabled Milton to get "to the head of [the epic] triumvirate." Homer took "the province of MORALITY," Virgil "POLITICS," but Milton surpassed them with "RELIGION."[35] At the end of the century Cowper, in his commentary on *Paradise Lost*, reiterates that Milton chose "the sublimest of all subjects," and affirms simply that Milton "is the Poet of Christians."[36]

As a modern classic, a British poet, and a Christian, Milton embodied his country's literary ideals and spoke as a living presence. His example and authority were constantly cited in discussions of current critical issues in poetry. For readers and writers of Addison's generation at the beginning of the century, of Thomas Warton's at mid-century, and of Johnson's in late century, Milton was likely to be at the center of literary controversy. He was himself largely responsible for the interest in blank verse, and in claims – in both critical essays and verse essays – that it had freed poetry from the troublesome bondage of rhyme. Although it was probably translations of Longinus that initiated critical interest in "the sublime," Milton was invariably cited, from Addison to Johnson, as England's great sublime poet, and *Paradise Lost* as the poem whose "characteristick quality" is sublimity.[37] Whether the age was discussing an irregular greatness, or the principle of decorum and the classical "rules," Milton was a central example. And for those critics, beginning at mid-century, interested in the question of original genius, Milton offered evidence of both profound originality ("things unattempted yet") and imitation. William Lauder is only an extreme and notorious example of an interest in Milton's "sources." Editors and commentators from Patrick Hume on annotated borrowings and allusions.

To judge then by the admiration of his achievement and the frequency of citation in discussions of literary theory, Milton would appear to be squarely in the mainstream of the age's literary culture. And yet in some deeper ways Milton was a kind of alien presence, in the poetic as well as the political landscape. He may have been his country's poet, but it was not clear that he had left any progeny.

To begin with, consider the eighteenth century's uncertain sense of the literary past. Literary history was still a new form in the eighteenth century. Dryden was the first poet-critic in English with a historical sense; Thomas Warton was the first to write a proper History of English Poetry. But even allowing for tentative efforts in a new form, it is still striking that eighteenth-century literary historians could not draw any clear line that led from Milton *to themselves*.

Milton's clearest affinities backward, in the eighteenth-century view, were with Spenser. Dryden reported that "Milton had acknowledged to me that Spenser was his original."[38] Patrick Hume was the first of many commentators to annotate parallels between Milton and Spenser. But to connect Milton with *later* writers proved more difficult. In his famous survey of English literary history (particularly the drama) from the Jacobeans to his own contemporaries in the epistle "To My Dear Friend Mr. Congreve," Dryden omits Milton completely.[39] Waller and Denham, in the standard eighteenth-century view, were the key intermediary figures between an older and a newer poetic tradition. By contrast, Milton seemed to Dryden a late example of an old tradition that was already being superseded and "refined."[40] Gray likewise saw Milton as something of a dead end. In his "sketches for a design" for a history of English poetry, in a letter to Thomas Warton,[41] the school of Spenser, including Drayton, Fairfax, Phineas Fletcher, Golding, and Phaer, "ends in Milton." Another school, "full of conceit," began under Elizabeth, was continued by Donne, Crashaw, and Cleveland, "carried to its height" by Cowley, "& ending perhaps in Sprat." Then follows the "School of France, introduced after the Restoration. Waller, Dryden, Addison, Prior, & Pope, wch has continued down to our own times."[42]

Warton, the recipient of Gray's sketch, had no more success in placing Milton. His unfinished *History of English Poetry from the Close of the Eleventh to the Commencement of the Eighteenth Century* (publ. 1774–81) did not carry the story past the Elizabethans. In his *Observations on the Faerie Queene* (1754, 1762), accounting for the decline of allegory from Spenser's day to his own, Warton notes that Elizabethan allegory gave way to a new species of poetry "whose images were of the metaphysical and abstracted kind." The older allegorical poetry made a brief attempt to return in Fletcher's *Purple Island* (1633), but a new kind of poetry succeeded, apparently the school of proto-Augustans, Waller and Denham,

in which imagination gave way to correctness, sublimity of description to delicacy of sentiment, and majestic imagery to conceit and epigram... The nicer beauties of happy expression were preferred to the daring strokes of great conception.

At the same time satire was "imported from France" (apparently by Dryden, Oldham, and others) and the muses' only themes were "polite life, and familiar manners" (by now we have clearly arrived at the age of Pope). In all this Milton is nearly forgotten, and appears only as a kind of afterthought: "The simple dignity of Milton was either entirely neglected, or mistaken for bombast and insipidity, by the refined readers of a dissolute age, whose taste and morals were equally vitiated.'[43] Virtually isolated in his own age, Milton in Warton's view had no immediate followers.

If Milton could not be placed in a succession of poets, he could still be compared to the leading exemplar of the dominant tradition. Though it now seems absurd to us, it became commonplace by about 1700 to think of Milton and Waller as the two great and contrasting English poets.[44] Each implicitly offered a model to the aspiring writer for "Sweetness" or for "Nobler Flights."[45] The comparison must still have had currency in 1746 when Collins used it to suggest his own literary affinities in the "Ode on the Poetical Character" he advances toward a Miltonic Eden, "greeting" Milton's glory, and "retreating" from Waller's "myrtle shades."[46] By this point, however, Waller's stature has diminished,[47] and with the general change of taste in the mid-eighteenth century Milton reappears and attracts followers:

A visible revolution succeeded in the general cast and character of the national composition. Our versification contracted a new colouring, a new structure and phraseology; and the school of Milton rose in emulation of the school of Pope.[48]

But it is one thing to attract a "school" in one's own lifetime, or in the following generation, and another for that school to arise some three-quarters of a century later. True, Milton found many mid-eighteenth century imitators. To say nothing of those inspired by *Paradise Lost* to attempt blank verse sublimity, "Il Penseroso," as Shenstone wrote to Graves in 1755, "has drove half our Poets crazy."[49] But even for the major mid-century poets, such as Gray and Collins, who admired and drew from Milton, his world, for both historical and personal reasons, seemed somehow beyond their reach.

Gray, recurrently concerned with the "Progress" (and the decline) of poetry in his day, makes Milton a symbol of the fire and amplitude that the modern poet cannot attain:

> not to one in this benighted age
> Is that diviner inspiration given,
> That burns in Shakespeare's or in Milton's page,
> The pomp and prodigality of heaven.
> ("Stanzas to Mr. Bentley," lines 17–20)

In the "Progress of Poesy" Milton is celebrated in terms that recall his own triumphant Christ who "rode sublime / Upon the seraph-wings of Ecstasy, / The secrets of the abyss to spy." But his eyes are since "closed" in "endless night,"[50] and now no "daring spirit" lives to wake the "lyre divine" (lines 95–97, 112–13).

Collins' much-discussed "Ode on the Poetical Character" likewise asks whether a poet can now inhabit Milton's "inspiring bowers." Early in the poem Collins wonders "Where is the bard" who can now take up the "hallowed work" of the Poetical Character. He himself vows and hopes, and pursues Milton's "guiding steps" – "In vain" (lines 70 – 72), for

> Heaven and Fancy, kindred Powers,
> Have now o'erturned the inspiring bowers,
> Or curtained close such scene from every future view.
>
> (lines 74 – 76)

As Collins and Gray suggest, that Milton seemed out of reach was partly a matter of time: he belonged to an earlier age that could not be recovered. Poets and critics who looked back toward the seventeenth century saw a great divide about the time of the Restoration. On the near side stood Dryden and Pope, distinctly contemporary poets. Milton, Thomas Warton argued, should be seen not as a contemporary, but as "an old English poet,"[51] still in touch with traditional – even medieval – English culture. The "old stories" of "traditionary beings" of folk tale and romance were "not entirely forgotten in Milton's younger days."[52] Milton himself had "a mind deeply tinctured with romance-reading" (I, 350). When he wrote his early poems, Warton suggests, "many traditionary superstitions not yet worn out in the popular belief, adhered to the poetry of the times. Romances and fabulous narratives were still in fashion, and not yet driven away by puritans and usurpers. To ideas of this sort, and they corresponded with the complexion of his genius, allusions often appear even in Milton's elder poetry."[53] But Milton was not simply the last medievalist or a latter-day Spenser. He looked upon romance materials with a loving and yet a critical eye. He "delighted," Hurd wrote, "with the Gothic Romances," but perceived their defects. He admitted them to his own work only "on the bye, and in the way of simile and illustration only."[54] He "tempered and exalted the extravagance of romance, with the dignity of Homer."[55] By such *tempering* Milton was able to preserve the best of the old, both in narrative and in drama:

It was happily reserved for the taste and genius of Milton, to temper the fantastic extravagance of the *Masque*, which chiefly consisted in external decoration, with the rational graces of poetry, and to give it the form and substance of a legitimate drama. (II, 308)

Thus Milton can still speak to a contemporary audience, for he respects the "rational graces" of modern poetry. Most poets, like Collins, found it difficult or even impossible, to marry the standards of modern poetry with the richer material of romance. Thus in the "Ode on the Popular Superstitions of the Highlands of Scotland" Collins must consign the "false themes" of superstition, folk tale, and romance to his Scots friend John Home, who has the good fortune to live in a region where the old stories are still alive in the popular mind. For the polite and "gentle" Collins and his readers, such materials must be hailed only "at distance."

If the mere lapse of time made Milton seem out of reach to eighteenth-century writers, so too did this extraordinary ability to reconcile the old and the new, the rational and the marvelous, and other apparent contraries. As Warton and others described him, Milton combined the strengths of older poetry – "warm imagination," "strong sensibility," a native vigor that used little art – with the advantages of modern poetry – correctness, exactness, decorum, learning, "arrangement and economy."[56] A poet like Spenser, to Warton's mind, is content to "engage the fancy, and to interest the attention by bold and striking images." Since he is not studious of "design and uniformity," he falls into "inconveniences and incongruities" and "careless exuberance" (I, 21 – 22, 23). But Milton surpasses Spenser by transporting the reader and satisfying the critic: he "engages" the "feelings of the heart" and "the cold approbation of the head" (I, 23 – 24).

From another angle, Milton was at once a man of genius and a man of learning, of native gifts and acquired knowledge. Many eighteenth-century observers did not expect these qualities to appear in the same writer, or, where they did, to conflict with each other. But this was not the case with Milton. Addison spoke for his age in remarking that "perhaps never was a genius so strengthened by learning, as Milton's."[57] His learning gave him full knowledge of ancient and modern poetry, but his genius freed him from the necessity of imitation. As Hayley saw it, "by the force and opulence of his own fancy he was exempted from the inclination and the necessity of borrowing and retailing the ideas of other poets... No poet, perhaps, who revered the ancients with rich affectionate enthusiasm, has copied them so little."[58]

"Exempted" catches the note of many of these comments: Milton seemed exempt from the laws of time and from the conditions that govern lesser poets. It is little wonder that a recurrent theme in the tributes to Milton from his death through the end of the eighteenth century is that Milton is literally inimitable. He is a "Mighty Poet" who soars "above humane flight" to accomplish a task Marvell thought impossible: "So that no room is here for Writers left, / But to detect their Ignorance or Theft."[59] He built, said Addison, on a grander scale than others: "No vulgar hero can his Muse engage, / Nor earth's wide scene confine his hallow'd rage."[60] By the mid-century "Milton alone could..." became a commonplace.[61] Most imitators, of course, failed:

"How few," admits Robert Lloyd, "Who copy Milton, e'er succeed."[62] It is precisely this view of Milton as exceptional that Lauder unsuccessfully sought to destroy in his *Essay* on Milton's imitations. Lauder concludes that, on his showing, Milton has at last been "reduced to his true standard," and "appears mortal and uninspired," "little superior" to other great English poets.[63]

If only Milton could do it, and only Milton had done it, then clear-sighted poets, not blinded by ambition, might well conclude that they could never hope to match his greatness. Perhaps, as Warburton warned, "all further improvements of the epic [were] at an end."[64] Or, as Hayley put it, despite a belief in progress one should not expect the arts to be progressive:

although in all the arts there are undoubtedly points of perfection much higher than any mortal has yet attained, still it requires such a coincidence of so many advantages depending on the influence both of nature and of destiny to raise a great artist of any kind, that the world has but little reason to expect productions of poetical genius superior to the Paradise Lost.   (*Life*, p. 208)

As cultural figure then, Milton presented an extraordinary challenge to the eighteenth century. Whether one considered his political character, his moral character, or his poetical character, one saw much to admire in Milton's career, ideas, and writings. And yet even his admirers had to concede that Milton was in some ways out of place in the eighteenth century. Those who attempted to apply Milton directly to contemporary politics, religion, or morals found themselves on the radical fringes, committed to extraordinarily rigorous ethical standards and an unfashionably other-worldly faith, righteously alienated in a land of evil.

The problem was similar if one looked to Milton as literary authority or literary model. Those who invoked him directly, imitated blindly, or admired uncritically, might be laughed at as mere copyists or Milton-olators. But in fact the best of Milton's eighteenth-century admirers realized that other strategies were available to them. The task for the post-Miltonic poet was to recognize both that Milton, like his own unfallen Adam, belonged to a world one could no longer inhabit, and at the same time that he spoke to perennial concerns. One then had to find a way to adapt Milton to new circumstances. For a poet, this involved a thoughtful and recreative kind of imitation, so, as Ben Jonson had put it, "to be able to convert the substance, or Riches of another *Poet*, to his own use."[65] Those who imitated too closely, or superficially, reproduced nothing more than a hollow echo of Milton's blank verse music or his Latinate diction. Greater poets realized that one had to rethink Milton, sometimes in a new mode, in order to discover the creative possibilities latent in his work.

PART II

After Milton: literary possibilities

At the end of *Paradise Lost* Adam and Eve look back at the "dreadful Faces" of angels barring the way to paradise, and forward to a "World...before them, where to choose." These lines resonate in the eighteenth-century imagination.[1] They may serve here as a metaphor for the eighteenth-century poet's response to Milton. By one account, the aspiring poet's way to life was blocked by the imposing face and fact of Milton and his achievement. By another account (my own) there lay before the post-Miltonic writer a world of literary possibilities. That world was perhaps not the same as Milton's wider realm. It was not a limitless world. But given the constraints of an enlightened age, of one's own talent and taste, many things were *possible*. Milton himself had left some avenues still open; had provided materials for adaptation; and had suggested other opportunities that later writers might take up.

Even an allegedly Milton-haunted poet like Gray sees a path open to him. At the end of "The Progress of Poesy" a "daring spirit" – Gray himself as Pindaric bard – still "wakes" the lyre. Against the admission that he is no Pindar (or Milton) Gray props his own assertion: "Yet shall he mount" (line 121). We are in danger of misreading Gray if we remember only "Beneath the Good how far" and not also recall the other half of the final line: "but far above the Great." We may likewise misread Collins' "Ode on the Poetical Character" by dwelling on the alleged despair and bleakness of its conclusion. As critics are now beginning to suggest, Collins' ambitious ode, though it acknowledges that Milton's particular poetic "bliss" was vouchsafed "to one alone / Of all the sons of soul" (lines 72–73), yet declares its own success: a sublime re-affirmation of poetry's divine origin and power in an age that values Collins' witty and urbane reformulation of old fictions.[2]

It is perhaps well to begin with the sharpest objection to my argument, with the claim, found in Eliot, Murry, and Bloom, that Milton in fact closed off certain literary avenues for a century or more. As we look back on literary history, few of us would deny that Milton seems to have been the last poet in English to make successful use of several traditional genres. Where is the eighteenth-century epic to compare with *Paradise Lost*, the pastoral elegy to match "Lycidas," the classical tragedy to stand with *Samson Agonistes*, the masque to equal *Comus*? Where, before Wordsworth and Keats, are there sonnets as good as Milton's? Are we not tempted to suggest that in some sense Milton *used up* or exhausted these traditional genres, or made them unavailable for creative use for a century and more? If these genres died out during the eighteenth century, can we identify Milton as the cause? My general reply to these questions is to note that it is difficult if not impossible to speak with confidence about unwritten poems. We do not yet know enough about literary history to explain why certain genres rise or fall in popularity, or exactly why a given poet adopts or avoids a given genre. But we do know enough to say that little compelling evidence can be produced to show that Milton *inhibited* the poets of the eighteenth century.

To substantiate these conclusions requires a closer look at eighteenth-century critical theory and literary practice. Furthermore, it requires that we try to look with their eyes rather than our own, to see not only the great achievements of the period – *Absalom and Achitophel*, *The Dunciad*, the *Life of Milton* – but also the literary aspirations and possibilities that presented themselves to the practicing writer in the ages of Dryden, Pope, and Johnson. Our goal is to recover the literary mentality of the post-Miltonic writers – what they saw when they looked back toward Milton, what they saw when they looked out at their own horizons of possibility. With the advantage (and disadvantage) of hindsight, we usually take a very selective view of a past literary period: we see the tallest surviving monuments. But to measure Milton's full impact on a century of English writers, we need to stand at ground-level, and sometimes to observe what may seem arid critical controversies, or literary ambitions that came to nought. Let us begin with the epic.

Epic

By some measures the epic was very much alive in the eighteenth century. Throughout the period it enjoyed great prestige as the highest of the genres. "A heroic poem ... is undoubtedly the greatest work of which the soul of man is capable to perform," wrote Dryden in the Preface to his translation of Virgil's epic in 1697.[3] Near the end of the eighteenth century Johnson could still say that "by the general consent of criticks the first praise of genius is due to the writer of an epick poem, as it requires an assemblage of all the powers which are singly sufficient for other compositions."[4]

Epics continued to be written throughout the century by some bad poets such as the everlasting Blackmore[5] and a decent minor poet such as Glover, whose *Leonidas* (1737) was popular enough to go through four editions in two years. Granted, the great English poets of the age did not write epic, but they never abandoned their ambition to write one. Dryden, obsessed with the heroic throughout his literary career, projected an epic on the Black Prince and on King Arthur in the 1670s and published a draft sketch of the poem in the 1690s. The epic was never written (Dryden complained that Blackmore stole his idea for a poem on Arthur), but the plan still seemed sound to Johnson a hundred years later: "That this poem was never written is reasonably to be lamented. It would doubtless have improved our numbers and enlarged our language, and might perhaps have contributed by pleasing instruction to rectify our opinions and purify our manners."[6]

Pope too hoped to write a heroic poem. His juvenile *Alcander* – 4000 lines written by age fifteen – is less significant than the *Brutus* he planned but left unfinished at the end of his life. William Hayley regretted that Pope, though "formed to fill the Epic throne," chose satire instead, and then turned to his epic project too late: "Had he possessed health and leisure to execute such a work, I am persuaded it would have proved a glorious acquisition to the literature of our country."[7] Among Pope's younger contemporaries both Thomson and Akenside shared his epic ambition: both projected heroic poems on the subject of Timoleon, the deliverer of Syracuse.[8] The greatest poet of the age to complete an epic was not an Englishman. Voltaire's *Henriade*, which appeared in 1728, though an attempt at a French national epic, was clearly designed to appeal equally to an English audience.[9] Although its reception was mixed, it no doubt helped keep alive the dream of an English national epic.

Another kind of evidence that the epic was not dead in the eighteenth century is that readers were still sensitive to its forms and understood its conventions.[10] Le Bossu's treatise on the epic (1675), a standard eighteenth-century authority, codifies and elaborates the discussion in Aristotle. The "Rules of Epic Poetry" were well enough known for Addison to begin his popular discussion of *Paradise Lost* by reference to them, and to take up the topics of the fable, characters, sentiments, and language. Critical discussions of epic were common for the rest of the century, as Blackmore, Kames, Blair, Trapp, and others surveyed ancient and modern epic and reviewed theoretical commonplaces (e.g. epic must be marvellous and yet probable, must excite admiration and teach virtue).[11]

The epic then looks very much alive in the eighteenth century. The form is understood and admired; old and new examples are regarded with great interest; the greatest poets still strive to use it. But the plain fact remains that, as contemporaries themselves recognized,[12] no great epic poems were written in the period. It is tempting to juxtapose failed eighteenth-century epic with Milton's seventeenth-century success, and to suspect a causal connection. Thus, one might suspect, Milton's great epic so awed the writers of the following century that they instinctively shied away from emulating him, or shrank from what they feared would be unfavorable comparisons. Milton deterred the great or "strong" poets, so it is said, and attracted only the second-rate or the "weak," who imitated him slavishly. A variant of this notion holds that, by the eighteenth century, there was "nothing left to be done." As Warburton put it, after Homer, Virgil, and Milton took morality, politics, and religion for their spheres, "all further improvements of the epic [were] at an end."[13]

This explanation of the failure of eighteenth-century epic is attractive. But is it true? There are reasons to think not. To begin with, the strong writers did not hesitate to declare their epic ambitions *publicly*. As early as 1676 Dryden gave notice in his published prefaces of his intention to write an epic. He continued to refer to the project in print as late as 1693 and 1700. Pope's plans were not so widely known, but he freely discussed *Brutus* with Joseph Spence in the 1740s, and reported to Spence in 1743 that the poem was "quite digested and prepared ... and even some of the most material speches writ in prose."[14] Even Collins, whose "Ode on the Poetical Character," in the standard reading, appears to admit his despair of attaining Miltonic heights, in fact declares that aspiration quite openly, and gives some signs of confidence that his sublime ode has succeeded.

Second, the great poets did not shrink from comparisons with earlier greatness; indeed, they courted comparisons between themselves and their epic predecessors, Dryden by translating Virgil and by adapting *Paradise Lost*, Pope by translating Homer and by declaring frankly how much he owed to Dryden, and by alluding throughout his career to Milton's great poems.[15] There is little reason to think that they were intimidated by Milton or his achievement. Both poets had long and extraordinarily successful careers; both have seemed to most of their readers strong, ambitious, and self-confident.

As for Warburton's announcement that the definitive epics had been written, many critics were not ready to agree. Hayley openly disputed Warburton's claim and hoped that his own *Essay on Epic Poetry* might give "spirit and energy to the laudable ambition of a youthful Poet."[16] He went on to propose that a new epic might be set in India, drawing on Indian mythology for machinery.[17] Gibbon suggested that an epic might be written about an explorer like Columbus.[18] An early critic proposed that the exploits in Spain of Pope's friend Peterborough might serve as an epic subject.[19] Whig poets had available William III or the Duke of Marlborough, perhaps the most famous English war hero of the century and the subject of a number of shorter panegyrics such as Addison's *Campaign* and Philips' *Blenheim*.

But a more promising subject – to judge by the projects of Dryden,

Blackmore, and Pope – seemed to be the heroes of earlier English history. Occasion might easily be found, as Dryden had suggested, to represent "the patrons of the noblest families" of the modern day "in the succession of our imperial line."[20] Hayley too regretted that England had no national epic to match other European countries, and urged Mason to sing his country's "dearest Worthies."[21]

Nor was the potential field limited to historical epic. Gibbon had proposed, *perhaps* ironically, that the "wonderful expedition of Odin," driven by the Romans from his supposed origin in Egypt to found a new religion and people in Scandinavia, "might supply the noble ground-work of an epic poem."[22] Hayley took Gibbon's suggestion seriously, and imagined that Gray could have written such an epic and adorned it with northern mythology, of which he had made a considerable study.[23]

Christian religious epic in some ways seemed to offer more opportunities. Milton had claimed little more than the opening chapter of Genesis. Many heroes of faith remained to be celebrated.[24] At least one good poet, Christopher Smart, had shown that David might be presented heroically, in a kind of epic hymn.[25] Dryden, Blackmore, and many others thought, despite Boileau's doubts,[26] that a modern epic poet could make very effective use of machines derived from the Christian religion.[27] And the Christian doctrine of miracles and the "irregular productions" of nature (such as comets) might provide all the marvels that an epic could require.[28]

Some critics went so far as to suggest that a modern epic could do without the supernatural altogether and still "attain the height of epic poetry by the same [means] as render Homer still the first of poets; by just representation of life and manners; by sublime descriptions of natural objects, by filling his action with the most striking incidents, the conditions of human affairs will allow; and above all by sublimity of sentiment."[29] An epic poet should not draw Homer's world but a world that a modern Homer might see. Goldsmith thought modern epic writers too enslaved to Homer and Virgil. Instead of taking a classical model, the epic poet, he urged, "should boldly follow nature in the dress she wears at present." Goldsmith saw no incongruity between the grandeur of epic and the refinement of enlightened Europe, either in style or in morality: "If, in an age like this, when all the social duties are perfectly understood, an hero was drawn in every circumstance of real dignity... such as results from the just conduct of the passions; who was great... from a finely regulated understanding: such an hero would fill the scene of an epic poem with more dignity, and interest us more than all the swift-footed Achilles's, or pious Eneas's of antiquity."[30] For Hayley, *Paradise Regained* is in some ways a better model for modern epic even than *Paradise Lost*: ''assuredly, there is no poem of epic form, where the sublimest moral instruction is so forcibly and abundantly united to poetical delight...It is admirably calculated to inspire that spirit of self-command, which is, as Milton esteemed it, the truest heroism, and the triumph of Christianity.''[31] Thus a modern epic writer might circumvent the common eighteenth-century objection to the brutal morality of traditional military epic.[32]

We then have grounds to doubt the conclusion that Milton's epic achievement blocked the way for eighteenth-century aspirants. Furthermore, we can find more plausible explanations for the failure of epic in the period. It is first worth recalling that great epic is always rare, always the exception. How many good epic poems, besides Milton's, were written in the sixteenth and seventeenth centuries? What prevented epic from remaining a vigorous genre was not Milton, or any single accomplishment, but a large-scale change in cultural conditions. Epic poetry, Horace Walpole wrote in 1782, ''is not suited to an improved and polished state of things.''[33] Thomas Blackwell thought modern epic impossible. Epic, he argued, requires the ''marvelous,'' but ''what marvellous Things happen in a well-ordered State?''[34] Several influential critics, perhaps influenced by the failure of Voltaire's *Henriade*, argued that ''the familiarity of modern manners...unqualifies them for a lofty subject.''[35] Ancient manners, Blair declared, afford superior materials for epic poetry.[36] After Voltaire, wrote Kames, ''no writer, it is probable, will think of erecting an epic poem upon a recent event in the history of his own country.''[37] War, Goldsmith argued, cannot be the subject of a modern epic because of the nature of modern warfare. Modern artillery and ballistics techniques and other technical advancements require the modern war hero to be a strategist and deployer of armies and weapons systems, not an Achillean warrior who meets his enemy in single combat. What is more, few in a civilized society are called upon to display the prowess of a soldier: ''skill in war, or courage, make but a virtue of a very subordinate nature among us.''[38]

Even biblical epic was challenged. It was one thing to write an epic about a nearly mythical pair in the primal garden, and another to write about plainly historical figures like the patriarchs. Shaftesbury was skeptical that Milton's great example could be fruitfully followed:

The War in Heaven, and the Catastrophe of that original Pair from whom the Generations of Mankind were propagated, are Matters so abstrusely reveal'd, and with such a resemblance of Mythology, that they can more easily bear what figurative Constructions or fantastick turn the Poet can think fit to give 'em. But shou'd he venture farther, into the lives and characters of the Patriarchs, the holy Matrons, Heroes and Heroines of the chosen Seed; shou'd he employ the sacred Machine, the Exhibitions and Interventions of Divinity, according to Holy Writ, to support the Action of his Piece; he wou'd soon find the Weakness of his pretended *Orthodox* Muse, and prove how little those Divine Patterns were capable of human Imitation.[39]

The loss of traditional epic machines and marvels, furthermore, was perhaps not so easily remedied by Christian writers as Blackmore hoped. Indeed, William Duff thought that poetry had sustained an "irreparable loss, since by this means those enchantments which are calculated at once to please, astonish, and terrify the imagination are utterly banished from all the haunts of the Muses."[40] Voltaire's rationalized machines – he used personified Vices and Virtues – met with Pope's guarded approval, but a contemporary of Goldsmith thought that they "failed of the intended effect ... The figures of policy, discord, fanaticism, and others of this kind, cannot raise what is called, in Epic poetry, the wonderful; because, as they are not operative, but allegorical figures, the mind explores the mystical meaning, with which it is satisfied."[41]

A chorus of voices was thus suggesting that, in Bishop Hurd's words, "some ages are not so fit to write epic poems in, as others."[42] The fault lay not in the inadequacy of the modern aspirant, or the intimidating success of a predecessor. Milton may have been the last in Europe to write an epic poem, perhaps because he inhabited, or at least remembered, a world from which the marvellous had not been banished. But even Milton seems to have recognized that classical epic conventions had to be modified in his age. He offers a radical critique of the classical epic hero and his virtues. Milton's virtues are not the Achillean ones of physical courage and prowess but rather the "better fortitude / Of patience and heroic martyrdom" (IX. 31 – 32). His hero is not the great man but (ultimately) the ordinary Christian in daily domestic life.[43] The real sphere of action is internalized. The true heroic acts are not deeds but motions of mind: faith, obedience, contrition, renewed faith. The hero is tested not in the heat of spectacular battle but in the performance of familial duties.[44]

Ironically, as Peter Hagin has argued, Milton's "new type of hero exercised ... negligible influence on the development of epic poetry" in the eighteenth century.[45] Glover and Blackmore continued to write epics of military action as if Milton had in no way discredited the form.[46] Pope's *Brutus*, in the sketch of it that Ruffhead presented, was to be full of traditional epic action – a council to plan a courageous voyage, storms, attacks by barbarians, battle against giants – and epic machinery of guardian angels.[47] Most theorists argued for Christianized epic but otherwise continued to think in essentially traditional fashion.

Even in this respect, then, Milton's example seems not to have deterred traditional epic ambitions in the eighteenth century. The point to make is that *Paradise Lost* may in effect be responsible for keeping the epic alive. Milton had demonstrated, in the face of failures by French and English writers, and doubts about the fitness of the age, that modern Christian epic might still be written.[48] If those ambitions bore little fruit, it is arguable that in some writers they were deflected into a newer genre, the novel, where the deeper features of Milton's epic helped shape the century's best long narratives.[49]

Pastoral

The pastoral, which like the epic undergoes an apparent decline in the eighteenth century, may be dealt with more briefly. By common consent among present critics, there is no major pastoral in the period comparable to the best work of the Renaissance pastoralists, Sidney, Spenser, or even Drayton. Milton's *Lycidas* (1637), the greatest of English pastorals (in our view), seems – with Marvell's slightly later poems – to be about the last of them, and to mark the exhaustion of the genre, at least until its resuscitation in the nineteenth century in the hands of Keats and Arnold. The very recovery of pastoral thus suggests that a different explanation must be found for the form's temporary decline in the eighteenth century. Johnson's notorious attack on *Lycidas* might suggest a widespread critical hostility to the form itself, focused on its most eminent example. But in a fuller literary history, as seen through the eyes of Johnson's contemporaries, the fortunes of pastoral in the eighteenth century were little affected by *Lycidas*.

It should be noted at the outset that pastoral is after all a minor genre for the Renaissance as well as the eighteenth century. In our eyes Milton used the form to write a major poem, but he is the exception. That pastoral should be a minor form in the eighteenth century should not surprise us. Second, pastoral, though minor, is by no means dead or even moribund in the age of Dryden and of Pope. As is well known, lively theoretical debate about the nature of the form was carried on in France at the end of the seventeenth century between those critics, headed by Rapin, who saw pastoral as an imitation of a shepherd's life in the golden age, and those, headed by Fontenelle, who insisted that pastoral should be an idealized image of contemporary rural life and manners. This debate was imported to England, where it was continued in the pages of the *Guardian*, in prefatory discourses, and in critical essays, with Pope, Gay, and Knightley Chetwode on one side, and Addison, Tickell, Ambrose Philips, and Thomas Purney on the other. Those staking out critical positions often did so to provide theoretical justification for their own pastorals, including Pope (1709), Philips

(1710), and Purney (1717). Surprisingly few pastoralists were content to produce imitations of Theocritus, Virgil, Spenser, or Milton. Two poems derivative of *Lycidas*, William Mason's *Musaeus* (1744), an elegy on the death of Pope, and Lyttelton's *Monody* (1747) on the death of his wife, were popular enough to appear in Dodsley's *Collection*. But most poets sought to correct or improve on the masters of the form, or to vary the subject matter. Thus Philips and Purney aim at recovering a simplicity and tenderness that Theocritus sometimes lacks.[50] Pope aims at introducing as much careful variety in four poems as Spenser has in twelve.[51] William Diaper attempts to vary pastoral subject matter in his *Sea-Eclogues* (1712), as does Moses Browne in *Angling Sports* (1729),[52] a collection of nine "piscatory eclogues," and Collins in his *Oriental Eclogues* (1742). Gay and Lady Mary Wortley Montagu found another way to vary or invert tradition through burlesque in *The Shepherd's Week* (1714) and *Town Eclogues* (1717). Later in the century writers experimented with pastoral drama – Boswell, a fellow Scot, thought Allan Ramsay's *Gentle Shepherd* of 1725 "the best pastoral that has ever been written"[53] – and pastoral ballad (Shenstone's *Pastoral Ballad* of 1743). The writer of *Guardian* No. 30 encouraged poets to write of English climate, soil, sports, and "our own rustical Superstitions." Spenser and Philips are offered as examples of an Anglicized Doric style, and models of a naturalized or indigenous pastoral.[54] Although we find little of interest in these poems (outside Pope's and Gay's), many (including Philips' and Mason's) had a high contemporary reputation.

If pastoral had a longer (even if unimpressive) eighteenth-century life than we sometimes remember, it is nonetheless striking that its progress seems to have had very little to do with Milton. Despite the fact that *Lycidas* was admired by poets and critics from Waller to Thomas Warton,[55] eighteenth-century pastoral theorists have surprisingly little to say about the poem. Like Pope, Purney, and Blair, they typically look to Theocritus, Virgil, and Spenser as the models, and are more likely to cite Ambrose Philips than Milton as the fourth great pastoralist.[56] Perhaps this is because theorists were more interested in a set of eclogues than in a single poem. Perhaps too the silence on *Lycidas* (and the relative rarity of *Lycidas* imitations) is due to the theorists' interest in generic purity. Although apparently an admirer of *Paradise Lost*, Purney says nothing of *Lycidas* in his Enquiry, perhaps because for him pastoral should aim at the "Simplicity and Tenderness" of Ambrose Philips. He probably disapproved of the turbulent passion in Milton's elegy, its aspirations toward a loftier style and a "higher mood," and the "digressions" on the corrupt clergy and on poetic fame. For Purney pastoral images should be limited, as those in *Lycidas* are not, to the "beautiful" and the "gloomy." He would throw out all words "that are *Sonorous* and raise a *Verse*" (p. 60). *Lycidas*, furthermore, is consistently allegorical. "Emblematical, allegorical, and refined thoughts," he says, are despite Spenser's example improper for pastoral (p. 50). Though he would have disagreed with Purney on the value of Philips' poems, Pope too thought pastoral should aim at "simplicity, brevity, and delicacy,"[57] and that, *pace* Spenser, it should avoid allegory and "matters of religion." In the hands of the best poets (Pope and Collins) pastoral was a supremely artificial form, self-consciously artful, polished to a high finish, modulated with particular attention to smoothness of diction and prosody. For such poets *Lycidas* could be no model, and had no influence.

Later in the century, when critics like Scott and Warton preferred *Lycidas* to Pope's *Pastorals*, they nonetheless conceded that Pope's were "correct" and Milton's "irregular." Warton admits Milton's "irregularities and incongruities," Scott his "incorrectness."[58] For neither of them could *Lycidas* serve as model. One can make allowances for his irregular numbers, but a modern poet, writing since "the improvement of our numbers," would avoid them. But their real objections centered on pastoral "fictions" or conventions. Warton finds that the fictions of pastoral, though commonplaces in Milton's day, are "obsolete" now.[59] For Johnson, the "inherent improbability" of pastoral always "forces dissatisfaction on the mind."[60] Though Scott admires a "well written eclogue" and challenges some of Johnson's strictures, he notes that the "pastoral idea" puts a strain on our credulity: "Satyrs and fauns can have no business on English ground...Mythological machinery is managed with so much difficulty, that in modern compositions it seldom fails to disgust."[61]

What late-century critics admired in *Lycidas* was its powerful feeling, a quality they found equally lacking in Pope's Golden Age swains and Philips' simpering rustics. Newton commends the poem for "the warm affection which Milton had for his friend, and the extreme grief he was in for the loss of him."[62] Warton praises *Lycidas* for its "passion" and Scott for its "mellowed sorrow."[63] It is not the "fiction" of the poem to which they respond but the reality it shadows. Warton praises the "natural painting" and the imagery which Milton "has raised from local circumstances" – the geography and superstitions of Wales and Cornwall (p. 35). Scott admires the way Milton has explored "real existence...selecting from its circumstances grand or beautiful, as occasion may require" (p. 59).

One reason these critics found eighteenth-century pastoral cold and fictional and may have looked to *Lycidas* for passion and realism is the rise of competing genres, poems of natural description such as Thomson's *Seasons*, and local or topographical poems such as *Cooper's*

Hill, *Windsor Forest*, and *Grongar Hill*. In both of these popular eighteenth-century genres, the poet's imagination (stimulated by memories of Milton's own "L'Allegro" and "Il Penseroso") explores "real existence" and attempts, far more than the conventional pastoral poet, to render a reasonably faithful transcription of the sights and sounds of an English countryside. These forms also readily accomodated the free-ranging moral reflection, meditation, and allegory that characterized Renaissance pastoral. Thus the narrowing of pastoral to elegance and smoothness, to manifest unreality or enervated rusticity, and the rise of new forms available to the poet who wanted to write about rural nature, combined to make *Lycidas* seem not a viable model but, as Warton put it, the work of "an old English poet."

Other competing genres were probably also making pastoral elegy seem obsolete. The poet who set out to write an elegy in the eighteenth century might choose from a number of current models, from the restrained "classical" lament such as Dryden's poem "To the Memory of Mr. Oldham" to the lofty and swelling ode such as "Anne Killigrew." By mid-century several stanzaic forms were fashionable, the Hammond stanza that Gray made popular with his "Country Churchyard" or the regular stanzaic odes of Collins (Horatian rather than Pindaric) such as the "1746" ode or the poems on the deaths of Colonel Ross and the poet Thomson.[64] The elegist who sought epigrammatic effects might choose the epitaph, as Pope and Johnson did. If he sought lyrical effects, he might write an elegiac song, such as Collins' popular "To fair Fidele's grassy tomb." Rustic simplicity might be found in Tickell's ballad, "Colin and Lucy," elegant dignity in his couplet elegy on Addison and Edmund Smith's couplets on the death of John Philips. Each conveys apparently straightforward and unaffected grief.[65] Another elegy in couplets, Pope's "Elegy to the Memory of an Unfortunate Lady," shares their strong emotional coloration, but strikes most readers as more artful, more theatrical, in its lament.

The eighteenth century was then rich in elegiac models. With very few exceptions, the successful elegies of the period seem more "natural" expressions of grief and loss than the pastoral elegy, less based on poetic "fictions." To put the point more carefully, while the pastoral elegy emphasizes its artificiality, the elegies of the eighteenth century, though they too are based on conventions, aim rather to conceal their art. Miltonic pastoral elegy, though it was adopted by a few monodists such as Lyttelton and Mason,[66] seemed to critics at the beginning and end of the century often to be a mechanical exercise. Purney, who wanted elegy to raise pity, found it insufficient "for a shepherd to make a mournful Speech" (p. 46). Johnson found it all too easy "to tell how a shepherd has lost his companion, and now must feed his flocks alone."[67]

To claim that pastoral is a dead form in the eighteenth century clearly overstates the case, but that pastoral declines in quality nobody would wish to deny. In the hands of some poets pastoral appears to go into a "tertiary" phase and become mock-pastoral. For others, like Pope, it becomes a kind of pure art song. And for still others, particularly after mid-century, pastoral in its earlier form, built on mythological fictions, could not survive into an enlightened age. But there is little reason to believe that Milton "exhausted" the form or intimidated subsequent pastoral poets. Pastoral takes a number of non-Miltonic forms in the period. Pastoral elegy survives, indeed revives, in the nineteenth century, in two great examples, but only by going back to classical roots ("Adonais") or by blending with another form, the topographical poem ("Thyrsis"). *Lycidas* leaves its real mark on eighteenth-century poetry not in the monodies it inspired but in the very diction, mood, and scenery of much of the best eighteenth-century verse. But that is another story.

Classical tragedy

Did *Samson Agonistes* help put an end to classical tragedy in England? It may have been the last great example of the form, but the evidence suggests that Milton's play is more likely to have prolonged the life of this genre than to have curtailed it. *Samson* was admired in the eighteenth century, enough for Johnson to complain that it had been overvalued. Edward Phillips and Toland called it an "admirable Tragedy,"[68] and Elijah Fenton thought it "not unworthy the Grecian stage when Athens was in her glory" (I, 246).[69] Monboddo thought it "the most faultless...of all his poetical works."[70] But *Samson* never seems to have attained great popularity, either as play or poem. At mid-century Hurd regretted that this "most artificial and highly finished" of Milton's poems was perhaps "for that reason...the least popular and most neglected."[71] Despite its "simplicity and dignity" it was neglected too in Milton's own day: "His Samson is at once the disgrace of his own age and of ours."[72] By the end of the century, according to Todd, *Samson* was still "not very popular even with the lovers of poetry."[73] It was not published separately until 1796.

Even if *Samson* was not popular among readers and was unknown to playgoers (except in its oratorio version),[74] the idea of classical tragedy was still alive and debated among critics and playwrights. Rymer vociferously asserted that the chorus was "the most necessary part of tragedy."[75] Nearly a century later Hugh Blair joined the continuing controversy concerning the exclusion of the chorus from tragedy. Blair himself approved the exclusion, although he would permit an entr'acte chorus with music and song.[76] Hurd defended the use of the chorus, citing the example of Milton, who attempted "to bring it into our language. His *Sampson Agonistes* was ... a master-piece. But even his credit hath not been sufficient to restore the Chorus."[77] The dramatist Richard Cumberland understood the original role of the chorus but found it unsuitable for modern imitations: "A man must be an enthusiast for antiquity, who can find charms in the dialogue-part of a Greek chorus, and reconcile himself to their unnatural and chilling interruptions of the action and pathos of the scene."[78] But Cumberland commends the classical tragedies of another admirer of Milton, William Mason, for making the chorus sing rather than speak. In his *Elfrida* (1751) and *Caractacus* (1759), "Written on the Model of the Ancient Greek Tragedy," Mason attempted to soften "the rigour of the old drama," and to "obviate some of the popular objections made to the antient form of Tragedy." His well-known *Letters on Elfrida* (1751) show an intelligent understanding of the strengths and limitations of Greek dramatic practices, and explain his own attempts to imitate and modernize: "I meant only to pursue the antient method, so far as it is probable a Greek poet, were he alive, would now do, in order to adapt himself to the genius of our times, and the Character of our Tragedy."[79] As the letters show, Mason's plays were conceived not in a narrow antiquarian spirit, but in the hopes of renewing the genre by adapting it, much like Pope in his Horatian imitations, to modern conventions and circumstances. Though Mason departs from Miltonic severity of design, he clearly found Milton inspiring. He very likely knew of Milton's plans for tragedies based on British history. One of Milton's own subjects, Edgar's murder of Ethelwold "for false wooing," became the subject of Mason's *Elfrida*.[80] The epigraph of *Caractacus* – "Nos munera Phoebo / Misimus; et lectas DRUIDUM de gente CHOREAS" – is taken from Milton's *Mansus*.[81]

Mason was not the only dramatist in the period to use the form. Richard Glover attempted blank verse Greek tragedy in *Medea* (1761). Johnson's *Irene* (1749) and Addison's *Cato* (1713) perhaps belong in the same genre. Though clearly designed for the modern stage, and lacking a chorus, they share classical subject matter and a strong concern for the unities of time and place. Among contemporary French dramatists well-known in England, Racine was the most prominent example of a classical or classicizing dramatist. His *Esther* (1689) and *Athalie* (1691) – the latter possibly inspired by Milton[82] – even made use of a chorus in the original private performances.[83] The success of Racine apparently encouraged even Dryden to project a tragedy "according to the manner of the Grecians,'' if a new theatre with a deeper stage could be built for the purpose.[84]

It is perhaps not surprising that there were few classical tragedies in England. Severely classical drama, closer to the spirit of the French theatre, ran counter to the English irregular genius as celebrated in Dryden's *Essay on Dramatic Poesy*. Variety of character and incident, underplots, and a mixture of comic and tragic actions had characterized most English drama since Shakespeare. A narrow neo-classical tradition, extending from Ben Jonson's Roman tragedies through Rymer to Addison, Johnson, and Mason, may have rivalled the Shakespearean line, but it failed to attract consistently large audiences.[85] In writing *Samson Agonistes* Milton quite consciously turned his back on most contemporary dramatists and audiences, who he thought had debased ancient tragedy by ''intermixing comic stuff with tragic sadness and gravity; or introducing trivial and vulgar persons, which by all judicious hath been counted absurd; and brought in without discretion, corruptly to gratify the people'' (Milton's Preface to *Samson Agonistes*). In Mason's view Milton held his own age in contempt and intended to ''put as great a distance as possible between himself and his contemporary writers.''[86] As a result, the age treated his poem ''with total neglect,'' and posterity had not done much better. Instead of following Milton's example, Mason concludes, a tragic writer should ''adapt himself more to the general taste'' (II, 182), as Mason himself did in attempting to revive classical tragedy in the 1750s. But in his day too a thriving English theatre was more interested in satisfying popular demand for spectacle, music, and song. Indeed, it was by means of musical accompaniment that scriptural subjects such as Samson were able to please audiences. Hurd wished that Milton had undertaken other tragedies based on scriptural subjects that he had noted in the Trinity MS. But it was Handel, through the new form of the English oratorio, who was able to interest a wide eighteenth-century audience in *Samson Agonistes*.[87]

That *Samson Agonistes* did not inspire more eighteenth-century classical tragedy, then, should not lead us to conclude that eighteenth-century dramatists despaired of emulating Milton. Milton's poem was an individual achievement, conceived and executed against the spirit of the age, and making no accomodation to stage practice. Aspiring playwrights after Milton would have been deterred from classical tragedy chiefly out of fear of popular neglect. The few who attempted the form in the eighteenth century – Addison, Johnson, Mason – knew they would have to make concessions to the taste of modern audiences. Even so, it may have been the joint example of Racine and Milton that encouraged English playwrights to attempt classical tragedy at all. Mason's plays, it seems likely, would not have been written without *Samson Agonistes*. Gildon thought *Aureng-Zebe* (1676) indebted to Milton's drama.[88] And as successful a play as *All for Love* (1677) – strikingly similar in several ways to *Samson Agonistes*[89] – may have taken its "classical" form in part because of Milton's recent example.

Masque

Comus, said T. S. Eliot in an essay on Ben Jonson, "is the death of the masque; it is the transition of a form of art...into 'literature'."[90] Nobody would disagree that *Comus* differs markedly from the Jacobean masques of Jonson and his contemporaries. Eighteenth-century critics noticed that *Comus* had less "music and machinery" and more "exquisite poetry" than any other contemporary masque.[91] But the causal sequence and the literary history implicit in Eliot's remark should not go unchallenged. Milton's poem is not a "transition" to anything; in the context of the history of the masque as a form it is an anomaly. If the court masque declines as a literary form, it is not because of Milton's achievement but primarily because the social and political conditions that sustained it at the courts of James I and Charles I radically changed. Designed, as recent critics have emphasized, to celebrate and flatter the Stuart autocracy in private performances at court and at great houses in which the courtiers and even the king himself might participate as masquers,[92] the masque was less likely to thrive under later monarchs. The eighteenth-century Hanoverians ruled not as absolute monarchs but through ministers, in a mixed state in which the role of the king was curtailed. Even the later Stuarts, Charles II and James II, developed a taste, both aesthetic and fleshly, for the pleasures of stageplays in the public playhouses. Though they permitted themselves to be flatteringly addressed from the stage, in the prologues and epilogues of the period, the kings were not the focus of the performance. If the descendant (or vestige) of the political element of the Jacobean masque is the Restoration prologue "To the King," then the descendant of the element of spectacle is the Restoration opera, a form that made use of increasing technical resources of the playhouse to achieve an impressive array of spectacular effects.[93]

Pace Eliot, it is proper to speak of the decline of the masque rather than its death. Although no poet of Jonson's caliber devoted considerable attention to the court masque after 1640, the Caroline masque writer William Davenant was still active after the Restoration, collaborating with Dryden on an operatic *Tempest* in 1667.[94] In 1684 Dryden began working on a masque on *Albion and Albanius*, designed to celebrate Charles II in much the same way Jonson had celebrated his father.

The allegorical "plot" presented the Restoration of 1660, the failed Rye House conspiracy of 1683, and the rout of the King's Whig opponents. Charles's death in 1685 proved only a temporary setback to Dryden's plans, for new scenes were quickly added to present the apotheosis of Charles and the coronation of his brother. *Albion and Albanius* was originally planned as a prelude to Dryden's play *King Arthur*, but when the play was delayed the masque was produced separately as an "opera" six times in June of 1685.[95]

Nor was Dryden's masque simply an outdated and nostalgic gesture. More than fifty years later James Thomson and David Mallet collaborated to produce a masque on *Alfred*, in which many of the Jacobean elements were retained. Commissioned by and privately presented to Frederick Prince of Wales at Cliveden, the Prince's country house, on August 1, 1740, *Alfred* had an explicitly political purpose, to celebrate both a traditional Whig hero and contemporary British naval power (the masque was the original setting for the song "Rule, Britannia").[96] The subsequent history of *Alfred* indicates the way in which the court masque, once an independent genre centered in the world of the court, was gradually absorbed by the public playhouses. In 1745 the masque was first presented on the public stage, in an operatic version set by Thomas Arne. In 1751, after Thomson's death, Mallet revised *Alfred* for a performance at Drury Lane in which Garrick played the lead. As a play with dances and songs by spirits and shepherds, it merged with the theatrical fare common on the eighteenth-century stage, in which music, song, and dance were regular elements. Retitled *Britannia*, it was performed as an afterpiece twelve times over four seasons in the late 1750s.[97]

That masques similar to Jonson's continued to be performed in the Restoration and early eighteenth century suggests that Milton's triumphant use of the genre neither deterred later writers from using the form, nor induced them to write a more "literary" masque. That *Comus* itself was adapted for presentation on the later-eighteenth-century stage suggests that it was a change in audience taste and in theatrical conventions, together with a change in the monarchy's own view of itself, that eventually made the court masque seem an outdated form. Late in the century Thomas Warton sees *Comus*, like *Lycidas*, as essentially the product of its own age, and the kind of work that would not be written in his day. Warton acknowledges that Milton introduced some "palpable absurdities" that would be avoided by "almost every common writer" in "the present age, correct and rational as it is," and notes that the masque "does not nearly approach to the natural constitution of a regular play."[98] He observes, however, that, compared to his Jacobean contemporaries, Milton had "reduced" the old masque "to the principles and form of rational composition" (p. 265). Still, Milton was writing in a different era:

the genius of the best poets is often determined, if not directed, by circumstance and accident. It is natural, that even so original a writer as Milton should have been biassed by the reigning poetry of his day, by composition most in fashion, and by subjects recently brought forward, but soon giving way to others, and almost as soon totally neglected or forgotten.[99]

To make creative use of *Comus*, eighteenth-century poets and dramatists could not simply replicate Milton's achievement. They had to adapt the masque to suit quite different cultural conditions.[100]

As this brief survey shows, then, the traditional genres in which Milton excelled do not die out in the eighteenth century. Granted, it is mostly minor poets who complete the period's epics, pastoral elegies, classical tragedies, masques, and sonnets.[101] Why the major poets avoid these forms or fail to complete their projected works can not be satisfactorily answered. We are probably misreading (or miswriting) literary history when we assign to a great writer the power to deter later writers from using certain forms. It is not the successful use of a form that puts poets off, but the embarrassing failure (like Blackmore's epics) or the change of taste that makes a poem like Herbert's "Easter Wings" seem "false wit." The great poet seems more likely to attract than to deter: Dryden is drawn to Shakespeare, to Juvenal, to Virgil; Pope is drawn to Milton, to Horace, and to Homer. What seems likely, in fact, is that the forms proved inadequate for a variety of reasons, having little to do with Milton's achievement and more to do with the cultural conditions of the age. When all is said and done, however, the major poets of the eighteenth century made their best use of Milton when they did not try to follow too closely in his tracks.

5 · ADAPTATIONS:
RE-MAKING MILTON

We can also measure Milton's impact on the eighteenth century, and the creative opportunities he offered, by examining a marked feature of the literary culture of the day – the extraordinary number and in some cases quality of adaptations of Milton's work. His poems were translated into Latin, or turned into couplets, or paraphrased into prose. They were set to music, illustrated, and altered for the stage. Granted, few adaptations if any attained the status of high art; none of them (in our eyes anyway) rival Milton's own work. They have been little studied as a literary phenomenon, perhaps because they have seemed a part of popular culture at best, a debasement or a dilution of the original texts. But their cultural significance should not be overlooked. Adaptations enabled Milton's works to reach a far wider audience; some proved extraordinarily popular; they also gave a number of writers the opportunity to bask in reflected glory, or (if they dared to "correct" or "improve" Milton in some small way) to stand on the shoulders of a giant.

Eighteenth-century adapters of Milton set out to translate his work into a different medium, or a different style, or to suit a different taste. In these respects they often resembled the century's many adapters of earlier writers, those like Dryden and Pope who updated Chaucer and Donne, or Garrick who adapted at least twelve and perhaps as many as 22 of Shakespeare's plays.[1] Adaptations of Milton may be distinguished from other adaptations in the period by their variety and their frequency. They can also be distinguished from parodies, the kind that make fun as well as the kind that merely imitate – for example, the numerous Spenserian imitations of the period. An adaptation, properly speaking, remodels the original, but retains its basic shape and language. Adaptations are likewise not to be confused with such poems as Pope's *Imitations of Horace*, where the later poet seeks to update topical references, to apply to London what the Latin poet originally applied to Rome. Such imitations rely on a reader's knowledge of the original poem, or recall it to him by means of parallel texts on facing pages, and please by artfully following, or departing from, the original. These poems are not designed, as Johnson noted, to please "common readers," for they require learning and the ability to notice both witty applications and witty divergences. By contrast, an adaptation does not require its reader (or spectator) to make an implicit comparison between original and remodeled poem. Although it assumes some prior knowledge – the Miltonic model's reputation serving to attract an audience – it now wants the audience's entire attention. Its goal is to win applause, both for the altered version and for the original, which the audience is now in a better position to understand and value.[2]

Much has been written to enumerate the many Miltonic adaptations in the eighteenth century. Marcia Pointon has traced Milton's mark on English painting.[3] R.M. Myers has looked at Handel's several settings of Milton's poems.[4] The eighteenth-century illustrations of *Paradise Lost*, from Medina to Blake, continue to attract attention.[5] The compilers of *The London Stage* provide documentary evidence to substantiate the popularity of the *Comus* adaptations by John Dalton and George Colman.[6] My concern is not with demonstrating the frequency of Miltonic adaptation but with assessing its cultural significance, not with describing illustrations and productions, but with attempting to discover or deduce the varied motives of the adapters as they set to work. If we can recover the motives of the adapters, we will be more able to determine the degree to which Milton left eighteenth-century writers frozen in gestures of homage and imitation, and the degree to which he opened up for them a range of literary opportunities.

Translations and corrections

One motive of Milton's adapters is fairly clearly to honor him and his work. This would appear to be the intention of those minor figures such as William Hog who turned *Paradise Lost* into Latin hexameters. Hog's translation appeared in 1690, only a generation after the English original, but it was neither the first nor the last. John Shawcross, following Todd, notes five different translations of *Paradise Lost* into Latin between 1686 and 1702,[7] another six between 1709 and 1753,[8] not counting reprintings, and his list is by no means exhaustive.[9] To put Milton into Latin is to make him speak the international language of literary culture, in which he may be read by all the learned men of Europe. Thus "T. P." presents "Our native Milton" to the "learned reader."[10] And William Hog seeks to spread the fame of a great British poem unknown abroad because written in English.[11] Furthermore, if Milton is the equal of his epic predecessor Virgil, as admiring critics routinely claimed, then the parity may be more clearly understood or symbolized if Milton's poem is cast in Virgil's own tongue, or as T. P. put it, "if Milton is represented as a Roman" (*donatus Romanus*). To display Milton in Latin is then to emphasize his classic status, and appears to spring from the same motive that led Patrick Hume in 1695 and other critics after him to amplify their commentaries on *Paradise Lost* by printing parallel passages from the classic epic writers. It also enables the translator, even more than the critic, to recover more fully the Latinity of Milton's syntax and diction.[12] Finally, to translate Milton into Latin is to make his work into a kind of monument, fixed in the permanence of a language that has ceased to change. In this respect the translators are like Newton and other editors who endow Milton, a recent modern writer, with the dignity of variorum editions and "authentic" texts.[13]

And yet, as the number of different translations alone makes clear, a Latin Milton is not simply designed to preserve Milton's image in selfless service to literature. To put Milton into Latin is in some sense to set one's stamp on him, and to give a virtuoso display of one's ability to turn hexameters. Even in the humble task of nearly-anonymous translator, a writer could feel that he was contributing, in his own name and in Milton's, to the stature of English letters. Dobson's translation has been called "about the greatest feat ever performed in modern Latin verse."[14] One should not assume, furthermore, that the audience of the translations was a small or elite one. Latin, after all, was still the possession of every well-educated man, and many eighteenth-century poets, including Addison, Gray, and Johnson, saw fit to write and even to publish poems in Latin. Interest in Renaissance neo-Latin poets such as Politian and Sarbiewski remained high.[15] The reader of the *Gentleman's Magazine* frequently came across Latin poems, and in 1746 and 1750 could have found eight different translations of the opening of *Paradise Lost* set out for his comparison.[16] Lauder's initial charges of plagiarism were made in the *Gentleman's Magazine* in 1747. It was in part the familiarity and accessibility of Latin translations of Milton that undid Lauder, when John Douglas and others showed that Lauder had inserted lines from Hog's translation into a text of the Latin poet Masenius.

A second motive for adapting Milton is to render him more accessible to a popular audience. This motive is clearly behind the various translations of *Paradise Lost* into heroic couplets, into "grammatical construction," or into prose. Those who translate the poem into Latin address a learned or at least a classically-educated audience. Those who translate "into English" as it were address an audience that found Milton's syntax and blank verse too difficult to follow. As early as 1699 one John Hopkins put Books IV, VI, and IX into rhyme for the benefit of those "ladies...who would taste the Apples, but care not for Climbing to the Bough."[17] Rhymed versions of Book I appeared in 1738 and 1740.[18] By mid-century even heroic couplets must have been too difficult for imagined audiences to read, or perhaps for the translator to write.

In 1745 the poem is "Render'd into Prose" in an edition entitled *The State of Innocence: And Fall of Man. Describ'd in Milton's Paradise Lost*[19] and "Rendered into Grammatical Construction" in 1773 in James Buchanan's *The First Six Books of Milton's Paradise Lost*. Buchanan's intended audience was "Ladies" together with "young gentlemen at our Latin schools" who had difficulty with the "construction, which is owing to the transposition or inversion of the words, as well as to ellipsis" ("Advertisement").[20] John Wesley thought some of the lines so "unintelligible" to his readers "of a common education" that he simply excised them altogether in his *An Extract from Milton's Paradise Lost* (1763, 2nd edn 1791). Cuts totalled 1870 lines, the most common of them involving obscure biblical or classical allusions, extended similes, complex syntax, or abstruse natural science.[21]

Editors like Hopkins, Buchanan, and Wesley make no pretense of creating literary texts to rival or even to complement Milton's own. Hopkins says he himself "would rather look on Mr. Milton plain ... than in the gawdy dress my Effeminate Fancy gave him" (Preface), and contents himself with the thought that his translation cannot harm "the Noble air of Mr. Milton's Style." The author of the prose paraphrase rejects the idea that his work is "superior or any Way equal to the Poetry of PARADISE LOST" (Preface). One may perhaps suspect such becoming professions of modesty. The ambitious and more talented of those who adapted Milton under cover of making his work accessible may well have been prompted by more self-regarding motives. At least one paraphraser baldly claimed that he was actually improving the poem. In 1756 appeared *A New Version of the Paradise Lost: or, Milton Paraphrased. In Which the Measure and Versification are corrected and harmonized; the Obscurities elucidated; and the Faults of which the Author stands accused by Addison, and other of the Criticks, are removed.*[22] This paraphraser retained blank verse, but presumed to "correct" Milton's prosody. His claim might be dismissed as effrontery, but we should note that it is not so very different from the work of a much better-known figure like Richard Bentley.

The ostensible purpose of Bentley's notorious edition of *Paradise Lost* (1732) was of course to restore the text to what Milton had himself written, or rather dictated. But Bentley's adversaries quickly charged that he sought not to restore but to correct. "It is plain," wrote Lewis Theobald, "it is the Intention of that Great Man rather to correct and pare off the Excrescencies of the *Paradise Lost* ... than to restore corrupted Passages ... The chief Turn of his Criticism is plainly to shew the World, that if *Milton* did not write as He would have him, he ought to have wrote so."[23] Indeed, Bentley's rewriting of allegedly corrupt passages, wholesale removal of alleged interpolations, and his own additions might suggest that we consider his edition as another of the many eighteenth-century *adaptations* of the poem, and a prime exhibit of the adapter as correcter. He adapts the poem to make it conform to his own notions of literary correctness. Christian truth must not be contaminated with pagan "trash" (IV. 659, 711). Poetry must be clear, regular, simple, and unambiguous. If necessary, Milton must be written to improve logical clarity (as in the case of his objections to "darkness visible" at I. 67), to achieve grammatical completeness (VIII. 504, 645), and clear syntax. All paradox and inconsistency must be purged. Thus "heaven's perpetual king" can in no way be "endangered" (I. 131). "Wedded love" may be a "mysterious *League*" but not a "mysterious Law," for "A *Law*, that's suppos'd *mysterious*, is no Law at all" (V, 750). Similes must be introduced only when the relevance of the comparison is clear (the "careful Plowman" at IV. 983 must go). Meter must be smoothly iambic.[24]

That *Paradise Lost* might be "improved" is as offensive an idea to us as it was to many of Bentley's contemporaries, including Zachary Pearce, who responded by defending Milton's text and demonstrating its poetic effectiveness. But the idea that Milton's work, written before an age of correctness, might be made more perfect, was an idea seriously entertained in Pope's day. Atterbury advised Pope himself to revise *Samson Agonistes*:

it deserves your care and is capable of being improv'd, with little trouble, into a perfect Model and Standard of Tragic Poetry, always allowing for its being a Story taken out of the Bible which is an Objection that at this time of day, I know is not to be got over.[25]

It is difficult to determine the tone of the remark: is the last part condescending, rueful, or ironic? What is clear is that Atterbury thinks the project worthy the attention of a great poet – already in 1722 the author of *The Rape of the Lock* and the *Iliad* translation – and likely to reflect well on him.

Thus we should perhaps consider more seriously the idea that to turn Milton's blank verse into couplets in the eighteenth century was implicitly to "correct" the poem, to subject it to contemporary rules governing prosody, and to re-assert the primacy of the couplet over blank verse.[26] Admittedly this enterprise shows a certain perverseness, since Milton had gone out of the way to denounce the modern bondage of rhyming, but as serious a poet as Dryden nonetheless saw profit in "tagging" Milton's verse. The popular belief that Milton would have done better to write in rhyme was widespread enough to call forth a satirical response directed at Bentley and other correcters,[27] and to provoke Johnson to declare that he "cannot prevail on [himself] to wish that Milton had been a rhymer."[28]

ADAPTATIONS: RE-MAKING MILTON

Milton on the stage

That making Milton more accessible – the ostensible motive – might also win some glory for the adapter seems clearer when we look briefly at the well-known stage adaptations of *Comus*. John Dalton's 1738 adaptation of Milton's masque was the most successful of many eighteenth-century alterations of Milton for the stage.[29] It was performed 11 times in its first season at Drury Lane, and retained a place in the repertoire for thirty years. Immediately published in 1738, it went through seven separate editions by 1762 and another four by the end of the century. Dalton's goal, so he says in his self-effacing poetic prologue, is merely to give Milton's "Beauties to the publick Eye." Acknowledging the inferiority of his "meaner phrase" to Milton's "nobler lays," Dalton nonetheless suggests that "Such Heav'n-taught Numbers should be more than read," and that he was able to remedy the defect. What he could do was enable Milton's "pure essence" to be seen "in action." Thus he proceeded to alter the poem for the eighteenth-century musical stage. He added a number of songs, some of them based on lines drawn from "L'Allegro" and "Il Penseroso." He supplied a new scene in which the lady's brothers are tempted by a female nymph, Euphrosyne (in the spirit of those contemporary adapters of Shakespeare who added to Prospero's island a young man, brother to Miranda, who had never seen a girl). Long speeches in Milton's text were distributed among several characters to enliven the pace and add variety. "We on his deathless trophies raise our own," Dalton says in the Prologue, perhaps more truly than he knew. His adaptation was so successful that it not only gave Milton's poem the name by which it has ever since been popularly known (it was previously known only as *A Masque...*) but in some ways it usurped the place of the original, which was published in a separate edition only once during the sixty years following the appearance of Dalton's version. More strikingly, several lines from Dalton's *Comus* not found in the original appeared *as Milton's* in the *Gentleman's Magazine* and in a popular *Poetical Dictionary*.[30]

Dalton's success did not exhaust the theatrical possibilities of Milton's poem. In 1772 a popular dramatist, George Colman the elder, collaborated with a popular composer, Thomas Arne, to redesign a stage *Comus* as a two-act afterpiece. This time the adapters reduced Milton's text to less than a third of its original length. They excised or contracted descriptive passages and the brothers' "divine arguments on temperance and chastity," though they insisted that they had cut no "circumstance" (i.e. plot element) contained in the original masque. Colman and Arne are more forthright about Milton's defects as a dramatist:

"Pure Poetry unmixt with passion, however admired in the closet, has scarce ever been able to sustain itself upon the stage." And it is chiefly the music, they insist, that enabled the masque to succeed in the theatre.[31] Though never as successful as the Dalton version, the Colman – Arne *Comus* went through 23 performances at Covent Garden in 1772. It was published seven times over a period of the next fifteen years.[32]

The Colman – Arne adaptation might seem to lie on the borderline between serious art and popular ephemera, creative use of Miltonic poetry and mere commercial exploitation. Of course the adapters were moved by the hope of making money for themselves and their company, and an honest desire to bring some stylish entertainment to their audiences. But they are of interest to the student of literary culture, since they seem to have been animated both by a wish to make Milton accessible to a wider audience, and by a final adapter's motive, the wish to realize some possibilities latent in the original, suggested but left undeveloped by Milton himself.

Other theatrical adapters quite clearly turned to Milton's work for this reason. Joseph Warton claimed in 1756 (with some exaggeration) that "L'Allegro" and "Il Penseroso," once obscure, were made "universally known" by Handel's settings. While it is clear that poets knew and used Milton's poems before the 1740s,[33] it remains true that editors like Newton, Warton, and Bowles honored Handel as "a composer worthy of the Poetry," instrumental in spreading the knowledge and appreciation of Milton among popular audiences.[34] Milton's scenes, wrote one observer in 1753, are "greatly heightened and assisted" by Handel's mimetic musical effects.[35] The success of Dalton's *Comus* may have encouraged Handel to attempt settings for "L'Allegro" and "Il Penseroso." In 1740 his collaborator Charles Jennens, the librettist for Handel's *Saul* and *Messiah*, re-arranged "L'Allegro" and "Il Penseroso" for musical performance. Aware that the two poems are organized quite similarly – the ritual exorcism, the invocation to the chosen goddess, followed by the parallel tracings of an ideal day, closing with the pleasures of music – Jennens saw that the contrast between "L'Allegro" and "Il Penseroso" might be sharpened by immediately juxtaposing a short passage from "L'Allegro" with its parallel in "Il Penseroso." This of course also suited the needs of vocal performance, for Jennens produced a series of arias whose contrasting tempi, rhythm, and keys yielded the requisite variety. Jennens was a remarkably faithful adapter, cutting the poems by about one third, making minor alterations in syntax, while otherwise leaving Milton's poetry intact.[36]

Perhaps aware too that Milton did not clearly resolve the tension created by opposing his cheerful and solitary men,[37] Jennens chose to bring out Milton's hints by adding his own formal resolution of opposites in *Il Moderato*, 48 lines divided into seven arias.[38] Milton's poems were extraordinarily popular in this musical version, and were printed at least four times over the next fifteen years.[39] By contrast, Milton's originals were published separately only once during the century.[40]

Samson Agonistes offered different opportunities. Since Milton had never intended his poem for the stage (for that reason he did not divide it into act and scene),[41] it was left to eighteenth-century adapters to prepare the play for the public theatre, and thus to realize (as they thought) the play's full theatrical potential. As we have already seen, classical tragedy continued to seem a viable form of drama to eighteenth-century writers, and Atterbury presumably intended Pope to alter *Samson* in order to make it suitable for the stage.[42] Atterbury's call, however, remained unanswered until 1798, when John Penn adapted the play by dividing it into separate scenes, omitting some choral speeches. He justified the abridgement by suggesting that the tragedy, "curtailed" as it was, acquired "that rational as well as theatrical rapidity of march which the example of the managers, in shortening our finest plays for representation, justifies us in communicating to it." Penn's purpose is not only to produce an acting text but (more ambitiously) to show the "true nature of the drama."[43] Penn evidently hoped that his alteration would attract the attention of theatre managers, though there is no record that a production was ever mounted.

Yet *Samson Agonistes* did have a successful stage life in the period, not as a tragedy but as an oratorio. In 1743, fresh from his triumph with "L'Allegro" and "Il Penseroso," Handel collaborated with Newburgh Hamilton to produce *Samson. An Oratorio*. It was Hamilton's hope, he wrote, that Handel's music might add "new Life and Spirit" to Milton's poem.[44] He made some substantial cuts, set some of Milton's lines to rhyme, and divided the text into dialogue, airs, and chorus, in three acts. He also supplied a new character, Micah, a friend to Samson, to whom he assigned some of the Chorus's lines, and created a Chorus of Philistines to match the Chorus of Israelites. Finally, Hamilton supplies some new airs: he drew on Milton's "Upon Time" as the basis for a song for the Israelite chorus, and the "Nativity Ode" for one of Samson's airs. Hamilton's Miltonic pastiche, as Winton Dean notes, is often very skillful, both faithful to the original and at the same time effective in the theatre.[45] *Samson* was a very successful theatre piece, second in popularity only to *Messiah*, performed eight times in its first season (more than any other oratorio) and was successfully revived in London in nine of the next 16 seasons until

Handel's death in 1759.[46] The libretto went through four printed editions in the space of a year,[47] and at least 14 further editions in the next twenty years.[48]

Despite his success with *Samson*, Handel did not go on to attempt an oratorio on *Paradise Lost*. But it was not for want of a text. In 1744 Mrs. Delany, later one of Richardson's correspondents, made what she called "a drama for an oratorio" out of Book IX of *Paradise Lost*.[49] Her libretto apparently remained more faithful to Milton's text than Hamilton's: "I would not have a word or thought of Milton's altered; and I hope to prevail with Handel to set it without having any of the lines put into verse [i.e., into rhyme] for the arias" (p. 278). For whatever reason, Handel rejected Mrs. Delany and London had to wait until 1760 to hear an oratorio based on Milton's epic. Benjamin Stillingfleet based his text on parts of Books IV, V, IX, X, XI, and XII, all set in the Garden. He cut out not only the scenes in Hell and Heaven, but the parts of the Father, the Son, and Satan.[50] It was set to music by John Christopher Smith, a younger contemporary and sometime assistant to Handel, and performed twice.[51]

Apparently working in ignorance of Stillingfleet's version, the minor poet Richard Jago (remembered now only for "Edge-Hill," 1767) also composed a libretto for *Adam. An Oratorio*. Like Stillingfleet's it is set in paradise, and is based exclusively on the human parts of *Paradise Lost*, Books IV–V and IX–XII. But the performances of the Stillingfleet–Smith work seem to have made it difficult for Jago to find a composer or theatre manager willing to mount yet another oratorio on *Paradise Lost*. The libretto was nonetheless published in Jago's *Poems, Moral and Descriptive* (1784),[52] with a hopeful "Advertisement" and a postscript "To the Composer." Jago is extraordinarily faithful to the "very words" of his original, even in the airs. His goal seems to have been to include as many of the well-known Edenic passages of the poem as possible, and to stitch them together into a simple version of the Fall. His Act I consists of set pieces from Book IV, both descriptive and interlocutory, including Eve at the pool, "Not that fair field of Enna," and "With thee conversing." Act II is built on the discussion in Book IX concerning the division of labor and the famous Morning Hymn from Book V. Act III opens after the Fall. After a brief chorus from Guardian Angels, Adam denounces Eve ("O Eve, in evil hour") before a reconciliation scene based on the end of Book X. In a final scene Eve's lament for her flowers leads abruptly to her reassurance ("In me is no delay"). Jago's art, by his own admission, consists in selecting and compiling Milton's lines into a brief compass. He makes no effort to produce a living drama which moves relentlessly to the Fall and finally to restoration. *Adam* is at best a series of tableaux, each of which expresses a single mood (praise, lament, anger, etc.).

Unlike the stage adaptations of *Samson* and *Comus*, the oratorio versions of *Paradise Lost* never successfully competed for attention with the original. While Milton's tragedy and masque may have become better and more widely known as a result of the stage versions, adaptations of *Paradise Lost* appear only to have sought to capitalize on the poem's own fame.[53] I defer until a later chapter the first, the most ambitious, and the most significant adaptation of *Paradise Lost* in the age, Dryden's *State of Innocence*.

I have excluded, on the grounds that they are not strictly speaking literary, the many adaptations of Milton's work made by the engravers and painters of the eighteenth century. A good deal has already been written, furthermore, not only about the illustrations of *Paradise Lost* in the period, but also about Blake's engravings for many of Milton's works, and about Henry Fuseli's Milton Gallery, a commercial venture of 1790–91. To be sure, illustrations of Milton were in most cases directly connected with editions of the poems.[54] But enough non-pictorial evidence has perhaps been gathered to show that Milton's works provided the materials for an unprecedented amount and variety of adaptation in the eighteenth century. Granted, many of the adaptations I have surveyed are undistinguished. But it might be noted that, while only very minor figures engaged in those adaptations where the primary motive seems to be to honor Milton or to make him more accessible, greater figures such as Bentley, Pope, Dryden, and Handel thought it worth their time to adapt Milton so as to "correct" or improve him, or to develop some possibility left only latent. Even those who humbly came to praise Milton, as I have suggested, could claim some small independent glory for themselves. Milton, it may be said, captured the imagination of his adapters. But he also liberated it.

Finally, the eighteenth-century adaptations of Milton might also help us to see more clearly a central characteristic of the period's culture. The eighteenth century may have been the last great age of adaptation. Every age adapts its predecessors, but the eighteenth century does so more pervasively and more openly than most. In the past we have too often taken this as a sign of exhausted invention (Shakespeare's popularity masking a moribund tragic tradition) or of obtuseness and even cowardice (Tate evading the stark ending of *Lear*). Viewed another way, however, adaptation represents both cultural continuity (tradition preserved and maintained) and cultural vigor (tradition renewed in contemporary terms). Purists may prefer their Milton unadulterated, but the price of purity may be a merely academic reputation. In the eighteenth century Milton was a national treasure. It was in large part the adaptations that brought him that recognition.

6 · NEW GENRES

Another way to measure Milton's *creative* influence is to turn from those genres which remained alive in the century despite or because of Milton's achievement, and the variety of adaptations that his work prompted, to new genres which we can reasonably consider inspired or encouraged by Milton's example. Some of the most successful and distinctive forms of the eighteenth century – the tetrameter hymn or ode, the mock-epic, the evening piece, even the novel – would not have taken the form they did or would not have been written at all without Milton. But it would be misleading to imply that Milton's influence was wholly beneficent. He was indirectly responsible too, as many literary historians have claimed, for a good deal of dull blank verse and windy religiosity. To account for the failure of a Milton-inspired "Christian poetry" is also part of the story.

The evening poem

It has long been recognized that Milton's paired poems, "L'Allegro" and "Il Penseroso," sired a tradition of octosyllabic verse in the eighteenth century. This tradition might properly be called a genre, since it combines formal features (tetrameter couplets, address to personified abstractions, especially in order to banish or invite) with common subject matter (rural description, pleasures proposed) under a prevailing mood (meditative-descriptive) and rhythm (light and delicate rather than Hudibrastic or Swiftian). Previous accounts of this tradition, including that of R. D. Havens, are adequate enough to require no more than a reminder here that Milton's poems inspired some of the best work of a number of poets just below the top rank. Sometimes these poems are called hymns, as with Thomas Parnell's "Hymn to Contentment" (1714). More commonly they are called odes, and include some of the best work of Collins, the two Wartons, Akenside, and Langhorne. Sometimes Milton's tetrameters combine with the emerging topographical poem (derived from Denham's *Cooper's Hill* and perhaps Pope's *Windsor Forest*) to produce the century's popular "hill poems," such as Dyer's *Grongar Hill* (1726). To be sure, many lesser talents followed the fashion. Much of the stuff produced deserves to languish unrescued in magazines and miscellanies, or to suffer the mockery of parody.[1] Most of it, like William Mason's "Il Bellicoso" and "Il Pacifico," is slavishly imitative. But for the better poets in the octosyllabic tradition, Milton served, in Leavis's phrase, as "the inspiring and emancipating genius."[2]

Perhaps the clearest case in point is the development in the eighteenth century of the evening poem, which we might consider a sub-genre of the meditative-descriptive poem. Sometimes entitled "Ode," sometimes written in pentameter lines or in stanzas rather than octosyllabics, this is a distinctly eighteenth-century tradition which includes one of the best poems of the period. Before Collins and Joseph Warton wrote their "Odes to Evening" in the 1740s, it would not generally have occurred to an English poet to think of evening as a subject for poetic description. Just a year after they wrote, James Hervey's extraordinarily popular "Contemplations on Night" found evening "gently darkening into night" a time "peculiarly proper for sedate consideration. All circumstances concur to hush our passions and sooth our cares, to tempt our steps abroad, and prompt our thoughts to serious reflection."[3] And within a generation poetic descriptions of the evening appeared in the works of most of the poets of mid-century – Thomas Warton, James Beattie, John Langhorne, John Dyer, David Mallet, Richard Jago, William Cowper, and many other lesser figures. There can be little doubt, I think, that the rather sudden appearance and establishment of this popular poetic form is due to the rediscovery of the pastoral Milton – not only the paired poems but especially the pastoral parts of *Paradise Lost* – and that the eighteenth-century ode to evening can be clearly traced to Milton as its progenitor.

Prior to Milton one finds no significant descriptions of a mild and meditative evening either in English or in classical poetry. In Mediterranean pastoral tradition, descending from Virgil through Spenser and Pope, evening is a brief transition between day and night, a period of cold shadows and threatening mists, and a time when sheep and shepherd must be hurried into shelter.[4] It is only when the poetical shepherd is located in a northern clime where summer evenings are long and mild, and is separated from his sheep, that he turns meditative observer and finds that the evening invites him to wander forth and sing her praise. The first English poet to transform his shepherd into an evening wanderer is Milton. Although neither of Milton's paired poems gives a full-scale evening scene, they supplied the elements which were later to become key features of the eighteenth-century evening poem. Consider a familiar passage from "Il Penseroso":

> Thee Chantress oft the Woods among,
> I woo to hear thy Even-Song;
> And missing thee, I walk unseen
> On the dry smooth-shaven Green,
> To behold the wand'ring Moon,
> Riding near her highest noon,
> Like one that had been led astray
> Through the Heav'ns' wide pathless way;
> And oft, as if her head she bow'd,
> Stooping through a fleecy cloud.
> Oft on a Plat of rising ground,
> I hear the far-off *Curfew* sound,
> Over some wide-water'd shore,
> Swinging low with sullen roar.
>
> (lines 63–76)

These lines set forth a dramatic situation which the evening poets were later to develop: a wandering poet-observer attuned to the still sad music of the dying day; a scene devoid of peril or threat and presided over by feminized spirits – Philomel, Cynthia, Melancholy, the "pensive nun...Sober, steadfast, and demure" – with whom the poet has some kind of chaste though subtly sexualized encounter. *Comus* develops the image of the pensive nun and adds a costuming detail to the scene – the loose-fitting and sober-colored livery. Evening there appears as "gray-hooded Ev'n / Like a sad Votarist in Palmer's weed" (lines 188–89). The final element, later to recur in numerous eighteenth-century evening poems, is the moon, herself a wanderer like the poet, seen sometimes in a clear sky but more often breaking through a veil of clouds.

Milton's most fully developed evening scenes, however, are not in the early poems but in *Paradise Lost*. Evening in unfallen Eden is *mild, still, dewy, brown, cool*, a gradual process whose approach is *sweet*.[5] Eve's love song to Adam gathers up the several elements found in "Il Penseroso" and adds to them the idea of gentle arrival: "sweet the coming on / Of grateful Ev'ning mild, then silent Night / With this her solemn Bird and this fair Moon, / And these the Gems of Heav'n, her starry train" (IV. 646–49).[6] The evening scene that eighteenth-century poets found most inspiring is an extended version of evening's approach. Milton sets the scene with a description of sunset:

> Meanwhile in utmost Longitude, where Heav'n
> With Earth and Ocean meets, the setting Sun
> Slowly descended, and with right aspect
> Against the eastern Gate of Paradise
> Levell'd his ev'ning Rays.
>
> (IV. 539–43)

Note especially here that Milton's sun, unlike the Virgilian or Mediterranean one, descends *slowly*. Nearly fifty lines intervene while Uriel glides "through the Even" on a sunbeam before the sun falls "beneath th'*Azores*," where it arrays "with reflected Purple and Gold / The Clouds that on his Western Throne attend" (596–97). Then follows the arrival of evening:

> Now came still Ev'ning on, and Twilight gray
> Had in her sober Livery all things clad;
> Silence accompanied, for Beast and Bird,
> They to thir grassy Couch, these to thir Nests
> Were slunk, all but the wakeful Nightingale;
> She all night long her amorous descant sung;
> Silence was pleas'd; now glow'd the Firmament
> With living Sapphires: *Hesperus* that led
> The starry Host, rode brightest, till the Moon
> Rising in clouded Majesty, at length
> Apparent Queen unveil'd her peerless light,
> And o'er the dark her Silver Mantle threw.
>
> (598–609)[7]

Again appear several elements from the "Il Penseroso" passage: the absence of peril; the feminine spirits (nightingale, moon, and evening herself); the moon breaking through clouds. The scene is pervaded by a diffused and chaste sexuality focused here on the nightingale's love song directed as it were to all the inhabitants of evening. A chaste eroticism is implied too in the sudden and startling revelation of the unveiled moon who throws her mantle over the darkness. What is new in the passage – and what Collins' contemporaries found especially suggestive – is, first, the emphasis on evening's stealthy, soft arrival, still (motionless, soundless) yet still (always, continuously) coming on; second, the development of the imagery of clothing (the purple and gold hangings around the sun's throne, evening's sober livery, the moon's mantle); and third, the sublimity of the moon's unveiling.

Both poets and editors in the mid-eighteenth century found this passage inspiring: "Surely there never was a finer evening; words cannot furnish out a more lovely description... for the variety of numbers and pleasing images, I know of nothing parallel or comparable to this to be found among all the treasures of ancient or modern poetry." So declared Newton in his 1749 edition of *Paradise Lost*.[8] Jonathan Richardson remarked simply that "Surely here is the most Inchanting Description of Ev'ning that ever was made."[9] Dennis and Thomson singled out the lines for admiring comment.[10] As early as 1702 the passage is cited by Edward Bysshe in his *Art of English Poetry* – a sort of *vade mecum* for aspiring poets, often reprinted – under the headings of "Evening" and "Moon" as examples of "the most natural and sublime thoughts of the best English poets."[11]

"Evening poets" were not long in making creative use of Milton's lines. When interested in describing the dying half-lights of evening they typically turned to Milton's "sober livery":

> Now sunk the sun; the closing hour of day
> Came onward, mantled o'er with sober grey;
> Nature in silence bid the world repose.
>> Parnell, "The Hermit," lines 43–45

> Arising awful o'er the eastern sky,
> Onward she comes with silent step and slow
> In her brown mantle wrapt.
>> Mallet, *The Excursion* (1728), I. 240–42

> When Evening dons her mantle grey
>> Robert Lloyd, "To the Moon"

> Now twilight veil'd the glaring Face of Day,
> And clad the dusky Fields in sober Gray.
>> Pope, tr. *Iliad*, XXIV. 427–28[12]

> Hail, meek-ey'd maiden, clad in sober grey
>> Joseph Warton, "Ode to Evening," line 1

> When evening in her sober vest
> Drew the grey curtain of the fading west.
>> Cowper, "Charity," lines 262–63[13]

John Ogilvie's "An Evening Piece" is a pastiche of Miltonic phrases and images:

> Now o'er the western skies, descending Eve
> Spread her grey robe, the solitary Hour
> To Silence sacred and deep-musing thought
> Came sweetly serious on the balmy gale,
> And stole the ear of Wisdom: – all was still,
> Save where the slow-trilling from the mantling bough,
> Night's plaintive warbler, to the echoing vale
> Pour'd her love-labour'd note: mellifluous lay![14]

Ogilvie derives syntactic patterns ("Now... came... on," "all... save") and other details (the grey robe, the nightingale, silence, perhaps even "mantling") from the Edenic evening in *Paradise Lost*, Book IV. But he adds phrases drawn from Satan's dream-seduction of Eve in Book V (the "night-warbling Bird," the "love-labor'd song"). Even the "balmy gale" appears to come from the "gentle gales" and "balmy spoils" that greet Satan's arrival in Eden (IV. 156–59).

As eighteenth-century poets develop the evening poem several features quickly become standard. The scene is silent, sober, and serene.

It is a time of half-lights, gradual dimming and decline. A favorite term to describe the effects of twilight is "glimmering."[15] The softening scene has power to calm the mind:

> Hail sacred hour of peaceful rest!
> Of pow'r to charm the troubled breast.
> (Anon., "Ode to Night" [1765][16])

> Dost thou not at evening hour
> Feel some soft and secret power,
> Gliding o'er thy yielding mind,
> Leave sweet serenity behind?
> While all disarm'd, the cares of day
> Steal thro' the falling gloom away?
> (Langhorne, "The Evening Primrose"[17])

> the still landscape sooths my soul to rest,
> And ev'ry care subsides to calmest peace.
> (T. Warton, *Five Pastoral Eclogues*, II. 22–23)

> And holy calm creeps o'er my peaceful soul.
> (J. Warton, "To Evening")

Once calm, the mind is prepared for "musing,"[18] particularly as the meditative observer wanders into the scene before him. As Thomson says, sunset is "the soft Hour / Of Walking" (*Summer*, 1379–80); as another poet puts it, the evening stillness "Invites us forth to solitary vales."[19]

Though sometimes entitled "Ode to Night," the poems in this Miltonic evening tradition should be distinguished from the better-known contemporary "noctural tradition," including such poems as Parnell's "Night-Piece on Death," Young's *Night Thoughts*, and Blair's *The Grave*. While the night-piece is typically rapturous, bold, and pre-occupied with death and immortality, the evening poem is mild, temperate, pre-occupied with the "pensive pleasures" of the mortal imagination. The mild evening poem may be further distinguished from a related form by its ruling deity. In one amatory tradition, ultimately derived from classical pastoral, the poet addresses the evening star as the harbinger of love. In English this traditional association is prominent in Spenser, and appears as late as Akenside's and Blake's poems "To the Evening Star." The dominant and more Miltonic tradition addresses not Hesperus but the chaste Diana. Its note is composure rather than passionate anticipation.[20] In this milder tradition epithalamic associations of the evening star are played down, and Hesperus is subordinated to the moon.

Indeed, it is very probably due to Milton's example that the moon became a standard part of the eighteenth-century evening poem.[21] Milton's lines on the Edenic moon seem to have been widely known and admired. James Hervey's moon, like Milton's, rises "in clouded majesty," and "at length...unveils her peerless light."[22] John Brown's throws her "glimmering faintness" over a sleeping world.[23] Although Pope had provided a description of a cloudless moonlit night in the celebrated night-piece at the end of Book VIII of the *Iliad*,[24] evening poets more commonly responded to the moon glimpsed as it breaks through the clouds. For this they went to Milton: "Mark the resplendent moon. / Breaking through a parted cloud!" (John Cunningham, "Day: A Pastoral" [1766]); "The silver moon, with majesty divine, / Emerges from behind yon sable cloud, / Around her all the spacious Heavens glow / With living fires!" (William Julius Mickle, "A Night Piece" [1761]).[25]

Mickle and Cunningham are no more than competent versifiers, working in an established mode.[26] The case for Milton's creative influence does not finally rest with them. The best of the century's evening poets helped establish the form in the 1740s. Though he responded to Milton's suggestions for a poetry of the evening, Collins developed the form in distinctive ways.

What sets Collins apart from the other poets who attempt the evening poem is his ability to combine external description and internal affect, together with his almost perfectly adapted vehicle, the unrhymed Horatian ode, in which evening seems ideally evoked. Like all other eighteenth-century evening poets Collins is indebted to Milton, whose "Ev'ning Ear" he honored in the "Ode on the Poetical Character" (line 64). But in the "Ode to Evening" Milton inspires his poetic descendant to a kind of vision and communion that even the master could not attain.

Editors have pointed out that Collins addresses Evening in Miltonic diction (drawn largely from "L'Allegro" and "Il Penseroso")[27] and in Miltonic verse form, his translation of Horace's "Ad Pyrrham." Ainsworth remarked long ago that Collins' "Ode" may have been inspired by the first two lines of Milton's description of evening,[28] but neither he nor later commentators have looked at what Collins did to develop the hints. To begin with, it is clear that Collins knew Milton's evening passage well, for in an early fragment, "Ye Genii who in secret state," he imitated it:

> Some times when Morning o'er Plain
> Her radiant Mantle throws
> I'll mark the Clouds where sweet Lorrain
> His orient Colours chose.
> ...
> But when soft Evning o'er the Plain
> Her gleamy Mantle throws...[29]

Here Collins tries to find a way to adapt Milton's startling line about the moon's silver mantle to other times of day. In another early fragment he attempts his own moonpiece:

> The Moon with dewy lustre bright
> Her mild Aethereal radiance gave
> On Paly Cloisters gleam'd her light
> Or trembled o'er th'unresting wave.[30]

The mantle disappears but the paly cloisters are derived from "Il Penseroso." Collins finished neither fragment, perhaps because he felt they were too imitative.[31]

Collins is also aware of the briefer Virgilian pastoral evening. His third *Oriental Eclogue* takes place at "Evening":

> While Ev'ning Dews enrich the glitt'ring Glade,
> And the tall Forests cast a longer Shade.
> (lines 3 – 4)

The original of these lines is perhaps Virgil's "maioresque cadunt altis de montibus umbrae" (the close of Eclogue 1), as Lonsdale suggests, filtered through a couplet from Pope's *Pastorals*: "When falling dews with Spangles deck'd the Glade, / And the low Sun had lengthen'd ev'ry Shade" ("Autumn," lines 99 – 100). What is significant, however, is that Collins finds the evening far more inviting than either Virgil or Pope: his dews "enrich" the shade. While Pope's lines come at the end of his poem, when the singers return to shelter, Collins' come at the beginning of his eclogue, when Emyra, "Amidst the Maids of *Zagen's* peaceful Grove" (line 5), begins her song. To emphasize the pleasures of the evening Collins in 1757 added two quite un-Virgilian lines to follow immediately his couplet on dew and shade: "What Time 'tis sweet o'er Fields of Rice to stray, / Or scent the breathing Maze at setting Day."[32]

When he came to write the "Ode to Evening" Collins returned to Milton and found a way to use Miltonic suggestion to accomplish what Milton himself had not done – a leisurely description of the natural process of nightfall. A number of details in the early part of the "Ode" might come from Milton's passage:

> O *Nymph* reserv'd, while now the bright-hair'd Sun
> Sits in yon western Tent, whose cloudy Skirts,
> With Brede ethereal wove,
> O'erhang his wavy Bed.   (lines 5 – 8)

The sun's tent seems to combine the western throne whose clouds are arrayed "with reflected Purple and Gold" (*Paradise Lost*, IV. 596 – 97) and the lines in the *Nativity Ode* where "the Sun in bed, / Curtain'd with

cloudy red, / Pillows his chin upon an Orient wave'' (lines 229 – 31).
Collins' pilgrim is a descendant of Milton's "Twilight gray." Silence
broken only by a single song (the bat or beetle) recalls Milton's solitary
"wakeful Nightingale." The procession of Evening's train – Hours,
Elves, Nymphs, and "Pensive Pleasures sweet" – suggests Evening's
attendants in Eden – Twilight, Silence, Hesperus and the starry host.
As in Milton (and the evening tradition generally) the poet's pure
encounter with the goddess is purged of all erotic associations. Eve is
chaste, modest, reserved, "genial" rather than generative. Her "folding
Star" (Hesperus) is attended by *"Pensive Pleasures"* (rather than erotic
ones) and prepares ("musing slow")[33] for a meditative retreat rather
than a night of love.[34]

Collins' poem, as many commentators have noticed, combines
natural process with allegorical procession. Evening is hailed as a
goddess, and yet she never clearly emerges from the scene she rules.
As Evening approaches her vale darkens and her dewy fingers draw "the
gradual dusky Veil," an image both allegorical and natural. By comparison with Thomson's poetry, however, natural detail in Collins, as
Hagstrum has written, "has been subjected to greater imaginative
modification ... The personified figure ... is more prominent, is attended
by a greater number of subsidiary personifications, and is a more
efficacious unifying force."[35] Hagstrum finds analogues for Collins'
practice in Italian painting, but Milton's own verse description of
evening may have provided a closer literary model. As we recall,
Milton's scene is filled with personified abstractions, yet their gestures
(slow arrival, clothing "all things" in gray, silent accompaniment)
struck at least one eighteenth-century observer as "an exact and curious
Description of a Moon-Light Night."[36] Particularly in the light of
Collins' manifest interest in the Miltonic moon's silver mantle, it may
not be fanciful to suspect that Collins' "gradual dusky veil," drawn over
the evening landscape, is his inspired re-writing of an admired Miltonic
line.

Recovering the full context of Collins' poem – its place in an "evening" tradition and its inspiration, both mediated and immediate, in
Milton – enables us to see the "Ode to Evening" more clearly, and
helps account for an ending which has seemed problematic to many
critics. The drawing of the veil is the key moment of the poem. At
what seems the climax of Collins' natural description of the arrival of
Evening, she disappears behind her own veil. Most commentators
are disappointed with the lines that follow, the cycle of the seasons
and the concluding stanza, objecting to the didacticism, the troop of
abstractions, the breaking of the spell, or the allegedly false intrusion
of social concerns in what has seemed a "solitude" poem.

But recent critics have suggested that the closing lines confirm Collins' ultimately "social" perspective, and represent his attempt to give transient evening a kind of "permanence."[37] Even Collins' defenders, however, have regarded the drawing of the veil as a sign of "dissipated vision" or the closing off of a scene. One critic sees failure and loss of poetic vision: as Evening departs, poet and goddess are separated.[38] And yet on another reading precisely the opposite is true. Collins carefully discourages us from seeing the veil as a curtain that screens the scene from the eye, as Akenside's "cloudy curtain of refreshing eve" is "clos'd" to shelter the poet's "eye-lids" from a visionary scene.[39] What happens at the end of the "Ode" is that the poet effects a union with his subject, joining her behind the dusky veil, disappearing into the evening, the last stage in a process that one critic calls "the radical elision of the perceiving subject."[40] At the close of the first section of the poem the poet had addressed Evening directly: "As musing slow, I hail / Thy genial lov'd return!" By the time the poet reaches the mountain hut, the "I" drops out of the poem:

> be mine the Hut,
> That from the Mountain's Side,
> Views Wilds, and swelling Floods,
> And Hamlets brown, and dim-discover'd Spires,
> And hears their simple Bell, and marks o'er all
> Thy Dewy Fingers draw
> The gradual dusky Veil.
>
> (lines 34–40)

It is not the poet who views, hears, and marks, but the "Hut," into which the poet has been absorbed. The veil falls on a scene into which the poet has receded. At the end of the poem, likewise, it is not the poet who offers praise:

> So long, sure-found beneath the Sylvan Shed,
> Shall *Fancy, Friendship, Science*, rose-lip'd *Health*,
> Thy gentlest Influence own,
> Any hymn thy fav'rite Name!
>
> (lines 49–52)

"Hut" has become the simpler and more primitive "Shed." "Sylvan" makes the shed seem almost a part of the natural scene, and perhaps invokes a buried memory of Milton's Edenic "Sylvan Lodge" (*Paradise Lost*, V. 376). The retreat to rural enclosure also suggests another Miltonic pattern: Penseroso's withdrawal to a "mossy cell" (line 169) as a locus of prophetic vision. The observing and devoted "I" has merged – as the elided subject again suggests – with the object of his observation and devotion. When we consider Collins' preoccupation elsewhere with being cut off, by veils or curtains, from sources of poetic power, we can see more clearly the "Ode to Evening" as a celebration of achieved vision. At the end of the "Ode on the Poetical Character" the "inspiring Bow'rs" on the Miltonic height are "o'erturn'd," and the scene "curtain'd close." When the veil is drawn at the end of "Evening" the poet is not shut out: he has imagined himself into the evening landscape. Evening's veil does not separate the poet from his worshipped object; rather it gently covers "all."

Ironically then, the visionary moment comes not with the unveiling of the goddess or in her sudden revelation to her votary, but with the dropping of a veil. More exactly, it is both a veiling and an unveiling at once. In this respect Collins' poem is like Milton's moonlit evening, where the moon first "unveil[s]" her light and then throws her silver mantle over the dark. Collins may well have understood how important such moments of unveiling were to the blind poet, who in his address to Light laments his "veil'd" vision (his eyes were "in dim suffusion veil'd," *Paradise Lost*, III. 26). Milton's blindness cut him off from "the cheerful ways of men" and the "Book of knowledge" itself, nature's works. Most poignant, perhaps, is the loss of seasonal and daily pleasure:

> Thus with the Year
> Seasons return, but not to me returns
> Day, or the sweet approach of Ev'n or Morn.
> (*Paradise Lost*, III. 40–42)

What was denied to Milton is made accessible to Collins. His poem celebrates nothing so much as Evening's "sweet approach" and "lov'd Return."

Mock-epic

Another commonplace of literary history is that *Paradise Lost*, though it did not help the eighteenth century to write great epic, led fruitfully and directly to the period's best mock-epics, *MacFlecknoe*, *Absalom and Achitophel*, *The Rape of the Lock*, and *The Dunciad*. Dryden and Pope thus honored Milton's poem by turning it on its head. This idea needs more careful scrutiny than it has received. A related idea, more recently suggested, is that *Paradise Lost* contains within itself the genesis of mock-epic.[41] By contrasting a false model of heroism (the Achillean Satan) with the "better fortitude" of Christian models (Adam, Abdiel, Christ), Milton's poem already contains a crucial mock-epic ingredient. As Dennis Burden has shown, Satan thinks of himself as the hero of his own epic quest.[42] Like Dryden's Flecknoe, he is swelled with his own self-importance. Milton critics also commonly point to the ways in which Satan and his council enact an infernal parody of God and the angels. A less common notion, deserving wider currency, is that there is a strong note of ridicule in *Paradise Lost*.[43] It is important to add here that eighteenth-century readers as early as Addison noticed this "ridiculous" element.

The first observers to find Milton's Satan a ridiculous mock-hero were his own God the Father and Son. As the War in Heaven begins, God turns "smiling" to his Son to say:

> Nearly it now concerns us to be sure
> Of our Omnipotence...lest unawares we lose
> This our high place, our Sanctuary, our Hill.
> (*Paradise Lost*, V. 721–22, 731–32)

The Son detects the Father's irony: "Mighty Father, thou thy foes / Justly hast in derision, and secure / Laugh'st at their vain designs and tumults vain" (735–37). And the mockery strikes home, for Belial in Hell argues that God "from Heav'n's highth / All these our motions vain, sees and derides" (II. 190–91).[44] The absurdity of Satan's vaunts to defeat the Almighty, to enjoy his freedom, and to reign in hell struck Addison as "big with Absurdity...bearing only a *Semblance of Worth, not Substance*," and therefore "incapable of shocking a Religious Reader."[45] Voltaire reported that the French found laughable the very idea of an epic poem on "the Devil fighting against God."[46] Equally laughable is the temptation as a subject for epic – "Adam and Eve eating an Apple at the Persuasion of a Snake," in Voltaire's bald description (*Essay*, p.132). Another eighteenth-century observer detected the absurdity of Satan's rebellion, though he found it a flaw in the poem. *Paradise Lost*, he says, "is founded upon a very absurd Supposition, that has not the least Appearance of Probability; but on the contrary, seems utterly impossible, viz. The Rebellion of the Angels against God, with a Design to dethrone him."[47]

As Addison also saw, Satan in Hell has only a "Mock-Majesty."[48] Critics of *Paradise Lost* have commonly noted that Satan, in offering to undertake the mission to earth, serves as a parody of Christ. The unholy trinity of Satan, Sin, and Death likewise parody the heavenly trinity. A self-designated epic hero, Satan is a paradigm of later pretenders such as Absalom, who believes himself a messiah, and Belinda, who thinks herself the center of the universe.

Eighteenth-century readers detected other elements of ridicule in *Paradise Lost*. Voltaire found the War in Heaven "low and ridiculous" and the Paradise of Fools in Book III a series of "low comical Imaginations."[49] Jonathan Richardson also comments on the "Ludicrous

Scene" of punning in the War in Heaven (note to VI. 206), and finds something "Ridiculous" in Satan's headlong fall "in many an airy wheel" onto Niphates (III. 741). Contemporary theorists acknowledged that some ludicrous scenes were an appropriate and traditional part of epic. Kames, for example, allows that "ludicrous scenes and images may be introduced [into epic narrative] without impropriety" for the purpose of supplying variety and relief.[50] The comical features of Homer's Thersites were duly recognized. But Milton, in eighteenth-century eyes, particularly emphasized the comic element in epic. Of all Homer's imitators, said Pope, "Milton...has given most into the ludicrous; of which his *Paradise of Fools* in the third Book, and his *Jesting Angels* in the sixth are extraordinary Instances."[51]

For Voltaire the metamorphosis of the devils into dwarfs, in Book I, is ideally adapted to "that ludicrous way of writing" called the "Mock-heroic" (pp. 138 – 39). Indeed, the several scenes of metamorphosis in the poem are all implicitly comic. Shape-changing is traditionally one of the devil's tricks, a sign both of his supernatural power and his dangerous treachery. But Milton typically presents it so as to reveal the comic, self-incriminating dimension. Satan himself feels the shame of his "foul descent" even before Eve's fall, "constrain'd / Into a Beast, and mixt with bestial slime" (IX. 163 – 65). After she eats he slinks – like a guilty dog – back into the thicket (784 – 85). Even at the level of simile Satan passes through a series of degrading shapes. As he approaches Eden, the narrator compares Satan first to a "prowling Wolf" (IV. 183), then a "Thief" (188), a cormorant (196), and later a toad at the ear of Eve (800). Satan's return to Hell in Book X is perhaps the clearest example of comic metamorphosis. After entering the hall disguised, Satan proclaims his own victorious return, and holds God up to ridicule: the idea that an offended creator has "giv'n up / Both his beloved Man and all his World" is, he says, "worth your Laughter" (X. 787 – 89). But God gets the last laugh, as Satan proudly awaits the applause of his followers: "So having said, a while he stood, expecting / Thir universal shout and high applause / To fill his ear" (X. 504 – 06). Then comes the comic peripeteia, as a kind of pratfall. Instead of applause, he receives "A dismal universal hiss, the sound / Of public scorn" (508), as the devils turn all to serpents. Satan himself falls too, the would-be supplanter of Adam and Eve now himself ironically "supplanted" and changed into an object, an example of Bergson's "mechanical encrusted on the living":

> His Visage drawn he felt to sharp and spare,
> His Arms clung to his Ribs, his Legs entwining
> Each other, till supplanted down he fell
> A monstrous Serpent on his Belly prone.
>
> (511 – 14)

For an analogue in mock-epic we can recall the comic punishment, shame, and degradation Pope administers to his victims: a foolish poet reduced to a mere "phantom" with a "brain of feathers, and a heart of lead" (*Dunciad*, II. 44); the sons of Dulness "a vast involuntary throng" who "Roll in her Vortex, and her Pow'r confess" (*Dunciad*, IV. 82 – 84); the maids in the Cave of Spleen, who, "turn'd Bottels, call aloud for Corks" (*Rape of the Lock*, IV. 54).

An eighteenth-century poet with an interest in mock-epic might well look upon Milton's Satan as the ancestor of all mock-heroes, the archetypal example of the vaunting self-important fraud, "Semblance of worth, not substance" (*Paradise Lost*, I. 529). It has long been recognized that Dryden and Pope allude to Milton's Satan as they present Achitophel, Absalom, Sporus, and Cibber. But critics usually assume that the allusion to Milton works either to bring out the evil, that is, to show Achitophel or Cibber threateningly allied with the forces of darkness, or to bring out the disparity between the magnitude of Satan and the pettiness of contemporary vice and folly. Perhaps, however, we need to remember that for many early eighteenth-century readers Satan was an ultimately comic figure. If so, then an allusion to Satan might serve to bring out fraudulence and (finally) impotence. Cibber on his exalted throne is no less (and no more) than Satan imitating the majesty of God.[52] When Lintot, like a "dab-chick," waddles "On feet and wings, and flies, and wades, and hops; / So lab'ring on, with shoulders, hands, and head" (*Dunciad*, II. 63 – 65), we should see him as no less (and no more) comical than Satan, who pursues his way through chaos "O'er bog or steep, through strait, rough, dense, or rare, / With head, hands, wings or feet... / And swims or sinks, or wades, or creeps, or flies" (*Paradise Lost*, II. 947 – 49).

Milton may have provided eighteenth-century poets with a mock-epic myth and a paradigm for an epic hero, but can we go on to say that *Paradise Lost* is responsible for the development of mock-epic as a genre? Is it more than coincidence that mock-epic rises and flourishes shortly after the publication of *Paradise Lost*? Perhaps the authors of *MacFlecknoe* (c. 1676), *The Dispensary* (1698), *The Splendid Shilling* (1706), and *The Rape of the Lock* (1712) sensed that a way left open to the modern poet was to invert or parody the epic, a path suggested by Milton's own poem. But we must be very cautious about imputing too much influence to Milton. Mock-epic as a genre pre-dates *Paradise Lost*, whether we consider classical examples (Homer's lost *Margites*, the *Batrachomyomachia*) or modern ones (Tassoni's *La Secchia Rapita*, 1622). Tassoni's poem, along with Boileau's *Lutrin* (1674), probably had a good deal more to do with the rise of English mock-heroic as a genre than did *Paradise Lost*. This is not to deny that Milton may have contributed to the popularity of the mock-epic form in the late seventeenth century and even helped determine the direction of its development. *Paradise Lost* very probably encouraged English poets to think of mock-epic as a partly comic and partly "serious" form, as a way to attack figures who could be seen as foolish frauds and at the same time as potential threats to civilized values. No doubt *MacFlecknoe*, *The Dispensary*, and *The Rape of the Lock* would have taken substantially the same form if Milton had not written. But *Absalom and Achitophel* and *The Dunciad* clearly owe much of their darker implications to *Paradise Lost*.

Paradise Lost also clearly opened up the possibilities of blank verse mock-epic, and seems to have encouraged poets like John Philips to aim for a variety of mock-heroic effects not limited to burlesque. In Philips' hands – and in the hands of the best poets of his century – mock-heroic was capable of subtle and delicate effects, ranging from ludicrous bathos to exquisite half-compliment. Philips himself was especially good at a kind of witty and knowing half-serious overstatement that steers carefully between the solemn and the facetious. It is to this solemn Cervantic irony that the poet Edmund Smith refers when he praises his friend Philips' verses: "So thy grave lines extort a juster smile."[53] Consider the following examples from *The Splendid Shilling*. First, a burlesque passage describing a raving (and thirsty) dreaming poet:

> But if a Slumber haply does Invade
> My weary Limbs, my Fancy's still awake,
> Thoughtful of Drink, and Eager in a Dream,
> Tipples Imaginary Pots of Ale;
> In Vain; awake, I find the settled Thirst
> Still gnawing, and the pleasant Phantom curse.
>
> (109 – 14)

The comedy of the passage derives in large part from the erotic dream conventions that Philips violates (moments earlier the poet has been dreaming much more conventionally of a "desperate Lady near a purling Stream, / Or Lover pendent on a Willow-Tree"). Burlesque sometimes involves direct allusion to Milton, as when the "witless Swain" in *Cyder*, like Milton's devils, bites into a grub-eaten apple, "'Till, with a writhen Mouth, and spattering Noise, / He tastes the bitter Morsel, and rejects Disrelisht" (I. 447 – 49).[54] Philips' allusion reverberates far, bringing together Milton's epic context (itself implicitly mock-epic), Virgil's middle-style georgic description of tasters whose mouths are distorted by the bitter flavor of water strained through poor soil (the likely origin of Milton's line),[55] with his own coarser rustic comedy. Elsewhere Philips describes that "Horrible Monster! hated by Gods and Men," a dun:

                                    his faded Brow
          Entrench'd with many a Frown, and *Conic* Beard,
          And spreading Band, admir'd by Modern Saints,
          Disastrous Acts forebode   (48–51)

This is more clearly mock-heroic, the ridiculous dun a faded reminder
of Milton's Satan, whose face "Deep Scars of Thunder had intrencht"
(*Paradise Lost*, I. 601), likened to the sun which "in dim Eclipse
disastrous twilight sheds" (I. 597). The dun is then compared, in a long
mock-epic simile, to a spider lying in wait for its prey. This time Philips'
interest is that of a miniaturist:

                              So her disembowell'd Web
          Arachne in a Hall, or Kitchin spreads,
          Obvious to vagrant Flies: She secret stands
          Within her woven Cell; the Humming Prey,
          Regardless of their Fate, rush on the toils
          Inextricable, nor will aught avail
          Their Arts, nor Arms, nor Shapes of lovely Hue;
          The Wasp insidious, and the buzzing Drone,
          And Butterfly proud of expanded wings
          Distinct with Gold, entangled in her Snares,
          Useless Resistance make; With eager strides,
          She tow'ring flies to her expected Spoils;
          Then with envenom'd Jaws the vital Blood
          Drinks of reluctant Foes, and to her Cave
          Their bulky Carcasses trimphant drags.
                              (*The Splendid Shilling*, lines 78–92)

This delicate passage is the kind of thing Pope might have written had
he tried blank verse mock-epic. Its interest is multiple: partly, the
disparity between the Latinate epic language and the humble event (the
"expanded wings" are from Milton's Satan, rearing off the pool in Hell,
Paradise Lost, I. 225); partly the vividness with which Philips develops
the traditional imagery of surprised entrapment, and the fineness of
feelings associated with doomed grace: "nor will aught avail / Their
Arts, nor Arms, nor Shapes of lovely Hue"; and partly the closeness
of the description, the attention to significant detail – the web literally
"disembowell'd," the "Humming" of the prey both a sign of its blithe
disregard and the means by which the spider catches it (cf. Pope's spider,
whose "touch, exquisitely fine, / Feels at each thread," *Essay on Man*,
I. 217–18). Our amused delight at the trivial subject is mixed with a
sense of exquisitely felt pain. Our response to the style is likewise mixed.
As a contemporary put it, "we are betrayed into a Pleasure that we could
not expect; tho', at the same time, the Sublimity of the Style, and
Gravity of the Phrase, seem to chastise the Laughter they provoke."[56]

This is a rather more complex account of mock-heroic than we might expect even now, implying the strong and active pressure of the high style upon the reader, chastising the laughter which the poem provokes.

Elsewhere Philips warns against lesser perils – the swine, snails, or wasps that can destroy an apple tree. The tone in the these passages from *Cyder* is mock-heroic, adorned with self-conscious pomp and mock-solemn moralizing, as when the "furious Mastiff" is bid to "vex / The noxious Herd [i.e. swine], and print upon their Ears / A sad Memorial of their past Offence," or when treacle is used to lure wasps:

> that with fruitless Toil
> Flap filmy Pennons oft, to extricate
> Their Feet, in liquid Shackles bound, 'till Death
> Bereave them of their worthless Souls: such doom
> Waits Luxury, and lawless Love of Gain!
> (*Cyder*, I. 432–36)

Only "Pennons" is directly borrowed from Milton (*Paradise Lost*, VII. 441) but the wasps provide a diminished reminder of the winged devils chained on the burning lake, their own "liquid Shackles" (Milton had of course earlier compared his devils to bees in *Paradise Lost*, I. 768–75).

Some eighteenth-century critical statements imply a sharp contrast between the heroic and the mock-heroic. The young Pope declared that "the *Ridicule* of [Milton's] Manner succeeds better than the *Imitation* of it."[57] Johnson later commented that "to degrade Milton's language [as Philips had] by application to the lowest and most trivial things gratifies the mind with a momentary triumph."[58] But, as Philips himself was able to demonstrate, mock-heroic in blank verse was a flexible device, capable of a wide range of effects. In the best eighteenth-century blank verse poems – Thomson's *Seasons*, Cowper's *Task* – the line between heroic and mock-heroic is difficult to draw.

Novel

Literary historians have long been tempted to link the decline of the epic and the rise of the novel, to speak of the novel as a kind of prose epic, and even to point to Tom Jones, Clarissa, and Amelia as the real Miltonic heroes of the eighteenth century.[59] To be sure, the novel like the epic is an encyclopaedic narrative. In its concern for characters in the middle station, and in private life rather than life upon the public stage, the novel would in some sense appear to be the inheritor of one part of the Miltonic legacy. And eighteenth-century English novelists, like their fellows the poets, regularly allude to Milton and especially to *Paradise Lost*. The passage from innocence through fall to recovery is a reasonably accurate precis of many an eighteenth-century novel. *Paradise Lost* no doubt encouraged reader and writer to think of the moral arc of human life in these terms. But we must be cautious not to overstate Milton's contribution. As recent critics are increasingly making clear, the eighteenth-century novel has roots in earlier literary and para-literary forms, from the ancient romance to modern confessional autobiography and Renaissance Spanish picaresque.[60] Such uses of *Paradise Lost* as there are tend to be intermittent rather than systematic or structural, and thematic similarities between Milton's epic and later novels operate at the most general level. But a discussion of Milton's creative influence and of the literary opportunities to which he pointed should nonetheless include some consideration of Milton and the novel.

In a recent and well-regarded critical account, Melvyn New suggests that the special form of major eighteenth-century fiction from Defoe through Smollett combines tendencies from an older romance tradition and a newer novel tradition, thereby mirroring a "world in intellectual transition" – a transition from a God-centered providential to a man-centered secular view of the world.[61] As New reads the major novels of the eighteenth century, the "claims of the romance" – that the world is patterned by an overarching order and governed by a manipulative providence – though present are no longer at the "theoretical center of narrative." A secular world view (whether psychological or socioeconomic) of man as the product of human or material forces has begun to "displace" the older view of man as "God's creature."

What effect did Milton and his epic have on this intellectual transition and on the literary form that the fiction writers of the eighteenth century developed in order to reflect that transition? My view is that *Paradise Lost* provided support to *both* the old romance tradition and the emerging novel form, and furthermore that it was ideally suited to promote an alliance between the two. We can readily enough find distinctive romance patterning in *Paradise Lost*: a plot unfolding within a world that "makes ultimate sense" (God brings good out of evil); an archetypal sequence of Innocence, Fall, Suffering, and eventual Salvation; Exile from the Garden and ultimate Return to a paradise within. This setting and drama plainly provided a powerful model for the writers of eighteenth-century fiction. The Young Man leaving Home is an ancient situation, but it is Milton's retelling that Fielding remembered when he described Tom expelled from Paradise Hall: "the world was all before him."[62] The Temptation of Innocence is another old romance pattern, but Richardson alluded repeatedly and consciously to Milton's version of the situation.[63] For a third example consider the use of symbolic settings. Like Fielding and Richardson most novelists draw sharp contrasts between the Garden and the City. Milton's fallen mortals, like the virtuous characters in eighteenth-century fiction, never find their salvation in the City. They all leave their gardens, undergo trials in the cities of men, and return at the end to a restored or transformed garden paradise, what Milton variously calls a "paradise within" or an "eternal paradise of rest."

Paradise Lost, then, in several ways would have helped to perpetuate romance patterns in English narrative. But Milton's poem is itself a transformation of epic and romance traditions, and would have provided support for a newer kind of narrative too. The arena for heroism in *Paradise Lost* is the private life, and significant action has been largely internalized. Milton's emphasis falls on faithfulness, patience, and on the performance (or misperformance) of domestic duties, the responsibilities one must discharge in obeying a parent or supporting a spouse. Such duties had long been preached in homilies and sermons. In the early eighteenth century they were increasingly urged on readers by secular moralists such as Defoe in *The Family Instructor* or Addison and Steele in *The Spectator*. As part of his campaign to improve public morals, Steele borrowed some of the glamor attaching to older literary models of conduct. A man, he argued, could display "Heroic Virtue" in the discharge of domestic and ethical responsibilities in "common life": "The Man who does all he can in a Low Station, is more an Heroe than he who omits any Action he is able to accomplish in a great one."[64]

Paradise Lost provided a model for exploring the domestic realm in either the tragic or the comic mode. *Amelia* is an example of Milton-inspired domestic tragedy. When Amelia insists on accepting the masquerade ticket despite Booth's initial objections and fears, she follows explicitly in Eve's footsteps and like her fails to avoid temptation (cf. the discussion and separation of Adam and Eve, *Paradise Lost*, IX. 273–89). *Pamela* on the other hand is an example of domestic comedy partly inspired by Milton, particularly in the latter part of the novel, after the marriage of Pamela and Mr. B., in which our attention is directed (perhaps not successfully) to matrimonial virtue. Like the unfallen Eve, Pamela makes a model wife to her Adam, both subservient to him and an example to restrain him.

For a narrative writer, then, the Miltonic legacy is an ambiguous or divided one. *Paradise Lost* might seem a tale of nascent domestic realism, in which a representative man and woman act out a psychologically plausible drama of betrayal and reconciliation. Or it might seem a romance of Innocence, Fall, and Redemption, where the emphasis falls not on the human pair but on the larger divine plan in which man, woman, and tempter are but actors. The prose fictions written in eighteenth-century England, as New suggests, do not fall cleanly into either category. Their special form, I would finally suggest, may be in part due to two elements in *Paradise Lost* that I have not yet considered.

New argues that eighteenth-century fiction (his example is Richardson's) reflects that "moment in Western thought when the antithetical ideas of man as God's creature and man as a radical product of his own autonomous will came together in uneasy and temporary alliance" (p. 241). I would add that Milton had provided a model for such a double view of man in his central notion of human freedom. In Milton's theological and narrative system God the Father has absolute foreknowledge of man's actions but does not exercise predestination. He leaves man free, "Sufficient to have stood, though free to fall" (III. 99). Milton lays unmistakable and unusual stress, both before the Fall and after it, on the point that man was free to choose to obey or disobey.

A second feature of Milton's narrative that might have encouraged a writer to blend the older romance and the newer novel traditions is his treatment of the context of moral choices. In the romance tradition, character changes typically occur not as "development" but in a "series of crucial leaps into states that were radically different from what had gone before...a fundamental reorientation of the soul."[65] In the novel, on the other hand, human actions are understood primarily as the product of "individual motive," and are typically set within a rich and extended dramatic context, in which psychological and other factors contribute to our sense of plausibility and clear motivation. Milton's narrative of the reconciliation in Book X of *Paradise Lost* (like the narrative of the fall in Book IX) blends romance and internalizing ways of presenting crucial moral choice. Adam's repentance after the Fall is represented by means of the traditional stages of conversion, "conviction of sin, contrition, confession, departure from evil, conversion to good."[66] And his later re-education at the hands of Michael is presented as a series of separate stages, in which Adam reacts to distinct "scenes" of the human future, first distrusting God's justice, falling into despair, and eventually interpreting correctly the promise of the rainbow. Thus, we mark off the stages of Adam's recovery and re-education, the "fundamental re-orientation" of his soul.

But the recovery (like the Fall) does not take place in a psychological vacuum. Milton takes extraordinary pains and considerable time to present the Fall as a psychologically plausible event that comes on gradually. His theology may incline him toward a "romance" view of the Fall as a "crucial leap" of a yet "sinless" Eve (IX. 659), but his concern for narrative inclines him toward an internalizing view of the Fall as a fully understandable human event, the last small link in a long chain. So too, the depths through which Adam passes before he can ask forgiveness of Eve are rendered not as allegorical stations of the soul but emotionally charged responses to a particular human situation. His extended re-education, finally, takes place over two books, far more space than Milton needed if he simply wanted to declare or symbolize Adam's regeneration, or to summarize the story of man up to the Incarnation and then the Last Judgment. Milton is concerned to enact – with some plausibility – the *process* by which Adam is prepared for the expulsion.

Compare the "education" of Joseph Andrews, who in a discontinuous series of stages, as it were, discovers that Adams is not the infallible moral guide he thought him to be. Or consider Tom Jones' sudden discovery in prison that he himself is to blame for his own misfortunes.[67] Yet in both cases we would also want to say that Fielding suggests that Joseph and Tom profit from their mistakes and gradually learn from experience.[68] Richardson's fictions painstakingly recreate the gradual process of psychological and moral self-discovery in Pamela and Clarissa. And yet to stress growth in self-awareness is to see only part of each novel. In some ways Richardson's heroines don't change. As Patricia Meyer Spacks has suggested, the central character of many eighteenth-century novels triumphs by remaining essentially the same.[69] Virtuous innocence resists temptation, continuously proving and proclaiming itself. The goal, as in romance, is one's starting point. Richardson and Fielding, like the other novelists, knew their Milton well and used his work profitably. By juxtaposing *Paradise Lost* and the major novels of the eighteenth century we can observe not only a pattern of significant allusion but a fundamental imaginative continuity.

"Christian poetry"

In *The Advancement and Reformation of Poetry* (1701) John Dennis urged that "the Moderns, by joining the Christian Religion with Poetry, will have the Advantage of the Ancients."[70] Three years later he looked forward to the day when "another Milton" might arise to advance "so necessary and noble a Work."[71] Until then, other poets "may do in a less proportion to other parts of the Old Testament" what Milton had already accomplished. In 1712 Dennis's friend George Sewell wrote that at the end of his life in 1708 the poet John Philips had still intended to write a poem "in solemn Style" on the Resurrection and Day of Judgment.[72] As Sewell noted, "Milton has given a few fine Touches upon the same [subject], but still there remains an inexhaustible Store of Materials to be drawn from the *Prophets*, the *Psalmists*, and the other *Inspired Writers*."[73] The stage was set, one would have thought, for a flourishing new "Christian" poetry based directly, like Milton's, upon scripture. And for the first third of the eighteenth century a group of

Milton-inspired poets produced a stream of biblical epics, "Last Day" poems, biblical paraphrases, and poems that continued or elaborated on *Paradise Lost*.[74] But the sad fact is that these Miltonic poets, the *best* of whom were Blackmore, Isaac Watts, and Young, produced very little of lasting value. In a recent account of the subject, David Morris unsparingly judges most poetry of "the religious sublime" in the period to be a failure.[75] Milton's influence on the eighteenth century was not everywhere fruitful, and it is part of our story to try to explain why this should be so.

In attempting to discover why, despite apparent opportunities and great hopes, Milton did not lead to a "school" of great religious poetry, we may begin with Morris's own "speculations" on the general failure of religious verse in the eighteenth century. Morris rightly rejects the conventional idea that the "rationalism" of the age prevented great religious poetry. Centuries of Christians would have found bizarre the claim that their religion was not amenable to rational demonstration. Johnson deeply feared death because, in his view, it was *rational* (and Christian) to do so.[76] Likewise, the period's tendency toward the impersonal, the abstract, and the general (in all literary forms) – as opposed to the Donnean dramatic and personal particular – need not (despite Morris's doubts) prevent great religious writing. The example of Johnson's *Vanity of Human Wishes*, one of the incontestably great religious poems of the century, should demonstrate that general statements and representative particulars can carry great emotional weight and force. And Morris himself concedes that the "generalized language" of the eighteenth-century hymn is able to explore "the personal aspects of religious experience" (p. 215). Religious poetry may fail, Morris argues, because its language aims at pictorial representation and yet we can never "see" the spiritual world. But as his own counter-example shows, a poet like Thomson who looks for the divine or the sublime in the material world may well succeed in visualizing it. The crucial factor may be a lack of drama. Seventeenth-century religious lyric is often built on a conflict, ultimately resolved, between man's will and God's. The eighteenth-century religious sublime poem aspires only to "compel awed attention" (p. 217). The degrees and varieties of conflict are infinite, those of awe soon exhausted.

Morris begins to account for the relative failure of religious poetry in the eighteenth century. However, his focus on the religious sublime inclines him to set aside some of the great religious writing of the period, not only the hymns of Watts, Wesley, Newton, and Cowper, which Donald Davie would rank among the century's best lyrics,[77] but Johnson's moral essays in *The Rambler*. In assessing the direction of religious poetry after Milton, perhaps the question to ask then is not why

Milton's admirers did not produce great work, but why the great religious writing of the age on the whole took a non-Miltonic form. For some notes toward an answer we can look at the works of two important and underrated Miltonists at the beginning of the eighteenth century, the critical theories of John Dennis, and the poetic theory and practice of Isaac Watts.

Dennis's lifelong project was to reform poetry by inspiring modern poets to incorporate the Christian religion in their work. This goal underlines his two most important critical works, *The Advancement and Reformation of Poetry* (1701) and *The Grounds of Criticism in Poetry* (1704). There were calls for a more Christian poetry before Dennis, and by others during his lifetime, but his arguments were the most systematic and insistent. The call to serve Urania, the Christian Muse, is found prominently in Du Bartas, and again in Cowley and Davenant.[78] But Dennis was probably inspired by Milton's own restatement of the common idea. In *The Grounds of Criticism* he quotes a long passage from *Reason of Church Government* in which Milton celebrates the power of the Christian poet:

it is of power, beside the Office of a Pulpit, to imbreed and cherish in a great People the Seeds of Virtue and publick Civility ... to celebrate in glorious and lofty Hymns the Throne and Equipage of God's Almightiness, and what he works, and what he suffers to be wrought with high Providence in the Church; to sing victorious Agonies of Martyrs and Saints, the Deeds and Triumphs of just and pious Nations, doing valiantly thro' Faith, against the Enemies of Christ; to deplore the general relapses of Kingdoms and States from Justice and God's true Worship.[79]

Poetry, Milton says in *Of Education* (in a passage Dennis quoted three times) can be put to "glorious and magnificent use ... both in divine and in human things."[80]

But poetry in Dennis's own day – the metaphor is obviously derived from Milton – is "miserably fall'n" (I, 328). His hope is to "restore Poetry to all its Greatness, and to all its Innocence" (I, 328). A reformed poetry would "reform the Manners" (336) and aid in the "great Design of Arts ... to restore the Decays that happen'd to human Nature by the Fall, by restoring Order" (333). Not only the metaphor is Miltonic. Milton had also deplored the writings of "libidinous and ignorant Poetasters" who produce "Corruption and Bane," "Vicious Principles in sweet Pills" (330). A true poetry, on the other hand, as part of learning, could "repair the ruins of our first parents by regaining to know God aright" (*Of Education*).

If Milton's arguments are Dennis's inspiration, his poems are Dennis's great example of the right incorporation of religion and poetry.

No poet is quoted more often, and *Paradise Lost* is repeatedly preferred to all other poems ancient and modern. Dennis is especially interested in poetry's ability to arouse "enthusiastic passions," and quotes chiefly from the parts of the poem that concern supernatural creatures, devils, angels, or God. After quoting *Paradise Lost*, V. 266–87 (the descent of Raphael), for example, he notes: "The Reader may see...that the Ideas of Angels are exceeding proper to raise Enthusiastick Admiration, as being the most glorious and admirable Beings of the Creation, and which lead the Soul immediately to its Creator" (347). Admiration is aroused, he says, first by "all things which have an Immediate Relation to the Wonders of another World" (347) and next by "the great Phaenomena of the Material World" (348). It is significant that Dennis has little interest in the human parts of the poem, never citing Book IX, and citing Adam only when he talks with Raphael, or when he sings the Morning Hymn. Johnson complained of the want of human interest; Dennis never looked for it. The only human virtue ("Emanations of Divinity...often beheld in Men," 354) he cites is Satan's fortitude (355). Dennis's angle of vision, I would suggest, had significant consequences: it led him and his readers to see above all the "sublimity" of the poem. And it kept him from developing a theory – which might have inspired later poets – of a Christian poetry concerned primarily with man.

Consistent with his interest in sublimity, Dennis finds little to admire in the last three books of *Paradise Lost*: "how flat, how low, and un-musical is the Relation of the Actions of fallen Man, in the tenth book, tho deliver'd by the Voice of Divinity?" (I, 351). The subject of the last two books "could by no means supply him with the great Ideas, nor consequently with the great Spirit, which the First, Second, and Sixth had done before" (II, 368). Instead of the "wondrous Works of God," the last books focus on "the Works of corrupted MAN," from which Michael "could draw no sort of Enthusiasm, and least of all that of Admiration and Terror" (I, 351). Note that Dennis shows no interest in the pious works of the faithful few, like Noah and Enoch, or the virtues of patience, temperance and "suffering for truth's sake" (XII. 569) that Michael recommends to Adam.

Although Milton clearly wanted to recommend an unspectacular Christian virtue, a "*better* fortitude," Dennis was still thinking in traditional epic terms, and thought that even Milton did not fully show "the true use that ought to be made of Religion in Poetry" (369). Milton, he says, only "happen'd upon" it in parts of *Paradise Lost*. *Paradise Regained* he regarded as a failure, since Milton's subject, Christ's impassive resistance to Satan's temptations, did not "promote the Violence of the Enthusiastic Passions."[81] Epic heroes, he argued, should display active virtues in "good and great Designs for the Welfare

of their Country'' (II, 113), in ''great Passions'' and ''great Actions.''
A ''suffering Hero'' cannot be proper for epic (or apparently for sacred)
poetry: ''*Milton* could make but very little, even of a Suffering God, who
makes quite another Impression with his Lightning and his Thunder
in *Paradise Lost*, than with his Meekness and his Stoicism in *Paradise
Regain'd*'' (II, 113). Dennis grants that Christ shows ''Greatness of
Mind,'' but such a virtue will only be admired by the few (II, 113). A
poet should choose a hero ''whose every Action may flow from ... noble
Principles.''[82]

Paradoxically then, Dennis who wanted a poetry based on the
Christian religion in fact promotes a sacred poetry built on pagan
models, in which God and Christ are simply more terrible and powerful
than their Greek counterparts, and Satan more angry and more
courageous than Achilles. Ignoring Milton's re-ordering of the epic,
Dennis admired the parts of *Paradise Lost* that most resemble the *Iliad*
(''Pride and Ambition, Rage and Revenge, and Fury''), and dismissed
Paradise Regained, based as it is on ''Patience, Resignation, Humility,
Meekness, Long-suffering, and the rest of those quiet divine Virtues
that adorn the Christian Scheme'' (II, 368). For a theorist who aspires
to a more perfect sacred poetry, this is a remarkable rejection of the
Christian virtues as a foundation for poetry.

Dennis provided a theoretical foundation then for a Christian poetry
that centered not on the suffering Christian in this world, but on the
mighty Christian God, Creator of the World and its Last Judge. Much
of the ''religious sublime'' that Morris rightly finds wanting, from Abel
Evans's *Prae-Existence* (1714) to Thomas Newcomb's *The Last Judgment*
(1723), fails perhaps because it follows Dennis's directions only too
faithfully. Had Dennis (or someone else) developed a critical theory for
a sacred poetry based not on the Christian God but on Christian man,
his trials, his patience and humility, his Miltonic ''better fortitude,''
the eighteenth century might have seen a quite different sort of Christian
poetry based on the lives of biblical heroes or on modern Christians.
Dennis's contemporary, Steele, argued in fact that ''True Greatness
of Mind'' must be based on ''Christian principles.'' In *The Christian
Hero* (1701), a popular work that went through twenty editions in the
century, Steele recommended ''that Sublime and Heroick Virtue,
Meekness, a Virtue which seems the very Characteristick of a Christian,
and arises from a Great, not a groveling Idea of things ... founded on
the extended Contemplation of the Place we bear in the Universe.''[83]
Dennis implicitly found such Christianity unpoetic: ''Leave the Virtues
of Patience and Long Suffering to be taught by Priests'' (II, 114). Priests
stood ready to teach those principles in sermons and homilies, as did
secular moralists in conduct books, essays, and novels. Dennis's Milton,

it must be conceded, led to no "Christian" poetry of lasting value. The best religious poetry of the period is not markedly Miltonic.

Some might argue that the best Christian verse in the eighteenth century is found in poems not ostensibly "devotional":

> Pour forth thy fervour for a healthful mind,
> Obedient passions, and a will resign'd;
> For love, which scarce collective man can fill;
> For Patience sov'reign o'er transmuted ill.
> (Johnson, "Vanity of Human Wishes," lines 359–62)

> No farther seek his merits to disclose
> Or draw his frailties from their dread abode
> (There they alike in trembling hope repose)
> The bosom of his Father and his God.
> (Gray, "Elegy Written in a Country Churchyard," lines 125–28)

These lines owe nothing to Milton. Nor do the extraordinary poems of Christopher Smart, whose inspiration was not English Christian poetry but the Hebrew poetry of the Bible as presented by Lowth and others. A third group of religious poets, the great hymn writers of the period, despite their admiration for Milton,[84] likewise tend to go directly to the Bible rather than to *Paradise Lost* for their inspiration. To understand why this should be so, it is worth examining the work of Isaac Watts, the first of the great eighteenth-century hymn writers and the best of the century's religious poets.

A prolific writer of tracts, sermons, and educational works, Isaac Watts' reputation as a literary figure is based on his hymns, his divine songs for children, and his *Horae Lyricae* (1706, rev. edn 1709), the first section of which includes poems "Sacred to Devotion and Piety." Watts was an admirer of John Dennis, and cites in the Preface to *Horae Lyricae* Dennis's "noble essay to discover how much superior is inspired poesy to the brightest and best descriptions of a mortal pen" (Watts, p. xcii).[85] Like Dennis, Watts also sounds the old call for a more "Christian" poetry: "It has been a long complaint of the virtuous and refined world, that poesy, whose origin is divine, should be enslaved to vice and profaneness; that an art, inspired from heaven, should have so far lost the memory of its birth place, as to be engaged in the interests of hell. How unhappily is it perverted from its most glorious design! How basely has it been driven away from its proper station in the temple of God, and abused to much dishonour!" (p. lxxxi). Like others before him, Watts reminds his readers that "many parts of the Old Testament are Hebrew verse" (p. lxxxv). Modern poets too might make "noble use" of Christian subjects, "dressing the scenes of religion in their proper figures of majesty, sweetness, and terror" (p. xcvi). The scenes he specifies encompass primarily the sublime mysteries of the faith and the works of a mighty God. Although Watts allows for a poetry based on the trials of the modern believer – ''the anguish of inward guilt, the secret stings, and racks, and scourges of conscience; the sweet retiring hours, and seraphical joys of devotion; the victory of a resolved soul over a thousand temptations'' (pp. xcvi – xcvii), he focuses, like Dennis, primarily on the supernal – ''the inimitable love and passion of a dying God; the awful glories of the last tribunal; the grand decisive sentence, from which there is no appeal; and the consequent transports or horrors of the two eternal worlds'' (p. xcvii). Among modern poets who have given ''happy examples'' of such poetry, he cites Corneille and Racine among the dramatists, and Cowley, Blackmore, and John Norris of Bemerton among poets. The name prominent by its absence is of course Milton's.

Why should Watts not have cited Milton as a great exemplar of Christian poetry? It is true that he commends Milton's ''noble measures'' as a means to maintain ''the dignity of the theme.'' But Watts does not admire uncritically. Miltonic blank verse, he says quite plainly, is not the model for his own ''essays without rhyme.''

The length of his periods, and sometimes of his parentheses, runs me out of breath. Some of his numbers seem too harsh and uneasy. I could never believe that roughness and obscurity added any thing to the grandeur of a poem; nor will I ever affect archaisms, exoticisms, and a quaint uncouthness of speech, in order to become perfectly Miltonian. It is my opinion that blank verse may be written with all due elevation of thought, in a modern style.   (p. cv)

The determined, almost defiant, independence of this judgment implies a felt pressure to join the ranks of the Miltonolators. The substance of the remark concerns prosodic technique, the observations of a practicing poet that a Miltonic manner does not serve his own ends. In the *Horae Lyricae* as in the hymns, Watts thought carefully about poetic and devotional ends. As preacher and poet he sought to ''diffuse virtue and allure souls to God'' (p. xcviii). The proper vehicle must advance and not impede these ends. This was even more important in hymns, designed ''to assist the meditations and worship of vulgar Christians'' (p. xcix). In many of his hymns, he wrote, he ''just permitted my verse to rise above a flat and indolent style... because I would neither indulge any bold metaphors, nor admit of hard words, nor tempt the ignorant worshipper to sing without his understanding.''[86]

For a devotional poet with Watts' designs, Miltonic form did not serve. Perhaps not surprisingly Watts preferred two common lyric forms (his major collection is subtitled ''Poems, Cheifly of the Lyrical Kind''), the common hymn measure and a chastened Pindaric ode stanza.

Miltonic matter was no more congenial. Watts' Calvinist theology is a good deal more severe than that of Milton, who rejected the doctrine of individual predestination and emphasized man's freedom to choose God. The titles of Watts' poems tell a different story: "Divine Judgments," "The Law Given at Sinai," "God's Absolute Dominion," "The Day of Judgment." Like the famous "O God our help in ages past," Watts' hymns tend to center on a contrast between "Man Frail" and "God Eternal." Ordinarily, however, Watts promises little "shelter from the stormy blast": his God is incensed, mighty, incomprehensible; flesh is but a "tottering wall," and man's earthly home the footstool of God, a mighty molehill, a "dwelling-place of worms." When Watts does recall the redemptive promise, he focuses on the mystery of the Incarnation and the Crucifixion – "His dying Crimson like a Robe / Spread o'er his Body on the Tree"[87] – in a manner that almost seems more Catholic than Protestant.[88] And yet Watts' primary source is always the Bible, not only the psalms but also the Song of Solomon, which provides the inspiration for a series of poems "dedicated to Divine Love." One finds almost nothing in Watts' religious poems – whether hymns or divine odes – that recalls Milton.

And yet Watts unquestionably admired Milton's poems and read *Paradise Lost* with "vast reverence": "His works contain admirable and unequalled instances of bright and beautiful diction, as well as majesty and sereneness of thought. There are several episodes in his longer works that stand in supreme dignity without a rival" (Preface, p. civ). Like Milton, Watts addresses the Christian Muse, Urania, and in a Pindaric ode on "The Adventurous Muse" praises Milton's "adventurous genius" that led him to sing "Themes not presum'd by mortal tongue." In a striking figure that anticipates Collins' "Ode on the Poetical Character," Milton is imagined not only singing the "lost Garden" but regaining it too ("Now the lost Eden he regains, / Keeps his own air, and triumphs in unrivall'd strains") and bearing with him the reader's "raptur'd mind to paradise." As a "noble hater of degenerate rhyme," Milton has shaken off his chains, and "built his verse sublime." Here Watts has attempted to follow him, not in divine poems but in several poems "Sacred to Virtue, Honour, and Frienship." Watts' most successful poem in Miltonic blank verse is his translation of Sarbiewski's ode on "The Dacian Battle." Cast in the form of a heroic eclogue sung by the shepherd Gador, not "of the heroic muse / Unknowing nor unknown," it treats, in a strenuous blank verse, of a victory won by the Poles over the Turks. Though Watts rarely alludes to Milton, his syntax displays a Miltonic compression and his diction is unusually Latinate. At the climax the shepherd sings of finding two "beauteous Youths, of richest Ottoman blood," joined in death. He honors them as Virgil honored the dead Nisus and Euryalus in Book IX of the *Aeneid* ("Fortunati ambo," lines 446ff):

> "Sleep, sleep, ye hapless pair,"
> Gently I cried, "worthy of better fate,
> "And better faith."

The words of course ironically recall Milton's address to the unfallen Adam and Eve, "Sleep on, / Blest pair; and O yet happiest if ye seek / No happier state" (IV. 773 – 75).[89]

In one or two other blank verse poems Watts attains an energetic blank verse. A passage on the Horatian theme of "True Courage" concludes with the death of the body and the ascension of the spirit, which "Breathes and flies upward, an undoubted Guest / Of the third Heaven, th'unruinable sky," an impressive Latinism that recalls Milton (who often uses "ruin" for fall) but is nonetheless original. Watts' other Miltonic blank verse poem is an epistle "To Mitio" on the pleasures and pains of married love, broadly based on the descriptions of Adam and Eve in Book IV. This poem largely fails, however, since its blank verse is prolix and dilute, without the compression and energy that animates Milton's lines.[90] Although Watts is sometimes praised for his handling of Miltonic blank verse, it must be said that he is rarely successful with it and rarely very Miltonic. This seems to have followed not from lack of talent but from principle: he took care, he said, not to "contract" or "cramp" the sense in his blank verse lines (Preface, p. xcviii). Too often the result of untangling Milton's tight syntax is a nerveless laxity, prose sense cut into five-foot strips. Watts is happier with shorter forms, common measure, sapphic, tetrameter, and reined-in Pindaric.

In each of the four forms I have examined – the "evening poem," the mock-epic, the novel, and the religious sublime poem – Milton's presence is readily detected. In only one case, the evening poem, is Milton clearly the progenitor. In the others he exerted significant shaping influence on an emerging form. But we must not, by focusing solely on genre, construe the question of influence too narrowly. Some of the richest evidence of Milton's creative pressure is found not in the genres in which he worked, or those he helped to shape, but in what might be called the informing power of a Miltonic paradigm or myth. It is to Milton's myth of a lost garden paradise that I now turn.

7 · REGAINING PARADISE

"The world was all before them"

Twenty years after the publication of *Paradise Lost* John Norris of
Bemerton first published a poem entitled "The Complaint of Adam
turn'd out of Paradise."[1] With Milton's lines in the background,
Norris's Adam complains:

> And must I leave thee now?...
> An *under-gardiner's* place, 'tis all I crave...
> Let me in *Eden* take one *farewell* round...
> O whither now, whither shall I repair?...
> The *World* can't recompense for *Eden* lost.

Like Marvell, Norris imagines an Adam in paradise alone,[2] but his
lament is clearly derived from Eve's words in *Paradise Lost*, regretting
the loss of her garden:

> O unexpected stroke, worse than of Death!
> Must I leave thee Paradise?...
>   ...O flow'rs,
> That never will in other Climate grow,
> My early visitation, and my last...
>   ...from thee
> How shall I part, and whither wander down
> Into a lower World...?
>   (XI. 268–83)

Fifty years later the young William Shenstone, already a sensitive
gardenist, adapted and expanded upon Eve's words in a poem he
entitled "EVE's Speech in *Milton*, upon her Expulsion out of Paradise":
"O Mournful Message! such transcendent Pain / Nor Death cou'd give,
nor Expectation feign! / Must I then leave these blissful Walks, and
Bow'rs...?"[3] Norris was by no means the only one in his generation
to brood on the exile from paradise. For illustrators one of the most
popular "scenes" in *Paradise Lost* is the Expulsion. All the major
illustrators from Aldrich in 1688 to Blake in 1807[4] conclude their series
with Adam and Eve being conducted from paradise by the angel
Michael:

They looking back, all th'Eastern side beheld
Of Paradise, so late thir happy seat,
Waved over by that flaming Brand, the Gate
With dreadful Faces throng'd and fiery Arms:
Some natural tears they dropp'd, but wip'd them soon;
The World was all before them, where to choose
Thir place of rest, and Providence thir guide:
They hand in hand with wand'ring steps and slow,
Through *Eden* took thir solitary way.

(XII. 641 – 49)

For some illustrators the moment is fraught with woe and terror; for others the prominent emotion appears to be regret, not unmixed with hope. Critics too commented frequently on the ending. Voltaire and Jonathan Richardson remarked how the expulsion gives the poem a fittingly complete close.[5] As Richardson noted, "This last Circumstance brings our Progenitors into the Condition in Which We Are, on *Even Ground* with Us, Wandring in Doubt and Uncertainty; in Sorrow, but Recompens'd with Comfort and Joy" (p. 535). But the persistence of sorrow troubled some like Addison, who found that the last two lines of the poem "renew in the Mind of the Reader that Anguish which was pretty well laid" (*Spectator* 369). Bentley was so troubled that he rewrote the last lines to emphasize the "Heavenly comfort" that "cheered" Adam and Eve on their "social" way.[6]

Other admirers "rewrote" Milton's lines too. "Wand'ring steps and slow" seems especially to have lodged in the memories of eighteenth-century poets. Imitations of the phrase are found in Thomson ("tottering steps and slow") and Mallet ("silent step and slow"),[7] three times in Pope,[8] Collins ("with gradual steps and slow"), Gray ("solemn steps and slow"), twice in Goldsmith,[9] and the early Wordsworth ("Our various journey, sad and slow").[10] Although the Miltonic phrase in its new contexts is often shorn of its elegiac or wistful tone, it retains the vivid sense of fateful motion charged with feeling, and almost arrested by the lingering adjective "...and slow." An equally resonant phrase is "the World was all before them." By 1705 it was apparently already a familiar tag. John Dunton's account of his "Bachelorship" in his *Life and Errors* (1705) begins: "Having now, as they say, the whole world before me."[11] To judge by eighteenth-century allusions, the phrase suggested not so much a brave new world as a beautiful world lost. In 1723, for example, Bishop Atterbury, preparing to leave for exile in France, wrote to Pope from the Tower, adapting Milton's lines to his own situation:

Some natural tears he dropped, but wiped them soon.
The world was all before him, where to choose
His place of rest, and providence his guide.[12]

When we remember that Atterbury, then aged 60, was leaving England for the first time, forcibly parted from his church and his lifelong friends, the allusion seems both to recall a lost paradise and to put a brave face on a bleak future. Johnson's youthful Rasselas, newly escaped from the Edenic Happy Valley, naively thinks a world of happiness lies before him: "I have here the world before me, I will review it at leisure: surely happiness is somewhere to be found" (ch. 16). But as Imlac helps him to see, and as the allusion to Milton reminds us, though one might "choose" a "place of rest," no "choice of life" ensures certain happiness.[13] "The world was all before us" is Burke's answer – only partly consolatory – to a friend's lamentation about their "future fortunes."[14] In Sheridan's *The Duenna* (1794), a sentence of banishment takes Miltonic form: "The world lies before you, so troop, Thou antiquated Eve, thou original sin."[15] The best-known allusion is probably Fielding's. As Tom Jones leaves Paradise Hall *we* know that he goes on to find good fortune and ultimately to return home, but at the moment of departure the narrator suggests little comfort from Milton's lines: "*The World*, as *Milton* phrases it, *lay all before him*; and *Jones*, no more than *Adam*, had any Man to whom he might resort for Comfort or Assistance." In determining "What Course of Life to pursue," Tom finds that "the Prospect was all a melancholy Void" (VII. 2).

In other writers the allusion to the expulsion scene is less explicit, but it is still plain that Milton's version of the loss of Eden haunted their imaginations. The forcible exclusion from a garden paradise lies at the heart of a number of important mid-century poems. Gray's distant prospect of Eton is also a distant prospect of Eden. Like fallen man Gray's narrator looks back through time and space to an enclosed "paradise" (line 98) where, like Adam, the schoolboys enjoy "spirits pure, and slumbers light, / That fly the approach of morn" (lines 49 – 50),[16] and where (like Adam and Eve until Michael reveals the future) they have as yet "no sense...of ills to come" (line 53). Like Satan Gray's narrator approaches this garden of innocence as one barred from it, able to feel its "gales" (line 15, cf. the "gentle gales" that meet Satan's approach to Eden),[17] allowed only "momentary bliss" of a "second spring" (lines 16, 20, cf. the "Vernal delight and joy" that drive from Satan "All sadness but despair").[18] Collins too, in the "Ode on the Poetical Character," as editors note, evokes Milton's Eden by name and description only to bewail his own exclusion from the "inspiring bowers." Even Goldsmith's lament for Auburn is perhaps modeled in part on Eve's lament for her lost paradise. Now a ruined garden, Auburn's "bowers of innocence and ease" (line 5) once required nothing more than Edenic "light labour" (line 59) to provide "innocence and health" (line 61). Now Goldsmith's emigrants take a "long farewell" from their "bowers" and "native walks," shuddering to face a savage world across the sea (lines 364–67). Their original is Eve, who dreads to "leave / Thee Native Soil, these happy Walks and Shades" and her "nuptial bower" for a "lower World, to this obscure / And wild" (*Paradise Lost*, XI. 270–71, 283–84). Like the emigrants, Goldsmith's narrator "still had hopes my latest hours to crown, / Amidst these humble bowers to lay me down" (lines 85–86). His hope too is modeled on Eve's lament for her paradise, "Where I had hope to spend, / Quiet though sad, the respite of that day / That must be mortal to us both" (*Paradise Lost*, XI. 271–73).[19]

The lament for a lost paradise in eighteenth-century writers is matched by an equally strong wish for a paradise regained. Goldsmith's *Traveller*, for example, is centered on the desire to find "Some spot to real happiness consigned" (line 60) – Goldsmith recurs five times to the idea of a blessed "spot." Is this "spot" or delimited place not based ultimately on the garden paradise which Milton calls a "delicious spot"?[20] Like Adam, Goldsmith's narrator must finally settle for a paradise within, "That bliss which centers only in the mind" (line 424). Indeed, it might be argued that the most pervasive and creative influence of *Paradise Lost* upon eighteenth-century poetry was not its Christianization of epic, or its diction and prosody, but its elaboration of a myth of the lost garden, somehow to be recovered. The action of much post-Miltonic poetry is the loss and subsequent regaining of a garden-like paradise, whether as literal rural place or as a composed and restored state of mind. M. H. Abrams has recently argued that in Wordsworth and the English Romantics man finds a paradise by uniting the mind and the "goodly universe." Milton's theological system is "naturalized" and secularized as a myth of the imagination.[21] But English writers did not need a Romantic revolution to see the poetic potential in Milton's myth. As in many other respects Romantic poets built on foundations laid in the eighteenth century.[22] The prospect of regaining a kind of paradise is the animating dream behind much of the best and most characteristic eighteenth-century poetry.

To be sure, the idea of an earthly paradise and of hopes for its recovery is ancient and widespread. Classical tradition provided the idea of the Golden Age or of the return of Astraea, still a potent myth for English poets in Pope's day. Some fancied they found a miniature image of that age in Horace's Sabine farm. Others looked to primitive societies: for Aphra Behn the natives of Surinam were like "our first Parents before the Fall."[23] The Bible and Christian tradition provided millennial hopes for a renovated world, newly invoked by the Saints and Fifth Monarchy Men in the Civil War. But it was not only Puritan fanatics

who imagined that an earthly paradise might be restored. As Ernest
Tuveson has shown, theologians and natural philosophers like Henry
More, Thomas Burnet, and William Whiston looked forward to the day
when "the World shall be restored to its Primitive State, and the Earth
itself shall be renewed."[24] For some including Burnet and Whiston the
millennium was still far in the future, and would require catastrophic
change in the present corrupt world. But for others, such as John
Edwards, Thomas Sherlock, and William Worthington, "the earthly
paradise is to be merely the last, culminating state in a series of
progressive stages which can be discerned in history."[25] Sherlock wrote
in 1725 of a "gradual working of Providence towards the Redemption
of the World from the Curse of the Fall."[26] Worthington wrote in 1773
that "natural and moral evil will...be removed and overcome, before
the consummation of all things...The latter ages of the world...will...
approach to the innocence and perfection of the paradisiacal state."[27]
Still other philosophical optimists – Leibniz, Spinoza, Bolingbroke –
challenged the very notion that the earth is any less Edenic now than
it ever was, on the grounds that a just God would not punish the
generations since Adam and Eve for the sins of their progenitors.[28]

That an Edenic garden might somehow be recovered was clearly
more than "in the air" in the eighteenth century. It becomes a powerful
idea not only in theological and philosophical writers, but also in the
poets inspired by Milton. Milton himself had made no optimistic
promises about the recovery of paradise on earth. He suggests that
Joshua, "whom the Gentiles *Jesus* call," will one day "bring back /
Through the world's wilderness long wandered man / Safe to eternal
Paradise of rest" (XII. 312–14), but such paradise will only be found
in heaven. The earth one day "Shall all be Paradise, far happier place
/ Than this of *Eden*, and far happier days" (XII. 464–65), but only after
the "dissolution" of the world. For fallen man the earth remains a fallen
place. Only with strenuous moral effort (of which few will prove capable)
can man hope to possess a "paradise within." What that moral effort
might require is suggested in *Paradise Regained*, in which Christ, "by
vanquishing / Temptation, hast regain'd lost Paradise" (IV. 607–08).
Through his disciplined triumph "A fairer Paradise is founded now /
For *Adam* and his chosen *Sons*" (IV. 613–14).

Despite Milton's soberly qualified hopes, eighteenth-century poets,
in their greater optimism, commonly turned to the version of the garden
myth in *Paradise Lost* as they entertained hopes of building their own
paradise within, or even of finding an earthly paradise in England's
green and pleasant land. The form which their paradise took was
modeled not on Milton's celestial city in heaven (an architectural world
of towers, doors, battlements, pavilions, and tabernacles) but the

"happy rural seat" of Eden.[29] And it is not the Miltonic task of re-building a paradise that they celebrate so much as its immediate pleasures.

The presence of Milton and the dream of a paradise regained can be detected in a number of common poetic genres in the period, reflecting the various particular shapes that the dream took. One way to recover paradise is to retreat from the world into contemplative (often rural) solitude, and to celebrate it in a "retirement" poem. A more active means might be called the exercise of enlightened perception or imagination, celebrated in a poem like Akenside's *Pleasures of Imagination*. Georgic poets sought to find an image of Eden in a still-pastoral English world of rural industry, as in Philips' *Cyder* or Dyer's *The Fleece*. And celebrants of marriage commonly saw the Edenic union of Adam and Eve as a model for a kind of paradise still possible on earth.

Retirement poems

Retirement poems are not only a post-Miltonic phenomenon. As Maynard Mack and others have reminded us, a large body of retirement literature, with strong classical origins, flourished in England in the seventeenth century well before *Paradise Lost* appeared. Yet it remains true that after about 1675 a retirement poem was more likely than before to be clearly set in a rural and Edenic scene to which the poet makes repeated reference. Henry Vaughan's "Retirement," for example, first published in 1678, celebrates a rural retreat: "If *Eden* be on Earth at all, / 'Tis that, which we the *Country* call" (lines 27 – 28).[30] Particularly if it also celebrated solitude (rather than Horatian or Epicurean sociability), an eighteenth-century retirement poem very likely reflected images of Milton's Eden. John Hughes's "A Thought in a Garden" (1704) draws on a variety of retirement traditions, but naturally includes Milton. The poem begins in a garden of flowers and "blossomed trees," but fancy readily brings thoughts of the original garden paradise. May "leads on the cheerful hours," as universal Pan, in Milton, "knit with the *Graces* and the *Hours* in dance / Led on th'Eternal Spring" (IV. 266 – 68). In this "elysium" (line 13) and "blest retreat" (line 1) the world seems new: Hughes's Adamic poet sees "a new world of flowers" (line 6). The Earth itself "seems new-born" (line 15).

At about the same time Marvell too celebrated a garden retreat (though written earlier than *Paradise Lost*, "The Garden" was first published in 1681), in which the retired man might enjoy Adam's unfallen paradise. But Milton's Eden seems to have made more of an impression than Marvell's on the eighteenth-century retirement poets. Lady Winchelsea's "Petition for an Absolute Retreat" (1713), celebrating a retreat from a world to a rural garden, is a prominently Miltonic dream. An enclosed garden, as in many a Roman poem, would afford her "Only plain and wholesome Fare" (line 33), but the details are Miltonic: "Fruits indeed (wou'd Heaven bestow) / All, that did in *Eden* grow, / All, but the *Forbidden Tree*, / Wou'd be coveted by me" (lines 34 – 37). Though she petitions for "absolute retreat," Lady Winchelsea does not (like Marvell) ask to be left alone. Like Adam (the first to raise objections to solitude) she wants a fit partner:

> Give me there (since Heaven has shown
> It was not Good to be alone)
> *A Partner* suited to my Mind,
> Solitary, pleas'd and kind.
>
> (lines 48 – 51)

Her vision of Milton's Eden (which she now hopes to recover) is based (rather more than Milton's) on the solace of human love: Adam and Eve, she says, "in some Grove, or flow'ry Lawn, / Spent the swiftly flying Time, / Spent their own, and Nature's Prime, / In Love; that only Passion given / To perfect Man, whilst Friends with Heaven" (lines 61 – 65). Indeed, her retreat would be yet more secure than Eden: "No intruders thither come" (line 8) to disturb their harmony. In the Eden she remembers and celebrates Adam and Eve are never separated: "They by no Domestick Cares, / From each other e'er were drawn" (lines 59 – 60). The crucial decision to work separately, prominent in Milton's account in Book IX, is here discreetly omitted. In the absolute retreat fallen passions are excluded: "Rage, and Jealousie, and Hate, / Transports of his fallen State, / (When by Satan's Wiles betray'd) / Fly those Windings, and that Shade!" (lines 66 – 69).

To be sure Lady Winchelsea's dream is not wholly earthbound. The delights of "the present Moment" yield to the higher pleasures of Contemplation as the soul views "the Height, from whence she came." Other retirement poets, following Milton's lead, put still greater emphasis on the spiritual rather than physical pleasures of garden retreat. Indeed, Milton's effect on the retirement genre is to spiritualize it by locating the real retreat within. An anonymous poet in 1730 gestures once toward "the Shade of yonder Grove," but the true scene of retirement is "the Temple of my Heart." Beginning with the classical idea (derived from Cicero) that the retired man is never less alone than when alone,[31] the poet works a Miltonic variation: in solitude he welcomes God as his "dear Guest."

> My *Eden* then be my Abode,
> And the great Visitant, my God!
> He only my Companion be,
> From whom I hope eternity!

The poet here conflates allusions to two of Milton's angels who visit
Eden, Raphael the "sociable spirit," referred to nine times as a "guest"
in *Paradise Lost*, and Michael, called a "great visitant" at XI. 225.[32]

Thomas Parnell too spends his "Hours of sweet Retreat" by "yonder
Mossy Seat," but the joys he celebrates are primarily internal: "Lovely,
lasting Peace of Mind! / Sweet Delight of human kind!"[33] While Lady
Winchelsea locates a recovered Eden in a rural retreat, Parnell like
Milton looks for a "paradise within":

> Lovely, lasting Peace appear!
> This World it self, if thou art here,
> Is once again with *Eden* bless'd,
> And Man contains it in his Breast.

And like Adam and Eve Parnell sings a hymn to the "great *Source of
Nature*." Although there are no unmistakable allusions to *Paradise Lost*,
the hymn is closely analogous to the morning hymn in Milton's Eden.
"These are thy glorious works, parent of good," sing Adam and Eve,
bidding the angels, sun, moon, fixed stars, elements, plants, and
animals to "sound his praise" (V. 172). Parnell, in contemporary
physico-theological fashion, declares that sun, moon, stars, seas, wood,
and field,

> All of these, and all I see,
> Shou'd be sung, and sung by me:
> They speak their Maker as they can,
> But want and ask the Tongue of Man.

In closing Parnell goes so far as to imagine that the contented man has
all but attained the bliss of Heaven. While Milton draws a sharp line
for fallen man between this life and the next, Parnell blurs that line.
He challenges the reader to "find a Life of equal Bliss, / Or own the
next begun in *this*."

Another retirement poet in 1730 draws on Milton's Edenic myth to
rewrite Pomfret's famous "The Choice" (1704), a poem celebrating
the choice of a contemplative life in resolutely earthbound "pleasure,
ease, and plenty." The anonymous author of "Retirement: A Divine
Soliloquy" sees in retirement an opportunity to recover the paradise
that Adam and Eve lost:

> Such was the blest Abode, the happy Clime,
> Where our first Parents sweetly spent their Time
> In mutual Love and Innocence, among
> The shady Bow'rs and Trees, and flow'ry Throng
> Of Eden's Paradise, before they fell.
> And turn'd their Heav'nly Garden into Hell.

> Thither again, my Soul, if thou wouldst know
> What Innocence and Love is, thou must go;
> And there, if thou woudst turn that Hell again
> To Paradise on Earth, thou must remain.
>
> (p. 15)[34]

The emphasis on "mutual Love" suggests that this Eden derives from Milton, whose Adam and Eve speak of "mutual love" as "the Crown of all our bliss" (IV. 728). But the union here celebrated is wholly spiritual. Milton's Eve and Pomfret's "obliging, Modest Fair" are transformed into the poet's soul.

One final example may illustrate how Milton's earthly paradise becomes a metaphor for a re-imagined paradise within. Isaac Watts' "True Riches," which first appeared as one of the songs "Sacred to Virtue, Honour, and Friendship" in his *Horae Lyricae* (1709), combines Horatian self-sufficiency ("'Tis enough that I can say / I've possest my self to day") with Milton's innocent sensuousness:

> I've a mighty Part within
> That the World hath never seen,
> Rich as *Eden*'s happy Ground,
> And with choicer Plenty crown'd.
> Here on all the shining Boughs
> Knowledge fair and useful grows.
>
> (lines 21 – 26)[35]

Milton's Tree of Knowledge here yields not apples but "Thoughts of larger Growth, / Rip'ning into solid Truth" (lines 31 – 32). As in Eden "Seraphs" might "feed on such Repast" (line 34), and "Angels," milder than Milton's Michael on the "Hill" of vision (XI. 377), alight on "Hills of Contemplation" and call the poet "up."[36]

Pleasures of imagination: Akenside and Young

Retirement from the world – to rural shades or to the contented mind – was but one way to recover paradise in the eighteenth century. For other poets Eden might be found in the world at large, if perceived by an enlightened eye. Despite the Fall, and in some sense in refutation of it, the world is still pristine and accessible to man's pure mind. Henry Brooke, for example, a late heir of the physico-theological tradition, saw the entire world as "Myriads of Edens":

> The florid theatres, romantick scenes,
> The steepy mountains, and luxuriant plains,
> Delicious regions! plants, woods, waters, glades,
> Grots, arbours, flowrets, downs, and rural shades,

> The brooks that sportive wind the echoing hills,
> The pearly founts, smooth lakes, and murmuring rills –
> Myriads of Edens! blissful, blissful seats!
> Arcadian groves, sweet Tempe's blest retreats,
> Delightful Ennas, and Hesperian isles,
> And round, and round throughout, Elysium smiles.
> (Universal Beauty, 1735, I. 137–46)[37]

But the most prominent example of a poet who discovers and recovers Eden through the exercise of man's unfallen mental powers is Akenside. His *Pleasures of Imagination* (1744) suggests that the world accessible to man's imagination is Milton's unfallen world. His raptured survey of "this goodly frame" (I. 1) recalls Raphael's dialogue with Adam, who likewise beholds the wonders of "this goodly Frame" (*Paradise Lost*, VIII. 15). Those to whom the great scene of nature is unveiled "partake the eternal joy" (I. 108) of those in heaven: "the men / Whom Nature's works can charm, with God himself / Hold converse" (III. 629–31), as Adam once in Eden could "converse" with Raphael (*Paradise Lost*, V. 230) and even "hold converse" with God his creator (VIII. 408).

Akenside's admiration for Milton is well-documented in the *Odes*. In an ode "On the Absence of the Poetic Inclination" (1745), later re-titled "To the Muse," he imagines that a song from Milton might persuade the muse, like Eurydice, to return: "from amid the Elysian train, / The soul of Milton shall I gain, / To win thee back with some celestial strain?" He has only to invoke Milton's name to feel his spirit kindle. He "gains" Milton's soul not by calling up the dead so much as by a kind of transmigration.[38] That Akenside was inspired by Milton is clearer yet when we examine their narrators. Like Milton's poem, Akenside's *Pleasures of Imagination* begins "from Heaven." His muse, like Urania, was present even before the original creation:

> Ere mountains, woods, or streams adorn'd the globe,
> Or Wisdom taught the sons of men her lore;
> Then liv'd the Almighty One: then, deep-retir'd
> In his unfathom'd essence, views the forms,
> The forms eternal of created things.
>
> (I. 62–66)

In like manner Milton's Urania, who "Before the Hills appear'd, or Fountain flow'd, / ...with Eternal Wisdom didst converse, / Wisdom thy Sister, and with her didst play / In presence of th' Almighty Father" (*Paradise Lost*, VII. 8–11). Later, when Akenside's narrator invokes Beauty, the "Genius of Ancient Greece" (I. 567), he reveals an ambition that matches (and seeks to match) Milton's: "Inspire my kindling bosom to the height / Of this untempted theme" (I. 572– 73).[39]

Like Milton too Akenside aspires to soar above the world, there to breathe "Aethereal air" (I. 42).[40] While Milton betrays some concern that his narrative aspirations might be of Satanic origin,[41] fearing that his presumption might lead to a fall (VII. 12 – 20), Akenside soars in full confidence through "The blue profound, and hovering round the sun / Beholds him pouring the redundant stream / Of Light" (I. 191 – 93). Despite the potentially Satanic associations of such flight Akenside reaffirms his innocence, and the Miltonic narrator as his model: "Thus," he says Miltonically, "with a faithful aim have we presum'd, / Adventurous, to delineate Nature's form" (I. 438 – 39), adding later, "Nor be my thoughts / Presumptuous counted" (I. 573 – 74).[42] Even the fallen poet recovers paradise.

Akenside's most remarkable use of Milton is to declare a paradise regained in his large-scale rewriting of the Edenic books of *Paradise Lost* (Books IV – VIII) in Book II of *The Pleasures of Imagination*. When Adam and Eve finish their Edenic meal, Raphael cautions them to be obedient. Adam's slightly wounded response – how could we possibly want obedience to God? – prompts Raphael's long theodicean narrative of the War in Heaven. In Akenside's *Pleasures of Imagination* the narrator's claim that all passions are delightful, when questioned – do sorrow and fear also delight us? – prompts a narrative, which, like Milton's theodicy, demonstrates that "the ways / Of Heaven's eternal destiny to man" are "just, benevolent, and wise" (II. 670 – 72). That narrative itself contains a fanciful allegorical vision modeled on Raphael's original descent to Eden.

Akenside's narrative is placed in the mouth of old Harmodius, who when a youth had bitterly lamented the death of Parthenia, and questioned the "awful will" of God that permitted such "cruelties" (II. 214 – 16). A celestial figure suddenly appears to him, descending like Milton's angels from the sky. Raphael had worn a pair of wings that "came mantling o'er his breast," and another that "Girt like a Starry Zone his waist" (V. 279 – 81). Akenside's vision, "the Genius of human kind" (II. 237), wears a transparent robe "mantling to his knee" and collected "around his waist / ... with a radiant zone of gold" (232 – 34). Though dressed to recall Raphael, the Genius speaks more like Michael, displaying "Displeasure, temper'd with a mild concern" (239), reproving Harmodius, and presenting a series of visionary "scenes."[43]

The first scene is an Edenic "sylvan theatre" (291),[44] a mountaintop paradise with a "flowery level" beside a clear stream. Like Raphael the Genius explains that this "primeval seat / Of man" (365 – 66) was created by God who breathed into each form "its portion of the vital flame" (319).[45] One sign of Akenside's claim that paradise is still within man's reach is that in his vision creation is continuous: "Nor content, / By one exertion of creative power / His goodness to reveal; through every age, / Through every moment up the tract of time / His parent hand with ever new increase / Of happiness and virtue has adorn'd / The vast harmonious frame'' (337–43).[46] Another sign is that he argues, following Milton, that all things, through time, "climb the ascent of being, and approach / For ever nearer to the life divine" (362–63). Although Akenside's account of the steady upward ascent to "higher scenes of being" might easily have been derived from Platonic sources, it seems likely, given the Edenic scene, that Milton's "One Almighty is, from whom / All things proceed and up to him return" (V. 469–70) and his dynamic "scale of Nature" (V. 509) are not far from Akenside's mind.

Third, in a remarkable adaptation of Milton's paradise, Akenside declares that man's mind itself, like the flowers in Eden, will "grow up and flourish" (553). From "the tender seeds / Of justice and of wisdom," if properly tended, will "evolve / The latent honours of his generous frame" (453–55).[47] Milton's unfallen man had within him the potential, if he remained obedient, of turning all to spirit and ascending to Heaven. With the Fall the mind was forever corrupted, and man redeemable only through Christ. For Akenside the mind still contains its Edenic potential. His flower metaphor might well have been inspired by Milton's elaborate comparison of upward spiritual movement to the flower that springs from leaves, stalk, and root (V. 479–82), but the details derive from Adamic gardening. In Akenside's vision of Eden a goddess is sent "to rear the blooming mind, / The folded powers to open, to direct / The growth luxuriant of his young desires" (II. 386–88), recalling the Edenic need to "direct / The clasping ivy where to climb" (IX. 216) and to restrain "Luxurious" growth (IX. 209). As Akenside makes clear, with strikingly similar language, these Edenic conditions still pertain for the man who learns the pleasures of imagination:

> What high capacious powers
> Lie folded up in man; how far beyond
> The praise of mortals, may the eternal growth
> Of Nature to perfection half divine,
> Expand the blooming soul?
>
> (I. 222–26)

Akenside here implies that the Fall has never taken place, that one can still participate, in the imagination, in an unfallen world.

The Genius's second visionary scene in Eden makes this elision or denial of the Fall explicit. An Adamic youth is seen attended by two "radiant forms," one a goddess representing Virtue, the other

112

Euphrosyne, originally one of the three graces, and here "the gentle queen / Of smiles, and graceful gladness" (II. 393 – 94).[48] Faced with a kind of "choice of Hercules," the youth prefers the young and beautiful Euphrosyne to the majestic and matron-like goddess, and as they depart longs for her return in lines that clearly allude to Eve's departure from Adam just before the Fall: "The younger chief his ardent eyes detain'd, / With mild regret invoking her return" (II. 405 – 06).[49] As she goes, furthermore, Euphrosyne carries "in her hand … a living branch / Rich with immortal fruits" (417), like Eve returning to Adam after the fall carrying "in her hand / A bough of fairest fruit" (IX. 850 – 51).[50] The Fall itself is elided as Eve's innocent departure and guilty return are collapsed into one moment. The youth is then reproved for his preference, and threatened by the Son of Nemesis, but his "fall" proves to be forgiveable, rather like the "fall before the Fall" that Adam undergoes in Book VIII when he reveals to Raphael his attraction to Eve's beauty. The Goddess warns the youth, as Raphael had warned Adam, of the dangers of preferring beauty to virtue. She then disarms the Son of Nemesis and grants the youth's wish that Euphrosyne be restored to him. Harmodius himself draws the moral: God has decreed "That Virtue's awful steps, howe'er pursu'd / By vexing fortune and intrusive pain, / Should never be divided from her chaste, / Her fair attendant, Pleasure" (II. 673 – 76). Thus Akenside's original question is in a roundabout way answered: for the virtuous even the passions of sorrow, pity, and terror are attended by a kind of pleasure.

Sorrow thus is acknowledged in Akenside's Edenic world, but it is not a serious threat to universal harmony. The Son of Nemesis may again visit the youth with pain, but the young hero is confident that he will survive his "trial" (II. 608). Unlike Adam and Eve who in the trial with Satan were found wanting, he finds heavenly favor: "well pleas'd on high / The Father has beheld you, while the might / Of that stern foe with bitter trial prov'd / Your equal doings" (II. 650 – 53). In later revisions of the poem Akenside takes a less sanguine view and more fully acknowledges the presence of evil in the world. The allegorical vision of Eden is dropped, and a new theodicy is introduced in Book III to explain why God "bade … The viper Evil, creeping in, pollute / The goodly scene" (III. 9 – 11).[51] But Book III, relating the story of Solon's resistance to Pisistratus, remained unfinished, and a fragmentary Book IV, despite a strongly Miltonic opening, breaks off after 130 lines.[52]

Johnson thought *The Pleasures of Imagination* an example of "great felicity of genius, and uncommon amplitude of acquisitions." Most modern readers pass over the praise and assent rather to Johnson's complaints about the poem's diffuseness. Reading Akenside's poem in its Miltonic context may render it more accessible because more focused. Both the didactic and the narrative elements of the poem emerge more clearly when we see them as an appropriation of and a response to the picture of man's native powers in *Paradise Lost*.

Edward Young published his *Night Thoughts* in the same year as *The Pleasures of Imagination*, but Young is in some ways Akenside's antithesis. Both poets are admirers and imitators of Milton; their works are both post-Miltonic theodicies. Akenside is the Platonist poet of the intellectual world, celebrating the powers and pleasures of the imagination. Young rejects the gloomy world of this life, whether natural or intellectual, in favor of Christian immortality. Paradoxically, however, opposites meet. Like Akenside Young displays a high confidence in man's immortal origin and end. Man is "a native of the skies" (*Night Thoughts*, V. 456), his a "Sky-born, sky-guided, sky-returning race! / Erect, immortal, rational, divine!" (VI. 418–21). Young also acknowledges but ultimately devalues the Fall, and like Akenside he affirms that paradise can be regained, though only in the Christian afterlife. Put another way, he insists as an orthodox Christian that the old Adam, even in his unfallen paradise, has been superseded by Christ, the new Adam. Young would have us not look back but ahead.

Young adopts Milton's fortunate Fall – the idea that man redeemed and restored is "happier" than he was in Eden, and God more glorious. "Death gives us more than was in Eden lost" (III. 533). "Redemption!" Young exclaims, " 'twas creation more sublime" (IV. 455). That Christ chose to die for man serves to exalt man as much as Christ, and make the world seem glorious: "How changed the face of nature! how improved! / What seem'd a chaos, shines a glorious world, / Or, what a world, an Eden, heighten'd all!" (IV. 502–04). But Young carries the notion of the fortunate Fall so far as to imply that the original paradise was inherently flawed. Adam is not so much man's once-immortal forefather, unique inhabitant of a paradise forever lost, as the first in "the long list of swift mortality" (IX. 2117). Young emphasizes not original harmony but original sin, when the passions were "seduced / By wanton Eve's debauch, to stroll on earth / And set the sublunary world on fire" (VII. 542–44). Devaluing Eden by blurring differences between the unfallen and fallen worlds, Young mockingly asks "And had your Eden an abstemious Eve?" (IX. 1774); recalling Eve's despair, he notes that even in Eden suicide "might prevail" (V. 453). In effect Young takes Eve's polemical view: "*Eden* were no *Eden* thus expos'd" (IX. 341).[53]

The first paradise was quickly lost, as any earthly paradise must be.[54] Pleasure's sacred stream, the narrator says, "Makes a new Eden where it flows; – but such / As must be lost, Lorenzo! by thy fall"

(VIII. 658–59). The only Eden that can endure is a heavenly paradise. Milton had imagined at least three kinds of recovered paradise – the millennial earth (XII. 464), the "eternal Paradise of rest" (XII. 314), and the "paradise within" (XII. 587). Young collapses these into one, "A fairer Eden, endless, in the skies" (IX. 386), "An Eden…a Paradise unlost" (IX. 1069), the true and eternal "garden of the DEITY" (IX. 1040).

An English Eden: Philips and Dyer

Akenside's Eden is located in the exercise of the imagination, Young's in the afterlife. For contemporary georgic writers it still survived in the natural world of agricultural England. The purist might of course wonder at once what an Edenic paradise can have to do with a fallen georgic world. From its classical beginnings georgic had dealt with the world of *labor*, in which a careful husbandman, sweating under Adam's curse, painstakingly worked and improved the soil, or guarded against disease and bad weather. It is the pastoral genre, not the georgic, whose subject is the world of otium, in which the herdsman has leisure for song, love, and fellowship. To be sure, Virgil's famous "O fortunatos nimium" (*Georgics* II) could make the farmer seem, by comparison with the towndweller and courtier, an inhabitant of the Golden Age. But even Virgil's fortunates are "hardened to toil and inured to scanty fare" ("patiens operum exiguoque adsueta").[55] Why then should an English georgic writer, still in the eighteenth century very conscious of genre distinctions and classical precedents, turn to the pastoral Milton for a model? Partly perhaps because Milton was an Englishman, and a modern classic. Partly because Milton himself had blurred the distinction between georgic and pastoral by making Adam and Eve gardeners, engaged in daily work to maintain their garden paradise. Partly too because the Edenic myth might endow England and English agriculture with even greater dignity and spiritual resonance. In fact John Philips and John Dyer remember both Virgil and Milton. Virgil provides the model for the didactic element – instruction in the arts of cider-making and sheep-shearing – and political framework, linking agriculture to national greatness. As *Cyder* (1708) and *The Fleece* (1757) demonstrate, Milton's version of the Edenic story gave literary shape and mythic resonance to their claims that a paradise might still be found in the orchards and pastures of rural England. Paradoxically, the world of the eighteenth-century georgic answers better to Milton's pastoral Eden than to traditional notions of georgic. The georgic laborer in Philips and Dyer more closely resembles an Adamic gardener than his descendants who must eat their bread in the sweat of their faces (*Paradise Lost*, X.

205; Gen. 3. 18), or the georgic Christ through whose efforts "*Eden* [is] rais'd in the waste Wilderness" (*Paradise Regained*, I. 7). To use Milton in this way is both to incorporate and yet to transform him, to honor him and yet wittily to rewrite him. In *Cyder* Philips sets out to do nothing less than to celebrate the innocent pleasures of that same delicious fruit by which our grandparents fell from Eden. Milton would have indignantly protested the complacent materialism and worldliness of his admirers. Yet his own Eden is very much a material garden, to be tended and enjoyed, if not actually cultivated. If the eighteenth-century georgic writers recognized the georgic spirit in Milton (which Anthony Low's recent book underlines), they may in fact have been extending and developing suggestions latent in Milton's work that a georgic paradise is to some degree recoverable.[56]

Cyder is Philips' most Miltonic poem but it is also his most Virgilian. The celebration of English cider is modeled directly on the *Georgics*, and particularly on the second book, in which Virgil instructs his reader in the growing of grapes and the making of wine. *Cyder* makes clear that Philips understood the *Georgics* to be more than, in Addison's words, "some part of the science of husbandry put into a pleasing dress."[57] For Virgil and for Philips a georgic is a profoundly political poem, grounding the stability and strength of a country in its farmers, celebrating the fertility of the earth, the joy of rural retirement, and the fruits of peace. *Cyder*, like the *Georgics*, is a post-civil war poem, looking back on a period of violence and disorder and now celebrating an achieved harmony. After fifty years of revolutionary plots, real or imagined, the killing of one king and the deposing of another, England in 1708, safely consolidated with Scotland, could rejoice with Pope that "Peace and Plenty tell a Stuart reigns" unchallenged. Anne is Philips' Augustus, guarantor of her country's happiness and power.

Both the didactic and political elements, then, Philips owes to Virgil.[58] To Milton the poem owes its verse form and its language – the muscular, taut, compact blank verse, the Latinate polysyllabic diction, exotic proper names, adjectives placed after nouns. Allusions to *Paradise Lost* are frequent.[59] Philips announces his debts as early as the opening lines:

> in *Miltonian* Verse
> Adventrous I presume to sing; Of Verse
> Nor skill'd, nor studious: but my Native Soil
> Invites me, and the Theme as yet unsung.
> (I. 3–6)

Philips takes as his theme "the Fruit of that Forbidden Tree" but wittily declares his intention to sing after his own fashion. *His* apples shine

> Tempting, not fatal, as the Birth of that
> Primaeval interdicted Plant, that won
> Fond *Eve* in hapless Hour to taste, and die
>   (I. 515–17)

With impishness that for Milton would approach impiety, Philips even associates himself with Eve, tempted by Satan and soon to fall. Eve says:

> Great are thy Vertues, doubtless, best of Fruits...
> Whose taste, too long forborn, at first assay
> Gave elocution to the mute, and taught
> The tongue not made for speech to speak thy praise.
>   (IX. 745, 747–49)

In Philips too the apple, "of more bounteous Influence, inspires / Poetic Raptures, and the lowly Muse / Kindles to loftier Strains; even I perceive / Her sacred Virtue" (I. 518–21). Inspiration is due not to the nightly visits of the muse, but to timely draughts of cider: "See! the Numbers flow / Easie, whilst, chear'd with her nectarious Juice, / Hers, and my Country's Praises I exalt" (I. 521–23). We here recall Milton's "inspires / Easy my unpremeditated verse" (IX. 23–24). "Hail Son of God," says Milton, "Thy Name / Shall be the copious matter of my Song" (III. 412–13). "Hail *Herefordian* Plant... Heav'n's sweetest Blessing, hail! / Be thou the copious Matter of my Song" (I. 624–26), says Philips rather, again allying himself with Satan – "O sacred, wise, and wisdom-giving plant" (IX. 679) – and with Eve – "O sovran, virtuous, precious of all trees / In paradise... henceforth my early care, / Not without Song, each morning, and due praise shall tend thee" (IX. 795–96, 799–801).

Elsewhere Philips applies Milton's weighty lines to matters of less moment. Raphael's sober warning to Adam after relating the War in Heaven and the "terrible example" of the "reward of disobedience" becomes in *Cyder* a warning that the farmer not omit his duty of tithing, lest he suffer the fate of a miser who withheld "The Clergy's Due," and whose fields were cursed with unwished-for rain, unseasonable frost, or drought. "Remember, and fear to transgress" (VI. 912), concludes Raphael. "Be Just, and Wise, and tremble to transgress" (II. 161), Philips wittily echoes. The delight in Philips' lines derives in part from his delicious awareness of his own mischievous transformation of Milton, reducing the "Forbidden Fruit, that cursed Fatal Fruit," as one disapproving contemporary put it, to mere cider apples,[60] and the commonsense triumph that restores to the symbolic pledge of man's obedience the concreteness and familiarity of "Red-streak" and "John-Apple." (We might note here that Milton's interdicted fruit is only twice called an "apple" in *Paradise Lost*, once when Satan contemptuously reports his triumph to the devils in Book X).

Philips' subject is consciously smaller than Milton's mythical fruit. But in his hands the apple and the life of the retired industrious farmer are simultaneously a "Large Subject" (I. 770), and a worthy foundation upon which to celebrate English agriculture and English political order. Indeed, the sense that the subject is both small and great lies at the center of *Cyder* and helps account for its peculiar combination of playfulness and ardor. It may also explain Philips' ambivalent attitude toward Miltonic verse: he will honor his subject, yet he will remember the disparity between English pippins and the fatal fruit.

He will also insist gently on the political differences between a royalist Tory and a republican. Toward the end of Book I Philips praises the retired life and the poets who have lived it – Virgil and Spenser. He would add Milton,

> had but He that first ennobled Song
> With holy Raptures, like his *Abdiel* been,
> 'Mong many faithless, strictly faithful found;
> ...
> But He – However, let the Muse abstain,
> Nor blast his Fame, from whom she learnt to sing
> In much inferior Strains, grov'ling beneath
> Th'*Olympian* Hill, on Plains, and Vales intent,
> Mean Follower.
>
> (I. 785–87, 791–95)

At the end of Book II Philips makes more clear his regret about Milton's politics. A passage on the dangers of drunkenness leads easily – with help from an allusion to *Paradise Lost*[61] – to the dangers of "Civil Broils" and to memories of the civil wars. Philips uses Milton's own words to condemn the parliamentary forces:

> Can we forget, how the mad, headstrong Rout
> Defy'd their Prince to Arms, nor made account
> Of Faith, or Duty, or Allegiance sworn?
> Apostate, Atheist Rebells! bent to Ill,
> With seeming Sanctity, and cover'd Fraud,
> Instill'd by him, who first presum'd t'oppose
> Omnipotence.
>
> (II. 498–504)[62]

The specific political differences between Milton and Philips may be less important, however, than a more general one, involving much larger assumptions about England. Milton's poem is based on a myth of lost innocence, to be recovered (if ever) through the mediation of supernatural powers. Though he once harbored hopes of writing a poem "doctrinal and exemplary to a nation" and embellished with the heroic deeds of his countrymen, by the time he wrote *Paradise Lost* Milton had abandoned secular political hopes and looked beyond England to the fallen state of all men. Philips' doctrinal poem is on the other hand profoundly patriotic, embellished with the deeds of native kings and heroes, and very much a poem of this world. In his myth England is "the Cyder-land." Whatever ills this "once Happy" land has suffered – Philips surveys English history from the warring pre-Conquest kings to the Wars of the Roses and the Civil War – the Cyder-land itself has magically remained "unstain'd with Guilt" (II. 514) and "obsequious still to Thrones."[63] Enemies to the throne are disloyal, and in accord with contemporary political thinking mere schismatics, while the loyalists are the true representatives of the nation. That the country has remained innocent, virtuous, and strong is due to its own genius and to the powers of "Nature" and "Fate" which luckily severed Albion from the continent and provided champions like Henry Tudor. That it enjoys the fruits of a fertile soil is due to Pomona and to the goddess Plenty who strews "from well-stor'd Horn, rich Grain, and timely Fruits" (II. 659). Queen Anne plays the role of Milton's God, joining England and Scotland with a single fiat:

> prudent ANNA said
> LET THERE BE UNION; strait with Reverence due
> To Her Command, they willingly unite,
> One in Affection, Laws, and Government,
> Indissolubly firm.[64]
>
> (II. 639–43)

Milton's verse and language are here put to profoundly unMiltonic ends: a celebration of a secular political order presided over by the granddaughter of Charles I, and praise not of the Creator but of the fruits of the earth, whose fame has reached "to the utmost Bounds of this / Wide Universe" (II. 667–68). The British navy, instrument of imperial power

> thro' the Ocean vast
> Shall wave her double Cross, t'extreamest Climes
> Terrific, and return with odorous Spoils
> Of *Araby* well fraught, or *Indus*'s Wealth,
> Pearl, and Barbaric Gold.
>
> (II. 653–57)

The language is Milton's but the vision of material splendor is Philips' version of a favorite English theme, found prominently in *Cooper's Hill*

and *Annus Mirabilis*, the glories of Thames-bound maritime trade.[65]
The ideological deviation from the Miltonic original is indicated by the
Satanic associations of Philips' commercial fantasy. The "odorous
Spoils / of *Araby*" derive from Satan's delight at the "odorous sweets"
and "balmy spoils" of Eden, compared by Milton to the winds that blow
"*Sabean* Odors from the spicy shore / Of *Araby* the blest" (*Paradise Lost*,
IV. 159–60). More impudently, the "Pearl, and Barbaric Gold" allude
directly to the riches of Satan's throne, said to outshine

> the wealth of *Ormus* and of *Ind*,
> Or where the gorgeous East with richest hand
> Show'rs on her Kings *Barbaric* Pearl and Gold.
> (II. 2–4)

What Milton presents as the tainted dross of the world Philips embraces
as the reward of English virtue.

Cyder concludes with a picture of England as an earthly paradise. As
in traditional accounts, based ultimately on Virgil's description of an
agricultural Golden Age,[66] the earth pours forth its fruits unbidden. In
repainting this old picture Philips supplies Miltonic details. English
swains need only "reap what Plenty strows" (II. 658) and "applaud"
as the juice of apples flows "in well blended Streams" (II. 662–63), like
Eden's stream that "Ran Nectar" (*Paradise Lost*, IV. 240). Milton's
"Nature boon" (IV. 242) reappears as Philips' "Boon Nature" (II.
443). Like the inhabitants of Milton's Eden, Englishmen enjoy "In
narrow room Nature's whole wealth" (*Paradise Lost*, IV. 207), not only
the "rich Grain" from their native fields but also the exotic treasures
of the east. Though the world outside their garden may suffer "baleful
Ills, caus'd by *Bellona*'s Wrath" (II. 664), English swains shall live and
work "unmolested" (II. 658). That work more closely resembles the
"pleasant labour" (*Paradise Lost*, IV. 625) of Edenic gardening than
the georgic labors of Virgil's "unrelenting toil" (*labor improbus*)[67] or
Milton's post-lapsarian world in which man eats his bread "in the sweat
of [his] Face" (*Paradise Lost*, X. 205). To be sure, Philips' cider-makers
must exercise industry and "necessary Care" (I. 44). But the "Pains"
are "little" (I. 216) and labor "it self rewards / With pleasing Gain"
(I. 418–19).

Philips' *Cyder* then provided not only an example of what an English
poet might do with Milton but also made Miltonic materials more
available for new use. By aligning the Satanic rebellion with the English
civil wars, and the divine restoration of order with Anne's royal arts
of reconciliation, Philips redirected attention from a mythical Eden to
a new Golden Age in this world and this England.[68]

In an age of agricultural revolution and incipient industrialization, how long might poets seriously claim that work in rural England was still Edenic? Dyer's *The Fleece* (1757), written half a century after *Cyder*, shows that the idea persists remarkably late, but only through careful and selective focus. It is primarily in the first two books of *The Fleece* that Dyer presents the pastures of rural England as a pastoral Eden:

> Pleasant Siluria, land of various Views,
> Hills, rivers, woods, and lawns, and purple groves
> Pomaceous, mingled with the curling growth
> Of tendril hops.[69]

As a painter and a hill-poet, Dyer is especially fond of "various views." The phrase comes from Milton's description of the hilltop paradise, "a happy rural seat of various views" (*Paradise Lost*, IV. 247),[70] but was effortlessly transferred to descriptions of the English countryside in topographical or country-house poems. To celebrate England's rural variety a poet need only enumerate its features, as Milton had before him in praising Eden: "Ye Hills and Dales, ye Rivers, Woods, and Plains" (*Paradise Lost*, VIII. 275), "sweet interchange / Of Hill and Valley, Rivers, Woods and Plains" (IX. 115 – 16).[71] The "purple groves / Pomaceous" obliquely recall both Philips, who coined the Latinate word (meaning "consisting of apples"),[72] and Milton before him, as is confirmed by the Miltonic "mingled with the curling growth / Of tendril hops."[73] The "delicious downs / Of Albion" (p. 63) call up Milton's "delicious Grove" and "delicious spot."[74] Dyer indeed does not hesitate to call the scene a paradise:

> such herds of kine
> ...
> What other paradise adorn but thine,
> Britannia? happy, if thy sons would know
> Their happiness.
>
> (Bk. I, p. 59)

Dyer's political motive – to encourage agriculture and to remind farm workers how well off they are – is aided by the allusion to imparadised Adam and Eve: "O yet happiest if ye seek / No happier state" (IV. 774), itself an adaptation of *Georgics*, II. 458 ("Oh happy, if he knew his happy State!" in Dryden's Miltonic translation).

Like Adam and Eve Dyer's shepherds at the sheepshearing festival eat an Edenic meal. Their fruits "of frugal store, in husk or rind" and "dulcet cream / Soft-temper'd" (p. 84) plainly derive from the meal that Eve prepared for Raphael's visit.[75] And their songs are the "Music of Paradise!"

which still is heard,
When the heart listens; still the views appear
Of the first happy garden, when content
To nature's flow'ry scenes directs the sight.
(Bk. I, p. 80)

Dyer does not forget, however, that the shepherd's life can be a difficult one, for "innum'rous ills ... rush around" his innocent lambs (p. 71): "thy bosom to a thousand cares divide" (p. 71). But by comparison with other sheep-raising countries, England is still a paradise, blest with a temperate climate:

With grateful heart, ye British swains, enjoy
Your gentle seasons and indulgent clime.
(p. 73)

Other lands are beset with famine, plague, and war, but "your mild homesteads, ever-blooming, smile / Among embracing woods; and waft on high / The breath of plenty" (p. 75).[76] England has "no golden mines, / no soft perfumes, nor oils, nor myrtles" – the furniture of a Mediterranean paradise – for they would only "Enervate" "The vig'rous frame and lofty heart of man" (p. 58). Its very fogs and damps are bracing: "Hail noble Albion ... round whose stern cerulean brows

White-winged snow, and cloud, and pearly rain,
Frequent attend, with solemn majesty:
Rich queen of mists and vapours! These thy sons
With their cool arms compress; & twist their nerves
For deeds of excellence and high renown.
(pp. 58–59)

Dyer here allows for some traditional affectionate grumbling about English weather, and even perhaps a kind of inverted mock-heroic recollection of an earlier queen of vapors, Pope's Dulness. But his claim for hardiness through trial and adversity (itself traditional) should be taken at face value. Dyer would have it both ways: rural England is still an Edenic garden of innocent pleasure, yet it is at the same time a wet northern land that strengthens moral sinews. By the same token Dyer discovers a kind of paradise in the fallen world of labor. Labor is the law of nature ("Ev'n nature lives by toil"), the active principle ("All live by action"), the source of value ("'Tis art and toil / Gives nature value... / Varies, improves, creates" – p. 97) and moral excellence ("man is born to care; / Fashion'd, improv'd, by labor"), and thus finally something for which man should be "grateful" (p. 124), a word with strong Miltonic associations.[77]

More revisionist yet is Dyer's implication that English sheep-raising and the wool trade can in some respects undo the effects of the Fall. The draining of Bedford Level in the fens of Cambridgeshire, for example, is presented as a "new creation." Once a "dreary pathless waste," it is now a garden thanks to the "godlike" Russell,

> who drain'd the rushy fen,
> Confin'd the waves, bid groves and gardens bloom,
> And through his new creation led the Ouze,
> And gentle Camus, silver-winding streams;
> God-like beneficence; from chaos drear
> To raise the garden and the shady grove.
> (Bk. II, p. 97)[78]

Like Milton's creator on the third day who gathered the waters "Into one place," "bid the ground be dry," and said "let th'Earth / Put forth the verdant Grass... / And Fruit Tree" (VII. 283 – 311), like Christ who "Rais'd" an Eden "in the waste Wilderness" (*Paradise Regained*, I. 7), Russell raises a garden out of chaos.[79] The fleece produced on these and other English pastures will help Britannia serve as clothier of the world, "to clothe the naked,"[80] as Christ clothed Adam and Eve. English woolens may then help to mitigate the effects of the Fall, to protect man against the cold and (recalling both Christ the good shepherd, and the origin of the wool) "to fold the world with harmony."[81]

Dyer is able to sustain his Edenic vision over the first two books of *The Fleece*, while his subject remains essentially pastoral, the care of sheep and the preparation of wool. In the latter two books spinning, weaving, tapestries, trade, and navigation take him from England's gardens into the world of commerce and the nascent British Empire. Milton's mythical garden no longer suits Dyer's needs, as he turns, like Philips before him, to the theme of British maritime power.

The fiction that agricultural England was still an Eden no doubt faded as the century progressed, perhaps because the realities of modern farming techniques, machinery, and commerce could not be contained in a Miltonic paradise. But if an observer contracted his gaze from the pastures and orchards to the landscape garden, where one's occupation was not work but the pleasures of ambulatory contemplation, he could still see the world through Milton's eyes, and imagine himself in a recovered paradise. It was a commonplace in eighteenth-century writing on landscape gardening as early as Switzer's *Ichnographia Rustica; or The Nobleman, Gentleman, and Gardener's Recreation* (1715) that Milton's descriptions of Eden had provided a model for the modern English landscape garden.[82] Milton's Eden served not only as a paradigm for the professional gardener to imitate as he designed and planted to allow for pleasing profusion and variety, "not nice Art / ... but Nature boon." It also helped enable the gardener's aristocratic clients to believe that as they walked through a Kent or Brown landscaped scene they had recovered some of the original innocence of Eden. Indeed, gardeners did not hesitate to declare quite explicitly, with Timothy Nourse in 1700, that the true purpose of agriculture and gardening at a country house was not simply to restore nature to its prelapsarian beauty but "to restore Man to his lost Station,"[83] or with Switzer in 1715 that the gardener aimed "towards the Redress of those Malignities" that came with the Fall.[84] The man who pursues the pleasures of gardening is "in" or "near" the "exalted State" of unfallen man. His soul is "elevated to unlimited Heights above, and modell'd and prepar'd for the sweet Reception and happy Enjoyment of Felicities" (pp. iv, 217). This claim, an obvious selling point for the enterprising professional gardenist, became a cliché.[85] Young, later in the century, despite his tendency in *Night Thoughts* to dismiss the original paradise, says elsewhere that a garden is both a promotion of a virtuous man's happiness, and a picture of it, in its culture, order, fruitfulness, and seclusion from the world. "A garden to the virtuous is a paradise still extant; a paradise unlost."[86]

Since landscape gardening and poetry were for Pope and others "sister arts" it is not surprising that these ideas had their impact on polite literature, and appeared in poems such as *Paradice Regain'd: or, the Art of Gardening* (1728),[87] and Gilbert West's *Stowe* (1731), among many others. That Milton's version of the Eden myth played a prominent role in the century's thinking about landscape is clear too in the frequent allusions to Milton by visitors to gardens. Even gardens as iconographically classical as Stowe and Stourhead were commonly viewed, as evidenced by allusions to *Paradise Lost*, through Milton's eyes.[88]

Miltonic marriage

For those not wealthy enough to retreat to their own Edenic rural landscape, another way equally Miltonic was still open to recover paradise. In 1709 Sir Richard Steele wrote to the woman who was soon to become his wife: "the Union of minds in pure affection is renewing the First State of Man."[89] Half-a-dozen years later a contributor to *The Censor* quoted lines from *Paradise Lost* displaying "our First Parents in the Perfection of their Love," and went on to remark that "we can scarce attain a closer View of the Joys in Paradise, than from the Union and uninterrupted Satisfaction of a virtuous Couple."[90] The joys shared by Adam and Eve, he implies, are still available to any modern "virtuous Couple."

The main source for this notion is Milton himself, whose "divine Hymn on Marriage," as Thomson called it,[91] was cited with extraordinary frequency in the eighteenth century.

> Hail wedded Love, mysterious Law, true source
> Of human offspring, sole propriety
> In Paradise of all things common else.
> By thee adulterous lust was driv'n from men
> Among the bestial herds to range, by thee
> Founded in Reason, Loyal, Just, and Pure,
> ...
> Perpetual Fountain of Domestic sweets,
> Whose bed is undefil'd and chaste pronounc't,
> Present, or past, as Saints and Patriarchs us'd.
> (IV. 750–55, 760–62)

Milton's lines praise the marriage of unfallen Adam and Eve, but serve also as a free-standing hymn. In form they are an address to married love from the narrator who interrupts his own story of Eden to praise marriage and to denounce hypocrites who find something "impure" in prelapsarian sexual love. The "perpetual" fountain of wedded love flows unceasingly for Adam and Eve, and for all married couples since, whether "present" or in the historical "past." At the Fall, of course, Edenic marriage is strained and nearly shattered, but as part of the restorative movement of the final books of *Paradise Lost* marriage too is reconstituted so as to preserve nearly all of its Edenic purity while retaining the traditional ends – mutual solace and "increase." When Eve laments that she must leave paradise, her "Native Soil" (XI. 270), Michael tells her that her paradise shall now be wherever Adam is: "Thy going is not lonely, with thee goes / Thy Husband, him to follow thou art bound; / Where he abides, think there thy native soil" (XI. 290–92). And as she prepares to depart she turns going into a kind of staying, and life with Adam into a kind of paradise: "In mee is no delay; with thee to go, / Is to stay here; without thee here to stay, / Is to go hence unwilling; thou to mee / Art all things under Heav'n, all places thou" (XII. 615–18). Her syntax – "with thee...without thee..." – recalls her famous song in Eden ("With thee conversing I forget all time... / but [nothing] without thee is sweet"), and manifests obliquely that she still will enjoy some of the pleasures and consolations of Eden in the lower world.[92]

If Milton inspired eighteenth-century hopes in a marital paradise, he also provided a model for what the ideal marriage should be. In 1739 William Smith digresses in his commentary on Longinus to note that

Adam and *Eve* in *Milton* are the finest Picture of conjugal Love that ever was drawn. In them is true warmth of Affection without the violence or fury of Passion; a sweet and reasonable Tenderness without any cloying or insipid Fondness. In its Serenity and Sun-shine, it is noble, amiable, endearing, and innocent.

Even when they quarrel, "*Eve* knows how to submit, and *Adam* to forgive. We are pleased that they have quarreled when we see the agreeable manner in which they are reconciled."[93] As part of a campaign to reform the manners of the age, the *Tatler* papers often praised married love and in so doing invariably cited Milton. In *Tatler* No. 40, for example, Steele quotes *Paradise Lost*, V. 12 – 13, "Leaning half-rais'd, with looks of cordial Love / Hung over her enamor'd" – and comments approvingly on Adam's "tenderness and guardian affection" for his sleeping spouse. Later in *Tatler* No. 263 he quotes the same lines as part of a longer passage which describes Adam awakening the sleeping Eve (V. 1 – 30). Steele notes especially the "fondness of the posture" and "the softness of the whisper." His intended audience appears to be his male readers who (in his view) need to treat their wives more gently, perhaps, than they are accustomed to do. In *Tatler* No. 149 this is made explicit. Steele cites the passage from Book VIII (lines 39 – 54) which describes how Eve would rather be taught by Adam than Raphael: "Her Husband the Relater she preferr'd / Before the angel, and of him to ask / Chose rather: hee, she knew, would intermix / Grateful digressions, and solve high dispute / With conjugal Caresses" (VIII. 52 – 56). Steele then offers Adam as a model to husbands, "a lecture to those of my own sex, who have a mind to make their conversation agreeable, as well as instructive, to their fair partners." Conversely, in *Spectator* No. 89 Addison quotes a passage describing Eve's "innocence and virgin modesty" (*Paradise Lost*, VIII. 500 – 11) and offers Eve as an example "to all her Daughters."[94]

Elsewhere in the *Tatler* Steele does not fail to quote and praise the hymn to marriage ("Hail wedded Love," in No. 79) and Eve's love song ("With thee conversing," in No. 98 and again in No. 114), giving each a conduct-book turn: "This additional satisfaction, from the taste of pleasures in the society of one we love, is admirably described by Milton." Perhaps in part due to Steele's encouragement and example, these two passages were regularly cited throughout the century by essayists from Isaac Watts to Lord Kames and imitated or borrowed by poets from Charles Wesley (for a love song to God) to Thomas Morell, the librettist of Handel's *Alexander Balus* (for the wedding of Cleopatra).[95] Called upon to celebrate a marriage, the eighteenth-century poet readily turned to Milton for an allusion. Upon "The Marriage of the Earl of A— with the Countess of S—," Pomfret offers appropriately idealizing compliment: "Since the first pair in Paradise were join'd, / Two hearts were ne'er so happily combin'd."[96] In a blank verse didactic poem entitled *The Nuptials* (1760), Richard Shepherd traces the origin of marriage to Adam's dissatisfaction with solitude in *Paradise Lost*, Book VIII.[97] And inevitably eighteenth-century husbands and wives, as Jean Hagstrum has noted, saw themselves as Adam and Eve. Mary Wollstonecraft wrote to William Godwin in 1796 suggesting that at their evening lesson he "sweeten grammatical disquisition after the Miltonic mode."[98] Apparently fond of this passage, she also alluded to it in an earlier love letter to Gilbert Imlay (p. 235). Only a few years later Wordsworth wrote to his wife Mary, "How often does that passage of Milton come to my mind: 'I chiefly who enjoy so far the happier lot, enjoying thee, preeminent &c'."[99] Implicit in many of these citations and imitations – and explicit in Pomfret – is the idea that marriages now made on earth can closely resemble that made in Eden.

Implicit too is the faith that a modern marriage need never go through the domestic hell of the Fall and mutual recriminations of *Paradise Lost*, Books IX and X. A misogynist tradition, reflected in Adam's outburst at Eve's faithlessless (X. 867 – 908), remained alive in the eighteenth century, found for example in *The Great Birth of Man; Or, the Excellency of Man's Creation and Endowments Above the Original of Woman* (1686),[100] in John Sprint's controversial 1699 wedding sermon, *The Bride-Womans Counselor*,[101] and perhaps as late as 1778, when an anonymous poem, *The Court of Adultery. A Vision*, took its epigraph from Adam's reproach to God for creating "this fair defect / Of nature," allowing man to be trapped in "female snares."[102] But far stronger in the period is the tradition of mutual love and tenderness that Jean Hagstrum has recently surveyed.[103] This was not to say, however, that Miltonic marriage in the eighteenth century was wholly a union of equals. Milton had made clear that the traditional Pauline injunctions – the man should love and the woman should obey – were still in force. For eighteenth-century marriage on the whole still implied subordination of wife to husband. On this point Adam and Eve served as both ideal and cautionary models. They are introduced as "not equal":

> For contemplation hee and valor form'd,
> For softness shee and sweet attractive Grace,
> Hee for God only, shee for God in him.
>
> (IV. 296–99)

Richardson and Newton both noted that Milton here followed Paul: "by Obeying her Husband she obey'd God, whose Substitute he was." Eve's hair was a sign "that she is in the Power of her Husband."[104] Most

eighteenth-century commentators had no doubt that Milton expected
the wife to submit to her husband's will. Despite the increasing interest
in companionate marriage charted by Hagstrum and Lawrence
Stone,[105] a husband's kindness was perhaps to soften but not to reduce
his underlying authority. Those who pleaded for mutual love between
spouses nonetheless insisted on a traditional male supremacy. Even
Steele cited the authority of both God and nature to argue that women
were placed "in a degree of inferiority" to men. A section on the duties
of a wife in Steele's often-reprinted *Ladies Library* insisted on the
"necessity of subordination and subjection." A wife must obey her
husband unless to do so were to violate God's laws.[106] Those who
resented male domination like Mary Astell nonetheless realized that
Milton gave no comfort to a woman whose husband proved unkind.
Despite his resistance to political tyranny, "not *Milton* himself wou'd
cry up Liberty to poor *Female Slaves*, or plead for the Lawfulness of
Resisting a Private Tyranny."[107]

To judge by eighteenth-century reactions, the greater danger was
not a cruel husband but an indulgent one. Here Adam provided a bad
example in failing to insist that Eve remain by his side on the fatal
morning when she proposed that they work separately. In an essay in
the *Universal Spectator* (Dec. 1731) on excessive "Nuptial Liberty," of
which the modern instance is the wife who insists on journeying to Bath
or Tunbridge "on pretence of her Health," Adam is cited as a warning:

> Let [the indulgent husband] bear in mind the following Speech in *Milton*,
> wherein *Eve* upbraids the Good-Natur'd *Adam* for his Indulgence:

> > Being as I am, why didst not thou the head
> > Command me absolutely not to go,
> > Going into such danger as thou saidst.
> > Too facile then thou didst not much gainsay,
> > Nay didst permit, approve, and fair dismiss,
> > Hadst thou been firm and fixed in thy dissent,
> > Neither had I transgressed, nor thou with me.
> > (IX. 1155–61)

The modern husband who makes Adam's mistake, so the *Universal
Spectator* continues, may find reason to reflect, with him: "Thus it shall
befall / Him, who to *Worth* in Women over-*trusting* / Lets her *Will*
rule."[108] This warning and the quotation from Milton was seasonable
enough to be reprinted at least three times within the next ten years –
once in the *Universal Spectator* and twice in the *Gentleman's Magazine*, where
the moral is drawn explicitly: "If all Husbands wou'd be more *firm* than
Adam, and more *fixt* in their *Dissents*, they will not be reduced to that
self-condemning thought, that their Vexation had not befel them, if they

had not ' – Woman Overtrusting / Let *her Will* rule.' "[109] If the husband stood firm a modern marriage then might avoid the Fall.

Perhaps the most remarkable use of Miltonic marriage, and of the resolute husband, comes in Richardson's *Sir Charles Grandison* (1753 – 54). Once immensely popular (its admirers included Jane Austen) the novel now has few readers, largely because its eponymous hero, Sir Charles himself, is usually found to be boringly virtuous, the ideal Christian gentleman, as pure as unfallen Adam. One potentially fruitful way to read the novel, in fact, is to accept this hostile characterization of it, and then to see it as a serious attempt to re-imagine and to re-create a moral world in Edenic terms. It seems likely that those who find *Sir Charles Grandison* boring might also find life in Milton's prelapsarian paradise boring. Conversely, the reader who can be brought to agree that Milton's Eden is a fully human world of moral choices might even find *Grandison* an ambitious – and an interesting – work of fiction.[110]

Milton is invoked early in the novel. In Letter 13 of the first volume Harriet Byron reports on her debate with the supercilious Mr. Walden about the respective merits of Homer and Milton.[111] In Letter 17 of volume three Sir Charles himself cites lines from *Paradise Lost* (VII. 500 – 11) to illustrate the claim that "Ladies must not be easily won" (II, 97). Later Grandison engages to teach Clementina to read Milton's works (II, 122, 144). After his marriage to Harriet, Sir Charles defends Milton against charges of unintelligibility (III, 245 – 46). Milton also enters the novel through the person of Sir Charles himself, conceived by Richardson as "a Man acting uniformly well thro' a Variety of trying Scenes, because all his Actions are regulated by one steady Principle." He is "A Man of Religion and Virtue … happy in himself, and a Blessing to others" (Preface, I, 4). The reader might object that no such ideal creature has existed in real life since Adam, but should also note that Richardson has in some ways suggested that Grandison in fact is a kind of Adam. At his return to his family he is described by Harriet in terms that recall the first man, "with fine curling auburn locks waving upon his shoulders … intelligence sparkling in his fine free eyes … manly stature and air and … noble aspect" (I, 359). The detail of Grandison's hair was striking enough to attract the attention of George Eliot[112] who took it as a sign of Sir Charles's moral superiority. But it may have had a more specific referent. When Adam is introduced in paradise the details of hair, eye, and manliness are similar:

> His fair large Front and Eye sublime declar'd
> Absolute rule; and Hyacinthine Locks
> Round from his parted forelock hung
> Clust'ring, but not beneath his shoulders broad.
> *(Paradise Lost*, IV. 300 – 03)[113]

And just as Adam's manly form is contrasted to Eve's gentle softness, so Sir Charles's male beauty is contrasted to the "womanly beauties" of his admirers. His name too may suggest Miltonic moral qualities: he is the *grandest son* of his grandparent Adam, who is himself called by Milton "the goodliest man of men since born / His Sons" (*Paradise Lost*, IV. 323–24).[114] And he displays Adam's exemplary virtue, filial obedience, in following his apparently arbitrary father's "prohibition" not to correspond with his sisters (I. 321).

Grandison's situation of course contains some unEdenic elements – a rakish father for example. But in the novel's central dilemma – Sir Charles is in love with two admirable women – we can perhaps see adumbrations of Adam in Eden. Sir Charles is obliged to choose between two goods, and as Mark Kinkead-Weekes observes is endowed with some of his creator's taste for moral casuistry – the settling of difficult "cases."[115] Adam too is something of a casuist. Although it involves no conflicting duties or goods, Eve's dream presents a special moral problem: if you dream evil thoughts, are you still innocent? Adam solves it with assurance: "Evil into the mind of God or Man / May come and go, so unapprov'd, and leave / No spot or blame behind" (V. 117–19). The dialogue on astronomy between Raphael and Adam in Book VIII largely concerns the question: under what conditions is scientific curiosity permitted? And the subsequent discussion of Adam's attraction to Eve's beauty attempts to draw the fine line between proper human love and uxoriousness. Eve's suggestion that she and Adam work separately presents a difficult case of conscience, where Adam must choose between two competing goods: protecting Eve's innocence by insisting that she not seek out trial, or endorsing Eve's freedom and responsibility to make moral choices. Each choice carries great risk.[116]

But at the moment in *Paradise Lost* most ripe for casuistical analysis – should he obey God or join the mortal Eve? – Adam is surprisingly unreflective. Within moments of the fallen Eve's return with apple in hand, he says to himself, "with thee / Certain my resolution is to Die" (*Paradise Lost*, IX. 906–07). Without really considering the choices open to him, Adam determines to join Eve. The "reasons" he subsequently offers himself and her are rationalizations for yielding to the attraction of the "Bond of Nature." But Milton conceived of alternative courses of action. Both Adam and Eve earlier imagine Eve dead "And *Adam wedded to another Eve*" (IX. 828, 911).[117] After the fact Adam laments that he "might have liv'd and joy'd immortal bliss" (IX. 1166). His situation, as the narrator says, only "*seem'd* remediless" (IX. 919). That remedy, in Milton's mind, would in fact have been divorce,[118] since Eve is no longer a "fit" companion. Adam could have gone to God and asked for a new mate.

It is precisely this alternative that Richardson seized on, in the novel's most explicit link between Grandison and Adam in Eden. In complimenting Sir Charles's unfailing rectitude, Harriet contrasts him to Adam at the Fall:

Do you think, my dear [she writes to Grandison's sister], that had he been the first man, he would have been so complaisant to his Eve as *Milton makes Adam* – To taste the forbidden fruit, because he would not be separated from her, in her punishment, tho' all *posterity* were to suffer by it? – No; it is my opinion, that your brother would have had gallantry enough to his fallen spouse, to have made him extremely regret her lapse; but that he would have done *his own duty*, were it but for the sake of posterity, and left it to the Almighty, if such had been his pleasure, to have annihilated his first Eve, and given him a second.

(II, 609)

It is usually assumed, even by the novel's modern defenders, that this passage is damaging both to Grandison and to Richardson, that it reveals the rigid inhumanity of the novel's hero.[119] Richardson himself seems to have felt that this image of an Adamic Grandison was problematic, for he has Harriet continue: "But, my dear, do I not write strangely? ... on re-perusing what I have written, I am afraid that you have taught me to think oddly" (IV, 362). This qualification perhaps shows that Richardson thought his readers would not agree that Adam should have divorced Eve. He himself had recently engaged in prolonged correspondence with Lady Bradshaigh concerning woman's subordination to man, in which she had defended Eve's actions in encouraging Adam to eat.[120] Richardson answered teasingly, only pretending (I think) to agree that Eve had acted out of love.[121]

But as we have seen Milton had left open the possibility that Adam might have divorced Eve. Perhaps he chose not to make that alternative as prominent as Richardson did because he left no doubt that Adam acted in error: he was "fondly overcome with Female charm" (IX. 999).[122] Modern readers of Milton are inclined to forgive Adam too hastily for his humanity, not noticing that he eats not out of love for Eve but love of himself: "How can I live without thee? ... to lose thee were to lose my self" (IX. 908, 959). They are also likely to find life in Eden boring and infantile, less than fully human. But if we observe Adam's flaws and if we take Milton's Eden seriously as a fully moral life in which obedience is being constantly tested, then we can wish that Adam had not eaten, and can at least imagine the possibility of a moral hero like Grandison who does not allow principle to be compromised, for whom there is "no gap between the moral demand and the instinctive repsonse."[123]

If Richardson, through Harriet's musing comparison, here attempts to imagine a modern Adam who would not fall, we can perhaps see that

in the novel at large he attempts to create a modern Eden. Like *Pamela,*
Sir Charles Grandison concludes with an ideal marriage, which serves as
the center of a moral circle. As Kinkead-Weekes has suggested, that
circle was wide enough to include the author and his intimates, to whom
the novel was recited, and who acted less like readers than friends of
Sir Charles, Harriet, and the others, passionately responsive to their
lives as they unfolded.[124] This family of the heart or renovated moral
community, however improbable it seems to us, was Richardson's
paradise regained. It is only fitting that the country house of Sir Charles
and Lady Grandison should be set in a park "planted by the ancestors
of the excellent owner," consciously modeled on Milton's Eden. The
park naturally has lawns, gardens, and vineyard, a winding stream, and
a plain villa with fine prospects – in short, Milton's "happy rural seat
of various views." The chief Miltonic detail, however, is the orchards.
Eden had been planted in a kind of natural amphitheatre,

> Cedar, and Pine, and Fir, and branching Palm,
> A Silvan Scene, and as the ranks ascend
> Shade above shade, a woody Theatre
> Of stateliest view.
>
> (*Paradise Lost*, IV. 139 – 42)

Above these ranks of trees came the "verdurous wall" itself, and higher
yet "a circling row / Of goodliest Trees loaden with fairest Fruit"
(146 – 47). Grandison's father, who had a "poetical" taste, apparently
laid out his orchards with Milton in mind:

It is planted in a natural slope; the higher fruit-trees, as pears, in a semicircular
row, first; apples at further distances next ... The outside of this orchard ... is
planted with three rows of trees, at proper distances from each other; one of
pines; one of cedars; one of Scotch firs, in the like semicircular order.

(III, 273)

The view "from the top of the rustic villa, which commands the
whole," consciously recalls Adam's "prospect large / Into his nether
Empire neighbouring round" (*Paradise Lost*, IV. 144 – 45). Grandison
thus still lives happily in the home of his Edenic "Grand Parents,"
enjoying the double-paradise of gentleman's landscaped park and happy
marriage.

Regaining paradise – this is the dream that unites poems as various
as Lady Winchelsea's "Petition," Akenside's *Pleasures of Imagination*,
Philips' *Cyder*, and even Richardson's *Grandison*. We may be tempted
to see this informing dream as a manifestation of the governing myth
of a secularizing and enlightened century, looking for its salvation in
a world of material and moral progress. But this misrepresents the spirit

of the post-Miltonic English writers. The Enlightenment thinkers in England broke less with their cultural past than did their fellows on the Continent. English culture remained firmly – if not profoundly – Christian. Indeed, one reason why eighteenth-century England, unlike France, suffered no shattering break with its past may be that it had available – through Milton's achievement – a powerful myth of paradise. This paradise might be attained not by building a new rational human order, but by looking backward. In proclaiming a paradise regained, eighteenth-century English poets do not secularize Eden so much as they seek to re-create the primal conditions of Adam and Eve.

PART III
The major writers

8 · DRYDEN

In earlier chapters I have presented some eighteenth-century images
of Milton the man, and surveyed his presence in the literary landscape
generally in order to substantiate the claim that Milton's influence, far
from intimidating later writers, was by and large fruitful for them. He
left open the traditional genres and helped to open a set of new literary
opportunities that were taken up by a wide range of writers from John
Philips and Isaac Watts to Akenside and Collins. Up to this point I have
largely deferred discussing the creative response to Milton on the part
of the period's major poets, to some of whom I now turn – Dryden,
Pope, Thomson, Johnson, Cowper.[1] An argument for Milton's
creative presence in the period stands or falls not on the work of lesser
figures but on that of the major writers.

Dryden's literary heritage

The writers who came of age after 1700 found a literary culture already
permeated by Milton – his myths, his ideas, his verse forms, his
language. Many of the century's lesser writers responded to that diffused
Miltonism and in turn reproduced a kind of derivative echo. What is
striking about the century's major writers is that they returned to the
source: they encountered Milton directly. This is equally true of the late
seventeenth century's one great Miltonic writer – John Dryden.

Milton and Dryden constitute one of the most intriguing pairings
in English literary history. Together they preside over a momentous
transition in English literature and in English culture generally. Both
Janus-figures, they are "betwixt two Ages cast, / The first of this and
hindmost of the last,"[2] the last men of the Renaissance, and at the
same time heralds of something quite new. Yet Dryden is clearly part
of that newer age – in his *Essay on Dramatic Poesy* he speaks largely
through Neander, the "new man" – in a way that Milton, for all his
influence on the eighteenth century and the Romantics, is not. Here are
two of our greatest poets, whose lives overlap by forty-three years, and
whose writing careers by twenty-five (1649 to 1674), yet we know little
about their relations with and attitudes toward each other. How well
in fact were they acquainted? When did Dryden first learn of Milton's
work? What effect did it have on his own? Should we think of them as

contemporaries and rivals, or as predecessor and successor, ancient and modern? Can we say that Milton in any way significantly deflected Dryden's career? Did Dryden suffer from the "anxiety of influence"? Would he have written the same works if Milton had not written? In the context of Milton's creative influence on a whole century of writers, the relationship between Milton and the first great writer to register his presence is worth re-assessing here.

We must be careful, however, not to assume that Milton stood at the center of Dryden's mind and art, whether as a blocking figure or as muse. Despite our expectation that Milton's grandeur must have commanded a major response from every reader, critic, and poet who followed him, Dryden may not have looked at the matter in this way. His career and his literary opinions and standards appear to have been well established by the time he would have been aware of Milton's work as a poet. Dryden and Milton were both Cambridge men, but in the eighteen years between Milton's departure from Christ's and Dryden's arrival at Trinity in 1650, Cambridge (and the nation) had changed utterly. Dryden had the opportunity to meet Milton in the 1650s, when they both worked in Cromwell's civil service. A "Mr. Dradon," almost surely the poet, walked with the other "Secretarys of the ffrench & Latin Toungs" along with Milton in Cromwell's funeral procession.[3] But Milton in the 1650s was known primarily as a controversialist. Milton's first volume of poems appeared when Dryden was fourteen, but there is no clear-cut evidence that he read it before 1660.[4] His literary tastes at Winchester and Cambridge included Cowley and Spenser, but not, so far as is known, the early Milton. He is said to have read *Paradise Lost* in 1668 or 1669, when he reportedly remarked, in apparent admiration and rivalry, "that Poet has cutt us all out."[5] He did not ask leave to "tag" Milton's verses until 1673 or 1674.[6] By 1668, and certainly by 1670, Dryden was already well-launched on his career as poet and dramatist. He was, after all, Poet Laureate, and had behind him the panegyrics on Cromwell and on Charles, his substantial and ambitious *Annus Mirabilis*, his *Essay on Dramatic Poesy*, and ten plays. His major heroic plays, *Tyrannic Love* (1669) and *The Conquest of Granada* (1670 – 71) build on his earlier attempts in the genre and show no sign of Milton's influence. Dryden's interest in the heroic clearly predates the appearance of *Paradise Lost*, and his famous remark in 1672 that "an Heroick Play ought to be an imitation, in little of an Heroick Poem" was made with the broad epic tradition in mind. In the essay "Of Heroique Playes" where the remark appears, he cites not Milton but Davenant, Cowley, Tasso, Spenser, and especially Virgil and Homer.[7]

Dryden's sense of his literary heritage was extremely broad. To locate him in relation to his past masters we must not limit ourselves to Milton, who was only one member of what Dryden thought of as the family of English poets.[8] Chaucer was its father; Spenser was descended from Chaucer, and Milton from Spenser.[9] Sometimes Dryden spoke of another lineal descent, from Harrington through Fairfax, to Waller and Denham.[10] Here he was perhaps thinking of a distinctly modern kind of poetry in heroic couplets, for elsewhere Waller and Denham are "those two Fathers of our *English* Poetry."[11] All these poets, together with the older Latin family extending from Ennius and Lucilius to Virgil and Horace, are in some sense Dryden's own ancestors and his acknowledged masters.[12] In drama too there are fathers and sons. Shakespeare, Jonson, and Fletcher are "our Fathers in wit," and Dryden and his contemporaries are their "Lawful Issue."[13]

Furthermore, Dryden's sense of literary lineage and of literary rivalry appears to have been more complex than any model of Oedipal struggle. He must have thought often about the problem of being a successor or latecomer, for he recurs strikingly to the idea of depleted patrimony in his early poetry:

> We thought our Sires, not with their own content,
> Had ere we came to age our Portion spent.
> (*Astraea Redux* [1660], lines 27 – 28)[14]

> Nature is old, which Poets imitate,
> And for Wit, those that boast their own estate,
> Forget *Fletcher* and *Ben* before them went,
> Their Elder *Brothers*, and that vastly spent:
> So much 'twill hardly be rapair'd again.
> (First Prologue to *The Wild Gallant* [1663], lines 43 – 47)[15]

And in his occasional criticism he frequently recurs to the related and more encouraging topics of emulation or rivalry. Unlike metaphors of succession or inheritance, emulation is unconcerned with temporal precedence. The successor follows a predecessor, and inherits what remains; the emulator assumes all writers in all ages to be his contemporaries, competing against each other. By the time of the *Essay on Dramatic Poesy*, Dryden, about to be named Poet Laureate, translates from the Roman historian Velleius Paterculus the idea that "Emulation is the Spur of Wit; and sometimes Envy, sometimes Admiration, quickens our Endeavours."[16] Or as Dryden was to put it near the end of his career, "Great Contemporaries whet and cultivate each other: And mutual Borrowing, and Commerce, makes the Common Riches of Learning, as it does of the Civil Government."[17]

To be sure, emulation sometimes meant imitative strife, and an imitator might fall short of his model. Yet even defeat can be honorable. Dryden quotes Longinus on this point:

We ought not to regard a good imitation as a theft, but as a beautiful idea of him who undertakes to imitate, by forming himself on the invention and work of another man; for he enters into the lists like a new wrestler, to dispute the prize with the former champion. This sort of emulation, says Hesiod, is honorable ... when we combat for victory with a hero, and are not without glory even in our overthrow. Those great men whom we propose to ourselves as patterns of our imitation serve us as a torch, which is lifted up before us to enlighten our passage.[18]

At other moments Dryden can forswear all thought of competition with an honored predecessor, and yet insist on the value of his own efforts too. "Peace be to the Venerable Shades of *Shakespear*, and *Ben* Johnson: None of the Living will presume to have any competition with them: as they were our Predecessours, so they were our Masters. We Trayl our Plays under them: but, (as at the Funerals of a *Turkish Emperour*) our Ensigns are furl'd, or dragg'd upon the ground, in Honour to the Dead." Yet as Dryden continues, he stands upon the dignity of the successor: "so we may lawfully advance our own, after-wards, to show that we succeed: If less in Dignity, yet on the same Foot and Title."[19] Elsewhere Dryden can freely and comfortably acknowledge his "masters," Virgil in Latin and Spenser in English, gaining a sense of dignity from the apprenticeship.[20]

Dryden's example shows how one can sensibly concede superiority to a predecessor yet not fall irrevocably into anxiety. Dryden returns to Velleius Paterculus for an idea that seems to have guided his own literary pursuits through much of his career:

as in the beginning we are fired with the ambition to overtake those whom we regard as leaders, so when we have despaired of being able either to surpass or even to equal them, our zeal wanes with our hope; it ceases to follow what it cannot overtake ... and abandoning the old field as though pre-empted, we seek for some new object of our effort.[21]

Dryden applies this idea most clearly to his own career in discussing the achievement of the Jacobean playwrights who preceded him and seemed to have exhausted all the dramatic possibilities:

There is scarce an Humour, a Character, or any kind of Plot, which they have not us'd. All comes sullied or wasted to us ... This therefore will be a good Argument to us either not to write at all, or to attempt some other way. There is no bayes to be expected in their Walks: *Tentanda via est qua me quoque possum tollere humo* [I must essay a path whereby I, too, may rise from the earth].[22]

Writing drama in rhyme, says Dryden, is the only way left free to him and his contemporaries, and he speaks with some pride that his age is "arriv'd to a perfection in it, which they never knew; and which ... 'tis probable they never could have reach'd."[23]

"The Genius of every Age is different" (the remark reveals Dryden's essential historicism).[24] We should remember the confident side of Dryden's thinking – that despite past greatness his age found its own way of excelling – as much as the opposing side – that, sadly, "The second Temple was not like the first."[25] In the context of Dryden's balanced (and sometimes ambivalent) attitude toward the achievements of his predecessors, and of his sense of the opportunities for friendly rivalry, Dryden's response to Milton has a special interest. Though we have little evidence to go on, and must therefore proceed cautiously, it is my contention that Dryden, a strong and self-confident poet throughout his career, was not threatened or intimidated by Milton and the achievement he openly recognized.[26] It is a measure of Dryden's resilience, persistence, and strength that he maintained his own independence from Milton, and particularly in the area of heroic poetry determined to follow his own imaginative path. "Abandoning the old field as though pre-empted, we seek for some new object of our effort."

Dryden's criticism of Milton

Aubrey reports that Dryden "very much admire[d]" Milton,[27] and yet Dryden's written praise of Milton's work is always measured out sparingly. The one exception is the preface to *The State of Innocence*, where Dryden may have been struck by the audacity of his rhymed dramatic version of *Paradise Lost*, and chagrined by the inevitable comparison, which could only work in Milton's favor: "what I have borrowed will be so easily discerned from my mean productions, that I shall not need to point the reader to the places: and truly I should be sorry, for my own sake, that any one should take the pains to compare them together; the original being undoubtedly one of the greatest, most noble, and most sublime poems which either this age or nation has produced."[28] *Paradise Lost*, he would grant, was a great poem, but he would also insist that its subject was not "that of a Heroique Poem, properly so call'd."[29] The event or outcome is "not prosperous," like that of all other epic works;[30] the devil is his hero, instead of Adam;[31] the "machining persons" are more numerous than the human.[32] Despite Milton's achievement, the way is still left open for a modern poet to write an epic, "properly so called."

Refusing what he called critical "Idolatry,"[33] Dryden is the first of a line of independent Milton critics – Watts, Pope, Johnson – who insisted on the critic's responsibility to offer praise and blame impartially. Already in 1685 one could feel the pressure of Miltonolatry, and Dryden pushed back against it: "Am I ... bound to maintain that there are no flats among his Elevations, when 'tis evident he creeps along sometimes, for above an Hundred lines together? cannot I admire the height of his Invention, and the strength of his expression, without defending his antiquated words, and the perpetual harshness of their sound?"[34] Such resistance is a mark of Dryden's integrity, but at times one finds lacking in his response to Milton that other characteristic of Dryden as critic: a generosity of spirit that locates the special strength or greatness of a writer and frankly confesses his pleasure in it. Juvenal, says Dryden winningly, "gives me as much Pleasure as I can bear."[35] Chaucer ("he must have been a man of the most wonderful comprehensive nature")[36] and Shakespeare ("the man who of all Modern, and perhaps Ancient Poets, had the largest and most comprehensive soul")[37] receive Dryden's full-hearted admiration. With Milton, the praise sometimes tends toward the perfunctory – "As for Mr. Milton, whom we all admire with so much Justice..."[38] – or the ambivalent.

The famous epigram printed in Tonson's 1688 edition of *Paradise Lost* is a case in point. Homer and Virgil first appeared, says Dryden, and finally Milton: "The force of *Nature* cou'd no farther goe: / To make a *Third* she joyned the former two."[39] To say that Milton combines Homer and Virgil is at once to magnify and subtly to reduce him. Furthermore, contemporary evidence from Dryden's prose suggests that he did not see the three poets as a triumvirate of equals. In the *Discourse on Satire* (1693) he notes, in strikingly similar language:

> But suppose that *Homer* and *Virgil* were the only of their Species [sic], and that Nature was so much worn out in producing them, that she is never able to bear the like again; yet the Example only holds in Heroick Poetry.[40]

Also in 1693 he remarks, "let *Homer* and *Virgil* contend for the Prize of Honour, betwixt themselves; I am satisfied they will never have a third Concurrent."[41] And when he does admit a third but inferior heroic poet, in the dedication to his translation of the *Aeneid*, it is not Milton but Tasso.[42] To say that Milton combines Virgil and Homer, that he "endeavours everywhere to express Homer", or borrows from his "master" Spenser, are of course traditional means of according praise. But to see Milton in dependent relation to earlier masters may also be a way of containing him. Since Spenser is also Dryden's avowed master, then Dryden and Milton are in a sense brother poets, and therefore more like contemporaries, rivals, and equals. If Virgil and Horace are the masters of Spenser and Milton,[43] then for Dryden to imitate Virgil and Horace directly is implicitly to return to Milton's own source and to put himself upon the same plane as his English predecessors.

Despite such gestures to declare a kind of parity in kinship, and despite his acute consciousness of poetic lineage, Dryden seems to have been reluctant to clarify his own lineal relation with Milton. In his famous survey of English drama from the Jacobeans to his own contemporaries in the "Epistle to Congreve," Milton is (appropriately) omitted. In the Preface to *Fables* Dryden describes one poetic line leading from Spenser to Milton,[44] another leading from Fairfax to Waller. Later in the preface Dryden conflates the two lines: "after Chaucer there was a Spenser, a Harington, a Fairfax, before Waller and Denham were in being."[45] Dryden could add his own name to the list, as heir to both lines, son of both Spenser and Waller. Milton, however, is father to nobody. The reason may be that in 1700 it was not yet clear who Milton's heir would be. Or it may be that for Dryden, as for many modern literary historians and syllabus-makers, the pattern is much clearer if you don't have to take account of Milton, a giant straddling the "line of wit."

Dryden's critical remarks about Milton, then, are a record of qualified praise, of some ambivalence, and of some evasiveness in clarifying Milton's place in relation to his own achievement. On the whole one senses resistance to Milton, and a determination on Dryden's part to preserve his critical and creative independence. That determination is perhaps clearer in Dryden's poetic confrontations with Milton, particularly during the decade after Milton's death. I find no evidence to bear out the suggestion that Dryden somehow felt freed by Milton's death, and that his greatest works were written only when he could escape from Milton's shadow.[46] The Dryden of about 1670, author of *Annus Mirabilis* or *The Conquest of Granada*, who in any case seems to have paid little or no attention to Milton, is an exuberant and daring poet. Dryden's career did undergo a change in the mid-1670s, as he began to move from heroic drama toward satire, but we have no strong evidence to conclude that Dryden was here abandoning a sphere in which Milton had excelled and shifting into another which Milton had not touched. Indeed, in some respects the opposite appears to be true. In the dedication to *Aureng-Zebe* (1676), perhaps the last of his heroic plays, Dryden declares he is weary of the stage. Further, he is not as well suited to it as his contemporaries. He will seek instead a new arena. "Some little hopes I have yet remaining...that I may make the world some amends for many ill plays by an heroic poem."[47] Only two years after the appearance of *Paradise Lost* Dryden announces his own epic ambitions. During the middle third of his career – from 1674 to 1687, during which he wrote *The State of Innocence*, *MacFlecknoe*, *Absalom and Achitophel*, and *The Hind and the Panther* – Dryden repeatedly experimented with Miltonic materials for consciously heroic but unMiltonic purposes.

The State of Innocence

In the context of Dryden's own successful career as a man of letters, especially in the 1670s, we may wonder why he attempted a project that must – in our eyes – have been doomed from the start. But in the context of Miltonic adaptation for the next hundred years Dryden's venture is understandable. He too would appear to have sought to "correct" *Paradise Lost* and to seize a dramatic opportunity that Milton had created or left open for him. What is especially remarkable about Dryden's adaptation is that it was published barely ten years after the original appeared, and well before it had won universal acclaim. Indeed, Dryden planned and apparently wrote the work as early as 1673–74. The Stationer's Register on April 17, 1674 shows an entry for a "heroick opera" entitled *The Fall of Angells and man in innocence*.[48] Unlike later adapters Dryden discouraged any public comparisons with *Paradise Lost* by altering its title, both in the published version and in all extant manuscripts, and by direct prefatory appeal in "The Author's Apology for Heroic Poetry and Poetic Licence." Acknowledging his debt (the "entire foundation, part of the design, and many of the ornaments"), Dryden would be "sorry, for my own sake, that any one should take the pains to compare them together."[49]

What *Paradise Lost* offered was promising material for a working dramatist. There is ample reason to believe that Dryden intended the opera to be performed. In the Preface he speaks of *The State of Innocence* as an "opera"[50] that was never "acted," but does not take the opportunity to excuse its failure to appear on the public stage by declaring, as Milton had in the preface to *Samson Agonistes*, that it was never intended for performance. Indeed, Dryden wrote no play or opera in his long career that was not intended for the stage. *Paradise Lost* is only one of a number of well-known works that Dryden adapted for the Restoration stage during the 1660s and 1670s: *The Tempest* (1667), Molière's *L'Etourdi* as *Sir Martin Mar-All* (1667), *Antony and Cleopatra* (1677), *Troilus and Cressida* (1679), and Sophocles' *Oedipus* (1679). Thorough stage directions in the printed version[51] clearly point to the kind of performance the opera could have received with the technical resources in the Restoration playhouse – descending machines (for falling angels), painted flats, trap doors (for the fall into Hell). Why the opera was not performed is not certainly known.[52]

Paradise Lost probably represented for Dryden more than theatrically promising material. Scott suggested that the real motive for the adaptation was literary rivalry: Dryden, he said, sought to "shoot in the bow of Ulysses...to exert [himself] upon a subject in which another had already attained brilliant success" (V, 95–96). "It was only the hope of excelling his original, admirable as he allowed it to be, which impelled Dryden upon this unprofitable and abortive labour."[53] Spurred on by emulation, Dryden perhaps sought to match himself against the poet who had "cutt us all out." It was only natural for him to use whatever advantage he possessed. Milton may have dictated the subject, but Dryden could choose the medium. The successful man of the theatre chose to cast Milton's story as a drama. The choice had the additional advantage of being Milton's own original and abandoned idea. Milton had also publicly asserted the dignity of blank verse and virtually thrown down a challenge to the modern slaves of rhyme.[54] What more appropriate than for Dryden to "tag" Milton's verses.[55]

The State of Innocence also gave Dryden an opportunity to make creative application of his critical objections to *Paradise Lost*. This can be seen most clearly in Dryden's alterations of his original. The devil is not the hero of *The State of Innocence*; he is given very little opportunity to attain even conventional heroic stature. Dryden omits not only Satan's flight through Chaos and his battle against God in the War in Heaven, but he also takes away or tones down many of Satan's most stirring lines. "Better to reign in hell, than serve in heaven" (*Paradise Lost*, I. 236), for example, is transferred from Satan to Moloch (I. i). The famous "All is not lost; the unconquerable will, / And study of revenge, immortal hate, / And courage never to submit or yield" (I. 106–08) is reduced to "Yet, not all perished; We defy him still, / And yet wage war, with our unconquered will" (I. i). The clear-eyed and resolute "Long is the way / And hard, that out of hell leads up to light" (II. 432–33) becomes the shrill and boastful "Through brazen gates, vast chaos, and old night, / I'll force my way, and upwards steer my flight." Dryden also brings out clearly Satan's jealousy. When Moloch rises to offer to undertake "this glorious enterprise," Lucifer cuts him off: "Rash angel, stay; / That palm is mine, which none shall take away" (I. i). Nor is Dryden's Lucifer successful. The ending of *The State of Innocence* is unambiguously optimistic. In *Paradise Lost*, as Dryden describes it, the foiled Adam is driven out of his stronghold, "to wander through the world with his lady errant."[56] In the adaptation, though Adam and Eve must depart the garden, the emphasis is more clearly not on Lucifer's triumph but on man's gain.

In other respects too Dryden has adapted Milton in order to answer his own critical notions. The "machining persons" in *Paradise Lost* are reduced in number (we never see God the Father, or the Son, or Sin and Death; the angelic host is reduced to Raphael, Gabriel, and Uriel, and in the process is distinctly humanized). Emphasis shifts, as Dryden thought it should in "proper" epic, to the human drama. Language is also updated. Gone are Milton's antiquated words, borrowed from

145

Spenser. In their place we find, to the displeasure of most readers, the language of Restoration lovers – Adam: "Let us locked in close embraces be." Eve: "Some restraining thought, I know not why, / Tells me you long should beg, I long deny" (II. ii) – and terse, ironic colloquialism, Adam complaining that he should be "tied up from doing ill," or lamenting the terms on which life has been granted to him:

> Why is life forced on man, who, might he choose,
> Would not accept what he with pain must lose?
> Unknowing, he receives it; and when, known,
> He thinks it his, and values it, 'tis gone.
>
> (V. i)

This is the vigorous Restoration idiom of Rochester's "Satire Against Reason and Mankind." Here as elsewhere in the opera Dryden, alert to the incongruities and even the comedy of the story, adopts a skeptical and worldly perspective on the Fall.[57] And those "flats of scripture" which Dryden found such heavy going largely disappear. The scriptural sections of *Paradise Lost*, Book III (the Council in Heaven), Book VII (the Creation), and Books XI and XII (biblical history) are omitted or substantially reduced in Dryden's adaptation.

One other significant change may also represent Dryden's criticism of Milton, implied but nowhere enunciated in his critical remarks. Milton provides a number of different grounds for his justification of God's ways to man: man's free will as the cause of the Fall; God's creative goodness; Christ's redemptive sacrifice; and the "paradise within" which will succeed and surpass the external paradise lost of Eden. It is striking that Dryden subverts all four of these grounds. Milton establishes free will as a cornerstone of his edifice, by having God himself declare that man was "Sufficient to have stood, though free to fall." But in *The State of Innocence* the matter of free will, foreknowledge, and predestination is vigorously debated between Raphael and Adam. Dryden seems intellectually stimulated by the issues, and takes care to present them in their full and difficult complexity. Adam, at the end of the debate, is not so much persuaded as dissuaded from further enquiry. The reader is left with the notion that the whole matter remains problematic.[58]

The reader of Milton is also persuaded of God's goodness through Raphael's account of the Creation. Partly because the stage has no leisure for such narrative digressions, Dryden omits this part of the poem. He focuses instead (as later adapters would) on the domestic drama – Adam and Eve in love; their separation, quarrel, and reconciliation – and gives us little sense of the backdrop, the beautiful garden that God has created for man. (Perhaps he would have counted on painted flats to convey what later adapters found delightful in the "Morning Hymn"). Nor do we hear anything of Christ's propitiatory sacrifice. His offer to save man (Book III) and his visit to the garden to judge, pity, and clothe him (Book X) both disappear from Dryden's version.[59] Finally, the promised "paradise within," compensation for the loss of Eden, is perfunctorily asserted. "For outward Eden lost, find Paradise within," says Dryden's Raphael simply, yet we are given no explanation about how man is to attain it, or how many men will ever seek it.

Was Dryden aware that he was undermining the force of Milton's theodicy? The question is perhaps unanswerable, but the fact remains that, to our way of thinking, Dryden's determination to heed the generic requirements of proper epic, and to "seek for some new object of our effort," unwisely led him to pare away not baroque excrescences but essentials.

Dryden's heroic poems: *Absalom and Achitophel*, *The Hind and the Panther*, and the *Aeneis*

It should be noted that *The State of Innocence* was popular enough with Dryden's contemporaries to circulate in numerous manuscripts (of which five are extant) and to justify eleven editions by 1703.[60] But in our eyes Dryden's deviation from his original is a measure of his failure. In *Absalom and Achitophel* the deviation may well be a measure of Dryden's success. The frequent Miltonic allusions, familar enough to most readers, no longer need to be pointed out. But we do need to assess their significance. In my view Dryden has not written a "miniature epic," nor does he present a contemporary re-enactment of the Fall.[61] Rather he has written a more purely political poem, worldly, shrewd, and pragmatic in its point of view, quite remote from the austere theology of Milton's epic. Despite occasional and oblique glances at contemporary politics, Milton's poem requires of its reader no particular acquaintance with seventeenth-century England. Despite the allegorical frame which places the action in Old Testament times, Dryden's poem continuously reflects on the events surrounding the Exclusion Crisis, and expects the reader to do the same. As I have argued elsewhere,[62] the poem calls not for obedience to the divine will, but for recognition of the political expediency in supporting the king: "What prudent man a settled throne would shake?" Charles, so Dryden asserts along lines that anticipate Halifax's famous "Character," has in his mildness preserved peace in his time, has through artful managing of men prevented a recurrence of civil war.

The difference between *Paradise Lost* and *Absalom and Achitophel* is perhaps seen clearest in Dryden's conclusion. The king's enemies, it is true, are discredited through allusions to Milton's Satan.[63] But David only superficially resembles Milton's God. The California editors claim that David appears as a "natural-supernatural character derived from the highest reaches of the epic poem. Like God the Father in *Paradise Lost*, the King denounces the ingrates and declares what will happen to them; since what he says is law, what he declares will happen, will happen. The Almighty nods consent and it is so ordered."[64] But close comparisons will show that David sounds not like God the Father but like Dryden's own witty and urbane narrator, ironic, skeptical, fully human. His voice is not tonelessly authoritative, his style not short and perspicuous, not the "concise and clear manner" that Addison admired in the speeches in *Paradise Lost*, Book III.[65] On the contrary, David jokes broadly ("Those heap'd Affronts that haughty Subjects bring, / Are burthens for a Camel, not a King," 951–52). He can be sarcastic: "If my Young *Samson* will pretend a Call / To shake the Column, let him share the Fall" (955–56). The modern sense of the word "Patriot," he notes ironically, is "one that would by Law supplant his Prince" (966). And he can add with contempt: "Never was Patriot yet, but was a Fool" (968). Elsewhere in his final speech David both comically understates ("A King's at least a part of Government," 977) and overstates ("From Plots and Treasons Heaven preserve my years, / But Save me most from my Petitioners. / Unsatiate as the barren Womb or Grave; / God cannot Grant so much as they can Crave," 985–88). His view of his enemies is satirical, his method ironic denigration and unmasking: "My Pious Subjects for my Safety pray; / Which to Secure they take my Power away" (983–84). If Dryden took a clue from Milton, it is not from God's speeches in Book III, but from his sardonic observations to the Son in Book V, as they observe Satan's preparations for rebellion, and the Son's reply: "thou they foes / Justly hast in derision, and secure / Laught'st at their vain designs and tumults vain" (V. 735–37). Other features, however, appear to derive from a courtier's knowledge of an informal king, too apt, says Halifax, to make "broad Allusions upon any thing that gave the least occasion."[66] When invoking a biblical analogy, David typically gives it the kind of comic, bawdy turn one might expect from Charles:

> Law they require, let Law then shew her Face;
> They could not be content to look on Grace,
> Her hinder parts, but with a daring Eye
> To tempt the terror of her Front, and Dye.
>
> (1007–10)

The story of Moses in Exodus 33 supplied Dryden with the contrast between God's "face" (his power or justice) and his "back parts" (his mercy), but in David/Charles's mouth the allusion is teasingly anatomical.[67]

Anne Ferry in effect recognizes these unMiltonic attributes of David's speech, though for her they are a sign that Dryden's poem has failed:

David's style... mixes solemn echoes of Genesis with a casual profanity and ironic verbal play imitative of upperclass speech in a worldly society. We do not... hear in David's utterance what the lines framing it declare to be a miraculously powerful language, purified by grace of the abuses that characterize human speech elsewhere in the poem.[68]

I would argue on the contrary that the attributes of David's speech should alert us that her conception of the king's role is mistaken. The king's speech is an exact index of his nature and function in the poem. He is not a divinely ordained redeemer (though Dryden would not deny that, ultimately, a king's rule is divinely sanctioned), but a humanly skilled politician.

By the same token Dryden should not be read as an essentially Miltonic poet, but as a man of a new era. Though he is heir to the same classical and theological traditions that shaped Milton, he is a far more worldly voice, acutely aware of his age and his audience. For the Milton of *Paradise Lost*, politics is practical theology. Every ruler, from the time of Adam, is an image of God and speaks with divinely ordained authority. For Dryden, politics is the art of the possible; kings, though ultimately (and remotely) supported by God, must be artful "managers."[69] To gain the desired end – political stability – the king and his propagandist will wittily manipulate the ceremonial symbols and traditional attributes of the office.

We are not accustomed to think of *The Hind and the Panther* (1687) as a heroic poem. Dryden called it simply "A Poem," the term he had earlier used on the title page of *Absalom and Achitophel* (and Milton has used as subtitle to *Paradise Lost*). The poem is usually bracketed with *Religio Laici* as Dryden's religious apologetics, or viewed formally as allegory and beast fable. In the epistle "To the Reader" Dryden calls it a "Satyr" aimed at the "refractory and disobedient" (note the Miltonic ring) among the Anglicans and the Dissenters. Six years later Dryden was to declare satire a species of heroic poetry.[70] The subject matter of *The Hind and the Panther* – "Matters... Religious or Civil" – is the traditional matter of epic. Dryden most openly acknowledges his heroic pretensions when he says that he has attempted to "raise" the first part of the poem, giving it "the Majestick Turn of Heroic Poesie."[71]

In this context it is worth remarking Dryden's appropriations from *Paradise Lost*, a religious-heroic poem published only twenty years earlier. It is not that Dryden emulates Milton or wants his poem to be compared with Milton's epic. Nor does he directly and openly – as in the tract and pamphlet wars of the day – answer Milton's radical Protestantism with his own Roman Catholic principles. But the effect of Dryden's allusion to *Paradise Lost* is implicitly to turn material from Milton's poem to his own purposes, to celebrate Rome and to discredit Protestantism in general through specific attacks not on extremists but on the established church.

In the 1680s Dryden was himself moving further and further from Milton's radical religious individualism. Despite his Puritan family background and university training, Dryden became a defender of the Anglican *via media* and in 1685 a convert to the authoritarian Roman church. To a believer who insists on the authority of the church, Milton's defense of the private conscience was theologically unsound and politically unstable. It is clear from *Religio Laici* and *The Hind and the Panther* that Dryden viewed Protestant extremists with sardonic hostility. But in 1687, in an Anglican country, the Christian extremes might still find common ground or a common enemy. James's famous Declaration of Liberty of Conscience granted to Catholics and to Dissenters all the religious freedom that Milton himself had asked for. In *A Treatise of Civil Power* (1659) Milton had insisted that no man (and no government) can determine for another a matter of conscience. Dryden's epistle "To the Reader" of *The Hind and the Panther*, in support of James's Declaration, defends the same liberties in explicitly political terms: "Conscience is the Royalty and Prerogative of every Private Man. He is absolute in his own Breast, and accountable to no Earthly Power, for that which passes only betwixt God and Him" (*Works*, III, 120). Dryden continued to see danger in an unchecked private spirit (see *Hind and the Panther*, I. 452–96), but in the poem his real target is the established church, either the most likely convert to a Roman view, or the most powerful adversary.

Hence Dryden does not devote much space, after the introduction of the allegorical beasts, to the Dissenters. We might suspect some reflection on Miltonic Protestantism in the account of the Independent Bear or the Presbyterian Wolf. Milton had at one time or other made a party with both sects. Dryden's remarks on the Wolf's affinity with a "common-weal" (I. 234) and its "antipathy to kings" (I. 177) would readily attach to a defender of regicide. But radical theological and political opinions are not Dryden's real concern. It is the Anglican Panther, nearest to the Roman church, who must be won over or discredited. To this end several of Dryden's many allusions to *Paradise Lost* are designed to associate the Panther with Milton's Satan.

To begin with, the Anglican church was itself conceived in an incestuous marriage between "A *Lyon* old" (Henry VIII) and the Panther's mother (Anne Boleyn); they begat "schism"; "sacrilege" and "schism" in turn begat "heresie." The series of unions, as the California editors point out, recalls the multiple incest of Satan, Sin, and Death. Later the Panther, invited to share the Hind's rural shed, first displays amazement and then affects civility. The California editors suggest allusions to the hypocrite Satan's meeting with Uriel (*Paradise Lost*, IV. 120) and his initial entry into Eden, where he is likened to a hireling wolf and a thief (IV. 183–93). We might also recall Satan's first approach to Eve, where he "abstracted stood / From his own evil, and for the time remained / Stupidly good, of enmity disarmed" (IX. 463–65). Still later, in Part III, the Panther offers Satan's defense of "necessity" ("the tyrant's plea") for the unjust penal laws (*Hind and the Panther*, III. 836; *Paradise Lost*, IV. 393–94).

For his defense of the Catholic Hind Dryden goes again to *Paradise Lost*, this time to the Council in Heaven. In a passage Scott found "Extremely beautiful," Dryden has the Hind assert Rome's authority by suggesting an analogy:

> So when of old th'Almighty father sate
> In Council, to redeem our ruin'd state,
> Millions of millions at a distance round,
> Silent the sacred Consistory crown'd,
> To hear what mercy mixt with justice cou'd propound;
> All prompt with eager pity, to fulfill
> The full extent of their Creatour's will:
> But when the stern conditions were declar'd,
> A mournful whisper through the host was heard,
> And the whole hierarchy with heads hung down
> Submissively declin'd the ponderous proffer'd crown.
> Then, not till then, th'eternal Son from high
> Rose in the strength of all the Deity;
> Stood forth t'accept the terms, and underwent
> A weight which all the frame of heav'n had bent,
> Nor he Himself cou'd bear, but as omnipotent.
>
> (II. 499–514)

Just as the Roman church alone makes claim to "unfailing certainty," so Christ alone, in Milton's account (*Paradise Lost*, III. 203–65) which Dryden clearly has in mind, accepted the sacrificial mission that the Father proposed. The other churches who make no claim to infallibility are less like the silent good angels than the mute and dismayed fallen angels who decline to volunteer for the dangerous mission proposed by Satan (*Paradise Lost*, II. 420–26). Dryden perceived the dramatic power of Christ's action (in Milton's version), suggestive of both divine power and humility, an apt combination for his own Hind. Though there are no close parallels in language between the passage and Milton's council scenes, Dryden's diction is strongly Miltonic (ruined state, millions, consistory, etc.). His appropriation of Milton is altogether free, bold, and striking.

To repeat, one would not wish to go so far as to claim that *The Hind and the Panther* "answers" *Paradise Lost*.[72] Dryden's brief account of the Fall is quite unMiltonic. As the California editors note, there is no Eve, no Satan, and no tree (p. 367). But this does not mean that Dryden is re-writing Milton. His interest at this point in his poem is not the state of innocence but the rise of persecution. He thus moves quickly from original "new made man" through "pride of Empire" to the "murth'rer Cain" (I. 274 – 79). Dryden's many debts to the traditional language and doctrine of contemporary controversy forbid us from seeing *Paradise Lost* as a major presence in *The Hind and the Panther*. What Dryden displays, here as elsewhere, is a fine and witty opportunism. That Milton's poem is put to the service of a church Milton found heretical and even beyond the bound of toleration is an ironic twist that Dryden must have savored.

From one vantage *Absalom and Achitophel* and *The Hind and the Panther* look like Dryden's experiments with epic narrative. In both poems he forsook straightforward history for extended allegory, and epic grandeur for stylistic flexibility, encompassing wit, the "Majestic Turn of Heroick Poesie," and a plainer style as well. In each case he found a way to write a modern, witty, heroic poem, using Miltonic materials for unMiltonic (even antiMiltonic?) purposes. But Dryden did not altogether abandon his ambition to write a traditional epic. Despite Milton's recent achievement, he still thought there was room for him. Despite Milton's redefinition of heroism as spiritual or moral, Dryden in the last phase of his career continued to assert that a modern poet might celebrate a Christian king or general.

In the eighteenth-century debate about the viability of epic in the modern world,[73] Dryden argued vigorously in the affirmative. In the *Discourse on Satire* (1693), like others after him, he questioned the current belief that an epic both Christian and classically proper was impossible. It is true, he conceded, thinking no doubt of Milton's "better fortitude of patience and heroic martyrdom" (*Paradise Lost*, IX, 31 – 32), that

in the severe notions of our Faith, the Fortitude of a Christian consists in Patience, and Suffering for the Love of God, what ever hardships can befall him in the World; not in any Attempt, or in performance of those Enterprises which the Poets call Heroique; and which are commonly the Effects of Interest, Ostentation, Pride, and Worldly Honour: That Humility and Resignation are our Prime Vertues; and that these include no Action but that of the Soul: When as, on the Contrary, an Heroique Poem requires, to its necessary Design, and as its last Perfection, some great Action of War, the Accomplishment of some Extraordinary Undertaking, which requires the Strength and Vigour of the Body, the Duty of a Souldier, the Capacity and Prudence of a General, and, in short, as much, or more, of the Active Virtue than the Suffering.[74]

Dryden's answer to this objection is that the *private* Christian must exercise patience, obedience, and submission, while a Christian *magistrate* must also display prudence, counsel, active fortitude, in short, all the classic epic virtues. Therefore an epic about "some Great Commander, Enterpris'd for the Common Good, and Honour of the Christian Cause," may well be written now.[75] If a system of machinery based on supernatural agents were needed, Dryden proposed the guardian angels in the Book of Daniel. The problem with most Christian machines had been that they had no independent power. In Daniel the guardian angels of the Persians, the Greeks, and the Jews are privy to God's "General Purpose, and Design" but not to all the "Secrets of Government."[76] Dryden claims his machines are his own invention, "whereof I have not had the least hint from any of my Predecessors, the Poets" (IV, 19). (But Milton had in fact endowed his angels with free will and limited knowledge of God's plans.)

Dryden goes on to give a "rude draught" of the epic poem he had long projected. We may note how unMiltonic it would have been: national rather than biblical, celebrating Arthur or the Black Prince; in rhyme rather than blank verse; with a successful outcome (Arthur conquers the Saxons; the Black Prince restores Spain to its lawful lord); an adequate number of human agents. While Milton portrayed the recurrent degenerations of mankind through history, Dryden would have paid compliments to his "Living Friends and Patrons of the Noblest Families" and forecast the triumphal "Succession of our Imperial Line."[77]

Although in 1693 Dryden could still assert that a Christian epic might be written, he had apparently all but abandoned hopes that he might write one himself.[78] In June of 1694 Dryden virtually sealed his fate by contracting with Tonson to translate the works of Virgil, and to begin no other new work until the Virgil was completed.[79] In choosing to translate Virgil Dryden returned to one of Milton's own masters, and gave the world a classically correct epic, prefaced by a discourse on the proper nature of the heroic poem. And yet Dryden's *Aeneis* may be influenced by Milton after all. In translating Virgil rather than Homer (whose "vehemence," he later said, was more suitable to his own temper),[80] Dryden selected for his epic hero *pius Aeneas* who, like Adam before him, teaches the Miltonic virtues of constancy, patience, and piety.[81] The poem's moral too is eminently Miltonic: "to infuse an awful Respect into the People, towards [their] Prince. By that Respect to confirm their Obedience to him; and by that obedience to make them happy."[82] And though he wrote in rhyme, Dryden in the course of composition apparently reconsidered the merits of blank verse for narrative. Richardson tells the story that Dryden praised *Paradise Lost* "Loftily" to a gentleman who then objected, "Why, Mr. Dryden, 'tis not in rhyme." "No," replied Dryden, "nor would I have done my Virgil in Rime, if I was to begin it again."[83]

9 · POPE

"Constant remembrance"

To a degree that readers have still not recognized, Milton was an animating presence in the life and works of Pope from beginning to end. In 1705, in one of the earliest surviving letters in the correspondence, the 17-year-old Pope displayed his youthful admiration for and knowledge of Milton by lending to a literary friend his copy not of *Paradise Lost* but of the much less known *Poems* of 1645.[1] A few years later, in 1711, while still at Binfield, Pope wrote to another friend that he keeps "pictures of Dryden, Milton, Shakespear, &c., in my chamber, round about me, that the constant remembrance of 'em may keep me always humble.''[2] And in his later years at Twickenham Milton was still symbolically present. After Pope's death in 1744 an inventory of his goods listed a marble bust of Milton, one of the few possessions about which he left specific instructions in his will. He asked that the bust, a gift of the Prince of Wales, go to his friend Lyttelton, a minor poet and fellow-admirer of Milton.[3] In Pope's life as a professional writer Milton also played an important role. Though not himself an editor of Milton, Pope was closely connected to several editions produced by his contemporaries. As the first volume of the *Odyssey* translation appeared in 1725, Pope's collaborator Elijah Fenton published his edition of *Paradise Lost* with a brief "Life." Pope owned and annotated a copy of Bentley's notorious 1732 edition; Newton later consulted it for his own edition.[4] While his friends the Richardsons were preparing their annotations on *Paradise Lost*, Pope offered minor editorial assistance.[5]

The best evidence of Milton's presence is of course Pope's own poems, from the *Pastorals* to the *Dunciad*, in which Milton speaks out loud and bold, or (to vary the figure) plays the roles assigned to him by a master of allusion. Pope's intimate and extensive knowledge of Milton's poems has been established beyond question.[6] The function of Pope's allusions to and parodies of Milton's individual poems has been much discussed, and his general debt assessed in broad surveys.[7] What I offer here is not new evidence about Pope's debt or allusions to Milton (though critics will no doubt continue to uncover heretofore unnoticed allusions), but a reconsideration of larger questions in the light of my general argument and in the context of the responses of Pope's

155

contemporaries to Milton: broadly speaking, how did Pope *respond* to Milton, to the pressure he exerted on an English writer? The broad answer is that, like his contemporaries, Pope was inspired by Milton to do some of his best work; he regularly discovered ways of using Miltonic materials for his own new purposes; and he seems to have been quite free of any taint of anxiety of influence or untroubled by the burden of the past. Rather, he found the means to convert Miltonic riches into an inheritance on which he might fruitfully draw.

But Pope was not, in his attitude toward his Miltonic inheritance, simply the replica of every English poet from Dryden to Cowper. For Dryden Milton was an older contemporary whose career overlapped his own for some twenty-five years. For Pope, born in the year of the sumptuous folio edition of *Paradise Lost*, Milton was already a classic. As I have suggested, Dryden could not decide quite where Milton "fit" in the English tradition, but for Pope there was no difficulty in seeing Milton solidly lodged in the line of Chaucer, Spenser, Shakespeare, Cowley, Waller, and Dryden himself.[8] Dryden was not certain that *Paradise Lost* was a heroic poem, properly speaking,[9] but Pope had no doubt that Milton belonged in the great tradition of European epic, and that he was the greatest of modern epic poets.[10] And yet for all his sense of Milton's priority (in time and in stature), Pope did not make of Milton an inaccessible hero (as Collins did) or a giant that one made no pretense to rival (as Thomson did). Indeed, Pope was perhaps the last poet in the century to imagine himself, at least potentially, the equal of Milton. When Walsh told Pope that the way left open to him was to be "correct" (words that Pope never forgot),[11] he did not mean that such a path was *faute de mieux*, compensation for a greatness no longer available. On the contrary, it was a way of achieving "greatness": "Though we had had several great poets, we never had any one *great* poet that was correct." Although no great poet who lacked correctness is named, Walsh in c. 1705 must have had Milton in mind. It was only a year earlier that Dennis had publicly praised *Paradise Lost* as "the most lofty, but the most irregular Poem, that has been produc'd by the Mind of Man."[12] One might then best aspire to equal Milton's greatness not by being "Miltonic" but by being correct.

From the beginning of his career to the end Pope was encouraged to compare himself to Milton. As early as 1705 Pope's older friend Sir William Trumbull writes, in response to Pope's loan of the volume of Milton's poems, that Pope is himself likely to equal Milton.[13] This is heady stuff for a boy of seventeen to hear, and it was coming from more than one quarter. In the same year old William Wycherly comforts Pope, then suffering from eye trouble, with what might appear the absurd flattery of reminding him that other great poets have borne such suffering: "You may better bear the weakness of your owtward sight, since it is recompenc'd by the strength of your immagination and inward penitration [sic], as your Poetic Forefathers were down from Homer to Milton."[14] Pope continued to receive such compliments from sycophants who assured him he "coughed like Horace" – to judge by the famous passage in the "Epistle to Arbuthnot" (lines 116ff) – and one suspects that he both laughed at them and was secretly pleased. It must have been flattering for his friend Jonathan Richardson the younger – who had just edited Milton – to prepare a variorum edition of Pope (for his own use). Pope himself, displaying appropriate modesty, draws the parallel, later writing to Richardson in 1737, "remembring how much a worse writer, far, than Milton, has been mark'd, collated, & studied by him."[15]

The next year Richardson's father reaffirmed the Milton parallel by drawing Pope "as Milton."[16] The portrait in profile clearly presents Pope's features but substitutes Milton's hair, falling profusely to the shoulder, as found in Richardson's own portrait of Milton engraved for the frontispiece of his 1734 *Explanatory Notes*.[17] Though never published, the sketch was clearly designed as a tribute to Pope, and must have been shown to him. In case he did not perceive the similarity, the portrait is inscribed with Milton's name (in Greek), and (perhaps added later by the younger Richardson) the legend "A. Pope, as Milton." Another portrait, etched the next year, assimilates the two poets even more fully. Set off by two clearly recognizable profiles of Milton and of Pope, a third head, laureated, in three-quarters profile, amalgamates features from the other two. Whether or not the composite portrait is designed to represent Richardson's ideal poet (as Wimsatt and Wendorf suggest),[18] it offers to the viewer the suggestion that, just as Milton's Edenic groves "look green in song" (both his own song and Pope's), so Milton himself lives on in Pope. Put another way, the voice and spirit that inhabited Milton in his generation now inhabit Pope in a later one. It is then only iconographically fitting that the dying Pope is represented by another contemporary artist, Francis Hayman, as attended on his deathbed (or welcomed into paradise) by Milton, Spenser, and Chaucer.[19]

The symbolic iconography of Richardson's portrait – both the Miltonized portraits and another in which Pope appears in the dress of Chaucer[20] – has an interesting parallel in Pope's own work. If Pope is in some way a later incarnation of his predecessors, one might view Pope's career as a successive "re-writing" of his masters. In the decade 1700–10 he imitated the English writers – Waller, Cowley, Chaucer, Spenser, and Dorset – in poems eventually published in the 1717 collection and 1727 *Miscellany*, along with the early translations and paraphrases of Latin writers. In the years 1715–25 he literally produced a re-written version of Homer. In the 1730s he "rewrote" Horace (and Juvenal and Persius) to make them say of modern London what they once had said of classical Rome.

Of the poets in this list who made up Pope's heritage, Milton and Dryden might be said to be conspicuous by their absence. And yet one could argue that it is the work of his two immediate predecessors that he most deeply imitates and re-writes. Dryden supplied Pope a supple and polished verse form and a set of generic possibilities, including mock-epic, verse essay, familiar epistle, and epic translation.[21] Milton supplied what Pope could not readily find in Dryden or in his classical predecessors, a coherent and strikingly unified oeuvre offering a comprehensive and systematic view of the world on Christian principles. It is not that Pope simply adopted Milton's (or anybody's) world view. But he could take his own bearings by constantly referring to it. In measuring, as he repeatedly did, the differences between a state of order and harmony and a state of chaos (whether political or personal) Pope had available to him in Milton the compelling poetic myth of a fall from Eden. Where Dryden was urbane, ironic, various, an elusive voice in his poems, "all mankind's epitome" – and Pope obviously learned much from this stance – Milton (especially the later Milton) was austere, earnest, single-minded, a righteous moralist, an insistent presence in his poems. Pope (especially the later Pope) drew equally on this stance. Finally, Milton offered a benchmark. Dryden was the great poet of the previous age, but by common consent Milton was the greatest English poet. To measure oneself by his mark was ambitious and risky, and Pope gave a great deal of thought to the opportunities and risks that the Miltonic imitator faced.

On the one hand imitating Milton might be a substitute for original thought and labor. It was only too easy for the would-be epic poet to save himself the trouble of invention by dressing his poems in Miltonic colors. Every epic needs machines: Homer can provide the lazy poet with gods, and Milton with devils.[22] The modern hack in search of a properly elevated and exotic epic diction could find all the "Hebraisms and Grecisms" he would need in Milton, "without the trouble of Learning the Languages."[23] But such unthinking imitations often succeed only in condemning themselves, particularly if the imitator has not carefully considered the demands of his own decorum:

The imitators of *Milton*, like most other imitators, are not *Copies* but *Caricatura's* of their original; they are a hundred times more obsolete and cramp than he, and equally so in all places: Whereas it should have been observed of Milton, that he is not lavish of his exotick words everywhere alike, but employs them much more when the subject is marvellous vast and strange, as in the scenes of Heaven, Hell, Chaos, &c. than where it is turn'd to the natural and agreeable.[24]

As Pope later said to Spence, Milton's high formal style could only succeed – even in Milton – with "strange out-of-the-world things."[25] For "natural and pastoral subjects," he argued (with Philips' *Cyder* in mind), "it does very ill."[26]

In some cases, indeed, Milton should not be imitated at all. The dramatic speeches in *Paradise Lost*, where Pope finds "such transposition and forc'd construction, that the very sense is not to be discover'd without a second or third reading," he thought should be "no example."[27] Affected archaisms were an "Imperfection" in Milton. In Pope's day they were found only in mechanical imitations, "where with the utmost Exactness, and not so much as one Exception, nevertheless was constantly *nathless*, embroider'd was *broider'd*, Hermits were *Eremites*..."[28] The danger of all such misuses of Milton was exemplified for Pope in the epics of Blackmore, frequently cited for illustration in *Peri Bathous*. Far from ennobling his own poem, a foolish imitator succeeds only in debasing the Miltonic original. Unlike Virgil, who was said "to have read *Ennius*, out of his Dunghil to draw Gold," the modern imitators "read *Shakespear, Milton*, and *Dryden*, for the contrary End, to bury their Gold in his own Dunghil."[29]

But it remained possible to use Milton intelligently. The judicious use of a "Mixture of some *Graecisms* and old Words after the manner of *Milton*, if done without too much Affectation," might enable the translator of Homer to achieve the required "venerable *Antique* Cast."[30] Milton's "unusual style" can help to "awaken our ideas" in the descriptive and "picturesque" parts of an epic.[31] The main principle in such imitation, Pope continues, is to bear in mind the requirements of the new work, and to make sure that Milton's style serves them:

A just and moderate mixture of old words may have an effect like the working old Abbey stones into a building, which I have sometimes seen to give a kind of venerable air, and yet not destroy the neatness, elegance, and equality requisite to a new work.

As Pope's architectural metaphor implies, the poet must not forget that he is constructing his own building. He may wish to use old materials, but he is ordering them to a new end. The true imitator is always a re-creator.[32]

Pope did more than reflect on the difference between good and bad Miltonic imitation. From his very earliest efforts to work left undone at his death Pope was himself "re-writing" Milton. As early as 1700 Pope deliberately imitated Milton in his first attempt at epic poetry, *Alcander, Prince of Rhodes*: "I endeavoured," he later told Spence, "in this poem to collect all the beauties of the great epic writers into one piece. There was Milton's style in one part and Cowley's in another, here the style of Spenser imitated and there of Statius, here Homer and Virgil, and there Ovid and Claudian."[33] It was more than Milton's style that the precocious twelve-year-old Pope sought to imitate: "I had flung all my learning into it, as indeed Milton has done, too much, in his *Paradise Lost*."[34] In the middle of his career he considered remodeling *Samson Agonistes* into a tragedy that might be played on the stage, though again the project, like *Alcander*, came to nothing. In 1737, when Richardson was drawing Pope "as Milton," Pope, perhaps in the same spirit, sent to Richardson a copy of a sonnet, allegedly by Milton, "Written upon Occasion of the Plague, and found on a Glass-Window at Chalfont." The sonnet (of ten lines) was in fact written by Pope himself, in skillful imitation of the style of some of Milton's political sonnets:

> Fair Mirrour of foul Times! whose fragile Sheene
> Shall as it blazeth, break; while Providence
> (Aye watching o'er his Saints with Eye unseen,)
> Spreads the red Rod of angry Pestilence,
> To sweep the wicked and their Counsels hence;
> Yea all to break the pride of lustful Kings,
> Who Heaven's Lore reject for brutish Sense;
> As erst he scourg'd *Jessides'* Sin of yore
> For the fair *Hittite*, when on Seraph's Wings
> He sent him War, or Plague, or Famine sore.[35]

Though sometimes dismissed as a mere hoax to attract the uncritical applause of Miltonolators (the poem was in fact printed, as a "very happy Imitation," in Birch's 1738 edition of Milton's works), this sonnet has considerable interest as a sign of what Pope responded to in Milton. Milton may have in part attracted Pope because in 1738 Milton was being recurrently invoked by the opposition to Walpole.[36] But Pope's Miltonic stance is essentially moral rather than political. He takes little trouble to reproduce Milton's outer form (the sonnet has only ten lines, and ignores Milton's characteristic Petrarchan rhyme scheme), though he catches well the exclamatory opening, the complex grammar and syntax (the sonnet, like Milton's "When I consider," is all one sentence), and the offhand use of biblical allusion.[37] What Pope best reproduces is his angry, even satiric tone of righteous indignation, and what one might call his dramatic stance: setting himself, with the "Saints," against a world of wickedness, while he with some satisfaction observes and even invokes or directs the wrath of God against his enemies. This was a tone and a stance that Pope himself was to adopt in the fragmentary "One Thousand Seven Hundred and Forty," a jeremiad in which Pope declares that "the plague is on thee, Britain" (line 75), and longs for deliverance by an honest and virtuous king.

It appears too in the exactly contemporary *Epilogue to the Satires* (1738), his own "Fair Mirrour of Foul Times."[38]

> O sacred Weapon! left for Truth's defence,
> Sole Dread of Folly, Vice, and Insolence!
> To all but Heav'n-directed hands deny'd,
> The Muse may give thee! but the Gods must guide.
>
> (II. 212–15)

Though the tone and style of the *Epilogue* are often described as Juvenalian, one suspects that Pope had Milton in mind in such passages as these where satire is both a sacred calling and a way of testifying to the faith of the "one just man" in a world of iniquity. The epic model is Milton's Abdiel:

> So spake the Seraph *Abdiel* faithful found,
> Among the faithless, faithful only hee;
> Among innumerable false, unmov'd,
> Unshak'n, unseduc'd, unterrifi'd
> His Loyalty he kept, his Love, his Zeal;
> Nor number, nor example with him wrought
> To swerve from truth, or change his constant mind
> Though single.
>
> (V. 896–903)

Pope's grand gesture at the end of the first Dialogue of the *Epilogue to the Satires* is equally principled and courageous.

In the second Dialogue Milton himself may well be Pope's model, the Milton of the defiant political tracts, the hero celebrated by the eighteenth-century commentators for his *Conscia Virtus*, his pride in his own integrity. As the second Dialogue concludes Pope "ope's" a Miltonic "Temple of Eternity" (line 235) where Truth "guards the Poet" and makes his verse "Immortal."[39] Though the world succumbs to Walpole's power of corruption, Pope remains at his station – "Yes, the last Pen for Freedom let me draw" (line 248) – in emulation of Milton before him who, resisting the restoration of the Stuarts as late as April 1660 – a month before Charles landed – imagines he may be uttering "the last words of our expiring libertie."[40] Pope held out little hope that his defiance would stem the tide. To the second Dialogue he appended a valedictory note:

This was the last poem of the kind printed by our author, with a resolution to publish no more; but to enter thus, in the most plain and solemn manner he could, a sort of PROTEST against that insuperable corruption and depravity of manners, which he had been so unhappy as to live to see.

Though the protest may have fallen on deaf ears, the poet derived some satisfaction: "The Poem raised him, as he knew it would, some enemies; but he had reasons to be satisfied with the approbation of good men, and the testimony of his own conscience." Again Milton is Pope's exemplar. Though recompensed for his efforts on behalf of liberty with nothing but impunity, Milton, in a well-known passage from the *Second Defense*, reflected, in words that Pope may well have recalled: "What I have done hath, of it Self, given Me a Good Conscience within [*bona conscientia*], a Good Esteem among the Good [*bona bonos existimatio*]."[41]

Another fragment, apparently written about the same time, suggests that Milton continued to be on Pope's mind in the late 1730s as an exemplary figure. In 1738 Pope published an "Epitaph. For One who would not be buried in Westminster-Abbey," obviously intended for himself:

> HEROES, and KINGS! your distance keep:
> In peace let one poor Poet sleep,
> Who never flatter'd Folks like you:
> Let Horace blush, and Virgil too.[42]

The Twickenham editors suggest that the lines were not meant to be taken "too seriously" (VI, 376) but we may suspect that even Pope's jokes are revealing. The epitaph preserves the same stance of righteous detachment found in the Miltonic sonnet. This "poor Poet" would not wish to lie in Poet's Corner, next to English royalty. On the contrary, he imagines that those same "HEROES" and "KINGS" – both alive and dead – will seek out his peaceful grave, whence he will spurn them. It seems more than coincidental that this little self-flattering fantasy should be published only a year after Milton, buried without a memorial stone in St. Giles, Cripplegate, finally had a monument erected in his honor in Westminster Abbey. Controversy had surrounded the monument, many still objecting to Milton's presence in the Abbey on political grounds. Though Pope did not approve of Milton's anti-royalist politics, his epitaph probably expresses not resentment, much less jealousy, but affirms that the true poet's dignity after his death does not depend on recognition by a king whom he righteously denounced in his lifetime.[43]

Finally, one other fragment shows that Milton remained a model to the last years of Pope's career. As late as 1743 Pope still aspired to write a proper epic poem. He told Spence a year before he died that the poem, to deal with "civil and ecclesiastical government," had been completely planned. Only a fragment of eight lines survives, but it is enough to show that Pope was in some way still attempting to "rewrite" Milton:

The Patient Chief, who lab'ring long, arriv'd
On Britains Shore and brought with fav'ring Gods
Arts Arms and Honour to her Ancient Sons:
Daughter of Memory! from elder Time
Recall; and me, with Britains Glory fir'd,
Me, far from meaner Care or meaner Song,
Snatch to thy Holy Hill of Spotless Bay,
My Countrys Poet, to record her Fame.[44]

The lines are in blank verse, and though not notably Miltonic, syntactically resemble the invocations to *Paradise Lost* – the delayed imperative "Recall" (cf. Milton's "Sing heavenly muse," also delayed until the fifth line), the self-conscious emphasis on the poet both proud and devoutly submissive, even the curious repetition of "Me" (cf. "Instruct me, for Thouknow'st... / What in me is dark / Illumine"), and the contrast between lofty and "meaner" song (cf. "The skill of artifice or office mean, / Not that which justly gives heroic name / To person or to poem. Me of these / Nor skilled nor studious, higher argument / Remains").[45] More significant is Pope's subject – the establishment of government in Britain by the eponymous Brutus and other fugitives from Troy. Milton knew this story,[46] and expressed hopes of one day writing of "Trojan keels ploughing the sea off the Kentish coast."[47] Milton's aspirations were later diverted from a national epic about the origins of Britain to a poem about the origin of all mankind. Pope, who would have known from Milton's early poems of his first ambitions, now offered to complete a project Milton had abandoned, and to supply his country with its own epic. The poet who despaired of Britain's present state might nonetheless seek to recall to his countrymen the heritage of "Britains Glory." And in so doing he would adopt a stance – "My Countrys Poet" – that had been distinctly associated with Milton.[48] It seems apparent that in his last years Pope liked to think of himself as England's national poet. In 1741 and again in 1743 a copper medal was struck with a bust of Pope on one side, and on the reverse "Poeta Anglus" with the date.[49] To complete *Brutus* would have laid unquestionable claim to the title that Pope's countrymen still assigned to Milton.

Neither Pope's youthful *Alcander* nor his *Brutus* were ever completed. *Samson Agonistes* was never "corrected." But one should not conclude from this that Pope's attempts to "rewrite" Milton were always abortive, or that Milton did not serve as a productive stimulus. *Alcander* was of course premature; the *Samson* project died stillborn perhaps because Pope, as he told Spence, resolved after an early attempt at a tragedy on St. Genevieve, "never to write anything for the stage."[50] And there is reason to believe that had Pope lived he would have completed *Brutus*. But the real record of Milton's creative influence on Pope lies of course in the completed poems, from the *Pastorals* to the *Dunciad*. What one finds there is in part recurrent Miltonic resonance, whose effect is to suggest a larger moral world; in part Miltonic materials fitted, like building stones, into Pope's "new works." But most significantly one finds Pope deliberately exposing the difference between Milton's poetic world and his own.

The early Pope: *Pastorals*, *Windsor Forest*, and *The Rape of the Lock*

Pope's *Pastorals* often disappoint those readers and critics coming to them from the tradition of Renaissance pastoral culminating in Milton and Marvell. His four poems seem smaller, tamer, academic, merely conventional. No one would claim that the *Pastorals* are major poems, but they have been defended for their conscious art – as a deliberately modest first step in the poetic progress toward epic, as display pieces showing off precisely calibrated versification,[51] as illustrations of a "Golden Age" theory of pastoral. So conscious a pastoralist knew perfectly well that his poems were different from *Lycidas*, more like Spenser's and Virgil's eclogues. To read Pope's "Winter," an elegy on Mrs. Tempest, who died "on the night of a great storm in 1703" (Pope's headnote), after reading Milton's elegy on the death of Edward King, "who drowned in his passage from Chester on the Irish Seas, 1637," is to observe a process of reorientation or course correction: Pope reins in the freedoms Milton permitted himself, and deliberately reclassicizes the form.

Why should a reader sense this? The evidence is perhaps slight but suggestive. Pope first evokes Milton unmistakably in *Summer*, where "And yet my Numbers please the rural Throng. / Rough *Satyrs* dance, and *Pan* applauds the Song" echoes Milton's earlier lines:

> Rough Satyrs danc'd, and Fauns with cloven heel,
> From the glad sound would not be absent long,
> And old Damoetas loved to hear our song.
> (*Lycidas*, lines 34–36)

Pope thus implies that he sings to the same audience.[52] In "Winter" the first of Pope's two speakers is named Lycidas, a conventional pastoral name to be sure, but not a common one, and in 1709 surely an allusion to Milton.[53] The elegiac peripeteia, from "*Daphne*, our Grief! our Glory now no more" (line 68) to "But see! where *Daphne* wondring mounts on high" (line 69) recalls Milton's equally sudden reversal: "And, oh ye dolphins, waft the hapless youth. / Weep no more, woeful shepherds ... / So Lycidas sunk low, but mounted high" (lines

164–65, 172). Daphne will now enjoy a heavenly pastoral, "Fields ever fresh, and Groves for ever green!" (line 72), just as Milton's Lycidas will now enjoy "other groves, and other streams" in heaven (line 174). But there the similarities end. Where Milton's poem opens abruptly, is "interrupted" twice by the lofty voices of Phoebus and St. Peter, and effectively imitates, in its irregular numbers and repeated questions, the turbulent passions of the mourning shepherd, Pope's elegy is firmly controlled. Framed at each end with two responsive singers, Thyrsis's song carefully preserves pastoral humility and laments in stately fashion through six consecutive 8-line verse paragraphs that, with Daphne dead, Love, Beauty, Pleasure, Sweetness, Music, and Glory (one paragraph each) are all "now no more." It is as if Pope set out to reimpose traditional restraints on a form that Milton had loosened. Like most poetic revolutionaries, Pope goes back to the roots of the form to recover its purity.

Windsor Forest more obviously solicits comparisons with its Miltonic predecessor, *Paradise Lost*. Many influences combine to shape Pope's poem – including Virgil, Isaiah, and celebrations (as in Denham and Dryden) of English maritime commerce – but my concern here is with Pope's evocation and reshaping of Milton's Edenic myth: "The Groves of *Eden*, vanish'd now so long, / Live in Description, and look green in Song." "These," says Pope, i.e. the "Forests" and the "green Retreats" of Windsor Forest, "were my Breast inspir'd with equal Flame, / Like them in Beauty, should be like in Fame" (lines 7–10). From these familiar lines Pope emerges as Milton's rival or emulator. If he succeeds, Windsor Forest will rival Eden "in Fame." But it will have one further advantage. Eden can "look green" now *only* "in Song." Windsor's "green Retreats" can be enjoyed in Pope's song *and* in Queen Anne's England. The rest of the poem will in fact bear out how Pope, like Philips before him and other georgic poets later in the century, finds an Edenic garden paradise that has survived the Fall.

Pope's garden, like Milton's, displays "Order in Variety," presided over by a woman. But by the end of the poem the mistress of Windsor acts more like Milton's God than his Eve: "At length great ANNA said – Let Discord cease! / She said, the World obey'd, and all was Peace!" (lines 326–27). Other differences suggest that Pope has reconstituted Milton's Eden for his own purposes. His poem contains no myth of the fall from innocence. There is no happy garden in Windsor's distant past. When the forest first appears in Pope's poem "in Ages past," it is "A dreary Desart and a gloomy Waste, / To Savage Beasts and Savage Laws a Prey" (lines 43–44). Pope imagines not decline from original innocence, but progress from barbarity to civilization. The progress is interrupted by "Intestine Wars" (line 325), but Anne's arts of

reconciliation bring about a peace that completely heals the breach.
Material prosperity and imperial power mean not a sacrifice of rural
simplicity, but an extension of its order. In Milton the Fall brought in
its wake the physical destruction of Eden. As Michael prophesies,

> then shall this mount
> Of Paradise by might of waves be moved
> Out of his place, pushed by the horned flood,
> With all his verdure spoiled, and trees adrift
> Down the great river to the opening gulf,
> And there take root an island salt and bare,
> The haunt of seals and orcs, and sea-mews' clang.
>
> (XI. 829–35)

Pope, remembering those painful lines, sees not destruction but
continuity.[54] Windsor's trees too "shall leave their Woods," says
Pope's prophetic Father Thames, "And half thy Forests rush into my
Floods." But while Milton's trees become drifting hulks (it is the
"mount," not the trees, that takes root as a bare island), Pope's are
transformed into mighty ships, bearing "Britain's *Thunder*, and her
Cross" (lines 385–87), both her worldly and her spiritual power. And
the final binding of Discord shall take place not at the end of time, when
Christ "shall surprise / The serpent, prince of air, and drag in chains
/ Through all his realm, and there confounded leave" (*Paradise Lost*, XII.
453–55), but in secular time: exiled by Peace "from Earth to deepest
Hell, / In Brazen Bonds shall barb'rous *Discord* dwell" (*Windsor Forest*,
413–14). Despite recent suggestions, Pope's commercial myth is not
intended to replace Milton's myth of spiritual regeneration.[55] Rather
it adapts Milton's description of a lost Eden to make it fit the earthly
paradise of Stuart England. Embracing the secular world, Pope sees
no need to choose between worldly prosperity and a more perfect moral
order, between an Edenic forest and an empire.

To revise or re-write Milton in this way, Pope found a useful
intermediary in John Philips, whose *Cyder* had recently celebrated, in
Miltonic blank verse georgic, the peace and order brought about by the
same "Anna," ruling through quasi-divine fiat. Philips' Anna had
said, only five years before, "LET THERE BE UNION" (II. 649). Pope's
says "Let Discord cease!...and all was *Peace*" (326–27), and the
resemblance is even closer in the manuscript, which reads "Let there
be Peace!"[56] This is the clearest example in the poem of what has been
called "double allusion,"[57] Pope alluding to a Miltonic parody and at
the same time to the Miltonic original behind it. In another instance
Pope's description of the murder of Charles I as a "Fact accurst" (321)
looks back through Philips' account of the same event as a "Fact /
Unparallel'd" (II. 507–08) to *Paradise Lost*, where "accurst" is a

common epithet and "fact," in the seventeenth-century sense of crime or evil deed, appears three times.[58] Philips' description of the retired happy man who turns from natural science to "Speculations deep / Of Good, and Just, and Meet, and th'wholsome Rules / Of Temperance" (I. 761–63), based in part on "Il Penseroso" and on *Comus* (cf. *Cyder*, I. 757–63 and "Penseroso", 171–74, *Comus*, 765–67), may have led Pope back to the early Milton to details with which to adorn his lines on the happy man and the retired poet.[59]

Philips' most important service to Pope, however, was to show him how Milton's epic materials might be adapted to georgic uses, and how his Edenic myth might be adapted to local circumstances. As Pope was remodelling *Windsor Forest* about 1712 he would have found in *Cyder* a poem that combined many elements that were to make up the final version of his poem; not only a recurrent allusion to *Paradise Lost*, but also the praise of rural retreat; the praise of English poets who had lived a life of retirement; the survey of the heroes and kings of English history from the violent past to the peaceful present; the celebration of England as a commercial and maritime power; and above all the suggestion that Eden might be found, or at least reconstituted, in England's green and pleasant land. What Pope did *not* take from Philips was his Miltonic blank verse. As he later told Spence, "Philips, in his Cyder, has succeeded extremely well in his imitations of Milton's style, but was quite wrong in endeavouring to imitate it on such a subject."[60] Having taken what he found useful in Philips (and in Milton before him) Pope cast the materials in heroic couplets, and put his own characteristic stamp on them. *Cyder*, for all its independence, remains a Miltonic imitation. *Windsor Forest*, for all its allusiveness, is a free-standing creation and a greater poem.

So much has been written about Miltonic allusion in *The Rape of the Lock* that there would appear to be very little left to say. But it is perhaps worth noting briefly how the Miltonic quality of Pope's poem, no doubt unintentionally, has been overstated. For the epic conventions he wished to parody Pope of course need not have gone to Milton, who was only the most recent exemplar of a long tradition with which Pope was already very familiar. Indeed, Pope's major source is no doubt Homer. Except for the machinery of the sylphs, added in the second edition, *The Rape of the Lock* could easily have been written without *Paradise Lost*. It is striking to recall that, unlike the *Dunciad*, the poem in fact contains very few direct allusions to Milton's epic. Only two (both concerning the sylphs) and possibly a third are felt as purposeful allusion. Pope's spirits "Assume what Sexes and what Shapes they please" (I. 70), in conscious imitation of Milton's angels (*Paradise Lost*, I. 423), and, like the angels in the war in heaven (Pope's own note draws the parallel) can suffer no permanent wound: "Airy Substance soon unites again" (III. 152).[61] Ariel's address to the "*Fays, Faeries, Genii, Elves*, and *Daemons*" (II. 74) perhaps recalls Satan's "Thrones, Dominations, Princedoms, Vertues, Powers" (V. 601). The other parallels are so minor, so distant, or so conventional in epic tradition, whether or not Pope was consciously recalling Milton, that they do not help establish an effective Miltonic presence in the poem.[62]

What Milton provided Pope was an occasion for some sophisticated parody, and, as Cleanth Brooks pointed out long ago, a chance to put his finger on an apparent flaw in Milton's scheme of supernatural machines. God assigns his angels the task of guarding the garden, and later of taking up arms against Satan's legions, but in each task they prove ineffectual, as if by God's own plan (who easily could have ordered otherwise).[63] In one case God prevents a battle between Uriel and the fallen Satan; in the other combatants are sent to fight in a war they cannot win, since each side is, quite literally, invulnerable. So too Pope's Ariel is assigned the task of guarding Belinda's heart (at one point he sounds like Gabriel in Eden),[64] but finds his "Pow'r expir'd" when an earthly lover is discovered lurking there (III. 144–46). As Brooks notes, what seems an unavoidable narrative defect in *Paradise Lost* is no flaw in *The Rape of the Lock*. An epic encounter between fops and belles in which Chloe kills Sir Plume with a frown, only to have him revive when he sees her smile in triumph, redeems the absurdity of Miltonic war.

At the same time the Miltonic parallel allows for more serious resonances. As many critics have suggested, Belinda seems an Eve, first tempted in a dream by a supernatural agent at her ear to know her "own importance," attracted to her own image in a mirror, succumbing to pride, suffering a "fall," but rejecting the consolation and advice offered her by Clarissa, who plays a role like Milton's Michael.[65] The point to make here is that Pope does not especially encourage us to see such similarities. Belinda at her toilet table shares only a kind of detached self-regard with Eve at the pool. Clarissa speaks not of redemptive motherhood but self-protection and survival. In each episode, further-more, the Homeric analogy prominently calls attention to itself. Pope finds room for both laughter and something close to tears, nearly Olympian bemusement and an acute sense of transience, but we must be careful not to import into *The Rape of the Lock* a moral drama in which grave Miltonic themes are thinly disguised in the language of wit and politeness. Twenty years ago Aubrey Williams warned against taking the poem too lightly. The pendulum may have swung so that we are now again in danger of taking it too gravely.[66] To see latent in Clarissa's speech the Miltonic suggestion that Belinda's fall, like Eve's, was "fortunate," since it enabled her to abandon a coquette's sterile role and embrace full womanhood, is to extend the limits of allusion farther than Pope licenses.

The danger of over-Miltonizing *The Rape of the Lock* is that it can blind us to the fact that Pope wants to take seriously what Milton would not have troubled himself with: certain polished social rituals which, rightly understood, can have aesthetic and even moral value, and wrongly used can produce disorder, moral shallowness, and frustration. Pope knows as well as anyone that the world of Belinda and Clarissa is a limited one – beauty and "good Sense" are a far cry from the set of traditional virtues that Michael urges on Adam or Sarpedon urges on Glaucus – but at the same time suggests that their world, like Belinda's toilet table, displays a kind of "mystic order" and does have its "own importance." Its value is felt most acutely when Pope shows its precariousness, when the symbolic frail china vessel is shattered into fragments, or transformed into the merely utilitarian pipkins, jars, and bottles of the Cave of Spleen. Williams is right to stress the *moral* implications in the "fall" of china, but we should not forget the way a vase functions too as an emblem of grace, beauty, delicacy, and civility – the qualities of a *social* order in jeopardy.

An Essay on Man

That the *Essay on Man* prominently alludes to *Paradise Lost*, invites comparisons with it, and even may be said to be a "transliteration" of Milton's themes into "rationalistic terms" have become established truths about the poem since Maynard Mack's Twickenham edition nearly thirty-five years ago.[67] But it remains to ask *why* Pope should have wished to re-write the poem in this way. Mack himself suggests hesitantly only that Pope may have sought, "instinctively," to make Milton's theme "available, possibly to himself and certainly to his age, as nothing else could have done," since Milton's own mode of mythical narrative had "lost, perhaps, its full imaginative availability for Pope and his age."[68] In Mack's view Pope's transformation is almost wholly one of form and treatment, while theme – God's ways are just, his world an ordered and harmonious whole, and man's role to submit without insisting on full knowledge – remains at least broadly "analogous."[69] Although Mack recognized some important differences between *Paradise Lost* and *An Essay on Man* – the latter is "distinctly a poem of the middle flight," and lacks Milton's "Magnificence" – what he stresses are the similarities. There is reason to believe, however, that Pope's allusions to Milton are designed to advertise the differences as much or more than the similarities, and that the *Essay* marks a more radical departure from *Paradise Lost* than Mack allows.

Pope was indeed the first to suggest significant differences. Whereas Milton's poem is obtrusively Christian, Pope's is only implicitly so. For Milton the principal justification of God's ways is the propitiatory sacrifice of Christ, but Pope leaves God's son wholly out of his poem.[70] Pope told Spence, furthermore, that he omitted from the *Essay* both the fall of man and the doctrine of the immortality of the soul – the very heart of Milton's poem – because they "lay out of my subject, which was only to consider man as he is, in his present state, not in his past or future."[71] Thus Pope was not simply translating Milton's mythical narrative into abstract terms, but was radically contracting his focus and taking on what may have seemed to him a more difficult task of vindication. One of Pope's first commentators, Joseph Warton, saw it in these terms. Pope's line "vindicate the ways of God to man" in his view "hinted...that he intended his poem for a defence of providence, as well as Milton: but that he took a very different method in pursuing that end; and imagined that the goodness and justice of the Deity might be defended, *without* having recourse to the doctrine of a future state, and of the depraved state of man."[72] Warton does not take the view that Pope's vindication simply *supplements* Milton's defense of God by re-arguing his case on purely philosophical grounds. On some key points, he says, Pope's case denies Milton's. If man is "as perfect as he ought" (I. 70), he is "as perfect a being as ever his Creator intended him to be; nor, consequently, did he stand in need of any redemption or atonement."[73] Pope's claim that the "gen'ral ORDER, since the whole began, / Is kept in Nature, and is kept in Man" (I. 171–72), is not "reconcileable to the doctrine of a lapsed condition of man, which opinion is the chief foundation of the Christian revelation, and the capital argument for the necessity of redemption."[74]

Modern critics have followed Warton in thinking that Pope challenges Milton's ideas and argues not Milton's but his own case in the *Essay*. Barbara Lewalski conveniently summarizes how Pope "alters Milton's themes." Both Milton and Pope might subscribe to the notion that "Partial Evil" is "Universal Good," but would understand the phrase quite differently. For Milton evil arises when God's creatures freely choose to disobey or to pervert God's ends. Good will ultimately result only because God will work good out of evil. Pope translates the idea from the plane of action to the plane of perception, from the evil that men do to the evil that men see about them in the system of things. They see systematic evil because their vision is "partial." From God's point of view, toward which the narrator and his reader aspire, such evil disappears in a vision of "universal Good." Milton's Adam likewise arrives at a vision of "goodness infinite, goodness immense! / That all this good of evil shall produce, / And evil turn to good" (XII. 469–71).[75] Pope's "good" is apprehended in the present, Milton's largely in the distant future, and Adam's rapture does not allow the reader to forget that, for now, man must live in a "world of woe" that is the consequence of his own doing.

Other important differences spring from this central one. The means to free choice – the central element in Milton's moral and theological system – is reason. As Lewalski notes, in Pope's system reason's role is to dictate submission: "To Reason right is to submit" (*Essay on Man*, I. 164). For both Milton and Pope reason can easily "misinform the will," but Milton seems to blame the will and Pope the intellect. "In Pride, in reas'ning Pride, our error lies" (*Essay on Man*, I. 123).[76] Passion too is assigned different values. For Milton it is always a danger. "Here passion first I felt," Adam reports to Raphael of his response to Eve. Raphael's answer is a grave warning: "In loving thou dost well, in passion not" (VIII. 585, 588). But for Pope passion is life's animating force, the very "elements of Life" (*Essay on Man*, I. 170): "Reason [is] the card, but Passion is the gale" (*Essay on Man*, II. 108). In Milton's un-fallen world Adam and Eve, if through the proper exercise of reason they obey God's will, can hope to rise to a higher state along what Milton imagines as a continuum. In Pope's always already fallen world the continuum is a hierarchy with fixed niches. One cannot climb closer to the angels. And yet one can hope to recover a kind of paradise, in the fallen world, that Milton reserves for the end of time, or for the mind alone.

Despite these differences Pope's man strikingly resembles Milton's. As Raphael tells Adam, man is created "perfect, not immutable" (V. 524): his kind of perfection lies in his ability to rise (or fall) in the exercise of his free will. Pope's apparently fallen man, if he is not perfect, is at least "as perfect as he ought" (I. 70). Though he can never approach angelic status, he is "created half to rise, and half to fall" (*Essay on Man*, II. 15). In several respects then – his "perfection" and his prospective enjoyment of a paradisal state – Pope's man appears to enjoy the condition of Milton's unfallen but mutable Adam and Eve. Indeed, critics since Joseph Warton have argued that the system of Pope's poem not only excludes the Fall, but actually contradicts it.

As Douglas Canfield recently re-argues the case, the *Essay* supplies no substantial evidence that man ever occupied a different niche, or was endowed with different powers. Nor does Pope suggest that any dramatic or catastrophic change has taken place since the Creation to correspond to the Fall in Milton's account. To be sure, there have been some gradual changes since man left the state of nature – he was, for example, not originally carnivorous. "Some change since all began" (*Essay on Man*, I. 147) refers not to the Fall, but to the few minor exceptions to the general laws of nature.[77]

For Canfield, as for Joseph Warton, the *Essay on Man* is not so much a redaction of *Pardise Lost* as a reinterpretation of it. Pope alludes to *Paradise Lost* "to draw attention to the unbridgeable gap between the theodicy of Milton's poem and that of his own."[78] Pope reinterprets the Fall as the perennial falls, the constant fallings off, of every man. Milton's theodicy is built around a single catastrophic event that irrevocably altered not only Adam and Eve but all their descendants, as well as the natural world itself. Pope's is built on a fixed and unchangeable system that is not effected by human actions.[79] In Milton the origin of evil is ultimately historical; in Pope it has always been part of the nature of things. This means on the one hand (as Canfield would put it) that we have always lived in a "fallen" world. But the emphasis can be reversed: the world we inhabit is no less Edenic than Adam's paradise.

Whether or not it is right to claim that Pope – like many other contemporary philosophers and poets – finds a way to deny the Fall; or whether Pope, in his own mind anyway, was not challenging orthodox beliefs, it can be argued that even the precisely limited focus of the poem – "man as he is, in his present state," without reference to his origin, his redemption, or his immortal end – so reduces the scope for theodicy as to constitute a significant difference from *Paradise Lost*. To limit his focus in this way required that Pope transform other elements of his Miltonic model as well. Perhaps the most visible element is the poet's stance in relation to his muse, his material, and his audience. Milton's stance had been made clear primarily in the poem's invocation and personal digressions at the beginnings of Books I, III, VII, and IX. He presented himself on the one hand as a mere mortal, low, dark, advanced in years, compassed round with dangers; and on the other as an inspired bard, aided by a celestial patroness, endowed with inward eyes that let him see things invisible to mortal sight. His subject could hardly be graver, and he takes it up with solemnity and reverence. Largely at odds with the world, he hopes to find fit audience though few.

In *his* invocation – with its prominent allusion to Milton's earlier invocation – Pope adopts a wholly different stance. Man of the world, familiar with "this scene of Man," Pope displays an air of breezy confidence that his own powers are more than equal to the expository task at hand. It will be a modest project, an occupation for the left hand, an amateur's cursory survey, a trial ("Essay"), an experiment ("Try what the open, what the Covert yield"). By comparison Milton's "advent'rous song" seems vast and ponderous. Bolingbroke, as Pope's muse, corresponds to Milton's Urania, but he is treated as an equal, a fellow gentleman-philosopher, a collaborator, even to be rallied out of his preoccupation with politics ("Awake, my ST. JOHN! leave all meaner things..."). Bolingbroke serves also as Pope's immediate audience, though Pope soon turns to address a wider audience of his fellow men.[80]

At the outset Pope announces his intention of undertaking Milton's task. In justifying the ways of God to man Milton could rely not only on his heavenly muse but also on other supernatural narrators (Raphael, Michael, even God himself) who carried much of his burden. Pope transposes Milton's theme into a wholly human argument, what one man of the world might say to another, based simply on "what we know" not as theologians or philosophers but as ambling observers:

> Eye Nature's Walks, shoot Folly as it flies,
> And catch the Manners living as they rise;
> Laugh where we must, be candid where we can;
> But vindicate the ways of God to Man.
>
> (I. 13–16)

Though semantically close to Milton's "justify," "vindicate" carries the additional sense of "to clear from censure, criticism, suspicion, doubt."[81] Pope's self-imposed task is then presented as more difficult than Milton's since the implicit charge against God's justice is more vividly imagined. It is also more audacious in implying that God might need an advocate, and that man might so serve. In Milton's poems, as Pope probably knew, it is God himself who "vindicates" the glory of his own name.[82]

Why "*But* vindicate"? Perhaps to preserve his amateur status, to keep the project from seeming too ambitious, perhaps to help signal the *difference* between his vindication and Milton's justification. Whatever else it does, the antithesis (Pope and his contemporaries were very sensitive to rhetorical antitheses) suggests some significant contrast between *vindicate* and the preceding verbs, *expatiate*, *beat*, *try*, *eye*, *shoot*, *catch*, *laugh*, *be candid*. "But" perhaps suggests too that vindicating God will not easily follow from a leisurely mental tour. How indeed are mere men, confined to human powers, without appealing to the stories and doctrines of scripture, to accomplish Milton's task?

Pope may not have fully solved the problem. He himself said that the author of the *Essay* "quits his proper subject, to insert his belief of a *future state*."[83] The lines at the end of Epistle I beginning "All are but parts of one stupendous whole" (I. 267–80) prove, he said, that the author is "quite Christian in his system, from *Man* up to *Seraphim*."[84] In such passages, transcending the limits of "what we know," Pope adopts an essentially theological perspective, laying claim to knowledge that he can only attain through faith.[85] Inconsistencies like these might be thought a sign of Pope's incomplete success.[86] By another account Pope confronts the problems involved in accomplishing Milton's task without Milton's tools, and deliberately juxtaposes the knowledge and comfort available to man as he looks down on the patterned plan of God's world, and as he looks out into the "mighty maze" itself.[87]

The Dunciad

It has been long recognized that *The Dunciad* often imitates or alludes to *Paradise Lost*, and that Pope's poem occupies the place in his work and career that *Paradise Lost* does in Milton's: it is his master work, his "epic," or (more properly) the mock-epic that stands in place of the epic he never wrote. The common view is that Pope uses allusion to *Paradise Lost* to suggest the ultimate dangers of Dulness, that she and her agents are aligned with the forces of evil: Cibber is a kind of Satan, the "Antichrist of Wit," and Dulness an anti-Logos whose "uncreating word" will finally destroy civilization. This view is perhaps most persuasively presented by Aubrey Williams in his still-influential study of *The Dunciad*, published nearly thirty years ago,[88] and is familiar to all students of the poem. It has more recently been restated by a Miltonist, Barbara Lewalski, who concisely summarizes the substantial number of parallels between *The Dunciad* and *Paradise Lost*, and argues that the "basis" for Pope's poem is "Milton's invented myth of Satan's offer to help the Anarch Chaos regain the portion of his realm taken over by the created universe" in *Paradise Lost*, II. 959–1010.[89] In such readings the presence of Milton in *The Dunciad* helps Pope to direct our attention from the comic surface to the ultimate seriousness of his subject.

In the last ten years, however, some critics have sought to re-emphasize that *The Dunciad*, both on its surface and in its very nature, is a comic poem, and that its subject is the Triumph of Wit over the comically bumbling forces of Dulness.[90] In this newer critical context it is worth re-examining the pattern of allusions to *Paradise Lost* in *The Dunciad* to show that on the whole they too are designed to be largely comic, to belittle the dunces, or to recall the old view (present in *Paradise Lost*) that even the devil – like his contemporary avatars – is an ass, to bring out not so much the similarities as the differences between Cibber and Satan, dunces and devils.

Take for example those allusions that most explicitly link Pope's hero to Satan. At the beginning of Book II Cibber sits enthroned:

> High on a gorgeous seat, that far out-shone
> Henley's gilt tub, or Fleckno's Irish throne,
> Or that whereon her Curls the Public pours,
> All-bounteous, fragrant Grains and Golden show'rs,
> Great Cibber sate.
>
> (1743, II. 1–5)

174

As Pope's own note indicates, the lines are a "Parody of *Milton*":

> High on a throne of royal state, that far
> Outshone the wealth of Ormus and of Ind,
> Or where the gorgeous East with richest hand,
> Show'rs on her Kings barbaric pearl and gold,
> Satan exalted sate.
>
> (*Paradise Lost*, II. 1–5)

To be sure, Pope goes on to refer to the "jealous leer" (II. 6) on Cibber's face (cf. Satan's "jealous leer malign," *Paradise Lost*, IV. 503) and to compare his reception by the devils to that accorded Camillo Querno when he was crowned "Antichrist of Wit" in Rome (lines 11–12). Too many critics hasten to assert, however, that it is Cibber, rather than Querno, who is named Antichrist. And few bother to draw attention to Pope's note explaining who Querno was and why he was called "Antichrist of Wit."

> He was introduced as a Buffoon to *Leo*, and promoted to the honour of the Laurel; a jest, which the Court of *Rome* and the Pope himself entred into so far as ... to hold a solemn Festival on his Coronation, at which it is recorded the Poet himself was so transported, as to weep for joy.　(*Dunciad*, II. 11n)

In the full context, then, "Antichrist of Wit" is not simply an allusion to Satan as Antichrist (Milton in fact never calls him that) but primarily to the mock-coronation of another buffoon poet welcomed with "glee" (line 9) by a court which recognized and took delight in his buffoonery. The solemnity of Querno's (and by extension Cibber's) title is the meat of the jest, Pope's jest, since it is he who promotes Querno from laureate to Antichrist, the mock-ruler of Rome and of the tribe of poets. The allusion to *Paradise Lost* has an equally comic effect, for it links Cibber directly with notorious dunces – Orator Henley and Richard Flecknoe – and shameless publishers, whose eminence in "gilt Tub," mock-throne, and pillory only exposed them to scorn and to figurative (or even literal) rotten eggs. Many critics assume too hastily that the allusion simply aggrandizes Cibber, when the larger effect is to diminish or belittle him.

Or consider the allusion in Book I (1729 text) where the hero (here Theobald) sits supperless in his garret:

> Studious he sate, with all his books around,
> Sinking from thought to thought, a vast profound!
> Plung'd for his sense, but found no bottom there;
> Then writ, and flounder'd on, in mere despair.
> He roll'd his eyes that witness'd huge dismay,
> Where yet unpawn'd, much learned lumber lay.
>
> (I. 111–16)

Again Pope's own note points to *Paradise Lost*: "Milt. *Round he throws his eyes That witness'd huge affliction and dismay.* The progress of a bad Poet in his thoughts being (like the progress of the Devil in *Milton*) thro' a Chaos, might probably suggest this imitation" (I. 115n, *Poems*, V, 77). Pope in fact alludes to Satan on the burning lake – (I. 56 – 57) – and to Satan in Chaos – (II. 927 – 50). Setting aside the fact that Satan swimming, sinking, wading, and creeping through Chaos is himself presented by Milton as a semi-comic bumbler, Pope's poet-hero emerges from the allusion not as a dangerous agent of evil but a desperate and incompetent hack.

What I have suggested about these two allusions might be said about many other allusions to *Paradise Lost* in the poem: in their full context they are largely comic or satiric. They induce in the reader not a sense of alarm (these duncis are doing the devil's work) but a sense of amused superiority; recognizing the allusion (as the duncis presumably do not), he laughs at their humiliation, incompetence, and impotence. At stake here is an important issue in Pope criticism (and criticism of eighteenth-century writers generally): the limits of allusion. When a poet alludes to a previous work, or event, or figure, does he intend to call up everything the reader might know or find out about that work, event, or figure? Does a poet often not edit his allusions so as to control his reader's response? Does the mere allusion to Satan mean that we should find Cibber to be dangerously Satanic, or to be Satanic in every way? (We should recall that Satan himself can easily be seen as a comic figure.) Does the use of the world "Antichrist" require or even urge us to adopt a gravely theological perspective on the poem? I suggest that it does not. The edited context – the mock coronation of Camillo Querno – should govern our response, and make us adopt the perspective of Pope Leo and his court who knew how to take pleasure in a fool. If we disregard the context and the predominant tone, and invoke the spirit of Pope's dark satires of the late 1730s, we can easily supply a Miltonic high seriousness to the entire *Dunciad* that Pope seems not to have intended.

To be sure, allusion is a potent tool, and sometimes seems to have a mind of its own. The poet may not always be able to prevent his reader from calling up the original context in its entirety, and of seeing Satan himself as Antichrist behind the jester "antichrist of wit." We have long been taught to see the inherent "ambivalence" of the mock-heroic metaphor, which tends – whether the poet wills it or not – to aggrandize and belittle at the same time.[91] Perhaps the poet may even wish to encourage or allow the wider associations into the reader's mind as a kind of under-meaning. But unless the poet is radically ambivalent – cannot decide whether Cibber is a buffoon, or more insidiously dangerous, or both – he will ordinarily make his primary meaning clear. And I would argue that Pope *primarily* wants us to see the dunces as comic bumblers.

Consider another feature of Pope's allusive technique that should discourage us from making fixed equations between Cibber and Satan. His allusions are by no means systematic. Cibber, for example, plays several roles, prominently including Aeneas. Among Milton's characters, he is associated with Adam (surveying the future as Adam did on his mount of vision)[92] and with Christ (beholding the kingdoms of Dulness as Christ beheld the kingdoms of the world).[93] Conversely, Satan is associated with at least five different figures in *The Dunciad*: Cibber, Bentley, Lintot, the deist, and the narrator himself.[94] Lintot in the publishers' race is like Satan laboring through Chaos[95] and at the same time is likened to the stately swan in Milton's account of the Creation.[96] Bentley in his brief introduction is like both Satan and Beelzebub – "Plow'd was his front with many a deep Remark"[97] – but he also nods like Milton's Michael[98] and is linked perhaps to the whale in Milton's creation account and through it back to Satan.[99] The *Dunciad* narrator invokes a hellish "darkness visible" to veil his "deep intent" as Satan hides his "dark intent" in the serpent's mazy folds (*Paradise Lost*, IX. 162). In the same passage the narrator, borne toward Chaos on Time's "rapid wing" (line 6), is linked with Milton, who in an early sonnet complained how Time has "stol'n on his wing my three and twentieth year" (Sonnet 7, line 2). Elsewhere (IV. 621) the narrator bids his muse relate "who first, who last resign'd to rest," exactly reversing Milton's epic narrator who asks his muse "who first, who last / Rous'd from their slumber" (*Paradise Lost*, I. 376–77). Though Pope's narrator pretends to celebrate the "Mysteries restor'd" of Chaos and Night, we do not doubt that his "deep intent" is otherwise directed. We also sense that Pope's allusive manner, though purposive, contains a strong element of free play, the delighted discovery of mock-parallels almost anywhere between his poem and Milton's epic, or Virgil's, or Homer's. His *Dunciad* is best read, I would suggest, not as Miltonic sublimity but as the "jumbled race" produced by a union of farce and epic (*Dunciad*, I. 70), or, as Ricardus Aristarchus himself suggests, as a "*Satyric Tragedy*," the satiric afterpiece that completes the epic "*Tetralogy*." *The Dunciad* then is both a fitting complement to Milton and epic tradition, and a witty parody of it. And it may stand as an epitome of Pope's response to Milton: Miltonic resonances, Miltonic building stones, but a "new world."

My reading of *The Dunciad* is inevitably "partial," stressing as it does the "comic" aspects of the poem at the expense of the "tragic." Pope in his later career was clearly capable of issuing stern warnings of disaster to his contemporaries, as I have suggested in my comments on the

Epilogue to the Satires. Nobody would want to deny that *The Dunciad* deals with a "serious" matter. The ever-present threat of Dulness, most dangerously imagined as a kind of mental torpor that allows the hard-won territory of civilization to be lost again to primal chaos, as the undifferentiated realm of Chaos in Milton is only held back by God's creative light. The Miltonic resonances of *The Dunciad*, especially in Book IV, have usually been thought to endorse such a "tragic" reading. My argument attempts a corrective: the Miltonic allusions, if we let their associations ramify, readily carry us into a Miltonic moral world, and themselves produce a narrowly "partial" view of Pope's poem. But a fully contextual reading of *The Dunciad* – in which the fourth book is a completion of the first three, the text is contained by an often antiphonal apparatus, and the poem is set into the frame of Pope's war against the dunces – suggests that Pope contains the Miltonic allusions, just as he contains the threat of Dulness. Even the "Miltonic" close of the fourth book – though it recognizes cultural decay – celebrates above all the Triumph of Wit.[100]

10 · THOMSON

In a selective survey James Thomson might stand as the characteristic Miltonic poet of the eighteenth century. He knew Milton's works thoroughly, borrowed from or alluded to them repeatedly, admired Milton openly. And yet, unlike Dryden for example, Thomson did not set himself up as a rival or emulator of Milton, whom he seems to have recognized as a higher order of poet. But such recognition carried with it no strong sense of intimidation, no suggestion that Thomson felt overpowered or overwhelmed by Milton's achievement. Like many another "Miltonic" poet he in fact looked on Milton as one of several models among classical, biblical, and native writers. For his greatest work, *The Seasons*, Thomson, as we shall see, often drew on Milton. His *Castle of Indolence* marks him also as an eighteenth-century Spenserian. And in his career as a tragic dramatist he adapted plays by Aeschylus (*Agamemnon*) and Shakespeare (*Coriolanus*). No single poet's career and no single genre had an exclusive hold on his imagination or his aspiration. Milton served him largely as a starting point. Thomson entertained thoughts of writing epic, though perhaps did not feel himself "in an Epic situation to execute it."[1] He attempted the masque form: his *Alfred* (1740), like *Comus*, began as a private performance before an aristocratic audience and later attained success on the public stage (and a place in national memory through its song "Rule, Britannia"). His greatest work, whatever its origins in Milton, is a free and independent creation, not contained by the Miltonic paradigm. In his use of the prosodic forms, the genres, and the myths of his predecessors, Thomson felt free to be eclectic, selective, and playful, and to transform what he found for his own purposes.

Thomson's blank verse

A brief look at Thomson's blank verse will suggest the nature of his indebtedness and his independence. It has long been recognized that Thomson's blank verse prosody has Miltonic origins and characteristics. R. D. Havens has pointed to Thomson's Latinate diction, his syntactical inversions, his use of adjective for adverb, and so on.[2] Havens goes so far as to claim that Thomson's "entire conception of the language and style of poetry seems... to have been moulded by *Paradise Lost*" (p. 140).

But there are good reasons to think that this overstates the case considerably. Thomson himself paid tribute to Milton in *The Seasons* as the "British Muse," but it is John Philips' blank verse prosody he salutes –

> PHILLIPS, *Pomona*'s Bard, the second thou
> Who nobly durst, in Rhyme-unfetter'd Verse,
> With BRITISH Freedom sing the BRITISH Song.
> (*Autumn*, 645–47)[3]

Milton, of course, is the first in the line of British blank verse singers, and Thomson thinks of himself as the third, who perhaps learned as much from the second as he did from the first. "Freedom" suggests primarily the release from the "modern bondage of rhyming"[4] but it perhaps also suggests the liberties Philips (and Thomson after him) felt free to take with Milton's prosody. These liberties include not only parody, but a rhythmic freeing as well, in which Milton's syntactic tensions are relaxed and lines are more loosely connected, with fewer pauses and impediments.[5] Johnson clearly recognized Thomson's prosodic independence: "His blank verse is no more the blank verse of Milton or of any other poet than the rhymes of Prior are the rhymes of Cowley. His numbers, his pauses, his diction, are of his own growth, without transcription, without imitation."[6]

It is a mistake to assume however, that Thomson's blank verse is uniform. He was aware of the need to vary his verse texture and of the ways that verse movement might be coordinated with subject matter. Consider a well-known passage from *Winter*:

> Wide o'er the Brim, with many a Torrent swell'd,
> And the mix'd Ruin of its Banks o'er spread,   95
> At last the rous'd-up River pours along:
> Resistless, roaring, dreadful, down it comes,
> From the rude Mountain, and the mossy Wild,
> Tumbling thro' Rocks abrupt, and sounding far;
> Then o'er the sanded Valley floating spreads,   100
> Calm, sluggish, silent; till again constrain'd,
> Between two meeting Hills it bursts a Way,
> Where Rocks and Woods o'erhang the turbid Stream;
> There gathering triple Force, rapid, and deep,
> It boils, and wheels, and foams, and thunders thro'.   105

Internal caesurae vary from none to three per line, so that the movement of the passage varies to reflect the movement of the river. In line 100, a line without pauses, the river spreads wide; in line 101 the spondee and trochees suggest the slowing down; and the tumbling iambs in 105 enact the violent rush between two hills. Confident arguments about sound matching sense are notoriously risky, as Johnson showed in his remarks on Pope's allegedly "representative metre."[7] But without claiming any exact correspondence between the placement of caesurae and the flow of Thomson's river, one can see that he employs the simple principles of prosodic variation and especially contrast to suggest movement and in particular satisfying climaxes.

More commonly Thomson will construct a series of short clauses and phrases that yield, at the end of the verse paragraph, to an unimpeded line:

> for, thronging, now
> Innumerous wings and in Commotion all.
> ...
> Infinite Wings! till all the Plume-dark Air,
> And rude resounding Shore are one wild Cry.
>> (*Autumn*, 847 – 48, 869 – 70, of migrating birds)

> With yielding Hand,
> That feels him still, yet to his furious Course
> Gives way, you now retiring, following now
> Across the Stream, exhaust his idle Rage:
> Till floating broad upon his breathless Side,
> And to his Fate abandon'd, to the Shore
> You gaily drag your unresisting Prize.
>> (*Spring*, 436 – 42, of the angler and his prey)

This expansive movement provides strong sense of closure, and tends to cause the blank verse to break, more than Milton's, into separate paragraph-length units.[8]

Occasionally Thomson chooses to be more Miltonic, to pack his lines more tightly, or to complicate their syntax, as in the passage on Willoughby's ill-fated Arctic voyage:

> Such was the BRITON's Fate,
> As with *first* Prow, (What have not Britons dar'd!)
> He for the Passage sought, attempted since
> So much in vain, and seeming to be shut
> By jealous Nature with eternal Bars.
> In these fell Regions, in *Arzina* caught,
> And to the stony Deep his idle Ship
> Immediate seal'd, he with his hapless Crew,
> Each full-exerted at his several Task,
> Froze into Statues; to the Cordage glued
> The Sailor, and the Pilot to the Helm.
>> (*Winter*, 925 – 35)

As Willoughby fails to find the northwest passage, syntactic and prosodic forward movement are appropriately halting, interrupted by parenthesis, held back by participial phrases ("attempted since ... seeming to be shut''). The active verbs are only two, and they tell Willoughby's story in a nutshell: ''sought...froze.'' The real action is in the participles, making the sailors immobilized and acted on rather than acting: ''caught...seal'd...full-exerted...glued.''[9] Thomson's purposes are here well-served by Miltonic verse movement. Without formally alluding to *Paradise Lost* the passage frequently suggests Milton not only in its use of adjective for adverb (''immediate seal'd,'' ''full-exerted,'' cf. ''falls horrible,'' line 925) but more effectively in its diction and syntactical rhythm (''he with his hapless Crew,''[10] ''attempted since so much in vain''[11]).

Several details oddly point to Satan and his ''hapless crew'' (*Paradise Lost*, V, 875) of fallen angels, chained not on a frozen but a burning lake, shut in ''regions of sorrow'' (I. 65) by ''bars of Hell'' (IV. 795), yet seeking ''passage'' (X. 304) to a new world. The details, however, do not add up to an ''allusion,'' nor does Thomson wish to imply that Willoughby is Satanic. Rather he freely appropriates Miltonic materials for his own purposes. The result is not mere Miltonic pastiche. The zeugmatic pattern (cordage...sailors, pilot...helm) freezes the men into position, subordinating them to the frames of the ship and of the rhetorical pattern. The concluding lines are pure Thomsonian *coup de théâtre*, no less effective for their being utterly implausible as an account of death in the Arctic.

Milton's blank verse then is not so much Thomson's model as it is a resource on which he can draw for particular effects. Frequently a consciously and conspicuously Miltonic passage conveys, against the backdrop of Thomson's basically middle style, the effect of mock-heroic. Thus the long passage in *Autumn* in which he describes the drunken feasting of fox-hunters aggrandizes the familiar:

> the strong Table groans
> Beneath the smoking Sirloin, stretch'd immense
> From Side to Side; in which, with desperate Knife,
> They deep Incision make...
> ...the mighty Bowl
> Swell'd high with fiery Juice, steams liberal round
> A potent Gale, delicious as the Breath
> Of Maia.   (lines 503–16)

Thomson's mock-heroic here sounds more like *The Rape of the Lock* than *The Splendid Shilling*, not so much the parody of Milton's manner as the use of it to make fun of fashionable or traditional English manners. When Thomson actually alludes to Milton it is mockingly to compare his beastly squires with Milton's devils, sitting ''frequent and full'' at their ''Divan'' (line 531, cf. *Paradise Lost*, I, 797, X. 457). Their drunken disputes lead them into the same ''endless Mazes, intricate, perplex'd'' (line 542) that bewilder the devils in their theological disputations (*Paradise Lost*, II. 561, "in wandering mazes lost"). In Thomson's "Argument" to *Autumn* the account of the fox-hunters is said to be "ludicrous."[12]

Other consciously Miltonic passages are not so much ludicrous as deliciously overstated. The description of the "villain" spider and the "heedless" fly in *Summer*, 267–80, for example, like the similar passage in *The Splendid Shilling* (lines 78–92), playfully inflates the event without making the principals comic, in an instance of pure linguistic or rhetorical play. Elsewhere the heightening is subtle enough that the reader hardly notices the drift from georgic middle style to a higher decorum. Early in *Spring* Thomson describes the dangers to young plants of the cold east wind

> before whose baleful Blast
> The full-blown Spring thro' all her Foliage shrinks,
> Joyless and dead, a wide-dejected Waste.
> For oft, engender'd by the hazy North,
> Myriads on Myriads, Insect-Armies waft
> Keen in the poison'd Breeze; and wasteful eat,
> Thro' Buds and Bark, into the blacken'd Core,
> Their eager Way. A feeble Race! yet oft
> The sacred Sons of Vengeance! on whose Course
> Corrosive Famine waits, and kills the Year.
> To check this Plague the skilful Farmer...
>
> (117–27)

Heavy alliteration (*baleful Bl*ast, *full*-*bl*own Spring...*Fol*iage *shr*inks, *d*ead, *w*ide-*d*ejected *W*aste), high diction (myriads, sacred sons of Vengeance), and melodramatic exaggeration (poison'd Breeze, kills the year) derive from heroic style, and function here to elevate Thomson's subject – the revolution of the seasons becomes a natural epic – and at the same time to arouse a knowing smile in the reader who recognizes that, as in Philips, the subject is after all both high and low. Only at the end of the passage does Thomson return to a georgic level, providing practical instruction in a plain expository language.[13] Miltonic diction and blank verse then allow Thomson at once to elevate his subject and to play with it. To identify this playful element in Thomson also helps to define his achievement and his place in eighteenth-century traditions. We usually think of Thomson not as a "laughing" poet but a sublime and "serious" one.[14] But *The Seasons* is a poem that encompasses both the sublime and the mock-heroic, both detached amusement and rapturous wonder. Milton's diction and prosody proved useful to Thomson in accomplishing both effects.

"Il Penseroso" and *The Seasons*

It was not only Milton's diction and prosody that provided Thomson a starting point for his own purposes. Although *The Seasons* was eventually to develop into an encyclopaedic poem of more than 5000 lines, its beginnings can in part be traced to Milton's 176-line "Il Penseroso".[15] In July 1725 while actively working on the first version of *Winter* (1726), Thomson wrote to his friend the poet David Mallet inclosing a draft of what was later to be published as a "Hymn on Solitude." It begins:

> Hail ever-pleasing Solitude!
> Companion of the wise and good!
> But from whose awfull piercing eye
> The herd of fools and villains fly
> O how I love with you to walk!
> And listen to your silent talk
> Which innocence and truth imparts
> And melts the most obdurate hearts.[16]

Thomson scholars since McKillop have been familiar with the poem's Miltonic origins, but they have not put adequate emphasis on the ways in which Thomson, far from simply following in Milton's tracks, took a few Miltonic steps and then boldly struck out on his own. From Milton Thomson takes the octosyllabic couplets, the formal opening invocation (cf. "hail, thou goddess, sage and holy, / Hail divinest Melancholy," "Penseroso," lines 11–12), and the closing petition. Milton's "These pleasures Melancholy give, / And I with thee will choose to live" becomes "O let me pierce your secret cell! / And in your deep recesses dwell" (lines 38–39).[17] After invoking the goddess Milton presents a series of scenes that gratifies the pensive/melancholic man as he moves through a landscape. Thomson centers rather on Solitude herself. He takes up Milton's invocation – "Come pensive nun…but keep thy wonted state, / With even step, and musing gait" – and sets the personified Solitude moving through a varied scene. "Missing" his goddess, Penseroso sets off alone. Thomson retains the vestigial walking poet, but the paradoxical "walking with Solitude" and listening to her "silent Talk" become metaphors for enjoying her delights. The activities of Penseroso's ideal day are in Thomson transferred to the personified Solitude, who wears "A thousand shapes" – Philosopher, Hermit, Shepherd, Huntress, Lover. That is, the pleasures of solitude may be found everywhere. While Penseroso walks through a landscape of green and grove, the details of Thomson's landscape are subordinated to or attributes of the allegorized Solitude: "Your's is the fragrant morning blush / And your's the silent evening hush" (lines 28–29). When the poets of the 1740s – Collins, Akenside, the Wartons – looked back to "L'Allegro" and "Il Penseroso" they could have found in Thomson a way of adapting Miltonic materials to help shape one of their characteristic lyric forms, the allegorical ode.

At about the same time – i.e. summer 1725 – Thomson may have been composing short "winter pieces,"[18] perhaps akin to a poem attributed to Mallet and printed under the title of "A Winter's Day" in 1729.[19] In any case, by the autumn of 1725 his developing poem on Winter, like the "Hymn on Solitude," was colored by Milton's "Penseroso." The "kindred glooms" of the published *Winter*'s opening appear in a passage quoted in a letter to William Cranstoun, c. October 1, 1725. That they are linked in Thomson's mind with Penseroso's "arched walls of twilight groves / And shadows brown" (lines 133–34) is clear from the same letter, in which Thomson cast Cranstoun as a Penseroso wandering through a later autumnal landscape:

I imagine you seized w^t a fine romantic kind of melancholy, on the fading of the Year. Now I figure you wandering, philosophical, and pensive, amidst the brown, wither'd groves...then again, when the heavens wear a more gloomy aspect, the winds whistle and the waters spout, I see you in the well known Cleugh, beneath the solemn Arch of tall, thick embowering trees, listening to the amusing lull of the many steep, moss grown Cascades; while deep, divine Contemplation, the genius of the place, prompts each swelling awfull thought...ther I walk in spirit, and disport in its beloved gloom.[20]

By the time Thomson published the first version of *Winter* in 1726 his conception of the poem had broadened. He still begins with a formal salute to an allegorical Winter and its train:

> With frequent Foot,
> Pleas'd, have I, in my cheerful Morn of Life,
> When, nurs'd by Careless *Solitude*, I liv'd,
> And sung of Nature with unceasing Joy,
> Pleas'd, have I wander'd thro' your rough Domains;
> Trod the pure, virgin Snows, my self as pure:
> Heard the Winds roar, and the big Torrent burst:
> Or seen the deep, fermenting Tempest brew'd,
> In the red, evening, Sky.
>
> (lines 6–14)

The observer is not wholly dispensed with, however. While many of the descriptions of winter issue from a non-localized eye ("See! where *Winter* comes...Lo!...Thick Clouds ascend"), Thomson, particularly in the opening sequence, locates them in a descendant of Penseroso:

> Now, solitary, and in pensive Guise,
> Oft, let me wander o'er the russet Mead,

> Or thro' the pining Grove; where scarce is heard
> One dying Strain, to chear the *Woodman*'s Toil:
> Sad Philomel, perchance, pours forth her Plaint,
> Far, thro' the withering Copse.
>
> (lines 40–45)

"Russet Mead" derives from "L'Allegro" ("Russet Lawns," line 61) and Philomel from "Penseroso" (line 56). In Milton's silent uninhabited groves no "rude axe" is heard ("Penseroso," line 136). In Thomson's more plaintive yet realistic version it is the laboring woodman (himself part of the scenery) who hears nothing. When night falls Milton's Penseroso stands watch in a "high, lonely tower" and dreams Plato's dreams or the sad tales of tragedians. As the year declines Thomson's penseroso-poet is borne aloft in thought by "Philosophic Melancholy." His tender emotions are aroused not by a theatrical scene but by suffering humanity.

> Then forming *Fancy* rouses to conceive,
> What never mingled with the Vulgar's Dream:
> Then wake the tender Pang, the pitying Tear,
> The Sigh for suffering Worth, the Wish prefer'd,
> For Humankind, the Joy to see them bless'd.
>
> (lines 68–72)

As night returns Penseroso retires to the "studious cloister's pale" and "high embowered roof" where organ music dissolves him into ecstasies and brings "all heaven before [his] eyes." Thomson's poet, in similar fashion, seeks contemplative withdrawal; but his retreat is sylvan gothic rather than monastic:

> OH! bear me then to high, embowering, Shades;
> To twilight Groves, and visionary Vales;
> To weeping Grottos, and to hoary Caves;
> Where Angel-Forms are seen, and voices Heard,
> Sigh'd in low Whispers, that abstract the Soul,
> From outward Sense, far into Worlds remote.
>
> (lines 74–79)

It is primarily when Thomson wishes to retreat that he invokes the "Penseroso" note. While the "ceaseless Winds blow keen" without, he seeks refuge in

> A rural, shelter'd, solitary Scene;
> Where ruddy Fire, and beaming Tapers join
> To chase the chearless Gloom: there let me sit,
> And hold high Converse with the mighty Dead.
>
> (lines 256–59)[21]

For much of the poem, however, Thomson is interested not in retreat but in imaginatively braving the elements, and describing the terrible beauty of winter storms and landscapes. For this Milton's paired poems gave him little. As Thomson revised *Winter* after 1726 the "Penseroso" element in fact is reduced, perhaps because the device of the wandering rural observer who occasionally takes refuge in a grove or tower did not permit the kind of extended geographical excursions and political reflections that Thomson added to the poem as it grew.

For *Summer* Milton provided a more useful framework. Thomson's plan, he wrote to Mallet in 1726, was to "contract the Season into a Day,"[22] a plan reflected in the "Argument" to the poem that first appeared in 1730: "As the Face of Nature in this Season is almost Uniform, the Progress of the Poem is a Description of a Summer's Day." Just as Milton had followed Allegro and Penseroso through an ideal day, so Thomson provides descriptions of dawn, noon, sunset, evening, and night, even taking the temporal scheme so far as to specify the hour.[23] At regular intervals through the first half of the first edition of *Summer* (1727), as the summer's day proceeds Thomson's observer moves through the scene in Miltonic fashion, especially recalling Penseroso when he seeks relief from the heat:

> Hence, let me haste into the mid-wood Shade,
> Where scarce a Sun-Beam wanders thro' the Gloom;
> And, on the dark-green Grass, beside the Brink
> Of haunted Stream ... lie at large.
>
> (lines 9 – 12)

> as thro' the falling Glooms,
> Pensive, I muse
>
> (lines 180 – 81)

> Nor undelightful is the humming Sound
> To Him who muses, thro' the Woods, at Noon.
>
> (lines 264 – 65)

> Welcome, ye Shades! ye bowery Thickets hail!
> Ye lofty Pines! ye venerable Oaks!
>
> (lines 356 – 57)

> Still let me pierce into the midnight Depth
> Of yonder Grove, of wildest, largest Growth
>
> (lines 403 – 04)

> Beside the dewy Border let me sit,
> All in the Freshness of the humid Air.
>
> (lines 487 – 88)[24]

Having borrowed the device of the pensive wanderer from Milton, Thomson uses it in *Summer* not to allude to his predecessor,[25] but (more independently) to provide a simple framework for his long descriptive survey. As Thomson expanded *Summer* in 1730 and 1744 he found less occasion to use the "Penseroso" model, no doubt in part because the long "View of Summer in the Torrid Zone" (lines 635–1100, 1746 version) was better presented as a mental flight than the observations of a rural wanderer. And in the final two sections of *The Seasons*, *Spring* (1728) and *Autumn* (1730), his poem having outgrown its Miltonic origins, Thomson found progressively less use for "Il Penseroso." His point of view becomes broader and more flexible, reflecting a variety of interests in the natural scene.[26] Milton's Allegro and Penseroso found everywhere materials to gratify their specialized imaginations; Thomson discriminates less, and thus is more easily pleased. All sensations in Milton's poems pass through a single filter. Thomson imagines other observers and their delights.[27] Thus, in *Summer* he tells the tales of Celadon and Amelia, Damon and Musidora; in *Autumn* of Lavinia and Palemon. In *Spring* the poet appears prominently only once as the localized observer: "Oft let me wander o'er the dewy Fields, / Where Freshness breathes... / ... as thro' the verdant Maze / Of sweet-briar Hedges I pursue my Walk" (103–06). Elsewhere the poet's friend Lyttelton becomes the observer, as *he* strays through Hagley Park (904–62). The cares of absent love are expressed not through the narrator but through an imagined "Lover" who "restless runs / To glimmering Shades, and sympathetic Glooms; / Where the dun Umbrage o'er the falling Stream, / Romantic, hangs; there thro' the pensive Dusk / Strays" (1025–29). In *Autumn* too the "I" figures as a prominent point of observation only in a passage that originally appeared in the 1726 *Winter*.[28] To the extent that the poem's increasing sprawl is controlled, it is not by means of the single Miltonic observer, or a rigorously limited viewpoint. What began as a meditative lyric after Milton's early manner became, especially after 1727, more open to other kinds of influence (from Virgil, from contemporary scientific and travel writing) and governed by a looser decorum, broadly speaking that of the eighteenth-century georgic but encompassing elements of the physico-theological survey.

Paradise Lost and The Seasons

Among the other poems that resonate through the full *Seasons* none in fact is more prominent than *Paradise Lost*.[29] And although for Thomson the decorum of "Il Penseroso" proved too limiting, he found in *Paradise Lost* at least two generic structures that proved useful organizing frames as *The Seasons* expanded: the choric hymn and the formal theodicy.

It has been recognized since the eighteenth century that Thomson's "Hymn" concluding *The Seasons* is broadly similar to the famous

"Morning Hymn" sung by Adam and Eve in Eden (*Paradise Lost*, V. 153 – 208).[30] Sambrook has recently gone so far as to declare that the Morning Hymn "could almost be read as a programme for Thomson's [entire] poem" (p. xxxiii). To be sure, as he notes, *The Seasons* as a whole, like the Edenic hymn or like Raphael's account of Creation in Book VII or Psalm 148 (the ultimate model), is designed in Milton's words to "magnify" God's works (*Paradise Lost*, VII. 97).[31] More particularly the "Hymn" is manifestly indebted to Milton's hymn for its central section (lines 37 – 93) in which Thomson bids "every living Soul" to join him in adoration:

> To HIM, ye vocal Gales,
> Breathe soft, whose SPIRIT in your Freshness breathes
> ...And ye, whose bolder Note is heard afar,
> Who shake th'astonish'd World, lift high to Heaven
> Th'impetuous Song, and say from whom you rage.
> (lines 40 – 47)

Adam and Eve had likewise bid all creation sing God's praise – angels, stars, sun, moon, but also "mists and exhalations," winds, trees, and birds. Thomson effectively includes each of Milton's categories, though he varies the order and provides additional sensory details. Despite the broad similarity Thomson borrows surprisingly few details from Milton.[32] Where Milton most effectively serves him is in supplying the notion (not found in Psalm 148) that created nature praises God not by anthropomorphically singing but simply by being itself – what Hopkins might have called "selving." Thus the winds breathe, and the pines wave their tops "in sign of worship" (94). This idea forms the basis for Thomson's free variation or re-creation: in his responsive world torrents "sound," fruits and flowers "soft-roll" their incense, forests "bend" and harvests "wave," each verb naturally appropriate and at the same time a "sign of worship." More generally, Milton's hymn supplied Thomson the notion that the "ceaseless change" of nature can "Vary to our great maker still new praise" (V. 183 – 84). Thomson echoes this note in the opening of the "Hymn" – "These, as they change, ALMIGHTY FATHER, these / Are but the varied GOD" (1 – 2) and confirms what was implicit in the *Seasons* as a whole: it is the "ceaseless change" of nature, traced through the course of the year, within an overarching harmony, that Thomson most celebrates.

Theodicy, the other generic structure in *Paradise Lost* that helped Thomson to shape *The Seasons*, is best seen at the end of *Winter*, the season that presents the most obvious challenge to the belief that God's ways to man are just. Despite a survey of wintry horrors that leave man in the "dreary Labyrinth of Fate" (1023), Thomson finds several means to justify providence, from the bracing health induced by clear winter days to the spring (both natural and immortal) which will surely follow, and the widening perspective in which "The great Eternal Scheme" will at last appear a "perfect Whole" (1046–47).[33] Perhaps appropriately the ultimate theodician claim – "Partial Evil" is "Universal Good" – comes only at the end of a very long poem. One might argue that it has been prepared for on numerous occasions when Thomson invoked the "larger Prospects" (*Winter*, 579) or the hope for "endless Growth and infinite Ascent" (*Winter*, 607) characteristic of his theory of spiritual evolution. But few readers of *The Seasons* would claim that the theodicean element is more than intermittently present.[34] The Miltonic theodicy, like the hymn, served Thomson as a means of encompassing his vast subject, but he did not feel bound by generic frames.

Thomson's theodicy, for example, despite its general debt to Milton, is based far more on the manifest goodness of the created world than on any thoroughgoing (and Miltonic) understanding of the role of evil in God's scheme. Put another way, in *The Seasons* there is no Satan, no Fall, and no Redeemer. Whereas Milton directs our attention to supernatural figures, Thomson finds everything in nature, and does without celestial or infernal machines. Sambrook observes that in *The Seasons* Thomson always "emphasizes God's immanence – never his transcendence" (p. 396). God's hand is often immediately present, but we are not asked to imagine him beyond his creation. Not only is Christ not present; Thomson makes no reference at all to the religious scheme founded on his Incarnation, Sacrifice, and Redemption – what after all remains the strongest argument in the Christian theodicy. Nor is there an incarnate principle of evil, a Satan who embodies or calls out the evil in men's hearts. The several examples of human malice and cruelty in *The Seasons* are not referred to any single principle or source. Perhaps this is explained by Thomson's assertion that evil only "seems" or is "deemed" to exist.[35] As he once wrote to Elizabeth Young, "There is no real Evil in the whole general System of Things; it is only our Ignorance that makes it appear so, and Pain and Death but serve to unfold his gracious Purposes of Love."[36] Milton, by contrast, affirmed that evil existed in the world, if not as an independent power then as the absence of good: those like Satan who fall away from God fall into evil.

Thomson clearly found Satan a powerful presence in *Paradise Lost*, for he often alludes to Books I and II in which Satan figures prominently, but he curiously (and repeatedly) neutralizes the opprobrium carried by the allusion and applies the lines to some innocent or at least amoral feature in the natural world. Thus Thomson alludes to the simile that compares Satan to a sleeping Leviathan in describing arctic sailors who moor their boat "Beneath the Shelter of an icy Isle / While Night o'erwhelms the Sea" (*Winter*, 1006–07, cf. *Paradise Lost*, I. 207–08). Elsewhere he remembers the comparison between Satan and the evening sun breaking through clouds (*Paradise Lost*, II. 488–94) in the description of grateful nature and bleating flocks after a summer afternoon storm (*Summer*, 1223–34). The similes comparing Satan to the sun eclipsed or shining weakly through "horizontal misty air" (*Paradise Lost*, I. 594–99) and the withered glory of the fallen angels to "forest oaks, or mountain pines" "scath'd" by lightning (*Paradise Lost*, I. 612–15) echo in Thomson's lines on the autumnal sun that glares through the fogs and "frights the Nations" (*Autumn*, 724) and the lightning-struck "Mountain-Pine…scath'd to Heaven" (*Summer*, 788–89).[37] Thomson's lines on the autumnal moon, "Full-orb'd," her "spotted disk" revealing "mountains…dales / And caverns deep, as optic tube descries" (1089–93), recall Satan's shield, compared to the moon

> whose orb
> Through optic glass the Tuscan artist viewed
> At evening from the top of Fesole,
> Or in Valdarno, to descry new Lands,
> Rivers or mountains in her spotty globe.
> (I. 287–91)[38]

Similes that compare Satan to "a black mist low creeping" (IX. 180) and a "wand'ring fire, / Compact of unctuous vapor, which the Night / Condenses" (IX. 634–36) reappear in Thomson's descriptions of an autumnal evening:

> humid Evening, gliding o'er the Sky,
> In her chill Progress, to the ground condens'd
> The Vapours throws. Where the creeping Waters ooze,
> Where Marshes stagnate, and where Rivers wind,
> Cluster the rolling Fogs, and swim along
> The dusky-mantled Lawn.
> (*Autumn*, 1083–88)

In Milton evening mists are repeatedly associated with Satan, who invades the garden "wrapt in mist / Of midnight vapor" to "glide obscure" (IX. 158–59), or with the fallen world when evenings bring "black air / …damps and dreadful glooms" (X. 847–48), and with the pain of the expulsion, when the cherubim descending from their high post are compared to "Evening Mist" which "Risen from a river o'er the marish glides, / And gathers ground fast" (XII. 628–30). But Thomson's mists suggest no malevolent supernatural agency. The scene is almost wholly naturalized, a scientific description of a damp autumnal evening on low marshy ground.

The effect of Thomson's many allusions is unusually complex. Typically he focuses not on Satan himself, but on familiar similes attached to him.[39] The reader is asked to register the Satanic associations but then to dismiss them since in Thomson's world evil agency is not required to account for lightning or mists. Satan is in effect consciously and deliberately recalled and then excluded from the poem. Hence perhaps the most striking of Thomson's allusions to Satan: "Welcome, kindred Glooms! / Cogenial Horrors, hail!" (*Winter*, 5-6). Here Thomson takes over Satan's own words, "hail horrors, hail / Infernal world" (*Paradise Lost*, I. 250-51), wittily implying at the outset of his poem that there would appear to be something diabolical about the man who can find winter congenial.[40] But Thomson quickly rejects the Satanic associations and establishes that winter is welcome in its way. The allusion is an especially clear example of the way in which Thomson feels free to turn Milton on his head.

Just as there is no Satan or Satanic principle in *The Seasons*, so there is no Fall. The myth that underlies *Paradise Lost* divides time into three periods, an Edenic paradise never again to be recovered on earth; a Fall into our world of woe; and future recovery of a "paradise within," or an eternal paradise at the end of time. Thomson's myth likewise provides for an innocent golden age at the beginning, and a final paradise of rest when "one unbounded Spring" will "encircle ALL."[41] Although he allows for a general and gradual decline from innocent beginnings to a more corrupt present, Thomson makes do without the crisis of the Fall.

His fullest account of the decline from Eden comes in *Spring*, where Thomson contrasts the "Prime of Days" (271), when "uncorrupted Man" still "liv'd in Innocence" (237, 242), with "these Iron Times" (274). As in *Paradise Lost*, one sign of the decline is the oppression of the seasonal cycle. No longer does the earth enjoy "Great Spring" all the year. Now summer brings "pestilential Heats," autumn "sickly Damps," and winter "his Waste of Snows" (318-29).[42] Storms without have their parallel within. Now, for Thomson, "the Passions all / Have burst their Bounds" in "foul Disorder," and "Convulsive Anger storms at large" (278-82), recalling Adam and Eve's rain of tears and "high winds worse within / ...high passions, anger, hate" that "shook sore / Their inward state of mind, calm region once / And full of peace, now tossed and turbulent" (*Paradise Lost*, IX. 1121-26). But Thomson nowhere explains how man has passed from one state to the other, as if reluctant to bind himself to a mythology or a theology that sees man natively corrupt and Eden irrecoverable. His account of the

Flood (*Spring*, 309 – 16) perhaps hints that he continues to hold out hope for a new beginning.

> Hence, in old dusky Time, a Deluge came:
> When the deep-cleft disparting Orb, that arch'd
> The central Waters round, impetuous rush'd,
> With universal Burst, into the Gulph,
> And o'er the high-pil'd Hills of fractur'd Earth
> Wide-dash'd the Waves, in Undulation vast;
> Till, from the Center to the streaming Clouds,
> A shoreless Ocean tumbled round the Globe.

Thomson relies on Thomas Burnet's *Sacred Theory of the Earth* for his science (the notion that the shell of the earth collapsed, and the waters under the earth poured forth),[43] but takes many verbal details from Milton. The rushing waters derive from the rain that "down rushed… / Impetuous" (*Paradise Lost*, XI. 743 – 44) and the shoreless ocean from his "sea without shore" (XI. 750). Other details derive, however, not from the account of the Flood in Book XI but the creation story in Book VII, which begins (like Burnet's narrative) with the "waters underneath" separated from "those above" by a firm "partition" (VII. 267 – 69). Thomson's "high-pil'd Hills" (313)[44] recall the mountains and "tumid hills" that "upheave" their backs in Milton (285 – 88). The wide-dashing waves suggest "the watery throng, / Wave rolling after wave" (297 – 98), and the disparting orb (in Thomson's final version) echoes the creative moment when like conglobed to like, and the unlike "to several place / Disparted" (240 – 41). That Thomson drew equally on two separate "floods" in Milton (both the original and the purgative) suggests that for him in some way the Deluge was not so much a cleansing as a creative renewal of the earth, and that Edenic conditions may in fact be restored. Man no longer enjoys eternal spring, but the central premise of *The Seasons* is that every season brings pleasures and a sense of God's presence: "the rolling Year / Is full of THEE" ("Hymn", 2 – 3).[45] Change itself gratifies. It is as if Thomson recalled Raphael's account of the "Grateful vicissitude" in Heaven (VI. 8) in which light and darkness lodge by turns; or, more aptly, Eve's song, which declares that "All seasons and their change, all please alike" (IV. 640).[46] What Eve says here of the several times of day (for as yet there were no seasons in our sense), Thomson – re-writing Milton – says of the entire "rolling Year."

Despite such manifest delight in man's natural conditions, Thomson is not naively "optimistic" or "complacent," though these charges continue to be lodged against him. Nor does he conceal the cruelty of the natural world which can stiffen the "Disaster'd" wanderer into a frozen corpse (*Winter*, 276 – 321) or bury pilgrims under a "Waste of burning Sand'' (*Summer*, 959 – 79). *The Seasons* as a whole makes plain the extent of ''the Wants and Miseries of Human Life'' (Argument to *Winter*), ''the sad Variety of Pain'' (*Winter*, 328), and ''shameful Variance betwixt Man and Man'' (331). As he surveys the human and natural worlds Thomson by turns finds cause for both distress and delight. Where Milton draws a sharp line between unfallen Eden, a world of innocence, delight, and divine presence, and our fallen world of depravity, woe, and divine displeasure, Thomson, having blurred the line of demarcation, sees around him both harmony and disharmony, enlightenment and darkness. For Milton the only recovery of paradise comes from Christ's intervention and from a ''paradise within.'' For Thomson the fallen world offers greater opportunities for redemption through displays of virtue and benevolence, or the gradual progress from barbarism to civilization.[47] But Thomson's difference from Milton – and his debt to him – can be seen most clearly in those climactic moments in *Spring*, *Summer*, and *Autumn* when a Miltonic garden paradise is regained.

Paradise unlost

At the end of *Spring* Thomson celebrates the pleasures of a ''pure and happy'' human love (''Argument''). He has gradually built toward this moment by describing how the animal world – both birds and beasts – responds to ''NATURE's *great Command*'' (634) with courtship and mating, and then ''th'infusive Force of Spring on Man'' (868). The ''Whole'' of the poem concludes, as he notes in the 1729 list of contents, with ''the Happiness of a pure, mutual Love, founded on Friendship, conducted with Honour, and confirmed by Children.'' As with many others in the eighteenth century, Thomson's ideas about mutual human love were colored by Milton, and it thus is not surprising to find significant allusion, at the end of *Spring*, to the nuptial bower of Adam and Eve. Like Milton, Thomson contrasts the calm happiness of his virtuous lovers with ''Raptures, Pangs, and Jealousies'' (from the list of ''Contents'') of what passes for courtship and love. Indeed, his juxtaposition of the ''warm Youth'' who leads a life of ''fever'd Rapture, or of cruel Care'' (1110) with ''the happiest of their Kind'' (1113) might have been suggested by Milton's brief dismissal of ''court amours'' and the ''starved lover'' singing to ''his proud fair'' in favor of wedded love, the source of both ''human offspring'' (*Paradise Lost*, IV. 750) and of the ''happiest'' love (774). And Milton's stress on the *mutuality* of ideal wedded love provided the theme which Thomson freely and independently develops:

> 'Tis not the coarser Tie of human Laws,
> Unnatural oft, and foreign to the Mind,
> That binds their Peace, but Harmony itself,
> Attuning all their Passions into Love;
> Where Friendship full-exerts her softest Power,
> Perfect Esteem enliven'd by Desire
> Ineffable, and Sympathy of Soul;
> Thought meeting Thought, and Will preventing Will,
> With boundless Confidence: for nought but Love
> Can answer Love, and render Bliss secure.
>
> (lines 1116–25)

Although Milton does not declare that the joys of wedded love were lost at the Fall, he nonetheless locates his highest praise of marriage in unfallen Eden, moments before the dream-temptation of Eve. That such joys are precarious is indicated by the elegiac note with which Milton-as-narrator blesses the lovers – "Sleep on / Blest pair; and O yet happiest if ye seek / No happier state" (IV. 773–75). For Thomson, it would appear, virtuous love can have nothing to fear, as his trans-formation of Milton's bower scene shows. Adam and Eve embracing sleep while on "their naked limbs the flowery roof [of their bower] / Showered roses" (771–73). As they sleep, Eve dreams of flying and of living the life of the gods, and wakes distressed. Spring likewise "sheds her own rosy Garland" (1169) on the heads of Thomson's lovers – thus securing the allusion to Milton's bower. But Thomson then makes Milton's Edenic day a metaphor for a whole lifetime of happiness:

> consenting SPRING
> Sheds her own rosy Garland on their Heads:
> Till Evening comes at last, serene and mild;
> When after the long vernal Day of Life,
> Enamour'd more, as more Remembrance swells
> With many a Proof of recollected Love,
> Together down they sink in social Sleep;
> Together freed, their gentle Spirits fly
> To Scenes were Love and Bliss immortal reign.
>
> (lines 1169–76)

For them old age will come with the mildness of a Miltonic evening, and the passage to death and immortal bliss will be as easy and joyous as falling asleep in Eden. Unlike Eve they will wake from their dreams to find themselves in Heaven. In Thomson's sanguine view virtuous lovers need never leave paradise.[48]

Thomson does not claim, however, that virtuous love guarantees a secure mortal passage. Another transformation of Milton's Edenic marriage suggests that the dangers to be faced are not the threat of temptation from within but the sudden and inexorable strokes of fate.

The tale of Celadon and Amelia (*Summer*, 1171–1222) is an ironic re-writing of Eve's dream and Adam's subsequent reassurance in Book V of *Paradise Lost*. These lovers, formed with both virtue and grace, love each other in perfect innocence:

> They lov'd. But such their guileless Passion was,
> As in the Dawn of Time inform'd the Heart
> Of Innocence, and undissembling Truth.
>
> (lines 1177–79)

To make these lovers clearly Miltonic, Thomson insists repeatedly on the mutuality of their wishes and eyes (1180–82) and locates them in Eden, where, "with each other blest, creative Love / Still bade eternal *Eden* smile around" (1193–94). The "harmonious Intercourse" of their life is interrupted not by a tempter but a tempest: "So pass'd their Life, a clear united Stream, / By Care unruffled; till, in evil Hour, , The Tempest caught them on the tender Walk / Heedless how far, and where its Mazes stray'd" (1189–92). Behind these lovers stands Milton's Eve, who had herself strayed "From her best prop so far, and storm so nigh" (IX. 433), and who "in evil hour" (IX. 1067) listened to the tempter/ serpent, repeatedly associated by Milton with "mazy folds" (IX. 161, cf. IX. 499). Thomson blends the actual temptation scene in *Paradise Lost* with the earlier dream-temptation, and has his Amelia, like Eve, weep in fear of present and future dangers: "her Eye / Fell tearful, wetting her disorder'd Cheek" (1198). Celadon plays the role of Adam, reassuring Amelia that she is innocent since there has been no "inward Storm" (1206). Milton's point is that, since God is reasonable and since reason is man's prime faculty, "Evil into the mind of god or man / May come or go, so unapproved, and leave / No spot or blame behind" (V. 117–19). Thus Adam and Eve emerge from the episode with calm restored. Thomson's point is Job's – the uncertainty of fate, or rather the mysterious and finally unfathomable ways of God. At the moment Celadon embraces the reassured Amelia, a bolt of lightning melodramatically strikes her to the ground, "A blacken'd Corse" (1216). Since we have been induced by the running Miltonic parallel to expect resolution of Amelia's fears, her sudden death is all the more shocking, and Celadon's speechless "Amazement" an image of our own. The moral seriousness of Milton's episode is perhaps cheapened in the retelling, since Amelia's fears and her self-awareness are by comparison with Eve's trivial. But Thomson might answer that in a fallen world Adam's confidence is misplaced. For Milton as for Thomson theodicy is based on reason: the justness of God's ways can be rationally understood. But Thomson makes the refinement of "reason's eye" a slow and difficult process. From the "dreary labyrinth of fate" (an antiMiltonic notion) God's ways in depriving lovers of their paradise may well seem cruel and unjust.

Elsewhere in *Summer*, as if to balance the tale of Celadon and Amelia, Thomson presents an earthly Eden where God sends not bolts of lightning but gracious messengers. The scene is no literal garden but a shadowy grove where the poet finds "the Haunts of Meditation," the scenes where

> Antient Bards th'inspiring Breath,
> Extatic, felt; and from this World retir'd,
> Convers'd with Angels, and immortal Forms,
> On gracious Errands bent: to save the Fall
> Of Virtue struggling on the Brink of Vice;
> In waking Whispers, and repeated Dreams,
> To hint pure Thought, and warn the favour'd Soul
> For future Trials fated to prepare;
> To prompt the Poet, who devoted gives
> His Muse to better Themes.
>
> (lines 522–32)

Here are the dreams of Adam and Eve, both those that calm – "For God is also in sleep, and dreams advise, / Which he hath sent propitious" (*Paradise Lost*, XII. 611–12) – and those that warn (like the dream-temptation). Here too are Milton's Raphael and his fellow angels sent "On errands of supernal grace" (VII. 573). In Thomson they come "to save the Fall / Of Virtue," but the line-ending encourages us to think, momentarily, while the word "Fall" itself stands at the "Brink," that such angelic visitors to a poet's haunts of meditation might well "save the Fall" itself. When in *Autumn* Thomson again takes up the theme of virtuous rural retreat he once more remembers an Eden visited by angels. "The pure Pleasures of the RURAL LIFE" is a very common theme in eighteenth-century georgic poems, as derived from Virgil's second Georgic. But Thomson gives it Miltonic coloring:

> This is the Life which those who fret in Guilt,
> And guilty Cities, never knew; the Life
> Led by Primeval Ages, uncorrupt,
> When Angels dwelt, and GOD himself, with Man!
>
> (lines 1347–50)

Edenic evenings

Thomson's appropriations of Milton's Edenic story mark his clearly as an eighteenth-century imagination. Like Philips before him, like Dyer and Akenside after him, Thomson found in rural English nature, especially in meditative retreat, traces of the Edenic paradise that Milton

declared had been lost. Like celebrants of English landscape gardening
he saw in Stowe a "fair Majestic Paradise" (*Autumn*, 1042). And like
the evening poets of mid-century, for whom he seems to have served as
a sort of mediator of Milton's influence, Thomson was inspired by
Milton's description of a moonlit evening in Eden (IV. 598 – 609). His
own two extended evening scenes (*Autumn*, 950 – 63, 1088 – 1102, and
Summer, 1647 – 98) are perhaps the subtlest and most poetically effective
indication that he can see in the natural world around him the kind of
serenity and harmony that Milton saw only in Eden.

The evening scene in *Autumn* is signalled first by deepening shade:

> But see the fading many-colour'd Woods,
> Shade deepening over Shade, the Country round
> Imbrown; a crowded Umbrage, dusk, and dun,
> Of every Hue, from wan declining Green
> To sooty Dark.
>
> (lines 950 – 54)

"Umbrage," "imbrown," "dusk" (as an adjective), and "dun" all
come from Milton.[49] Thomson notices above all the softening light:

> Mean-time, light-shadowing all, a sober Calm
> Fleeces unbounded Ether; whose least Wave
> Stands tremulous, uncertain where to turn
> The gentle Current; while illumin'd wide,
> The dewy-skirted Clouds imbibe the Sun,
> And thro' their lucid Veil his soften'd Force
> Shed o'er the peaceful World.
>
> (lines 957 – 63)

Almost substantial, even liquid, Thomson's sunlight is made gentler
by being filtered through the veil of clouds. In the literary background
we may sense Milton's "silver mantle" of moonlight thrown over the
dark. Thomson's re-writing combines pre-Newtonian scientific theory,
empirical observation, and a Miltonic appreciation for the beneficence
of heaven-directed light.

Later, as in Milton, twilight yields to the moon:

> Meanwhile the Moon,
> Full-orb'd, and breaking thro' the scatter'd Clouds,
> Shews her broad Visage in the crimson'd East.
> Turn'd to the Sun direct, her spotted Disk,
> Where Mountains rise, umbrageous Dales descend,
> And Caverns deep, as optic Tube descries,
> A smaller Earth, gives all his Blaze again,
> Void of it's Flame, and sheds a softer Day.
>
> (lines 1088 – 95)

Again light is first made "soft" before it is shed on the world below. Like Milton's queen, Thomson's benign moon suggests a force in nature to counterbalance darkness and cold. The compensatory movement implied by the moon's soft light becomes even clearer as the passage concludes:

> Now thro' the passing Cloud she seems to stoop,
> Now up the pure Cerulean rides sublime.
> Wide the pale Deluge floats, and streaming mild
> O'er the sky'd Mountain to the shadowy Vale,
> While Rocks and Floods reflect the quivering Gleam,
> The whole Air whitens with a boundless Tide
> Of silver Radiance, trembling round the World.
>   (lines 1096–1102)

Thomson's full moon is a mix of Popean splendor and Miltonic humility. The moon stooping through the passing cloud derives from "Il Penseroso,"[50] but the tide of silver radiance recalls Pope's *Iliad*.[51] In a typically Thomsonian sequence, then, "shorten'd Day" (line 1082) and obscurity give way to "softer Day" (line 1095) and finally to the sublime moment of full illumination.[52]

Thomson's other evening scene appears in *Summer*. Again the larger shape or rhythm is from darkness to light:

> Confess'd from yonder slow-extinguish'd Clouds,
> All Ether softening, sober Evening takes
> Her wonted Station in the middle Air;
> A thousand Shadows at her Beck. First This
> She sends on Earth; then That of deeper Dye
> Steals soft behind; and then a Deeper still,
> In Circle following Circle, gathers round,
> To close the Face of Things.
>   (lines 1647–54)

The station in the middle air may suggest the kind of allegorical painting Jean Hagstrum adduced as analogues to Thomson's word-painting, or William Kent's 1730 frontispiece to *The Seasons*, in which a goddess strews petals on the earth from the middle sky.[53] But the confessed deity quickly blends with her element, and her "thousand Shadows" never attain pictorial form. The epithet "sober" (subdued in color, sedate in demeanor), later to become a favorite term in the evening tradition, no doubt derives from Twilight's "sober Livery" in Milton. The shadows at Evening's beck perhaps correspond to the spirits (Twilight, Silence, the starry host) that animate Milton's Edenic evening scene.

But Thomson's real concern here is not with Milton, nor is it with personified evening. The passage suggests a predominant interest in effects of light, color, and gathering darkness. The light in Thomson's world is not so much Milton's "holy Light" as it is the natural light analysed in Newton's *Opticks*.[54] In the "Hymn to Solitude" Thomson describes the way "Evening scenes decay, / And the faint landskip swims away." In "To the Memory of Sir Isaac Newton," the sequence of colors in the rainbow is made to match the succession of colors through the day, from "flaming RED" and "tawny ORANGE" through yellow and green,

> Then the pure BLUE, that swells autumnal skies,
> Ethereal play'd; and then, of sadder hue,
> Emerg'd the deepen'd INDIGO, as when
> The heavy-skirted evening droops with frost
> While the last gleamings of refracted light
> Dy'd in the fainting VIOLET away.
>
> (lines 106–11)[55]

The same concern with fading light appears as Thomson's *Summer* evening scene continues, but here his focus is more clearly centered on the observing eye within the scene:

> Evening yields
> The World to Night; not in her Winter-Robe
> Of massy Stygian Woof, but loose array'd
> In Mantle dun. A faint erroneous Ray,
> Glanc'd from th'imperfect Surfaces of Things,
> Flings half an Image on the straining Eye;
> While wavering Woods, and Villages, and Streams,
> And Rocks, and Mountain-tops that long retain'd
> Th'ascending gleam, are all one swimming Scene,
> Uncertain if beheld.
>
> (lines 1684–93)

Winter's "Mantle" is all that suggests a Miltonic origin here, and the only survival in the scene from the allegorical tradition. The passage is a fine example of Thomson at his best and most creative, describing a scene of fading light in a way that Milton never does, even in "Il Penseroso" with its loved half-light. Thomson tries to capture the moments just before total darkness as they appear to "the straining Eye" under natural conditions in which the scene dissolves ("one swimming Scene") and wavers because all outline has been lost.[56] The inability to discern the clear outlines of the natural scene is recurrent in *The Seasons*,[57] and serves as an index of man's failure to "see" with reason's eye the grand eternal scheme. But man in *The Seasons* is never left without a guide for long. To clarify the scene Thomson turns on the lights as the passage concludes:

> Sudden to Heaven
> Thence weary Vision turns; there, leading soft
> The silent Hours of Love, with purest Ray
> Sweet Venus shines; and from her genial Rise,
> When Day-Light sickens till it springs afresh,
> Unrival'd reigns, the fairest Lamp of Night.
>
> (lines 1693–98)

Weary vision is here freshened, as the natural scene is re-inhabited by allegorical presences. Here Venus, the evening star and the traditional harbinger of love, leads a dance of the Hours. Like Milton's queenly moon, Venus "unrival'd reigns, the fairest Lamp of Night." Her pure ray corresponds to the flood of moonlight in the *Autumn* evening, each a sudden revelation from above and a sign of Heaven's beneficent scheme.

Most of the elements in Thomson's *Summer* evening have their origin (or their analogue) in Milton – personified Evening, the sober color and mood, Hesperus/Venus, gray dusk yielding to a flood of light, even the pensive observer. And yet the whole is plainly Thomson's own creation. Not only has he recombined and transformed Miltonic materials, but he has established a new perspective on them, not the omniscient point of view of Milton's inspired epic narrator, or the self-conscious and selective eye of "Il Penseroso," nor yet the passive eye of the descriptive nature poet. Thomson's eye is adventurous, active, seeing now a wholly naturalized scene and now its emergent allegorical spirits. It is acutely attuned to effects of light, especially as they obscure or clarify the patterns that he seeks always to comprehend behind the seasonal face of things.

The Seasons stands then as a monument to the fruitful influence of Milton's poetry. There is no doubt that Thomson's finest poem – and one of the major poems of the century – was largely inspired by "Il Penseroso" and *Paradise Lost*, and in part built with materials quarried from Milton's poems, and re-shaped for their new use. To concede that *Paradise Lost* is an incomparably greater poem than Thomson's major work is only to say what could be said of almost all post-Miltonic poems. Thomson's work, neither in his own eyes nor in ours, can be said to compete with Milton's. In *Paradise Lost*, because of Milton's rigorous and coherent conception, every element has its place and function. Thomson's imagination is less disciplined, cheerfully eclectic, and his poem governed (if that is not too strong a word) by a looser conception of decorum. But what Thomson accomplished, with Milton's help, he did better than anybody else. Milton may have pointed the way, but it remained for Thomson to devote a poet's eye to what Johnson called "the appearances of things as they are successively varied by the vicissitudes of the year.'' And as Johnson went on to say, paying proper tribute to Thomson's originality, ''The reader of *The Seasons* wonders that he never saw before what Thomson shews him, and that he never yet has felt what Thomson impresses.''[58]

11 · JOHNSON

For Thomson, as for Dryden and Pope before him, and many lesser writers at mid-century, Milton's works served not to oppress but to stimulate the poetic imagination as it responded to Milton's stances – the wandering observer, the defiant champion – or his central myth of a lost garden. But there is another side to the story. It is not that Milton also intimidated the same writers by his massive achievement, or left them in despair of matching his greatness. True, especially at mid-century, English poets became increasingly self-conscious, unsure of their audience, finding problematic their relationship both with immediate predecessors (Dryden and Pope) and admired Renaissance masters (Spenser and Milton). But Collins and Gray found ways to turn that self-consciousness to account, and to tap Milton's power even as they declare that a Miltonic poetry is no longer possible. It is rather that Milton left two enduring images, in his life and his work, with the power to trouble a Christian culture still deeply affected by the conditional promise of salvation and the ever-present possibility of damnation. One image centers in Milton himself: unceasing dedication to high and holy purpose, unshakable faith and a sense of divine guidance. This image could of course inspire emulation, but one might well despair of emulating so high an ideal. The other centers on Milton's Satan, in almost every way the poet's antithesis, trapped in a hellish prison largely of his own making, afflicted by despair and convinced that he can never find a place at God's table. It is this Satan – not the defiant Romantic Satan, heroically proud and self-assertive – that preoccupies the later eighteenth century. Johnson and Cowper may stand as two late-eighteenth-century examples – they write within twenty-five years of Blake's *Marriage of Heaven and Hell* and *Milton* – of writers for whom Milton indeed provokes both admiration and anxiety. That anxiety, however, is not prompted by Milton as a writer but by the strength and substance of his Christian beliefs.

Johnson and the biographical tradition

Since its publication in 1779 commentators have found Johnson's *Life of Milton* remarkable for its author's antipathy to his subject. The most common explanation among contemporary critics was that Johnson's response to Milton was essentially based on "the virulent malignity of his political resentment," as Blackburne shrilly put it in his *Remarks on Johnson's Life of Milton* (1780).[1] Or as the poet Cowper wittily noted, "A Pensioner is not likely to Spare a Republican."[2] Cowper's friend William Hayley, an admirer of Johnson, likewise observed "how far the virulence of political hatred may pervert a powerful mind."[3] But Hayley was also able to recognize that Johnson had in fact written a "truly eloquent and splendid encomium" on *Paradise Lost*. He was perhaps the first of many critics to comment on the striking contradictions in the *Life*, where, as he says, "an ill-subdued propensity to censure is ever combatting with a necessity to commend" (p. 13). Recent critics have continued to note the disparity between Johnson's disapproval of Milton's character, religion, and politics, and his high praise for much of the poetry. They note too the "fascinating contradictions"[4] in the discussion of *Paradise Lost* itself, and have offered some tentative or partial explanations for them. In my view the contradictions in the *Life* do indeed reveal Johnson's animus toward Milton, but we have to go beyond previous explanations – political hatred, the uncritical adulation of readers and credulity of earlier biographers, or ambivalence about the sublime – in order to understand fully Johnson's reaction. The *Life of Milton* is Johnson's mighty contest with an equally strong writer who compels both his disapproval and his admiration. Although Bate has suggested that Johnson, a strong and independent critic, was "unable to be intimidated," I would argue that for once Johnson had in this "mighty poet"[5] more than met his match. Whatever anxiety Johnson feels, however, is produced not so much by Milton's literary works as by his achievement as a man – his self-discipline, devotion, and religious conviction.

To stress the personal and psychological roots of Johnson's hostility is not to reject other explanations. Political disapproval was doubtless partly responsible for the tension and pressure that characterize the *Life*. Milton was not only a loud opponent of Johnson's own monarchical principles and of the established Anglican church; he actually justified the murder of the "unhappy Charles,"[6] and was an enemy, so Johnson claimed, to the very system of subordination and obedience to legitimate authority that constitutes proper government. Milton's political principles are mistaken; moreover, in Johnson's view they are not even intellectually respectable. Although the famous paragraphs on Milton's "political notions" are offered as brief summary and not as careful analysis, it is nonetheless striking that Johnson treats the evidence in a heavily partisan manner.

For example, when Milton turns against the Presbyterians, whom he had previously supported, Johnson sees not consistent principle, or even a genuine change of heart, but mere "humour." "He that changes his party by his humour is not more virtuous than he that changes it by his interest; he loves himself rather than truth" (I, 106). Johnson was much more generous or tolerant in his observations on Dryden who, he simply said, had "changed with the nation" (*Lives*, I, 334). He reports too with contempt that "it is not known that Milton gave any better reason" for his republicanism than that "a popular government was the most frugal, for the trappings of a monarchy would set up an ordinary commonwealth." To this remark Johnson can triumphantly reply that "it is very shallow policy that supposes money to be the chief good." Milton's remark in fact derives from Toland, who reports it as a "pleasant story," that is, a joke, Milton's light response to the question "what made him side with the republicans?" Not only does Johnson misjudge or willfully misinterpret a light-hearted remark, but he stubbornly pretends that Milton never gave a better reason. Instead Johnson relies on slightly-hedged conjectural interpretation and on suspicion. He "is afraid" that Milton's republicanism was founded "in an envious hatred of greatness." "It is to be suspected," he suggests, "that Milton felt not so much the love of liberty as repugnance to authority." Here Johnson probably seeks to refute such biographers as Toland who had celebrated Milton as a defender of liberty.[7] But Johnson refuses to admit that Milton's principles, however mistaken, might be sincerely professed. In so doing he also refutes the conclusion of sympathetic biographers from Aubrey to Newton – even when they did not share his politics – that Milton acted out of pure zeal and high principle.

This respect for a man of opposing principles, which Fenton and other biographers display, is present in fact in two of Johnson's own early biographies in the *Gentleman's Magazine*. In the *Life of Blake* Johnson pays handsome tribute to the famous Parliamentary admiral Robert Blake as a good, courageous, and principled man. "When the civil war broke out," Johnson says,

Blake, in conformity with his avowed principles, declared for the parliament, and thinking a bare declaration for right not all the duty of a good man, raised a troop of dragoons for his party... He continued, on many occasions, to give proofs of an insuperable courage, and a steadiness of resolution not to be shaken.[8]

In another early biography Johnson likewise praises the Puritan Francis Cheynel as a man of integrity in almost identical terms:

When the war broke out, Mr. Cheynel, in consequence of his principles, declared himself for the Parliament; and as he appears to have held it as a first principle, that all great and noble spirits abhor neutrality, there is no doubt but that he exerted himself to gain proselytes, and to promote the interest of that party which he had thought it his duty to espouse.[9]

Repeatedly Johnson notes Cheynel's sincerity. He is "a man who thinks his cause just" (p. 196). He was doubtless "incited by a sincere belief" (p. 197). He could "suffer as well as act in a cause he believed just" (p. 208).

What accounts then for Johnson's "inconsistent hostility" (as Hayley describes it, pp. 128–29), whereby he represents as honorable in Blake "the very principles and conduct which he endeavours to make infamous and contemptible in Milton?" Blake is celebrated for maintaining his post and discharging his trust even after Cromwell assumed power. "It is not," Blake had said, "the business of a seaman to mind state affairs, but to hinder foreigners from fooling us." And yet Milton is censured for "continuing to exercise his office under a manifest usurpation." Perhaps some of this inconsistency can be explained by Blake's simple devotion to his non-political duty, and to his success in instilling in the fleet, by means of his loyalty, "the surest foundation of unanimity and steadiness" (p. 54). Furthermore, Blake "did not approve the death of Charles I" but on the contrary "declared he would venture to save him." Perhaps too we should remember that the *Lives* of Blake and Cheynel were written early in Johnson's career, at a time when he took some pride and pleasure in railing at oppressive governments – in *London*, for example, or *Marmor Norfolciense*. In the years since Johnson's early biographies Blake and Cheynel had remained of merely historical interest, while Milton's fame as a poet and a vindicator of political liberty had grown louder and wider, thanks in large part to the efforts of a few well-placed writers and editors.

Johnson himself had used the editions of Toland, an early champion of Milton's politics, and his successor-editors at mid-century, Birch and Newton, who celebrated Milton's "love of liberty." He disapproved of Thomas Hollis's efforts to distribute Milton's "democratical works" in the 1760s and 1770s.[10] No doubt Johnson knew too that popular "Whig" histories of the English Civil War – by Mrs. Macaulay, John Wilkes, and others – kept Milton's name before the public in a favorable light.[11] Though such radical Whigs were few in number, Johnson may well have thought that such a vocal group, with access to the press, constituted a real threat to English political stability; and that the praise of Milton's politics needed to be answered in print. As Hollis's biographer, Francis Blackburne, noted in 1780, "Dr. Johnson's peace of mind required that this recovering taste of the public [for seventeenth-century republican writings] should not ripen into appetite, particularly for Milton's works."[12]

Political animus clearly contributed to Johnson's portrait of Milton, but even Hayley concluded (rightly, I think) that "Johnson's rancour against Milton" is not merely political. One other striking feature of Johnson's portrait suggests that political rancor is not the sole cause of his hostility. Although Johnson condemns Milton's political principles and his rebellious political temperament, he finds no evidence that these principles have corrupted or even colored Milton's poetry. Every reader of the *Life* must find it curious that Johnson does not observe any similarity between the rebellious Satan and Johnson's own view of the rebellious Milton, whose principles were founded "in an envious hatred of greatness, and a sullen desire of independence; in petulance impatient of controul, and pride disdainful of superiority." In these phrases we now find it difficult not to hear a description of Satan, but Johnson's conclusion is by no means that Milton was "of the devil's party." Indeed, for him Satan is not a critical problem. The devil speaks as a rebel should, yet he always condemns himself: "there is in Satan's speeches little that can give pain to a pious ear" (I, 173).

Perhaps Johnson chose not to read Satan biographically because it was simply inconceivable to him that the poet could intend to present the devil sympathetically. Perhaps too Johnson's critical method encouraged him to see literary effects not as reflections of biographical fact but as products of particular powers of mind – Milton's power of displaying the vast, Cowley's agile and elastic mind, Dryden's vigorous genius and strong reason, Pope's good sense.[13] Whatever the reason, Johnson's judgment of Milton the politician seems to have little to do with his strictures on Milton's works. To account for them we need to consider another motive.

In the *Life of Milton*, as in all his critical writings, Johnson is concerned to adjust reputations, to correct misjudgments, to insist on "impartial criticism" and "rational esteem" in place of "false approbation" and "blind confidence."[14] The target of Johnson's critical attack then is often not so much Milton, whose greatness he elsewhere freely admits, but adulatory critics and readers in the middle and latter part of the eighteenth century for whom "the divine Milton" could do no wrong.[15] Johnson insists that Milton's poems be judged on their own merits. Hence faults in his juvenilia must be admitted. "Nothing but veneration for his name could now procure a reader" for Milton's familiar Latin epistles and academical exercises (I, 149). Hence Milton's minor poems, very much in vogue in Johnson's day, need to be seen without prejudice: "Those who admire the beauties of this great poet sometimes force their own judgement into false approbation of his little pieces, and prevail upon themselves to think that admirable which is only singular" (I, 163). And hence the famous judgment on *Lycidas*: "Surely no man could have fancied that he read *Lycidas* with pleasure had he not known its author" (I, 165).[16] *Samson Agonistes* likewise is "too much admired... only by a blind confidence in Milton" (I, 189). Johnson's wish to arrive at a more correct judgment does not always work against Milton.

Paradise Regained, he says, is too much "depreciated." "Had this poem been written, not by Milton but by some imitator, it would have claimed and received universal praise" (I, 188).[17]

Such a concern to adjust critical reputation may lie behind Johnson's involvement in the still puzzling Lauder episode. In 1750 Lauder published his *Essay on Milton's Use and Imitation of the Moderns*, charging Milton with plagiarism from modern Latin writers. He had attracted the attention of Johnson, who contributed a Preface and a Postscript to Lauder's *Essay*. The incident is an embarrassing one for admirers of Johnson, since Lauder was soon after exposed as a fraud, and because Johnson's customary objectivity seems to have failed him here. The evidence is by no means conclusive, but Hawkins reports that Johnson was pleased when he first looked over the proof sheets while Lauder's *Essay* was in press: "I could all along observe that Johnson seemed to approve, not only of the design but of the argument, and seemed to exult in a persuasion, that the reputation of Milton was likely to suffer by this discovery."[18] To be sure, Hawkins is here largely speculating, and insists that Johnson was "not privy to the imposter." Indeed, when fraud was demonstrated, Johnson dictated or wrote for Lauder a letter of public confession,[19] and later said that in "the business of Lauder" he had been deceived.[20] We cannot, I think, fairly convict Johnson of malice in the Lauder episode, but we can conclude that he was not suspicious enough early enough,[21] and we need to ponder further why he might seem to "exult" in Lauder's charges.

This determination to correct midjudgment extends itself to Milton's previous biographers and their estimate of the man. Johnson was evidently concerned at the hagiographical tone that some biographies, particularly that by Richardson ("the fondest of all Milton's admirers") had taken. His judgments often implicitly contradict the opinion of an earlier biographer. For example, without citing Toland by name, Johnson assumes the reader's familiarity with his praise of Milton's love of liberty, and suspects on the contrary that it is a hatred of authority. Without naming Phillips, Johnson asserts that Salmasius, after his defeat at Milton's hands, was "dismissed, not with any mark of contempt [as Phillips had said], but with a train of attendance scarcely less than regal" (I, 115). Elsewhere Johnson more explicitly corrects earlier biographers, particularly where they have apparently exaggerated, extenuated, or conjectured needlessly. Milton, he notes, "is said to have read all the Greek and Latin writers" (Newton had in fact made this claim).[22] Johnson brusquely asks: "With what limitation this universality is to be understood who shall inform us?" (I, 91). Again, "it is told that in the art of education he performed wonders" (I, 99). This time Phillips is the target of Johnson's dry irony: "Those who tell or receive these stories should consider that nobody can be taught faster than he can learn.'' The "slow and tardy reputation'' of *Paradise Lost* had likewise encouraged previous biographers to conventional laments about the neglect of genius and the uncertainty of literary fame. Johnson insists on a fresh look: "Has the case been truly stated? Have not lamentation and wonder been lavished on an evil that was never felt?'' (I, 142). The conclusion of Johnson's brief analysis of the facts is that the poem's sale was very good given the circumstances, and is proof of "the prevalence of genius'' (I, 144).

Correcting earlier biographers is again not always to Milton's disadvantage. The deist Toland, perhaps not a disinterested witness, had said that Milton made use of the rites of no "particular sect among Christians'' (p. 151). Johnson replies that "prayer certainly was not thought superfluous by him, who represents our first parents as praying acceptably in the state of innocence, and efficaciously after their fall'' (I, 156). Johnson also mocks biographers for thinking it necessary to conceal Milton's days as a schoolmaster. "This is the period of his life from which all his biographers seem inclined to shrink. They are unwilling that Milton should be degraded to a schoolmaster'' (I, 98). But such evasions are quite unnecessary. Phillips, he says, laboriously "extenuate[s] what cannot be denied, and what might be confessed without disgrace. Milton was not a man who could become mean by a mean employment'' (I, 109). Johnson of course might have had his own reasons for asserting the dignity of schoolmasters, or of those who had been forced by economic necessity to open a school.

Just as Milton needs no apology, so a biographer need not excuse or conceal his own failure to turn up a fact. Whence Milton drew the original design of *Paradise Lost*, says Johnson, "has been variously conjectured by men who cannot bear to think themselves ignorant of that which, at last, neither diligence nor sagacity can discover'' (I, 133). Johnson on the other hand frequently confesses his own ignorance. He is "far from hoping to discover'' why Milton changed booksellers after the publication of *Paradise Lost* (I, 146). He knows "nothing particular'' of Milton's "intellectual operations'' as a statesman (I, 134).[23]

Finally, Milton's worshipful and credulous biographers do not or will not see Milton's human foibles. While Richardson "discovers always a wish to find Milton discriminated from other men'' (I, 138), Johnson in the interests of realism and honesty wants to level Milton with the rest of humanity, to present him not as a superman or a saint, but as a man who shares the "common weaknesses of mankind'' (I, 110). Thus Milton is "like many other authors'' in amusing himself "with little productions'' (I, 125). His mind is like "every fertile and copious mind'' (I, 139). His sudden bursts of inspiration, which Richardson marvels at, are quite like what happens "to every man in every mode of exertion, manual or mental" (I, 139). As Cowper was to note petulantly, in an unpublished annotation on Johnson's *Life*, "Let us by all means make an ordinary man out of him if we can."[24] Milton's conquest of the mighty Salmasius produced nothing more than the common result: "as controversialists are commonly said to be killed by their last disputes, Milton was flattered with the credit of destroying him" (I, 115). Like the exempla of human foibles in the *Rambler*, Milton's eager return to England when war broke out, whereupon he became an obscure schoolmaster, but serves to illustrate the disparity between "great promises" and "small performance" (I, 98). His unhappy marriages serve to illustrate the unrealistic expectations of "conjugal advantage." At such moments in the *Life* Johnson the detached and impartial observer is fully in control of his materials. To the moralist, Milton is useful "to point a moral, or adorn a tale."

Johnson Agonistes

Johnson finds Milton merely mortal in part then to correct the blind adulation of readers and biographers. But we may perhaps begin to sense that he cuts him down to size in order to serve not a general moral purpose but to answer his own psychological needs. We may find a clue in Johnson's remark, late in the *Life*, that "the reader feels himself in captivity to a higher and a nobler mind" (I, 190). Johnson, we may recall, was accustomed to think of conversation as a kind of contest or combat in which he could exercise his skills. Burke, he once said, "calls forth all my powers." In Milton too Johnson as it were found a formidable and intimidating opponent. I do not mean to suggest that Johnson was motivated by anything so petty as envy, a charge quite unfairly leveled at him by at least one nineteenth-century Miltonist.[25] His motive, I suspect, was more subtle and disturbing. As Bate reminds us, Johnson once wrote that "it is not only difficult but disagreeable to dwell on things naturally great." The writer becomes "degraded in his own eyes by standing in comparison with his subject, to which he can hope to add nothing."[26] Or as Johnson put it in *Rambler* 86, "It is ... always dangerous to be placed in a state of unavoidable comparison with excellence, and the danger is still greater when that excellence is consecrated by death [or, we might add, critical canonization]." He that succeeds a celebrated writer, has the same difficulties to encounter. But the biographer has advantage over the controversial combatant: he can exert complete control over the shape of the encounter between strong minds. Here Johnson was well served by his typical practice of establishing the powerful presence of the biographer in the biography, as impartial observer or judge, continually intruding to interpret or generalize. Unlike the popular "life and letters" biographers (Mason, in his life of Gray, for example), or the earlier biographers of Milton, who let the poet speak for himself,[27] Johnson always intervenes between Milton and the reader – to paraphrase, to summarize, and only rarely to provide extended quotations without appending his own observations.[28]

The relationship between Johnson and his subject here proposed might seem to provide support for claims that Milton *as a great writer* oppressed and intimidated the imagination of Johnson and his contemporaries. But such an explanation is, I think, too simple. It is not the fact of Milton's great achievement as a writer that troubles Johnson. Rather it is the kind of man Milton was, and the kind of book he wrote. Writing a biographical preface to Milton's works compels Johnson to consider certain aspects of his own experience and character that make him profoundly uncomfortable. Consider first Milton the man, who served to remind Johnson of his own fears and failings.

In some obvious ways, of course, Milton was utterly unlike Johnson. As Hayley notes, "never were two spirits less congenial, or two Christian scholars, who differed more completely in their sentiment of poetry, politics, and religion. In temperament, as well as in opinions, they were the reverse of each other; the one was sanguine to extreme, the other melancholy in the extreme" (p. 222). But in other respects the two were in fact remarkably similar. To speak generally, both, as Hayley concedes, were "equally sincere in their attachment to Christianity, and both distinguished by noble intellectual exertions in the service of mankind" (pp. 222 – 23). Both were men of deep and wide learning.[29] Their talent lay not in "doing little things with grace" but in works of larger size and weight. Born almost exactly one hundred years apart, their careers surprisingly coincide. Each was long and late beginning, and did not win fame until past the age of forty. Each was at one time an obscure schoolmaster, a lexicographer, a political controversialist, and a champion of free speech.[30]

In temperament too some deep similarities are masked by the obvious differences. Each was fiercely proud and independent, a strong and dominating personality, demanding of himself and others. Each is remarkable not just for his published works but for the active power of mind displayed in them. Boswell speaks of Johnson's superiority in "the art of thinking";[31] Johnson says there is more "thinking" in Milton and Butler "than in any of our poets."[32] Each was, as Johnson describes Milton at the end of the *Life*, "naturally a thinker for himself, confident of his own abilities, and disdainful of help or hindrance." Indeed, as we read some of the phrases from the final paragraph of the

Life of Milton, we might imagine we are reading an oblique self-portrait of the young and struggling Johnson himself, before he had won fame and a pension: "From his contemporaries he neither courted nor received support...His great works were performed under discountenance." Is his image of Milton in some way an idealized image, in the older Johnson's eyes, of those bitter and rebellious years in his own early life?

If Johnson reflected upon these similarities between his own career and that of Milton, he may have been troubled by the comparison. Not because he had failed to win significant success in his own outward career, but because he felt such a failure in his inward career. As we know from Johnson's biographers and from his own words, he was continually distressed by his laziness, his intemperance, and his religious fears. Milton, by contrast, as Johnson describes him, is a man of extraordinary self-discipline, methodical habits, and temperance:

His domestick habits, so far as they are known, were those of a severe student. He drank little strong drink of any kind, and fed without excess in quantity, and in his earlier years without delicacy of choice. In his youth he studied late at night; but afterwards changed his hours, and rested in bed from nine to four in the summer, and five in winter. The course of his day was best known after he was blind. When he first rose he heard a chapter in the Hebrew Bible, then studied till twelve; then took some exercise for an hour; then dined; then played on the organ, and sung, or heard another sing; then studied to six; then entertained his visiters till eight; then supped, and, after a pipe of tobacco and a glass of water, went to bed.   (I, 152)

The regularity of Milton's life may have provided occasion for Johnson to reproach himself. His skeptical reaction to the Miltonic regimen – "So is his life described; but this even tenour appears attainable only in Colleges" – combines incredulity and self-extenuation.

More troubling to contemplate may have been Milton's "full conviction" of Christian truth. Johnson had no doubts about Milton's faith, but was concerned about his religious independence. His paragraph on Milton's beliefs seems to reflect the anxiety of a Christian who found rigorously imposed duties necessary:

To be of no church is dangerous. Religion, of which the rewards are distant and which is animated only by Faith and Hope, will glide by degrees out of the mind unless it be invigorated and reimpressed by external ordinances, by stated calls to worship, and the salutary influence of example.

One reason for this remark is Johnson's felt need to leave the world a better place, to let slip no opportunity of reminding the reader of his duty, but clearly too Johnson is here describing his own needs for "external ordinances" and "stated calls to worship." Milton, on the contrary, had "the full conviction of the truth of Christianity ... regarded the Holy Scriptures with the profoundest veneration ... and lived in a confirmed belief of the immediate and occasional agency of Providence" without participating in any form of "visible worship," whether public or household prayers. This troubling example of unsupported faith is interpreted in the light of Johnson's own experience. Milton omitted family prayers, he believed, not out of principle, but "neglect."

The neglect of it in his family was probably a fault for which he condemned himself, and which he intended to correct, but that death, as too often happens, intercepted his reformation.

As Birkbeck Hill first noted, in this sentence Johnson is clearly "thinking of himself" (I, 156n).

Conviction and action were for Milton one: "his studies and meditations were an habitual prayer." But for Johnson the disparity between the preaching of a writer's works and the practice of his life was the cause for much self-criticism and theme of much of his best moral writing. Milton insisted that a good poet be "a true Poem ... a composition, and patterne of the honourablest things."[33] And, as Johnson admiringly notes, Milton preserved in "private and familiar" life that reputation "which his works had procured him" (*Rambler* 14). While Johnson lamented the gap between promise and performance in himself (promises made publicly about the long-delayed Shakespeare edition, or privately, about his personal conduct), Milton at an early age "promised to adorn his native country by some great performance" (I, 134), and lived to fulfill that promise.

What seems to have struck Johnson most strongly about Milton, and what may have troubled him most of all, was the extraordinary self-confidence that most of the biographers remark.[34] If his portrait has one single dominant feature, it is Milton's high "opinion of his own merit" (I, 104), and his "consciousness of his powers" (I, 134).[35] His early compositions met with applause, and "exalted him in his own opinion and confirmed him in the hope" that he "might leave something written to after-times, as they should not willingly let it die" (I, 94). "It appears in all his writings that he had the usual concomitant of great abilities, a lofty and steady confidence in himself" (I, 94). "He seems to have been well acquainted with his own genius" (I, 231). So certain is Johnson of this feature of Milton's character that he permits himself to imagine Milton's reaction to the slow reception of *Paradise Lost*: "I cannot but conceive him calm and confident, little disappointed, not at all dejected, relying on his own merit with steady consciousness, and waiting without impatience the vicissitudes of opinion and the impartiality of a future generation" (I, 144). Such conjectures, rare in Johnson's biographies, suggest a powerful wish to see in Milton the image of an ideal.

Boswell notes that Johnson too had a "noble consciousness of his own abilities, which enabled him to go on with undaunted spirit."[36] Perhaps, however, as George Irwin has speculated, "it was only an intellectual consciousness, a superficial awareness. He could not feel his superiority at the deeper emotional level, because he lacked that inner confidence which comes only with self-acceptance."[37] Perhaps too Johnson was aware that his great abilities had, so it seemed to him, produced so little of good. Milton could look back on a life of great achievement, "a life passed, as his conscience assured him, in the faithful discharge of arduous and irksome duties" (Hayley, p. 73). But Johnson, looking back, reflected again and again, as many commentators have reminded us, on the ominous warning implicit in the Parable of the Talents. That Milton had reflected on the same parable in *Reason of Church Government* – "remembring...that God even to a strictnesse requires the improvement of these his entrusted gifts"[38] – and in the sonnet on his blindness – "That one talent which is death to hide / Lodged with me useless" – may have unsettled Johnson the more.

To consider Milton's disciplined faith and his life as a writer would have provided Johnson an occasion for some painful self-scrutiny. Reading *Paradise Lost* was apparently just as burdensome. Jean Hagstrum suggested thirty years ago that it may have been the poem's characteristic quality, its sublimity, that both attracted and repelled Johnson. Along with Burke, Johnson admired Milton's power of "displaying the vast, and...aggravating the dreadful," but his high regard for rationality made him distrust sublime astonishment, in which the mind is filled and overwhelmed, while reason is suspended.[39] Johnson seems to have been more comfortable about the sublime when enthusiasm and astonishment receded to "rational admiration."[40] Furthermore, his own religious fears made him oppressed by Milton's use of "poetical terrour." While Milton actually introduced God the Father and God the Son as speaking agents, Johnson is reluctant even to name them in his discussion of the poem. Their characters simply do not admit of critical "examination." To imagine the Fall, or Heaven, or Hell plainly terrified Johnson:

Of the ideas suggested by these awful scenes, from some we recede with reverence, except when stated hours require their association; and from others we shrink with horrour, or admit them only as salutary inflictions, as counterpoises to our interests and passions. Such images rather obstruct the career of fancy than incite it.   (I, 182)

Milton boldly confronts and vividly describes what Johnson fears even to call to mind. Milton daringly writes of the "good and evil of eternity," but for Johnson these ideas are "too ponderous for the wings of wit."

The pressure exerted by Milton's power and his subject leads also to some extraordinary contradictions in Johnson's account of *Paradise Lost*. In accord with his normal critical procedure in the *Lives*, Johnson displays the poem's "excellencies" and then proceeds to discuss its "defects and faults." What is unusual in this *Life* is that Johnson frequently presents as a defect what he had earlier cited as an excellence. Thus the poem is said to be "perpetually interesting." And yet, later, "the want of human interest is always felt." "Scarcely any recital is wished shorter," but "none ever wished it longer." Its purpose is "the most useful": "to vindicate the ways of God to man; to show the reasonableness of religion, and the necessity of obedience to the Divine Law." The poet's "moral sentiments ... excel those of all other poets." And yet the poem "can give little assistance to human conduct." Its truths, after all, are "too important to be new." But then the praise of Abdiel's fortitude "may be accomodated to all times,"

and Raphael's reproof of Adam's curiosity after the planetary motions, with the answer returned by Adam, may be confidently opposed to any rule of life which any poet has delivered.

"Yet..." and "but..." constructions are of course common in Johnson's prose, and he characteristically considers the evidence for both sides of a question.[41] But the reversals of direction and the contradictions in this part of the *Life of Milton* are extraordinarily frequent and intense.

Some critics suggest that the contradictions are more apparent than real. A poem may be "interesting" (affecting, moving), and still want "human interest," since fallen creatures like ourselves have so small a share of the story.[42] Or as Robert Folkenflik ingeniously suggests, perhaps Johnson considers *Paradise Lost* from two different perspectives, as a work "abstracted from its effects on the hearer" (in which it succeeds admirably) and as a work that "relates the reader to the poem" (in which it fails).[43] Such explanations, however, will not explain away the tension in Johnson's criticism. The *Life* is less a record of Johnson's balanced conclusions about the poem's merits than a dramatization of his struggle with it.[44] "Whatever be the advantage of rhyme [and in two long paragraphs Johnson has just argued the superiority of rhyme to blank verse in English] I cannot prevail on myself to wish that Milton had been a rhymer." Johnson's verb is significant: Milton robs him of his usually magisterial control over his subject and his own reaction. Johnson cannot "prevail on himself" any more than he can prevail over

Milton. The language of power suggests Johnsonian combat: "Such is the *power* of his poetry that his *call* is obeyed without *resistance*." When we are no longer able to peruse the poem – for "its perusal is a duty rather than a pleasure" – we "*retire* harassed and overburdened", and we "desert" a poet whom we acknowledge our "*master*" (I, 183–84).

In self-defense Johnson might well seek to deny the power of Milton's example by giving him feet of clay, or by leveling Milton with himself and the rest of humanity. But such is Johnson's honesty that he cannot conceal that Milton is after all an extraordinary man, and his great poems an extraordinary achievement. Repeatedly in the paragraphs on *Paradise Lost* Johnson presents Milton as an exceptional poet. "The moral of other poems is incidental and consequent; in Milton's only it is essential and intrinsick" (I, 171). "Before the greatness displayed in Milton's poems all other greatness shrinks away" (I, 172). The poem has "by the nature of its subject, the advantage above all others, that it is universally and perpetually interesting" (I, 174). "There is perhaps no poem of the same length from which so little can be taken without apparent mutilation" (I, 175). His moral sentiments "excel those of all other poets" (I, 179). And repeatedly Johnson recurs to the same idea that he censures in other biographers: Milton raises our *wonder*. "Whoever considers the few radical positions which the Scriptures afforded him will wonder by what energetick operations he expanded them to such extent and ramified them to so much variety" (I, 183). "When he cannot raise wonder by the sublimity of his mind, he gives delight by its fertility" (I, 178). The poem, after all, even with its faults, is a "wonderful performance" (I, 188).

The man is no less "wonderful" than the poem. Nature had bestowed upon him more bountifully than upon others "the power of displaying the vast, illuminating the splendid, enforcing the awful, darkening the gloomy, and aggravating the dreadful" (I, 177). In Johnson's mind Milton seems actually to have become the ideal poet that Imlac enthusiastically describes in *Rasselas*, ch. 10, the master of history, morality, physiology, "the master of his language in its full extent." Although Johnson at first laughs at Milton's fears and aspirations – "however inferior to the heroes who were born in better ages...he might still be the giant of the pygmies" (I, 138) – Milton emerges from the *Life* quite frankly as a "hero."[45] "Like other heroes," however, "he is to be admired rather than imitated," an apparent exception to human laws.[46] Before him criticism must at last "sink in admiration."

12 · COWPER

The poet William Cowper was outraged by Johnson's *Life of Milton*: "Oh! I could thresh his old Jacket 'till I made his Pension Jingle in his Pocket."[1] Johnson's politically-inspired hostility, so he thought, required immediate correction. Cowper urged his friend Hayley, then at work on a new *Life of Milton*, to "censure and expose the cruelty of that literary cossack's strictures."[2] Unlike Johnson's, Cowper's admiration for Milton's character and work was almost unqualified. And yet like Johnson he in some ways seems troubled by Milton, and for similar reasons.

Cowper *the poet* seems on the whole undismayed and unintimidated by Milton's poetic achievement. Although Cowper's poetry may at first seem modest, unassertive, consciously minor, that modesty in fact conceals a kind of strength. His poetic output was substantial, his versatility great, his range extending from religious lyricism to Horatian urbanity, from conversational couplets to a free ruminative blank verse. Donald Davie has noted that we find in Cowper's verse "the fullest image in poetry of the public life of his times".[3] Pope was perhaps as important a poetic influence on Cowper as Milton. Yet for Cowper the fearful Calvinist, as for Johnson, Milton was a source of terror. Like Johnson, Cowper was deeply drawn to and deeply disturbed by *Paradise Lost*. He also shared Johnson's vivid apprehension of the threat of eternal damnation. Cowper, I would argue, looked at *Paradise Lost* with the eyes of *religious* (not poetic) anxiety. On the one hand he was terrified by the Satan he identified with; on the other, like his contemporaries who celebrated gardens and marriage, he found in Milton's Eden an image of the "domestic happiness" that could perhaps still be constructed so as to ward off his fears of damnation.

Cowper the Miltonist

Cowper deeply admired Milton's work, and knew it well. "Few people," he wrote late in his life, "have studied Milton more, or are more familiar with his poetry than [mys]elf."[4] He first read Milton at age fourteen in the 1740s, and memorialized the moment in a famous passage in *The Task* (IV. 709–17). Cowper's first poem, the "Verses written at Bath on Finding the Heel of a Shoe" (1748), is a parody, in

217

the manner of John Philips, of Miltonic blank verse.[5] His mature poems, as Havens and others have shown, are frequently marked by Miltonic borrowings and allusions. Cowper's blank verse is to some extent (by his own admission) modeled upon Milton's example. In a letter to Unwin he praised the "Music" of *Paradise Lost*[6] and declared, in a Preface to his own blank verse translation of Homer, that Milton furnished "an example inimitable indeed, but which no writer of English heroic verse without rhyme can neglect with impunity." Of Milton's prosodic principles Cowper consciously adopted the practice of shifting caesurae, to avoid monotony and to gain a "dignity and variety," and of elision.[7] And yet Cowper insisted that his blank verse was his own, and no mere imitation of Milton or of Thomson:

Milton's manner was peculiar. So is Thomson's. He that should write like either of them, would, in my judgment, deserve the name of a copyist, but not of a poet. A judicious and sensible reader therefore ... will not say that my manner is not good, because it does not resemble theirs, but will rather consider what it is in itself.[8]

Cowper's declaration of poetic independence seems straightforward and unaffected, not a sign of creative anxiety but of confidence in himself and the judicious reader, with perhaps some annoyance at the lazy response of the undiscriminating. And his claim is upheld by modern readers, who agree that Cowper's staple blank verse – natural, easy, diffuse, conversational[9] – is quite unlike Milton's. When Cowper *is* Miltonic, the verse has the effect of deliberate, conscious allusion.

In his later career Milton came to occupy Cowper even more. In conjunction with Hayley's *Life* Cowper himself projected a new edition of Milton's poetry, "on the plan of Boydell's Shakespeare," a lavish illustrated edition. Fuseli was to serve as illustrator, and Cowper as editor, giving a correct text, translating Milton's Latin and Italian poems, selecting notes from his editorial predecessors, and adding his own original notes and commentary.[10] Cowper began with the translations, which he completed in 1792. He likewise translated and defended the complimentary pieces (by Francini, Salsillo, and others) printed by Milton with his 1645 volume and censured by Johnson.[11] But Cowper tired of the project. The commentary on *Paradise Lost* was abandoned after Book III.[12]

One other piece of evidence shows spectacularly that Milton was often on Cowper's mind. Near the end of his life, in 1793, Cowper reported to Hayley that he had dreamed of meeting Milton. In the dream he had had the feelings of "an affectionate child" for a "beloved father." He resolved to accost Milton, who received him with complacence. Cowper then praised *Paradise Lost*, and Milton responded,

"Well, you for your part will do well also."[13] The language of the dream is striking, particularly since Cowper, then an old man of 62, quite explicitly casts himself as Milton's young son. Far from being stern and intimidating, Milton is mild, accessible, and reassuring. Relations with fathers then, even imaginative and dream fathers, need not be dominated by Oedipal rivalries and fears. The dream *may* suggest that Cowper sought approval from his poetic father. But since by 1793 Cowper had won substantial fame and approval from his public and had his literary career behind him, we may suspect that the dream has as much religious as literary significance. If the old Puritan father is a fantasized figure for the Calvinist God, then Cowper may in effect have dreamed of standing before a generous lord who assured him that at the bar of Judgment he "will do well."[14]

The dream may be a sign that Milton was not only a literary model but that he played an important role in Cowper's religious life. Afraid for much of his adult life that he was eternally damned, Cowper at an early point began to identify with Milton's Satan. During his first attack of insanity in 1763, described later in his autobiographical memoir, Cowper was driven to the "dark and hellish purpose of self-murder." To punish him for his despair, Cowper feared that "Divine Vengeance should plunge me into the bottomless abyss." The phrase appears to recall Satan's fall, "hurled headlong... / To bottomless perdition" (*Paradise Lost*, I. 45 – 47). It was "Satan and my own wicked heart," he thought, who furnished him with "weapons against myself."[15] At another time, he remembered, "I seemed to myself to pronounce those words from Milton, 'Evil be thou my Good.' I verily thought that I had adopted that hellish sentiment, it seemed to come so directly from my heart."[16] Cowper never fully lost the fear that Satan inhabited his heart. In the very late "Lines Written on a Window Shutter at Weston" (1795), composed when he was about to leave forever a long-loved haven, Cowper again found Satan's words in his mouth:

> Farewell, dear scenes, for ever closed to me:
> Oh, for what sorrows must I now exchange ye!
> Me miserable! How could I escape
> Infinite wrath, and infinite despair!

The lines combine Satan's "Farewell happy fields" (I. 249) and his later lament, "Me miserable! Which way shall I fly / Infinite wrath and infinite despair?" (IV. 73 – 74).[17]

The Commentary on *Paradise Lost* is also haunted by Satan. In his brief and fragmentary notes on Book I Cowper is especially sensitive to the plight of the damned. At the first description of Hell (I. 50 – 74) he comments feelingly:

The poet proceeds enumerating, as he would never cease, the horrors of the scene, deepening them still more and more as he goes, till at last he closes all with that circumstance of most emphatic misery, the immeasurable distance to which these apostate spirits had fallen from God, and the light of heaven.

At II. 618 he comments on Milton's Hell as if he himself had experienced it: "the poet seems to have contemplated the horrid scene, till, as in a dream or vision, he saw it. His description of Hell is not only a map, but a natural history of it."

Cowper's manifest anxiety leads him to an oblique confession of inadequacy, though what emerges – for the only time in his career – is his sense of *literary* inadequacy in the face of Milton. At the close of Satan's first speech to his legions (I. 663) Cowper comments:

It was doubtless a happiness to have fallen on a subject that furnished him with such scenery, and such characters to act in it, but a happiness it would not have been to a genius inferior to Milton's; such a one, on the contrary, would have been depressed by it, and in what Milton reaches with a graceful ease, would have fallen short after much and fruitless labor.

We may speculate that Cowper left his Commentary unfinished after Book III because he was unwilling or unable to examine closely the speeches of Satan in Book IV, particularly the opening speech in which Satan chooses his own damnation with the fateful words, "Evil be thou my good" (IV. 110).[18]

Recovered paradise

The Task was written in part as defense against such terrors, and as therapy for them.[19] The poem sets out to praise the retired life in the countryside. In retirement man may study best how to see God's hand in the "form / And lineaments divine" of nature (III. 721–22)[20] and may recover what he can of the original paradise. In a poem entitled *Retirement* (1782) written several years before *The Task*, Cowper noted that "in spite of sin and woe, / Traces of Eden are still seen below" (27–28). The retired spirit will search the page of scripture and find in it the most important theme, "ourselves and our recov'ry from our fall" (138). Seeking God's "favour," he will find the earth "start into a second birth," and "enjoy an Eden e'er it fails" (353–64).[21] Book III of *The Task*, "The Garden," the most Miltonic part of the poem, provides the clearest image of that recovered paradise.

Allusions to *Paradise Lost* are especially frequent in Book III. Adam and Raphael's dialogue on astronomy offers a warning against un-directed speculation. Let man, Raphael warns, seek knowledge in order "to read his wondrous works" (VIII. 68) and refrain from free "wandering thoughts" that might occupy the mind, "And render us in things that most concern / Unpracticed, unprepared, and still to seek" (187, 196–97). Cowper too warns that "God never meant that man should scale the heav'ns" (221):

> In his works
> Though wondrous, he commands us in his word
> To seek *him* rather.
>
> (222–24)

And yet all too often, Cowper notes, "Our wayward intellect, the more we learn / Of nature, overlooks her author more" (236–37). Cowper then goes on to single out Newton, Hale, and Milton as "Sagacious readers of the works of God" (253). Elsewhere in Book III Cowper alludes repeatedly to the well-known personal "digressions" in Books I, VII, and IX.[22] Compare, for example:

A.

> Here much I ruminate, *as much I may*
> With other views of men and manners now
> (*The Task*, III, 121–22)

> ... or years damp by intended wing
> Depressed, *and much they may*, if all be mine
> (*Paradise Lost*, IX. 46)

B.

> *Me* therefore, *studious of* laborious ease
> (*The Task*, III, 361)

> *Me of these*
> Nor skilled nor *studious*
> (*Paradise Lost*, IX. 41–42)

C.

> while *sedulous* I seek t'improve
> (*The Task*, III, 367)

> Not *sedulous* by nature to be indite
> Wars...
> (*Paradise Lost*, IX, 27–28)

D.

> And at this moment *unassay'd in song*
> (*The Task*, III. 451)

> *unattempted* yet *in prose or rhyme*
> (*Paradise Lost*, I. 26)

E.

> Much *yet remains*
> *Unsung*, and many cares are yet behind
> (*The Task*, III. 605–06)

> Half *yet remains unsung*
> (*Paradise Lost*, VII. 21)

The allusions are all slight but unmistakable. Taken one at a time, each is perhaps negligible. Cumulatively, they help establish the mock-heroic note of the poem[23] and associate Cowper with the Miltonic narrator of *Paradise Lost*.

Especially in the light of this association, it is surprising to find Cowper in the opening lines to Book III associate himself with Milton's *Satan*. As he begins the book called "The Garden" Cowper recalls the approach of Satan to the original garden:

> As one who, long in thickets and in brakes
> Entangled, winds now this way and now that
> His devious course uncertain, seeking home;
> Or, having long in miry ways been foil'd
> And sore discomfited, from slough to slough
> Plunging, and half despairing of escape;
> If chance at length he find a greensward smoothe
> And faithful to the foot, his spirits rise
> He chirrups brisk his ear-erecting steed,
> And winds his way with pleasure and with ease.
> (1–10)

Cowper's proem, a long epic simile, is virtually a tissue of Miltonic echoes, all of them significantly involving Satan, as he approaches Eden in Books II, III, IV, and IX:

A.

> *As one who long in* populous city pent
> (*Paradise Lost*, IX. 445)

B.

> So on he fares, and to the border comes,
> Of Eden … whose hairy sides
> With *thicket* overgrown
> (IV. 131–36)

C.

> But further way found none, so *thick* entwined,
> As one continued *brake*, the undergrowth
> Of shrubs and *tangling* bushes had perplexed
> All path of man or beast that passed that *way*.
> (IV. 174–77)

D.

> *If chance* with nymph-like step fair virgin pass
> (IX. 452)

E.

> Satan with less toil, and now *with ease*
> Wafts on the calmer wave by dubious light
> (II. 1041–42)

F.

> Down right into the world's first region throws
> His flight precipitant, *and winds with ease*
> Through the pure marble air *his* oblique *way*
> (III. 562–64)

To these six allusions we can add the suggestion of Satan struggling his way through Chaos, plummeting through vacuity, and foundering over a boggy Syrtis (II. 932–50).[24] Cowper has naturalized the scene, and translated it from Milton's mythical world to the English countryside of muddy roads and disappearing tracks, but the Miltonic original is clearly perceived. Cowper's first readers, innocent of his "Satanic" past, no doubt saw these allusions as part of the mock-heroic framework. But informed as we are, we cannot fail to find special significance in them. Cowper's fears have not been wholly purged. Even light-hearted allusions to Satan are in Cowper a sign of ill-concealed anxiety.

As he goes on to describe "The Garden," however, Cowper is not the invader of Eden, but its inhabitant, an Adamic gardener.[25] The gardener's work, much of it pruning the over-luxuriant growth (as in Eden), is only "such as may amuse / Not tire" (406–07), like that of Adam and Eve, who sit down

> after no more toil
> Of their sweet gardening labors than sufficed
> To recommend cool zephyr, and made ease
> More easy, wholesome thirst and appetite
> More grateful.
> (IV. 327–31)

Seasonal change (which came with the Fall) is denied, for fruits with proper sheltering will ripen for Cowper's gardener in summer or winter (427–29). With the help of a coldframe (Cowper recurs throughout *The Task* to images of shelter or protective enclosure) the cucumber will bloom "vivid green" in the middle of winter (525). In a greenhouse exotic flowers from Portugal and the Indies bloom "warm and snug," "Unconscious of a less propitious clime" outside (567–68).[26] The timid hare, like the animals in Eden, lives there a friend to man.[27]

223

Like Milton's Eden, Cowper's garden is a scene of "domestic happiness," the "only bliss / Of paradise that has survived the fall" (41–42). Like his eighteenth-century contemporaries Cowper could look on marriage as a kind of earthly paradise. In a poem written five years before *The Task* and sent to Unwin, Cowper praised the "Marriage Bond Divine" for bringing about "a Second Eden" on earth. What he singles out (appropriately enough for a bachelor friend of the family) is not the intensity of intimate union but "Friendship, Love, & Peace."[28] In *The Task* Cowper's point of view remains that of the privileged guest. His recovered earthly paradise is an asexual one, cozy and domesticated, "Friendly to Thought, Virtue, and to Peace" (291). The "self-sequestered man" will have a female companion (more or less like Mrs. Unwin) to provide him a "warm but simple home," a cup of tea, and to share "his pleasures and his heart" (386–90). In Eden Adam would pass on to Eve the fruits of his angelic interviews:

> Her husband the relater she preferred
> Before the angel, and of him to ask
> Chose rather; he, she knew, would intermix
> Grateful digressions, and solve high dispute
> With conjugal caresses.
>
> (VIII. 52–56)

In his garden too Cowper will choose a book "not sullenly perus'd / In selfish silence, but imparted oft / As aught occurs that she may smile to hear, / Or turn to nourishment, digested well" (393–96).

Evening is a time of particular Edenic pleasure. Like many other eighteenth-century poets of the evening, Cowper was inspired by the famous evening in *Paradise Lost*, Book IV. His evening piece in Book IV of *The Task*, entitled "The Winter Evening," suggests the vespertinal pleasures of the "self-sequestered man." A formal "Address to Evening," it begins as a lyric invocation and an appeal for favor:

> Come, Ev'ning, once again, season of peace;
> Return, sweet Ev'ning, and continue long!
> Methinks I see thee in the streaky west,
> With matron step slow-moving, while the night
> Treads on thy sweeping train; one hand employ'd
> In letting fall the curtain of repose
> On bird and beast, the other charg'd for man
> With sweet oblivion of the cares of day:
> Not sumptuously adorn'd, nor needing aid,
> Like homely featur'd night, of clust'ring gems;
> A star or two, just twinkling on thy brow,
> Suffices thee; save that the moon is thine

No less than hers, not worn indeed on high
With ostentatious pageantry, but set
With modest grandeur in thy purple zone,
Resplendent less, but of an ampler round.
Come then, and thou shalt find thy votary calm,
Or make me so. Composure is thy gift.
And, whether I devote thy gentle hours
To books, to music, or the poet's toil;
To weaving nets for bird-alluring fruit;
Or twining silken threads round iv'ry reels,
When they command whom man was born to please;
I slight thee not, but make thee welcome still.

(IV. 243–66)

The clearest indication that Cowper is remembering Milton's Edenic evening is the tag phrase "bird and beast," a simple inversion of Milton's "Silence accompanied, for Beast and Bird, / They to thir grassy Couch, these to thir Nests, were slunk" (*Paradise Lost*, IV. 600–02). The poet as votary of course recalls Joseph Warton and Collins, but the slow and stately arrival of evening ("With matron step slow-moving")[29] more closely resembles the formal appearance of Milton's evening ("Now came still Evening on") than the imperceptible approach of Collins' goddess. Cowper's Evening remains a pictorial figure, standing free of the scene, a fair matron, queenly yet modest, graciously offering her gifts of repose and oblivion. Like Milton's moon, she brings a protective veil, her "curtain of repose" answering the Miltonic "Silver Mantle."[30]

Like previous Evenings, Cowper's is female and at the same time gently de-sexualized. Traditionally chaste and virginal, she is made here a matron who puts the world to bed. As befits her age and dignity, Evening is dressed not as a glaring resplendent beauty, "sumptuously adorned" with "ostentatious pageantry," but simply, modestly, a crystalline "star or two" to set off her fine features. It is tempting, of course, to see Cowper's Evening as another oblique tribute to Mrs. Unwin, that comfortable and maternal protector who provided Cowper the "sweet oblivion" which enabled him to forget his fears of damnation. She "whom man was born to please" gently rules the parlor just as Evening dominates her scene. Each in effect brings the gift of "composure." The true votary of Evening will either be found "calm" (and thus deserve her presence) or be made so (and thus submit to her, confessing his need). Composure is the internalization of evening. Cowper's scene, indeed, is almost wholly interior. Only once does he provide description of the external setting – the Thomsonian detail of the "streaky west." Natural description is suppressed in favor of allegorical personification. Cowper is concerned above all with the effects of the evening on the poet, safely lodged in the comfortable parlor and (more important) secure in his calm and composed mind.[31]

But how much of Eden can the gardener in fact recover? Cowper is finally ambiguous on the point. Retreat, he says near the end of Book III,

> Cannot indeed to guilty man restore
> Lost Innocence, or cancel follies past,
> But it has peace, and much secures the mind
> From all assaults of evil; proving still
> A faithful barrier, not o'erleaped with ease
> By vicious custom, raging uncontroll'd
> Abroad, and desolating public life.
>
> (III. 677–83)

The retreat is not only geographical, an escape from the evils associated with "public life" in London. As the allusion to Satan's invasion of paradise helps bring out – "Leaps o'er the fence with ease into the fold... / At one slight bound high over leaped all bound" (*Paradise Lost*, IV. 181, 187) – the danger is also internal:

> When fierce temptation, seconded *within*
> By traitor appetite, and arm'd with darts
> Temper'd in hell, invades the throbbing breast,
> To combat may be glorious, and success
> Perhaps may crown us; but to fly is safe.
>
> (684–88)

Cowper has not rid himself of all Satanic impulses, "temper'd in hell," and must barricade himself within garden walls but also by "constant occupation" (693). The retired man, he had defensively insisted earlier, is not "idle" (353); he is sedulous not to "leave unemploy'd / The mind [God] gave me" (368–69). Such constant, obsessive occupation, it appears, is a defense against Satanic temptations and terrors from within. Unlike Eve, who, warned to avoid temptation (IX. 364), nonetheless sought out "Matter of glorious trial" (IX. 1177), Cowper will take Adam's advice: "to fly is safe."

Yet paradoxically, psychic retreat or contraction still leaves the gardener free to enjoy "Health, leisure, means t'improve it, friendship, peace" (691), a paradisal "bliss" (694) of "guiltless joys" (698). This paradise, furthermore, is "free to all men," a "universal prize" (724). Cowper, however, has little hope that men will heed his recommendation; most will still be attracted to the corrupt city. It is striking that Book III of *The Task* ends not with a celebration of the garden paradise, but with a satiric picture of London, the "crowded coop" (834) awaiting its destruction. The reason may in part be that for Cowper London is not simply a distant threat: it lies within him. He confesses his own attraction to the city "in whom I see / Much that I love, and more that I admire, / And all that I abhor; thou freckled fair, / That pleasest and yet shock'st me" (837 – 40). It is on London that Cowper projects his worst fears of damnation, for the city is

> more obnoxious, at this hour
> Than Sodom in her day had pow'r to be,
> For whom God heard his Abr'am plead in vain.
> (846 – 48)

The final image then is of an unrelenting judge. From this perspective too we may note that such fears have even invaded the garden itself. The passage in which Cowper describes pruning is written with peculiar and perhaps telltale vigor, and rhetorically heightened with a series of words that hint at Milton's "disobedience":

> No meaner hand may *dis*cipline the shoots,
> None but his steel approach them. What is weak,
> *Dis*temper'd, or has lost prolific pow'rs,
> Impair'd by age, his unrelenting hand
> Dooms to the knife …
> … The rest, no portion left
> That may *dis*grace his art, or *dis*appoint
> Large expectation, he *dis*poses neat
> At measur'd *dis*tances, that air and sun,
> Admitted freely, may afford their aid.
> (413 – 17, 421 – 25)

The comparison of man's life and a flower is of course traditional ("he cometh forth like a flower, and is cut down," Job 14. 2). "Disgrace" and "disposed" hint at the granted or withheld grace and God's "unsearchable dispose" (man proposes, God disposes). Is Cowper's pastoral gardener not in fact the Calvinist God of righteous judgment, dooming some with an unrelenting hand, measuring out to others the air and sun of his heavenly countenance?[32]

Cowper's own Calvinist fears may be the primary prompting for these lines, but Milton helped to shape them. "What is weak, / Distemper'd, or has lost prolific powers, / Impair'd by age" recalls Milton's "What in me is dark / Illumine, what is low raise and support" (*Paradise Lost*, I. 21 – 22), and his later fear that age or years may have damped his intended wing (IX. 44 – 46). Milton confesses weakness, and asks for support from his heavenly muse. Cowper envisages no such support for the weak or impaired. The remarkable series of words – discipline, distemper'd, disgrace, disappoint, disposes, distances – that apply both to gardener and judge, again allude to Milton, this time to a famous "alliterative crescendo" introducing Book IX of *Paradise Lost*: discourse, distrust, disloyal, disobedience, distance, distaste.[33] In the midst of his recovered garden paradise, Cowper thus remembers the Fall, his own vulnerability, and the relentlessness of divine rewards and punishments.

AFTERWORD: Notes toward an eighteenth-century theory of literary influence

In this book I have argued that Milton's presence in the works of eighteenth-century writers is clear and unmistakable. Many writers sought to follow in his footsteps, and to work in the genres that he had used – the epic, the pastoral, the masque, classical tragedy, and sonnet. Others saw possibilities for new genres suggested by Milton's own work, or saw opportunities to adapt Milton's poems for a new audience or medium. Pope and Dryden can be said to have "re-written" Milton's poems, transforming them so as to reflect new sensibilities and new concerns. What most often prompted a creative response from eighteenth-century writers is Milton's myth of a lost paradise: poets from Philips to Dyer, and Pope to Cowper, responded to Milton by suggesting that, in one way or other, paradise was yet unlost.

As a coda to my central argument for Milton's creative presence in the eighteenth century, I want to suggest briefly that we need to re-examine our ideas about literary influence in general, and in particular about the so-called "burden" that a rich literary tradition, or a great individual writer, placed on the shoulders of all literary latecomers. We have in fact long known about some of the ways in which writers can relieve or lighten the burden, and find room for creative movement. Fifteen years ago the late W. K. Wimsatt argued characteristically, in a symposium on the topic of "Freedom and Necessity in Lyric," that literary freedom might well flourish best in a period when past models are strongest. The eighteenth-century poet, he claimed (himself renewing a very traditional argument), continually found ways to imitate the past – through parody, through writing variations on an old theme, through a fusion of the contemporary and the past, through a distillation of tradition – that constituted free invention, or re-invention.[1]

Second, a good writer does not passively receive the past. As Eliot argues in his famous "Tradition and the Individual Talent," a poet cannot "inherit" tradition, but must "obtain it by great labour." That labor, Eliot says, "involves...the historical sense...a perception, not only of the pastness of the past, but of its presence."[2] We might concede that third-rate poets merely yield to the past, or rather to some contemporary version of it, simulating the manner of their betters without the labor of re-discovering or re-inventing a tradition and a style for themselves. We might even grant the point, often made these days by literary theorists, that any writer is radically circumscribed, shaped or even chosen by the prison house of his own language, by the literary and cultural voices that speak through him, by the past poems that constitute his own poems. But the best writers, so Eliot implies, none-theless *choose* to join a tradition, and to renew it by changing it, if ever so slightly. By consciously choosing and actively renewing, they declare their freedom.[3]

Consider the example of Pope. As John Paul Russo and others have shown, Pope always saw himself quite self-consciously as part of a rich literary cultural tradition. Indeed, he found his very "identity" by affirming his place in the "tradition."[4] Furthermore, Pope shows strikingly little sense of being intimidated or burdened by the achieve-ment of his predecessors. In his early poems, it is true, he frequently displays a diffidence about his abilities. He merely follows, so he says, in the footsteps of the ancients; he keeps to the pastoral shadows and avoids loftier themes; he is but "The last, the meanest" of the sons of the old bards. But those same poems – particularly *Windsor Forest* and the *Essay on Criticism* – strike most readers as performances of a poet who has mastered the forms in which he chooses to write. The pro-fessions of diffidence, as I have argued elsewhere, are not merely rhetorical gestures. They seem to reflect a genuine as well as becoming hesitancy to assert himself forcefully. And yet they also enable Pope to reduce his exposure to attack, to find strength in lowliness. They are precisely the note which the young poet might wish to sound as he presents his claim to join the line of his elders and masters. These professions culminate in the 1717 *Preface*, in which, without seeming to, Pope laid the foundation for the poetic "monument" that he spent the remainder of his life constructing.[5] By the time of the "Epistle to Dr. Arbuthnot" (1735) Pope, no longer an apprentice but a famous and successful poet, was able to speak with seemingly artless directness of the poet's easy relationship with his predecessors. Encouraged by a circle of older writers, including Walsh, Garth, and Congreve, Pope ventures to publish his work. The same judges who befriended "great Dryden" (Pope thus establishes a link with the greatest of his immediate predecessors) now open their arms to receive "one Poet more" (line 142). Far from feeling oppressed and excluded by a lofty and remote tradition, Pope emphasizes continuity and intimacy: the contemporary representatives of a living tradition are his dear friends.

Pope found other means to lighten or dissolve the burden of the past. One way was freely and openly to acknowledge one's debt. Thus Pope told Spence that he "learned versification wholly from Dryden's works, who had improved it much beyond any of our former poets."[6] Another way was to see that past not embodied in a single master but in several models. Dryden was only one of his masters. Pope learned equally from, and paid equal homage to, Homer, Virgil, Horace, and the writers of the Old Testament. Supplied with many predecessors, he felt dominated by no single one of them. Indeed, he might combine them (as in *Messiah* and *Windsor Forest* Isaiah complements Virgil), or play them off against each other (as Virgilian epic and Drydenian satire produce a "jumbled race" in the *Dunciad*). Or, as Howard Weinbrot has recently argued, he responded to the several different traditions of formal verse satire, associated with the poems of Horace, Juvenal, Persius, and Lucilius, by mingling them eclectically.[7] A third way was to develop a strong sense of himself in his own *present*, and to project a distinctive public personality. The squire of Twickenham who "lives among the great," literary genius of the political opposition, a successful and self-made businessman "indebted to no single man alive" need feel no inadequacy when he retires, in his imagination, to the company of his literary masters.

Armed with such self-confidence, Pope could paradoxically draw systematic parallels between his own life and career and those of his predecessors. Thus he told Spence that after attempting an epic on Alcander he turned next to a set of pastorals, "so that I did exactly what Virgil says of himself" (in Eclogue 6, where Tityrus, fain to sing of kings and battles, is urged instead of sing a "lay fine-spun").[8] And his career did in fact follow the Virgilian progress, from pastorals (1709) to the georgic *Windsor Forest* (1713) and then the epic *Dunciad* (1728). In the 1730s, as many critics have observed, Pope through his Horatian Imitations and his villa at Twickenham made of his very life an *imitatio Horatii*.[9] Pope often took great pains to emphasize the parallels, even at the risk of drawing hostile fire. Though the broad similarity betwen his work and that of Dryden in couplet satire, mock-epic, and epic translation was clear enough, Pope appended to the *Dunciad* in 1729 a formal "Parallel of the Characters of Mr. Dryden and Mr. Pope, As Drawn by certain of their Contemporaries."[10] While aligning, on facing pages, attacks on their "Politicks, Religion, Morals" and even "Names bestow'd," Pope contrives to have Dryden's reputation and authority discredit the abuse while he himself deplores the petty attacks that the great writer (Dryden in one generation, Pope in the next) must endure.

Our own critical tradition then – and the example of Pope – offer reasons for us to doubt that a rich heritage need oppress the writer or his imagination. Indeed, they offer reasons for us to see creative opportunities in the renewal of that past. We can find similar claims in eighteenth-century critical tradition. As critics and theorists from Dryden to Bishop Hurd considered the problem of following great literary geniuses in the near, middle, or distant past, they characteristically found room for what they aptly called "original imitation."

It is true that eighteenth-century critics often expressed the view that the arts suffered from an inevitable decline since the days of the first classics. Poetry, Hugh Blair stated in 1783, was "more vigorous" in its early days than in its "modern state."[11] William Duff spoke for many when he argued that "original genius," more common in early periods of society, "will seldom appear in a very high degree in Cultivated Life."[12] Bate's *The Burden of the Past* gathers eloquent testimony to illustrate a strong strain of regret and sense of failure in the period: how can we ever match the achievements of the ancients? What is there left to say or do that they have not already done better? But by isolating the century's broodings on the idea of decline, Bate and others risk overstating their "resignation" and "despair." If, however, we look again at what contemporary critics said, and what practitioners accomplished, we can find abundant evidence to demonstrate (what Bate himself intermittently concedes) that writers in the eighteenth century were on the whole "courageous, occasionally cheerful...at all times clear-headed and unillusioned" (p. 40). Fully aware of their condition as "moderns," they understood that "enlightenment" meant gains as well as losses. They were not willing (even if they had been able) to give up Christian truth, politeness, rationality, and correctness in order to recover all the rough vigor of agreeable fictions and the boldness of primitive poetry. Modernity was a condition which one simply had to acknowledge. If certain kinds of poetry were no longer possible, this was not a reflection on one's own talent, but on the impersonal forces of cultural change and development. The limitation, properly understood, might serve as a discipline. By defining the field and the work that was *possible*, it might focus and stimulate creative efforts. At their most confident, eighteenth-century writers thought they had succeeded: "The present Age of Wit obscures the last" (Dryden, "To Congreve").[13] "Denham and Waller improved our versification, and Dryden perfected it."[14] Pope's Homer "tuned the English tongue."[15]

To recall such expressions of confidence in the possibilities – and the fact – of contemporary achievement, is not to reinstate the old and discredited view of the eighteenth century as complacent and self-satisfied, but to redress an imbalance that Bate's book has, no doubt unintentionally, produced. Taken as a group the major writers of the century seem self-assured and bold. Their attacks of self-doubt and self-questioning are perhaps no more frequent or more intense than those of any writers since the end of the Renaissance. They may have been the first, as Bate argues, to feel and to explore as a group the problem of the latecomer. But their strategies for lightening the burden of the past and for adapting or converting its riches for their own use deserve more attention than they have received.

Some eighteenth-century critics in fact responded by denying that the "latecomer" faced a problem at all. In a French treatise on poetry and painting, for example, translated into English in 1748, the Abbé Dubos argued that poets of genius go not to their predecessors but to nature for their subjects. And the "characters of life" are unlimited. New combinations or qualities or circumstances can always be invented.[16] The same argument for the inexhaustible supply of nature is found five years later in Johnson's *Adventurer* No. 95. Probably familiar with Dubos' treatise, Johnson rejects the common complaint that "all topics are preoccupied." The scene of man, continually changing, "will always furnish writers with new images and the luxuriance of fancy may always embellish them with new decorations." The passions operate so variously,

that the show while we are busied in delineating it, vanishes from the view, and a new set of objects succeeds, doomed to the same shortness of duration with the former: thus curiosity may always find employment, and the busy part of mankind will furnish the contemplative with the materials of speculation to the end of time.[17]

Or as Johnson puts it in a contemporary *Rambler* essay, the world of "fiction" – a "boundless region of possibility" – has "surely a thousand recesses unexplored, a thousand flowers unplucked, a thousand fountains unexhausted, combinations of imagery yet unobserved, and races of ideal inhabitants not hitherto described."[18] A few years later William Duff, in his *Essay on Original Genius* (1767), builds on this familiar notion:

It may be said indeed, and it is true, that the stores of nature are inexhaustible by human imagination, and that her face is ever various and ever new.[19]

Despite the achievements of "illustrious predecessors," the "uncommonly original genius" (he names Collins, Gray, and Akenside among other contemporaries) can still select objects "which the eye of Fancy hath never explored."[20] Johnson's highest critical praise is reserved for those writers who are both natural and *new*, for those poets who give expression to sentiments that one has never seen written before but has somehow always felt (e.g. Gray), or who "trace a new scheme of poetry" (e.g. Denham, Thomson).

A second strategy is to concede that an illustrious predecessor has often preempted a topic and won those honors accorded to successful performance, and to convert that previous success into a kind of challenge. As we have seen in the case of Dryden, the ancient idea of *aemulatio* was still very much alive in the eighteenth century, and encouraged writers to think about literary imitation not as servile copying but as rivalry, as friendly combat. Writers might be drawn to such competition by a great writer, or by a subject on which earlier writers had won fame. The death of Antony and Cleopatra, Dryden says ambiguously in the Preface to *All for Love*, has attracted "the greatest wits of our nation, after Shakespeare" (were they attracted by Shakespeare, or by the subject?) Emulative contest is a friendly combat. The spirit is not that of the deadly duel for supremacy but the individual performance. In some sense the writer competes against himself. Dryden is encouraged to write about Antony and Cleopatra because many other writers had tried the same theme before him: "their example has given me confidence to try myself in this bow of Ulysses amongst the crowd of suitors; and, withal, to take my own measures, in aiming at the mark."[21] There is room for any number of competitors. They all have the "same motive": not to win or outdo each other but to fashion a vehicle that embodies "the excellency of the moral." Dryden is interested not in measuring himself against other writers, but in taking "my own measures." He is taking his own path, but he is also taking the measure of *himself*. In the concentration of the emulative moment, the writer is conscious only of himself. The other suitors and Ulysses himself disappear: he succeeds who thinks he can.[22] As a critic too Dryden sets writers against each other in friendly combat. Dryden's model is the funeral games for Anchises in the *Aeneid*, in which everybody gets a prize. Dryden himself plays the role of generous, fair-minded Aeneas: in the Preface to his *Fables* he compares ancient and modern writers in order to award a prize to both winner and "loser."[23]

Dryden is not an isolated example. His favorite classical source on emulation, Velleius Paterculus, continued to be quoted throughout the eighteenth century,[24] as did the better-known Longinus. One path to the sublime, Longinus says in chapter 13, is "an Imitation and Emulation of the greatest Orators and Poets that ever flourished":

Nor is such Proceeding to be look'd upon as Plagiarism, but in Methods consistent with the nicest Honour, an Imitation of the finest Pieces, or copying out those bright Originals. Neither do I think that *Plato* would have so much embellished his Philosophical Tenets with the florid Expressions of Poetry, had he not been ambitious of entering the Lists, like a youthful Champion, and ardently contending for the Prize with *Homer*, who had a long time engross'd the Admiration of the World.[25]

It is in this way that one may win the greatest prize, "Glory and Renown." In such competition, even defeat "is attended with Honour" (p. 38). A modern competitor may still hope to equal or even surpass his original. At the end of the eighteenth century Gilbert Wakefield finds it difficult to choose between Horace and his imitator Pope. After quoting from one of Pope's Horatian epistles, Wakefield notes: "It is not easy to decide the contest of superiority between the original and the copy in these verses. To me the imitation appears more humorous and sprightly; and the model more sedate and dignified."[26]

To be sure, there is another side to the story. Bate cites Hume on the way in which the fire of emulation can be "extinguished" by an "excess" of both admiration and modesty.[27] A great predecessor can freeze the would-be emulator in awe, or make him doubt his own genuine abilities. But Hume's sober reflections do not still the widespread expressions of confidence in the period that, through a proper emulation, an imitator can himself be an original. Hurd, for example, deplores "this anxious dread of imitation in polite and cultivated writers."[28] Young in his well-known *Conjectures on Original Composition* (1759) shared some of Hume's concerns about the intimidating power of "illustrious examples." But he urged nonetheless that a writer imitate them: not by imitating their works, but by imitating *them*: "He that imitated the divine Iliad does not imitate Homer; but he who takes the same method which Homer took for arriving at a capacity for accomplishing a work so great…Imitate; but imitate not the composition, but the man."[29] Young was saying little more than Trapp had said earlier, in his *Lectures on Poetry*. The modern epic poets should not "transcribe" the poems of Homer and Virgil into their own. They should rather follow the example, and the spirit, of Milton, who avoided such copying: "Let them improve and form themselves, as much as possible, by their Genius, their Judgment, and their Way of Writing and Thinking: To do this, is to imitate [in the proper sense]."[30]

Such exhortations to imitate the man but not his works are linked with the idea that, as Hurd put it in his dissertation "On Poetical Imitation," the "supreme merit of poetry" lies not in its subject or even its design but in its "execution."[31] Or as the dramatist Dryden wrote in defense of his habit of borrowing a story, "the employment of a poet is like that of a curious gunsmith or watch-maker; the iron or silver is not his own, but they are the least part of that which gives the value; the price lies wholly in the workmanship."[32] When a good poet borrows, says Warton in praise of Milton, he knows how to "make a borrowed thought or description his own, by the propriety of the application."[33] Again and again in the century critics return to that phrase: make it your own. Nature is after all everywhere the same, and we "can say nothing New, at least we can say nothing Better, than hath been said before; but we may nevertheless make what we say our *Own*."[34] Henry

Felton asks that a proper imitator "enter into the *Thoughts*" of the ancients, "and *imbibe* their *Sense*."[35] Jonathan Richardson seems to be saying the same thing – albeit more clearly – when he distinguishes between relying on what authorities (for very good reasons) have said or done, and returning to first principles oneself.

What he sees excellent in others he must not implicitly follow, but make his own by entering into the reason of the thing, as those must have done who originally produced that excellence; for such things happen not by chance.[36]

The writer who enters into the thoughts of his models, and thereby seeks to equal them, will not simply reproduce what he finds. He will wish, as Hurd puts it, to "add much of his own":

he must improve the *expression*, where it is defective or barely passable: he must throw fresh light of fancy on a common *image*; he must strike out new hints from a vulgar *sentiment*. Thus, he will complete his original, where he finds it *imperfect*: he will supply its *omissions*: he will emulate, or rather surpass, its highest *beauties*. Or, in despair of this last, we shall find him taking a different *route*; giving us an equivalent in a beauty of another kind, which yet he extracts from some latent imitation of his author; or, where his purpose requires the very same representation, giving it a new form, perhaps a nobler, by the turn of his application.[37]

Such a capacity for improvement struck Dryden as especially English. With his own *Fables* and the example of Chaucer in mind, Dryden remarked that "the Genius of our Countrymen in general [is] rather to improve an Invention, than to invent themselves; as is evident not only in our Poetry, but in many of our Manufactures."[38]

In consequence, the imitator can not only equal but may even surpass his original. Inverting the common theme that the first poets took possession of the best subjects, and thus of the highest fame, Hurd finds the advantage goes to the latecomers:

the first essays of genius, though ever so original, are overlooked; while the latter productions of men, who had never risen to such distinction but by means of the very originals they disgrace, obtain the applause and admiration of all ages.[39]

As Duff put it, the modern genius has the advantage over his predecessors, for he can "render his Works more perfect and accurate" through his use of critical learning, sound judgment, and the laws of writing" (p. 284). Thus Lucilius yeilded to Horace, the poets of the age of Louis XIV obscure the fame of their predecessors, and Pope's reputation surpasses that of older English satirists. By virtue of his advantages (for example, the "force of *judging right*," the imitator "shall almost lose his title, and become an inventor" (Hurd, II, 231).

Just as the imitator may become an inventor, the latecomer may become the equal of his predecessor. An early remark in Pope's letters suggests that we should perhaps rethink our usual metaphors for literary influence. In 1706 Pope wrote to Walsh that "A mutual commerce makes Poetry flourish; but then Poets like Merchants, shou'd repay with something of their own what they take from others; not like Pyrates, make prize of all they meet."[40] We speak of the poet as a son or heir (as if he had been created or chosen by a predecessor/benefactor). As Pope defines the relationship of poet to predecessor, he emphasizes that the poet both chooses his poetic father and stands on the same footing with him. The metaphor of mutuality makes predecessors into contemporaries who coexist in the same timeless world of Poetry; the metaphor of repayment absorbs literary history into a single poetic reservoir, from which the poet may take and into which he will give. One may thus borrow without incurring a permanent debt.[41]

In another way too, great poets are all contemporaries or (more accurately) stand on an equal footing with their honored predecessors. For as Dryden and others commonly remarked, one's models were themselves imitators. Dryden repeatedly observed how Homer taught Virgil, how Spenser was Milton's "Original." Neither Ovid nor Chaucer were "great Inventors," but copied "*Grecian* Fables" and tales from Boccaccio. It is the special "Genius" of his own countrymen, Dryden thinks, rather "to improve an Invention, than to invent themselves." The "greatest man of the last age," says Dryden of Ben Jonson, was a "professed Imitator" and a "learned Plagiary."[42] As a modern translator, Dryden consciously stands in a continuous line of imitators, adapters, modernizers, correcters. Nor is he the last. In the next age, "Another Poet...may take the same Liberty with my Writings."[43]

Dryden's contemporary, William Congreve, took a similar view of his own predecessors. *The Way of the World*, produced in the same year as Dryden's *Fables*, was modeled in part on Terence's Roman comedy. But Terence, he says in the Preface, "copied *Menander*; and *Menander* had not less Light in the Formation of his Characters, from the Observations of *Theophrastus*, of whom he was a Disciple; and Theophrastus, it is known was not only a Disciple, but the immediate Successor of *Aristotle*, the first and greatest Judge of Poetry."[44] And a dozen years later George Sewell notes that John Philips, an imitator of Milton, was also a careful analyst of Milton's own imitations: "There was not an Allusion in his *Paradise Lost*, drawn from the Thoughts or Expressions of *Homer*, or *Virgil*, which he could not immediately refer to; and by that, He perceived what a peculiar Life, and Grace, their Sentiments added to *English* Poetry."[45] In their several ways Dryden, Congreve, and Philips all testify to the fact that at least from late antiquity the greatest writers are re-writers.

This means that the modern poet, though least and latest, may more readily join a tradition. Thus Pope honors Milton and Virgil, and joins their company, by going back, as they did, to the Homeric source, or by letting allusion obliquely assert the complex of interfiliation. His Miltonized Homer declares the continuity of epic tradition, and his mock-epic allusions enable a reader of a single line of the *Dunciad* to call up Dryden or Milton – behind whom stand Virgil and Homer.

For all their concern about "the burden of the past" then, critics and theorists of the eighteenth century also developed and sustained a conception of original imitation that enabled them to look to past literary greatness as a body of patterns and materials that could be refashioned for the use – and the fame – of modern writers. To tell the whole story would require more space than the present inquiry permits. A separate inquiry would be needed to develop a full theory of literary imitation and influence valid for the eighteenth century, and perhaps the nineteenth as well. Another more historical inquiry would be needed to set Milton among the *several* masters – Homer and Virgil, Horace and Juvenal, Chaucer and Spenser, Ovid and Lucretius, Jonson and Shakespeare – with whom the eighteenth century conducted a continuous conversation and friendly competition. My limited inquiry has here attempted only to demonstrate how Milton's greatest eighteenth-century imitators re-thought his metaphors of fall and recovery, his myth of a garden paradise, his ideas of freedom, choice, marriage, and moral purity to create poems that, for all their debt to Milton, remain free-standing imitative originals.

NOTES

Introduction

1. *The Anxiety of Influence: A Theory of Poetry* (New York, 1973), pp. 32–33. I refer to Bloom's *Anxiety* rather than his more recent books on influence, since it is the first, the best-known, and the most complete statement of his critical theory. In subsequent books up to *The Breaking of the Circle* (1982) Bloom's basic ideas about the influence of great predecessors remain constant.

2. Quoted in Eliot's 1947 essay on Milton, repr. *Milton Criticism: Selections from Four Centuries*, ed. James Thorpe (New York, 1950), p. 314.

3. "A Note on the Verse of John Milton," originally published in *Essays and Studies*, 21 (1936), 32–40, repr. in *Milton: A Collection of Critical Essays*, ed. Louis Martz (Englewood Cliffs, N.J., 1966), p. 12. Eliot grants that much of the responsibility devolves not on Milton but on the bad poets.

4. "Milton," repr. in *Milton Criticism*, p. 311.

5. "Ben Jonson" (1919), in *Selected Essays*, 2nd edn (London, 1934), p. 160.

6. *Revaluation* (London, 1936), p. 103.

7. *The Influence of Milton on English Poetry* (Cambridge, Mass., 1922), pp. 66, 415.

8. J. W. Good's *Studies in the Milton Tradition* (Urbana, 1915, repr. 1971) is marked by a similar "pre-Romantic" bias.

9. See John Guillory, *Poetic Authority: Spenser, Milton, and Literary History* (New York, 1983), for a discussion of Milton's sense of his own authority.

10. For a discussion of the rupture that separated the early Humanist imitators from the classical past, see Thomas Greene, *The Light in Troy: Imitation and Discovery in Renaissance Poetry* (New Haven, 1982).

11. See Greene, *The Light in Troy*, pp. 40–45, and G. W. Pigman, III, "Versions of Imitation in the Renaissance," *Renaissance Quarterly*, 33 (1980), 1–32.

12. For distinctions among allusion, echo, and other kinds of resemblance, see Roger Lonsdale, "Gray and 'Allusion': The Poet as Debtor," *Studies in the Eighteenth Century*, IV, ed. R. F. Brissenden and J. C. Eade (Canberra, 1979), pp. 31–55. See also John Hollander, *The Figure of Echo* (Berkeley, 1981). What I call "theft" has been legitimized by some writers. Greene and Pigman note that one imitative theory in the Renaissance involved the concealment of one's model. See Greene, *The Light in Troy*, p. 75, and Pigman, on dissimulative *imitatio*, "Versions of Imitation."

13. See especially Christopher Ricks, "Allusion: The Poet as Heir," in *Studies in the Eighteenth Century*, III, ed. R. F. Brissenden and J. C. Eade (Canberra, 1976), pp. 209–40.

14. "Milton," *Proceedings of the British Academy*, vol. 33, repr. in *Milton Criticism*, p. 313.

15. *Life of Johnson*, ed. G. B. Hill, rev. L. F. Powell, 6 vols. (Oxford, 1934–50), IV, 34.

16. See William Hayley, *Life of Milton* (2nd edn, 1796), pp. 150–51, on the proem to Book VII.

17. "Life of Milton," in *Lives of the Poets*, ed. G. B. Hill, 3 vols. (London, 1905), I, 175.

18. *The Life of John Milton*, in *The Early Lives of Milton*, ed. Helen Darbishire (London, 1932), pp. 258–59.

19. *Paradise Lost* (1773 edn), I. 311. The note is not in the 1749 edition.

20. *Paradise Lost*, III. 682–89. Hayley, *Life of Milton*, pp. 131–32.

21. *Samson Agonistes*, line 566, in *Paradise Regain'd, ... Samson Agonistes: And Poems upon Several Occasions*, ed. Thomas Newton (1752), p. 233.

22. *Samson Agonistes*, line 594. Cf. line 695.

23. Hayley, *Life of Milton*, p. 168.

24. For Hayley, see *Life*, pp. 162, 200. For Thomas Warton, see *Poems on Several Occasions* (London, 1785), pp. 355n, 366n. For Upton, see Thomas Warton's *Critical Observations on Shakespeare* (1748), p. 144. Many of the biographical readings of eighteenth-century commentators can be conveniently consulted in Todd's 1803 variorum edition.

25. *Longinus on the Sublime*, tr. William Smith (1739), p. 19, repr. facs. edn, intro. W. B. Johnson (Delmar, N.Y., 1975).

26. Hayley, *Life of Milton*, p. 224.

27. Newton, *Life of Milton* (1749 edn), I, xviii–xvix; Hayley, *Life of Milton*, p. 85.

28. *Early Lives*, p. 182.

29. *A Dissertation on Reading the Classics* (1713), p. 213. See also Richard Hurd, "On the Idea of Universal Poetry": "his love of liberty, the ruling passion of his heart, led him to throw off rhyme." *Works*, 8 vols. (London, 1811), II, 24.

1 Milton's politics

1. George Sensabaugh, *That Grand Whig, Milton* (Standford, 1952), Caroline Robbins, *The Eighteenth-Century Commonwealthsman* (Cambridge, Mass., 1959). Sensabaugh's view of eighteenth-century British political history, essentially the old "Whig" interpretation, would be sharply challenged by recent historians. Nor can it be shown that Milton was ever "firmly established as a great spokesman of the Whig party" (p. 180). That Johnson's view is still assumed to represent "the eighteenth century" is clear from J. A. Wittreich, who in his edition of Hayley's *Life* claims that "the eighteenth century managed to eschew Milton's politics when it was not angrily rebuking the poet for being a surly and acrimonious republican" (1970 edn, p. v).

2. William Winstanley, *The Lives of the Most Famous English Poets* (1687), p. 195. Public authorities agreed. The *First Defense* and *Eikonoklastes* were confiscated and burned at the Old Bailey at the Restoration in 1660 by order of the Commons and the King. See J. M. French, *Life Records of Milton* (New Brunswick, N.J., 1956), IV, 322–23, 328–30. Newton gives the details in his *Paradise Lost* (1749), I, xxxi–xxxii. In the late 1670s a proposed

edition of Milton's *Letters of State* was suppressed. See J. M. French, "That Late Villain, Milton," *PMLA*, 55 (1940), 102–15; Maurice Kelly, "Addendum: The Later Career of Daniel Skinner," *ibid.*, 116–18. In 1683 his books were denounced in Convocation and publicly burned at Oxford. See *The Judgment and Decree of the University of Oxford Past in Their Convocation July 21, 1683, Against Certain Pernicious Books*. See French, *Life Records*, V, 262–63.

3. See the opinions of Anthony à Wood (1691), Addison (1694), Pierre Bayle (1697), Thomas Yalden (1698), Bishop Burnet (after 1700), and Thomas Hearne (1707), conveniently collected in John Shawcross, *Milton: The Critical Heritage* (London, 1970).

4. *The Sum and Substance of a Latine Tract Entitled… A Defence of the Royal Power &c. Against John Milton* (1703), p. A2.

5. The brief life of Milton is an abridgement of Wood's account, with all praise deleted. See M. Manuel, *N & Q*, n.s. 7 (1960), 426.

6. *Critical Review*, 5 (1758), pp. 320–21. If the *Review* attacked Milton through traditional Whig rhetoric of "liberties" and "constitution," David Hume censured him from a "Tory" angle. In the *History of England* Hume regrets that Milton, though a great poet, "was deeply engaged with those fanatics, and even prostituted his pen in theological controversy, in factious disputes, and in justifying the most violent measures of his party." *Critical Heritage*, II, 237.

7. *Biographica Britannica* (London, 1760), V, 3114n, 3118.

8. "Life of Milton," in *Lives of the Poets*, ed. G.B. Hill, 3 vols. (London, 1905), I, 157.

9. Note, however, that Johnson may have remembered (and endorsed) Aaron Hill's denunciation of Milton as "a hater of power only because born under the necessity of obeying it" (*Works*, 2nd edn [1753], I, 373). For further discussion of Johnson's *Life*, see ch. 11, below.

10. *The Early Lives of Milton*, ed. Helen Darbishire (London, 1932), pp. 13–14.

11. *Early Lives*, p. 31. Darbishire attributes the anonymous "Life" to the poet's nephew, John Phillips. But Maurice Kelley has disputed her claim and assigned it to Cyriack Skinner. The unnamed publisher of a 1692 English translation of the *First Defense* implicitly apologizes for Milton's harsh "Personal Reflections," but asks the reader to "consider the time when these things were written, and the occasion," when Milton was "under a necessity of vindicating whatever his Masters had done." *A Defence of the People of England*, tr. Joseph Washington (1692), p. 3.

12. *Paradise Lost* (1725), p. xiv.

13. *Early Lives*, pp. 215, 257.

14. Even Bayle's *General Dictionary*, though clearly hostile to Milton's politics, devotes much of its space to Milton's own view of himself. See VII, 568.

15. Newton, 1749 edn of *Paradise Lost*, I, p. xxi. See also pp. xv, xxviii, li.

16. *Paradise Lost* (1749), I, li.

17. Newton (1749), I, li–lii. Cf. Milton's own implicit defense in the *Second Defense* (*Complete Prose Works* [Yale edition], vol. IV [1966], pp. 552–53), and his contrast of "knight in arms" and writer in Sonnet 8. Compare the "Yorkshire Freeholder" who in 1783 objected to Johnson's treatment of Milton: "when he [i.e. Milton] offered his services to Cromwell, he

thought he was discharging his duty to his country.'' *Remarks on Dr. Johnson's Lives of the… Poets*, abstracted in the *Critical Review*, 55 (1783), p. 155n.

18. Newton (1749), I, li.
19. *Early Lives*, p. 214.
20. *Ibid.*, p. 153. The origin of this idea may be found in Aubrey, whose ''Minutes of the Life of Mr John Milton'' were gathered for Wood: ''His being so conversant in Livy and the Rom: authors and the greatnes he saw donne by the Rom: comonwealth & the virtue of their great Comanders induc't him'' to prefer a free state to a monarchy (*Early Lives*, p. 14.) Or in Milton himself, who regularly saw the great figures of his own time as Catos and Brutuses. Zera Fink, *The Classical Republicans* (Evanston, 1945), p. 90.
21. From James Thomson in his 1738 edition, who called it ''an admirable Defence of the best of human Rights'' (p. iii), to the popular historian William Harris, in his *Historical and Critical Account of the Lives and Writings of James I and Charles I* (1758), new edn, 5 vols. (London, 1814), I, 275. See below, n. 47.
22. ''Life,'' in *Paradise Lost* (1749), I, 16.
23. Newton (1749), I, pp. A5–A8.
24. ''Rege sub Augusto fas sit laudare Catonem.'' Quoted in Thomas Warton, *Poems on Several Occasions*, p. 590. The translation is mine. ''Sub Augusto'' alludes to the fact that George II, the reigning monarch in 1737, was christened George Augustus. Controversy over the monument continued, as witness a poem in the *Gentleman's Magazine*, 18 (1748), 134: ''Frown not, ye royal shades, that Milton's name / Among your sacred tombs a place does claim.''
25. As his memoirist Francis Blackburne put it, ''whatever may have been said of [Hollis's] principles, [he] was attached to the *mode* of the Revolution, as well as to the principles of it.'' *Memoirs of Thomas Hollis*, p. 94.
26. *Memoirs*, p. 93.
27. *An Abstract of the History and Proceedings of the Revolution Society in London* (1789), ''November, 1788,'' p. 4.
28. *Life of Milton* (2nd edn, 1796), p. 6.
29. Caroline Robbins' *The Eighteenth-Century Commonwealthsman*, concerned with the ''transmission, development, and circumstances of English liberal thought'' from 1660 to 1776, concedes that republicans were in fact no more than a ''fringe'' in eighteenth-century politics, and that they had little or no impact on practical politics (pp. 133, 320, 383). Though she admits the real inheritors of Commonwealth ideas were very few, Robbins tends to blur this point by fleshing out her summary of ''republican'' thought with a great many establishment Whigs, supporters of ''Revolution'' (i.e. 1688) and ''Liberty,'' and with culture heroes such as Newton, Locke, and Somers. In a more recent study Margaret Jacob also notes that radicalism was only a fringe element in eighteenth-century England. See her *The Radical Enlightenment: Pantheists, Freemasons, and Republicans* (London, 1981).
30. *A Complete Collection…* (1698), pp. 150–52. Even Toland, however, conceded that his addressee, Thomas Rawlins, might ''disapprove of

Milton's Sentiments in several cases" (*Early Lives*, p. 196). See also the life by the Anonymous Biographer, where Milton is presented as "an Advocate for Liberty against Tyranny & Oppression" (*ibid.*, p. 30).

31. The 1761 edition included additional notes by its sponsor, Thomas Hollis. Richardson, Birch, and Hayley all quoted Toland.

32. No. 161, November 6, 1731. The author instances Milton's campaigns for divorce, liberty of the press, and against rhyme and political tyranny. Cf. Johnson on Milton: "petulance impatient of controul" (*Lives*, I, 157). Giles Jacob in 1719 referred to Milton as "Defender of the Power and Liberty of the People" (*Poetical Register*, p. 183). A writer in *The Old Whig* in the 1730s lamented that "the spirits of a *Sidney*, a *Milton*, or an *Harington*" cannot be found among the day's "coffeehouse politicians." *The Old Whig*, 2 vols. (1739), II, 428 (no. 102).

33. Editor's preface, *Eikonoklastes* (1770).

34. *Memoirs*, Appendix, p. 574.

35. *Memoirs*, p. 148.

36. Another admirer of Hollis, Sylas Neville, recorded in his diary, upon seeing the bust of "the truly great & fine Milton" in Westminster Abbey, that his "immortal labours in the cause of liberty ought to have been mentioned in the inscription as well as his divine poem." *Diary*, ed. B. Cozens-Hardy (London, 1950), p. 27.

37. The Society for Constitutional Information, whose purpose was to revive a knowledge of "lost rights" and to diffuse knowledge of "the great principles of Constitutional Freedom," reprinted and distributed Thomson's Preface to Milton's "justly admired speech for the liberty of unlicens'd printing" and the "Letter from Mr. Wall to John Milton," first published by Baron in 1756. *Tracts Published and Distributed Gratis by the Society for Constitutional Information* (London, 1783). For information on the Society, see Robbins, *The Eighteenth-Century Commonwealthsman*, and Eugene Black, *The Association: British Extraparliamentary Political Organization, 1769–93* (Cambridge, Mass., 1963).

38. For an overstated claim, see David Erdman, *Blake: Prophet Against Empire* (Princeton, 1954), pp. 34–35. However, Milton's reputation as a defender of tyrannicide was kept alive by the numerous eighteenth-century editions of the Leveller Edward Sexby's *Killing No Murder* (1650), which praises "the learned Milton" and invokes his defense "that if God commanded these things, 'tis a sign they were lawful and are commendable." The political uses and fortunes of this tract are traced by Olivier Lutaud, *Des Révolutions d'Angleterre à la Révolution Française: Le Tyrannicide & Killing No Murder* (The Hague, 1973).

39. *Poems on Several Occasions* (1785), pp. 587–88. Cf. his endnote to "Il Penseroso": "He helped to subvert monarchy, to destroy subordination, and to level all distinctions of rank" (p. 95).

40. *Memoirs of My Life*, ed. Georges Bonnard (New York, 1966), p. 185, and Hayley, *Life of Milton* (2nd edn, 1796), p. vii.

41. Johnson thought Milton's plan for the education of children was "impractical." See Boswell, *Life of Johnson*, ed. G. B. Hill, rev. L. F. Powell, 6 vols. (Oxford, 1934–50), III, 358.

42. *History of England*, VI (1781), Preface, p. vii.

43. *A Modest Plea for the Property of Copy Right*, in *Critical Review*, 37 (1774), 214–21.

44. Thomas Hollis: "Milton the poet and Milton the politician were two different men. The latter is known to few in comparison with the numerous acquaintance of the other... Many are the prejudices of the present age against Milton's theological, ecclesiastical, and political principles" (*Memoirs*, pp. 509, 516). Richard Baron complained in 1756 that Milton's works were not well known (*Eikonoklastes*, editor's preface). See also Warton's edition of *Poems on Several Occasions*, pp. 587, 588; and the advertisement to the 1791 edition of *A Readie and Easie Way to Establish a Commonwealth*.

45. *Memoirs of Hollis*, p. 93. *The Tenure of Kings and Magistrates* was twice reprinted with contemporary politics in mind. A 1689 edition, "With Som Reflections on the Late Posture of Affairs," endorsed the right of "the People" to choose William as king in 1688. A 1784 edition was "Particularly Recommended, at this time, to the Perusal of the Men of Ireland," then restive under British rule. For bibliographical details, see John Shawcross, "A Survey of Milton's Prose Works," in *Achievements of the Left Hand* (Amherst, Mass., 1974), p. 313.

46. *Areopagitica* served as the basis for two unacknowledged paraphrases in the 1679–81 period, Charles Blount's *A Just Vindication of Learning* (1679) and William Denton's "An Apology for the Liberty of the Press" (1681). The Licensing Act was renewed again in 1692, but lapsed in 1695. Later attempts to pass a new bill failed. See Laurence Hanson, *Government and the Press, 1695–1763* (Oxford, 1936), and F. S. Siebert, *Freedom of the Press in England, 1476–1776* (Urbana, 1952). *Areopagitica* was adapted again in 1693 by Blount in *Reasons Humbly Offer'd for the Liberty of Unlicens'd Printing* and by Matthew Tindal in 1698 in *A Letter to a Member of Parliament*, later abridged as *Reasons Against Restraining the Press*. See Ernest Sirluck, "*Areopagitica* and a Forgotten Licensing Controversy," *RES*, 2, n.s. (1960), 260–74. Thomson's edition of *Areopagitica* appeared in 1738, one year after the Stage Licensing Act, when fears arose that a new press licensing law might be passed. The editor of a 1772 edition of *Areopagitica* warns of an impending design by "the foes of Public Freedom" to "restrain the Liberty of the Press" (pp. v–vi). Again in 1792 an editor finds reprinting "at this period peculiarly necessary" (n.p.), the courts having apparently reasserted the right to license books, perhaps in fear of the spread of radicalism across the Channel. Editions also appeared in 1791 and 1793.

47. *Areopagitica* (1772), p. xi.

48. Francesco Cordasco speculates that Milton's absence from the *Letters* "seems almost intentional, as though *Junius* were taking pains to remove from his acknowledged compositions any Miltonic indebtedness." *N & Q*, 195 (1950), 251–52.

49. See Black, *The Association*. See also Isaac Kramnick on "The Ambivalence of the Augustan Commonwealthsman," in *Bolingbroke and his Circle: The Politics of Nostalgia in the Age of Walpole* (Cambridge, Mass., 1968), pp. 236–60.

50. J. G. A. Pocock, *The Machiavellian Moment* (Princeton, 1975). Milton (b. 1608) and Harrington (b. 1611) were almost exact contemporaries. Both

were "aristocratic republicans" rather than democrats. Milton drew on some of Harrington's ideas on mixed government in *The Readie and Easie Way*, though he resisted Harrington's proposal for a rotating council. Both were in danger after the Restoration (Harrington was actually imprisoned), befriended by Andrew Marvell, and edited by John Toland. For one eighteenth-century comparison (in Harrington's favor), see Aaron Hill, *Works*, 2nd edn (1753), I, 374.

51. *Political Works of James Harrington*, ed. J. G. A. Pocock (Cambridge, 1977), p. 204.

52. But see Zera Fink, who in *The Classical Republicans*, pp. 90–122, argues for Milton's theoretical consistency.

53. Harrington later codified his political ideas into *A System of Politics*, posthumously published in 1700. Toland's edition of Harrington was frequently reprinted (in 1737, 1747, 1758, 1771). See Pocock (ed.), *Political Works*, p. xiii.

54. Christopher Hill has recently suggested that Harrington's ideas thrive in the eighteenth century because they are "firmly rooted in the world as it actually existed, in social transformations which appeared stronger than ideology," and that they accord closely with Whiggish defenses of property, trade, and empire. See *The Experience of Defeat: Milton and Some Contemporaries* (New York, 1984), pp. 327–28.

55. See John Brewer's study of the social and economic bases of radicalism in *Party Ideology and Popular Politics at the Accession of George III* (Cambridge, 1976), and "English Radicalism in the Age of George III," *Three British Revolutions: 1641, 1688, 1776*, ed. J. G. A. Pocock (Princeton, 1980), pp. 323–67. See also Pocock's review of Hill's *The Experience of Defeat*, in *TLS*, December 28, 1984, p. 1494.

56. Warton, *Poems on Several Occasions*, pp. viii–ix.

57. *Life of Milton*, pp. 176–77.

58. *Ibid*.

2 Milton's moral idealism

1. *Second Defense, Complete Prose Works*, IV, Pt. 1, p. 625.

2. *The Life of Milton*, in *The Early Lives of Milton*, ed. Helen Darbishire (London, 1932), p. 211.

3. *Life of Milton* (2nd edn, 1796), p. 52.

4. John Shawcross, *Milton: The Critical Heritage* (London, 1972), II, 89.

5. *Correspondence of Samuel Richardson*, ed. Anna Laetitia Barbauld, 3 vols. (London, 1804), I, 2; Hill, *Works*, 2nd edn (1753), I, 374.

6. Even Milton's staunchest eighteenth-century champions regret his bitter "Resentments" against his adversaries (Toland, in *Early Lives*, pp. 114–15), the "coarse asperity of his ecclesiastical disputes," and "personal invective" (Hayley, *Life of Milton*, pp. 75, 110–11). The standard defense was that seventeenth-century conventions of literary controversy permitted such coarseness. See, for example, Thomas Newton, *Life of Milton* (1749), I, xlix.

7. A reviewer of Harris's *Historical and Critical Account of Charles I* deplores Milton's acrimony and rancor against the King, calling them "stains in

the moral character of Milton, which all the splendor of his intellectual merit will never brighten." *Critical Review*, 5 (1758), 320.

8. For a survey of the Lauder controversy, see the selections in Shawcross, *Critical Heritage*, II, 135–98, and a series of articles by Michael Marcuse: "The Lauder Controversy and the Jacobite Cause," *Studies in Burke and his Time*, 18 (1977), 27–47; "The Pre-Publication History of William Lauder's *Essay on Milton's Use and Imitation of the Moderns in his Paradise Lost*," *PBSA*, 72 (1978), 37–57; "Miltonoklastes: The Lauder Affair Reconsidered," *Eighteenth-Century Life*, 4 (1978), 86–91; "The *Gentleman's Magazine* and the Lauder/Milton Controversy," *Bulletin of Research in the Humanities*, 81 (1978), 179–209; "'The Scourge of Imposters, the Terror of Quacks': John Douglas and the Exposé of William Lauder," *HLQ*, 42 (1979), 231–61. For reactions to Johnson's attack, see Francis Blackburne, *Remarks on Johnson's Life of Milton* (1780, repr. 1974).

9. *Pro Populo Anglicano defensio contra Salmasium* (1651), *Pro Populo Anglicano defensio secunda* (1654), *Pro se defensio contra A. Morum* (1655).

10. *Second Defense, Complete Prose Works*, IV, 611, 613, 620.

11. *Reason of Church Government, Complete Prose Works*, I, 810.

12. *Ibid.*, p. 804.

13. Toland quotes the sonnet (*Early Lives*, p. 165). Cf. Milton's *Second Defense:* "there was propos'd a Greater good for a Lesser Loss; An Opportunity of Acheiving the most noble and Usefull duty, with the bare Loss of my Eyes; Which Duty, as it is more Solid in it self than any Glory, so it ought sure to be far more Desirable and Preferable." Quoted by Richardson, *Early Lives*, pp. 249–50. I have ignored Richardson's italics.

14. *Early Lives*, p. 84.

15. *Ibid.*, p. 243.

16. See Marcia Pointon, *Milton and English Art* (Manchester, 1970), pp. 250–51.

17. See Richardson, *Early Lives*, pp. 207, 213, and Hayley, *Life of Milton*, p. 21.

18. *Conjectures on Original Composition*, ed. M. W. Steinke (New York, 1917), p. 44.

19. Published in 1674 as *Epistolarum Familiarium Liber Unus*, and frequently quoted by Toland, Richardson, and Hayley. The letters were also included in editions of Milton's prose works.

20. Quoted from the translation in Hayley's *Life of Milton*, pp. 118–19.

21. *Early Lives*, pp. 276, 284, 289.

22. *Ibid.*, p. 250.

23. *Ibid.*, p. 289.

24. Newton, *Life of Milton* (1749 edn), I, xlix.

25. *Paradise Lost* (1749), VII. 25n.

26. *Lives of the Poets*, I, 140.

27. See Hayley, *Life of Milton*, p. 131.

28. Quoted by Richardson, *Early Lives*, p. 223.

29. *Ibid.*, p. 250.

30. From the *Apology for Smectymnuus*, quoted by Richardson (*Early Lives*, p. 247) from Toland's edition, Complete Collection, p. 175. The entire passage is italicized in Richardson, his normal procedure when quoting Milton directly. Cf. also *De Doctrina Christiana*, II. 9, on man's duty toward himself,

where Milton underlines the importance of "Contentment" (being "inwardly satisfied" with the lot assigned by Providence) and "the love of an unspotted reputation."

31. From *Reason of Church Government*, quoted by Richardson, *Early Lives*, p. 248. Conscious of what animates him, Milton offers the same advice to Cromwell at the end of the *Second Defense*: "revere yourself" (*teipsum denique reverere*). Quoted in Hayley, *Life of Milton*, p. 134. Edward Young, in a treatise on *Original Composition* in which Milton is several times cited, urges the young writer to "reverence thyself." Was the precept, which Young says is borrowed "from ethics," perhaps chosen with Milton in mind? (*Conjectures on Original Composition*, p. 56.)

32. *Early Lives*, p. 194.

33. Newton, *Life of Milton* (1749 edn), I, lii.

34. *Milton's Paradise Lost. A New Edition* (London, 1732, facs. repr. 1974), Preface, n.p.

35. *Early Lives*, pp. 283, 284. Richardson alludes to 1 Thess. 2. 19 and Romans 8. 16.

36. "Life of Milton", in *Lives of the Poets*, ed. G. B. Hill, 3 vols. (London, 1905), I, 94.

37. Richardson assures his reader that Milton was "not Sour, Morose, or Ill-Natur'd," *Early Lives*, p. 212.

38. "Enthusiasm was the characteristic of his mind." Richardson, *Early Lives*, p. 208.

39. *Ibid.*, pp. 212, 224.

40. *The Nature, Folly, Sin, and Danger of Being Righteous Overmuch* (London, 1739). Robert Burns's epigraph to his "Address to the Unco Guid, or the Rigidly Righteous" is a free poetic expansion (as his note indicates) of the warning from Ecclesiastes.

41. *A Treatise of Human Nature*, Bk. III, Pt. iii, sec. 2.

42. *Prose Works*, ed. Herbert Davis *et al.*, 14 vols. (Oxford, 1939–68), II, 2. Cf. VI, 134: "*Cato* and *Brutus* were the two most virtuous men in *Rome*."

43. On Cato as an eminent political and moral hero, especially in the period 1700–1740, see J. W. Johnson, *The Formation of Neo-Classical Thought* (Princeton, 1967), pp. 95–105.

44. *Life of Milton*, p. 26; cf. *Early Lives*, p. 213.

45. "A Letter Concerning Enthusiasm" (1708), in *Characteristics of Men, Manners, Opinions, Times*, 3 vols. (1714, repr. 1968), I, 53. Cf. III, 33: "Even VIRTUE itself [is]a noble *Enthusiasm* justly directed."

46. *An Earnest and Serious Answer to Dr. Trapp's four Sermons, &c.*, p. 5. I quote from a pamphlet without a title page in the Columbia University Library. The sermon reached a fourth edition in 1772.

47. Guilhamet goes so far as to argue that *Paradise Lost*, with its emphasis on Satan's guile and hypocrisy, Adam and Eve's spontaneous worship, and the narrator's own "unpremeditated verse," is "the single most influential work" contributing to "the development of the idea of sincerity." *The Sincere Ideal* (Montreal, 1974), p. 40.

48. *Works* (1820), IV, 10–11.

49. *Works*, 3 vols. (1773), I, 592–93, quoted in Guilhamet, *Sincere Ideal*, p. 63.

50. Quoted in Guilhamet, *Sincere Ideal*, p. 67.

51. "Of Civil Power," *Complete Prose Works*, VII (rev. edn), 242–43.

52. *A Treatise of Human Nature*, Bk. III, Pt. iii, sec. 2. Cf. also "To love the glory of virtuous deeds is a sure proof of the love of virtue," in "Of the Dignity and Meanness of Human Nature," in *Of the Standard of Taste and other Essays*, ed. John Lenz (New York, 1965), p. 145. On a proper self-esteem, see also Pope, *Essay on Man*, IV. 255–56; *Spectator* 172; Shaftesbury, *Characteristics* (1711, repr. 1968), II, 118–19.

53. "Life of Milton," in *Lives*, I, 177, 179.

54. Newton, *Life of Milton* (1749 edn), I, xlvii. Richardson, in *Early Lives*, p. 285. John Aikin honors Milton as the first of poets "who have contributed to raise and purify the sentiments of mankind." *Letters of a Father to his Son*, 2 vols. (1798–99), II, 268–70.

55. See Johnson, *Rambler* 60, and Robert Folkenflik, *Samuel Johnson, Biographer* (Ithaca, 1978).

56. *Letters of Samuel Johnson*, ed. R. W. Chapman (Oxford, 1952), I, 240. "If nothing but the bright side of characters should be shewn, we should sit down in despondency, and think it utterly impossible to imitate them in anything." Boswell, *Life of Johnson*, IV, 53.

57. Johnson, in *Lives*, I, 155.

58. "I am not Justifying his Principles, but his Sincerity." Richardson, in *Early Lives*, p. 217.

59. Newton, *Life of Milton* (1749 edn), I, xi.

60. Richardson finds in Milton the attributes of Aristotle's magnanimous man: "Natural Greatness, Warmth and Vigour of Mind, together with an Openness and Generosity, all which is True Magnanimity." *Early Lives*, p. 215.

61. On the problematic nature of heroes for the eighteenth century, see *The English Hero, 1660–1800*, ed. Robert Folkenflik (Newark, Del., 1982), and esp. J. W. Johnson, "England, 1660–1800: An Age without a Hero?" (pp. 25–34).

3 Milton as literary hero

1. William Hayley, *Life of Milton* (2nd edn, 1796), p. 3.

2. John Jortin, *Remarks on Spenser's Poems* (1734), p. 171.

3. *The Life of John Milton*, in *The Early Lives of Milton*, ed. Helen Darbishire (London, 1932), p. 211. Richardson alludes to *Paradise Lost*, III. 29.

4. *Ibid.*, p. 83.

5. Edward Phillips, *Early Lives*, p. 53. Blackmore repeats the cliché: "the great Ornament and Glory of his Country," *Essays on Several Subjects* (1716), I, 277; James Paterson calls Milton "an Honour to the British Nation," *A Complete Commentary on Paradise Lost* (1744), p. 1. The origin of this tradition may well be the distich by Selvaggi, printed with Milton's 1645 *Poems*, and later adapted by Dryden (see below, p. 142).

6. Fenton, "Life," in *Paradise Lost* (1725), p. xxi.

7. Paterson, *A Complete Commentary*, p. 1.

8. It is now thought that the so-called "Tonson edition" of 1688, published by Tonson and by Richard Bentley, was encouraged by Francis Atterbury (who supplied Oxford subscribers and may have acted as literary advisor

to the illustrator Medina) and his Christ Church colleague and designer Henry Aldrich, who provided at least two plates. See M. D. Ravenhall, *Milton Quarterly*, 16 (1982), 29–36, and J. T. Shawcross, *Milton Quarterly*, 9 (1975), 43–46. The story of Somers' sponsorship, which probably dates from Tonson's dedication of the 1705 *Paradise Lost* to Somers, was refuted publicly by Richardson in 1733 and privately by Atterbury, who, in a hand-written note in a copy of the 1705 *Paradise Lost* insisted that it was not Somers whose encouragement occasioned the folio edition: "Not so! for I first started this Design to Tonson; and he undertook it, at my Instance." See Maynard Mack, *Collected in Himself* (Newark, Del., 1982), p. 425. A copy of the 1678 third edition of *Paradise Lost*, heavily annotated in Atterbury's hand – as if for use in making a new edition – survives in the Beinecke Library at Yale.

9. "The slow sale and tardy reputation of this poem have always been mentioned as evidences of neglected merit and of the uncertainty of literary fame, and inquiries have been made and conjectures offered about the causes of its long obscurity and late reception. But has the case been truly stated?" Johnson goes on to argue that the early sale of *Paradise Lost* was in fact "an uncommon example of the prevalence of genius." "Life of Milton", in *Lives of the Poets*, ed. G. B. Hill, 3 vols. (London, 1905), I, 142.

10. *Reason of Church Government*, in *Complete Prose Works*, I, 820.

11. Johnson, *Lives of the Poets*, I, 142.

12. See below, ch. 9.

13. *Early Lives*, p. 288.

14. Voltaire's praise of Milton in his *Essay on Epic Poetry* (1727) may have helped Englishmen to this sense. See below, p. 47.

15. Cowper's edition of the *Iliad*, 2 vols. (London, 1810), I, xxiii.

16. *A Review*, 8 (1711), no. 63, pp. 254–55.

17. *Poems on Several Occasions* (1785), p. 589.

18. From Newton's Preface. The compiler of the index was probably Alexander Cruden. See Christopher Bentley, "The Earliest Milton Word-Index," *Milton Quarterly*, 9 (1975), 47–48.

19. Massey, *Remarks on Milton's Paradise Lost* (1761), p. A2. Joseph Warton, in *Adventurer* No. 101 (1753), speaks of "the high rank which Milton has deservedly obtained among our few English classics" (in John Shawcross, *Milton: The Critical Heritage* [London, 1972], II, 226). Cf. William Wilkie's "Phebus and the Shepherd" (1768), where Milton is the "First classic of the English Tongue" (*Chalmers' English Poets*, XVI, 189); and James Buchanan, who calls *Paradise Lost* "the first English classic" in the "Advertisement" to his *The First Six Books of Milton's Paradise Lost Rendered into Grammatical Construction* (1773).

20. *Early Lives*, p. 318.

21. For "classick" as a noun, Johnson gives "An author of the first rank: usually taken for ancient authors." This meaning (and the use of "classic" as a noun) dates, according to *OED*, from 1711.

22. II, 108. Cf. Dennis: "If I were to recommend a *British* Poet to one who had been habituated to *Homer* and *Virgil*, I would for the Honour of my Country, and of my own Judgment advise him to read *Milton*." *Reflections on... An Essay on Criticism*, in *Critical Works of John Dennis*, ed. E. N. Hooker

(Baltimore, 1939), I, 108. Elsewhere Dennis calls *Paradise Lost* "the poem that has done most Honour to England" (*Critical Works*, II, 297), and "an Honour to *Great Britain*, and an Ornament to Human Kind" (II, 121). Cf. also a letter to the *General Advertiser* in 1750 on the occasion of the *Comus* benefit for Milton's granddaughter, repr. *London Stage*, IVa (1962), 185–86, 188.

23. Vol. 17 (1747), p. 567.
24. *Lives of the Poets*, I, 181.
25. *Rambler* 140, in *Works* (Yale edition), IV, 383.
26. "Life of Milton," in *Lives of the Poets*, I, 191; cf. Pope on Milton's "exotic style" (in conversation with Spence, *Observations, Anecdotes*, ed. James Osborn, 2 vols. (Oxford, 1966), I, 197; Addison, *Spectator* 297, and Dryden, in *Of Dramatic Poesy and other Critical Essays*, ed. George Watson, 2 vols. (London, 1962), II, 46.
27. Watson (ed.), *Of Dramatic Poesy*, II, 150. Cf. John Hughes, "Of Style" (1716), in *Poems on Several Occasions with Some Select Essays in Prose*, 2 vols. (1735), I, 250.
28. From *Reason of Church Government*, quoted in Richardson, who also notes Milton's wish to "Enrich and Adorn his Native Tongue" (p. 313).
29. *Reason of Church Government*, Preface to II, quoted in Hayley, *Life of Milton*, p. 39, who notes that Milton "appears, on every occasion, a sincere and fervent lover of his country," and finds a parallel in *Epitaphium Damonis*, lines 172–78 (Hayley, *Life of Milton*, p. 40).
30. *Observations on the Faerie Queene*, 1807 edn, II, 287.
31. "Conjectures on the Origin of Paradise Lost," published with the *Life*, p. 233.
32. See John Shawcross, "A Survey of Milton's Prose Works," in *Achievements of the Left Hand* (Amherst, Mass., 1974), p. 342. The *History* was begun c. 1646 (see Shawcross, "A Survey of Milton's Prose Works," pp. 343–44).
33. *Critical Works*, I, 214.
34. *Early Lives*, p. 290.
35. *The Divine Legation of Moses Demonstrated* (1738), repr. in Shawcross, *Critical Heritage*, II, 99. William Massey elaborated Warburton's point in *Remarks upon Milton's Paradise Lost* (1761), pp. iv–v.
36. *Latin and Italian Poems of Milton*, ed. William Hayley (London, 1808), p. 190.
37. Johnson, *Lives of the Poets*, I, 177.
38. Watson (ed.), *Of Dramatic Poesy*, II, 271. Milton had himself owned Spenser "a better teacher than *Scotus* or *Acquinas*." *Areopagitica*, *Complete Prose Works*, II, 516.
39. For more on Dryden's sense of Milton's place in literary history, see below, ch. 6.
40. Watson (ed.), *Of Dramatic Poesy*, II, 32, 84–85.
41. *Correspondence*, ed. P. Toynbee and L. Whibley, 3 vols. (Oxford, 1935), III, 1122–25.
42. Cf. Gray's note, in "The Progress of Poesy," to line 66: "The Progress of Poetry from Greece to Italy, and from Italy to England." Gray finds that Milton, though he stands in the tradition of Spenser, as it were died without issue. "Spenser imitated the Italian writers; Milton improved on them: but this School expired soon after the Restoration, and a new one

arose on the French model, which has subsisted ever since." "Phaer" is apparently Thomas Phaer, a sixteenth-century translator.

43. 1807 edn, II. 105–08.

44. The comparison must have occurred to the publisher Humphrey Moseley, who in 1645 published poems by Milton and by Waller. Born only two years apart, the poets were each friends of Henry Lawes, who composed music for both.

45. *The British Apollo*, 1, May 25, 1708, n.p. See also Francis Atterbury's 1690 Preface to the *Second Part of Mr. Waller's Poems*, in *Poems*, ed. G. Thorn-Drury (1893), I, xviii; and the *Athenian Mercury* for January 16, 1692, reprinted in Shawcross, *Critical Heritage*, I, 98. See also Nahum Tate's "A Poem, occasion'd by the late Discontents and Disturbances in the State" (1691), *Poems on Affairs of State*, vol. IV (1709), p. 309; and Sir Thomas Pope Blount's *De Re Poetica, or Remarks upon Poetry* (1694), p. 137.

46. Cf. Sackville, "To Mr. Pope. On Reading Mr. Addison's Account of the English Poets," comparing Waller's "Softness" and Milton's "Fire" (*Chalmers' English Poets*, XII, 135), and Leonard Welsted, who declares in 1712 that he has "a fondness" for Waller but "adoration" for Milton. See his "Remarks on Longinus," in *Works*, ed. J. Nichols (1787), p. 422. Schoolboys in Bath in 1717 published translations into Latin of several excerpts from Waller and Milton. See *Scholae Bathoniensis Primitiae, seu Excerpta Quaedam e Walleri & Miltoni Poematibus* (London, 1717). Cf. also *London Magazine*, 28 (1759), 101–02, 155–57; 29 (1760), 99.

47. But cf. the *Biographica Britannica* (1747–66), vol. 6, pt. 2, p. 4099, where Waller is still called "the most celebrated Lyric Poet that ever England produced."

48. Thomas Warton, Preface to *Poems upon Several Occasions by Milton* (1785), pp. x–xi.

49. *Letters of William Shenstone*, ed. Duncan Mallam (Minneapolis, 1939), p. 318.

50. Cf. the end of "The Bard": "Deep in the roaring tide he plunged to endless night."

51. Preface to *Poems upon Several Occasions*, p. xxi.

52. *Observations on the Faerie Queene*, I, 167n.

53. *Poems upon Several Occasions*, p. xx.

54. *Letters on Chivalry and Romance* (1762), repr. in Shawcross, *Critical Heritage*, II, 257–58.

55. Warton, *Observations on the Faerie Queene*, II, 192.

56. *Ibid.*, I, 23.

57. In *Spectator* 160 Addison distinguishes between the class of "natural Genius's" (Shakespeare is his modern example) and a second class of geniuses "that have formed themselves by Rules" (Milton and Bacon are the modern examples). Addison's remark is quoted later by Philip Neve, *Cursory Remarks on Some of the Ancient English Poets, Particularly Milton* (1789), repr. in Shawcross, *Critical Heritage*, II, 360. For other remarks on Milton's learning-and-genius, see Lord Monboddo, *Of the Origin and Progress of Language* (1773–92), repr. in Shawcross, *Critical Heritage*, II, 268n; and James Beattie, *Essays*, repr. in Shawcross, *Critical Heritage*, II, 285–86.

58. *Life of Milton*, pp. 246, 274. Cf. also pp. 208, 273.

59. "On Paradise Lost," printed with the second edition of *Paradise Lost* (1674).

60. "Account of the Greatest English Poets," in *Chalmers' English Poets*, IX, 529–30.

61. See Walter Harte: "Milton alone could Eden lost regain," in "Macarius; or the Confessor," in *Chalmers' English Poets*, XVI, 390–92; and Christopher Smart: "bard divine, / Whose greatness who shall imitate?", in "The Hop Garden," Bk. I, in *Chalmers' English Poets*, XVI, 38. Cf. Judith Madan, who in "The Progress of Poetry" (1731) speaks of Milton's description of Eden, "which he alone could sing." Repr. *London Magazine*, 28 (1759), 101–02, 155–57.

62. Robert Lloyd, in *Chalmers' English Poets*, XV, 90–91.

63. *An Essay on Milton's Use and Imitation of the Moderns in his Paradise Lost* (London, 1750), p. 163.

64. *The Divine Legation of Moses* (1738), repr. in Shawcross, *Critical Heritage*, II, 99.

65. *Timber: or, Discoveries* (1641), in *Ben Jonson*, ed. C. H. Herford and P. and E. Simpson (Oxford, 1947), VIII, 638.

4 The traditional genres

1. See below, ch. 7.

2. Collins' gloom needs to be reassessed. For some pregnant hints see especially John Sitter, "Mother, Memory, Muse, and Poetry after Pope," *ELH*, 44 (1977), p. 325; and Marshall Brown, "The Urbane Sublime," *ELH*, 45 (1978), p. 296.

3. *Of Dramatic Poesy and other Critical Essays*, ed. Geeorge Watson (London, 1962), II, 223.

4. "Life of Milton," in *Lives of the Poets*, ed. G. B. Hill, 3 vols. (London, 1905), I, 170.

5. *Prince Arthur* (1695), *King Arthur* (1697), *Eliza* (1705), and *Alfred* (1723).

6. "Life of Dryden," in *Lives of the Poets*, I, 386.

7. *Essay on Epic Poetry* (London, 1782), pp. 67, 286 (Hayley's own notes to his poetic *Essay*). Johnson thought the world had lost little in Pope's *Brutus*, but it is perhaps significant that he objected not to the form but the subject, a "ridiculous fiction" ("Life of Pope," in *Lives of the Poets*, III, 188–89). Joseph Warton doubted that *Brutus* would have succeeded because Pope's strengths were those of a "philosopher" rather than a "poet" (*Essay on the Genius and Writings of Pope* [1756, repr. 1974], pp. 280–81).

8. *James Thomson, 1700–1748: Letters and Documents*, ed. A. D. McKillop (Lawrence, Kansas, 1958), p. 74; *Gentleman's Magazine*, 63 (1793), p. 885.

9. Voltaire's *Essay on Epic Poetry* was published in English in 1727 prior to its appearance in French. The *Henriade* was translated into English three times by 1762. See the edition by F. D. White (Albany, N.Y., 1915).

10. One late-century observer, however, thought that full-scale epic, because it demanded a great deal of its reader, could no longer be "an entertainment suited to the general taste of the people." John Millar, *An Historical View of the English Government*, 4th edn (London, 1818), IV, 334.

11. The most compendious survey of eighteenth-century discussions of epic is H. T. Swedenberg, Jr., *The Theory of the Epic in England, 1650–1800* (Berkeley, 1944).

12. As early as 1727 Voltaire noted that *"Milton* is the last in *Europe* who wrote an *Epick* Poem,'' dismissing all subsequent examples as unsuccessful attempts. See White's edition of Voltaire's *Essay*, p. 129. Horace Walpole, who thought epic inherently absurd and *Paradise Lost* a "monster," declared that the genre had been degenerating ever since Homer and that it had finally died in Ossian (*Horace Walpole's Correspondence*, ed. W. S. Lewis, vol. 1 XXIX, pt. 2, [New Haven, 1955] p. 256). In 1787 John Millar commented that the epic in English had been declining "for more than a half century," and that the "late adventureres in this field... seem greatly inferior to their predecessors... They are a sort of minor poets, destitute of that creative power... but straining to be sublime." *An Historical View of the English Government*, IV, 333.

13. *The Divine Legation of Moses*, quoted in John Shawcross, *Milton: The Critical Heritage* (London, 1972), II, 99. Cf. Duff, on "the real difficulty of attaining complete originality in the province of the Epopoea" after Homer. *An Essay on Original Genius* (1767, repr. 1964), p. 278.

14. *Observations, Anecdotes, etc.*, I, 137, 153.

15. See below, chs. 8 and 9.

16. *Essay on Epic Poetry*, I, 41–48, and Hayley's notes, p. 120.

17. Hayley worried, however, that British campaigns in India might not offer a "subject truly noble" (notes, p. 297).

18. *Critical Observations on the Design of the Sixth Book of the Aeneid* (1770), in *Miscellaneous Works*, ed. John, Lord Sheffield (London, 1796), II, 502.

19. William Coward, *Licentia Poetica* (1709), as quoted in Swedenberg, *Theory of the Epic*, p. 70.

20. Watson (ed.), *Of Dramatic Poesy*, II, 92.

21. *Essay on Epic Poetry*, V, 288.

22. *Decline and Fall*, ch. 10, Everyman edn, ed. Oliver Smeaton (London, 1929–33), I, 236n. Gibbon says drily that though the story is "pleasing," since it deduces the enmity of the Goths and the Romans from "so memorable a cause," it cannot "safely be regarded as authentic history." Wordsworth later meditated an epic on the migration of Odin, whom he identified with Mithridates (*Prelude* [1805], Bk. I, lines 185–89).

23. *Essay on Epic Poetry*, V, 298.

24. Cumberland's *Calvary* was inspired by Milton (see Swedenberg, *Theory of the Epic*, pp. 128–29). That poem, like Aaron Hill's *Gideon*, may have been a critical failure, but we can reasonably attribute such failure to inadequacy in the poets rather than inherent defect in the subject or genre.

25. Cowley asked "what worthier *subject* could have been chosen among all the *Treasuries* of past times" than the life of David (1688 Preface), but his *Davideis*, of which he completed only four books of a projected twelve, did not answer his own *"Idea"* of a divine poem in epic form. *Poems*, ed. A. R. Waller (Cambridge, 1905), pp. 12–14.

26. *L'Art Poétique* (Paris, 1674), III, 177–92.

27. Blackmore, "Essay upon Epick Poetry," in *Essays upon Several Subjects* (London, 1716), p. 74.

28. *Ibid.*, pp. 34–35.

29. Henry Pemberton, *Observations on Poetry* (London, 1738), p. 164.

30. From a review of Kedington's *Critical Dissertations upon the Iliad*, in the

Critical Review (Jan. 1760), repr. in Goldsmith, *Collected Works*, ed. Arthur Friedman, 5 vols. (Oxford, 1966), I, 217. Cf. Trapp, who urged epic poets not to imitate Homer's and Virgil's subjects, but to follow Milton's example and "open a Way entirely new ... Whoever attempts an Heroic Poem, must form a new Plan." *Lectures in Poetry* (1742, repr. 1969), pp. 351–52.

31. *Life of Milton*, p. 220.

32. On eighteenth-century uneasiness about martial epic morality – with its implicit worship of violence and revenge – see C. J. Rawson, *Henry Fielding and the Augustan Ideal Under Stress* (London, 1972), pp. 158–59, 168–69.

33. A letter to Mason, June 25, 1782, in Lewis (ed.), *Horace Walpole's Correspondence*, XXIX, pt. 2, p. 256.

34. *An Enquiry into the Life and Writings of Homer* (1735, 2nd edn, 1736, repr. 1976), p. 26.

35. Lord Kames, *Elements of Criticism* (London, 1762), III, 235–36n.

36. *Lectures on Rhetoric and Belles Lettres* (1783), ed. Harold F. Harding (Carbondale, Ill., 1965), II, 41.

37. *Elements of Criticism*, III, 236.

38. *Critical Review*, 9 (1760), in Goldsmith, *Collected Works*, I, 223.

39. *Characteristics*, 5th edn (London, 1732), I, 358–59.

40. *Critical Observations on the Writings of the Most Celebrated Original Geniuses in Poetry* (London, 1770), pp. 303–04n.

41. *The Art of Poetry on a New Plan* (London, 1762), II, 364, published by John Newbery and possibly edited by Goldsmith, according to Swedenberg, *Theory of Epic*, p. 105.

42. *Letters on Chivalry and Romance* (1762), Letter 10, in *Works* (1811, repr. 1969), IV, 330–31.

43. Perhaps we can say that the poem offers both a traditional and a new version of epic. If we look at the poem with Christ, not Adam and Eve, in its center, we have the triumph of one warrior, superior in strength and purity, over a determined antagonist.

44. The choice of a private world means, as Thomas Greene notes, that the Miltonic hero is detached "from the community, the City of Man in this world," and discovers that he is not the independent master of his own fate. His actions depend finally on the will of a higher power. *The Descent from Heaven* (New Haven, 1963), p. 407.

45. Peter Hagin, *The Epic Hero and the Decline of Heroic Poetry* (Bern, 1964), p. 44.

46. Blackmore adapted the epic to the conditions of his day in a different way. For him "nothing ... should be an integral part of an Epick Poem, but what is easy, natural, and probable." *Essays upon Several Subjects*, p. 25.

47. Owen Ruffhead, *The Life of Pope* (1769, repr. 1968), pp. 410–24.

48. See David Morris, *The Religious Sublime* (Lexington, 1972), pp. 44–45.

49. See below, ch. 4.

50. Modern pastoralists, Purney says, should avoid imitating the classics and should "trust their own genius." *A Full Enquiry into the True Nature of Pastoral* (London, 1717, repr. 1948), intro. E. Wasserman, p. 71. His fourth chapter in Part IV is entitled "That there may be several sorts of Pastorals."

51. According to Pope, "the year has not that variety in it to furnish every month with a particular description, as it may every season" ("Discourse

on Pastoral Poetry,'' in *Poems*, Twickenham edition, I, 32). In his own poems Pope varies not only the season but also the time of day (morning, noon, sunset, midnight), the scene (valley, river's side, hill, grove), the passion (happy love, hopeless love, faithless and absent love, grief), and the format (singing contest, monologue, dialogue, and one singer with audience).

52. Browne notes approvingly that Rapin had allowed that pastoral "may contain more subjects than Virgil has made use of" (p. xxi). His eclogues of fisherman and fowlers were popular enough to reach a third edition in 1773. Browne's fifth eclogue was praised in the *Gentleman's Magazine* as the "best Imitation of Milton's Lycidas that has yet appear'd." *Gentleman's Magazine*, 10 (1740), 253.

53. *Life of Johnson*, ed. G. B. Hill, rev. L. F. Powell, 6 vols. (Oxford, 1934–50), II, 220.

54. See A. J. Sambrook, "The English lord and the happy husbandman," *Studies in Voltaire and the Eighteenth Century*, 57 (1967), 1357–58.

55. George Sherburn, "The Early Popularity of Milton's Minor Poems," *MP*, 17 (1919–20), 259–78, 515–40.

56. See especially Purney's *Full Enquiry*. *Lycidas* is not mentioned at all in Chetwode's "Preface" to Dryden's translation of Virgil's pastorals, in Pope's "Discourse", the *Guardian* papers on pastoral, or Blair's survey of the genre in his *Lectures*. Browne mentions Milton as a modern pastoralist, along with Spenser, Fletcher, Philips, and Congreve ("Preface" to *Angling Sports*).

57. "Discourse," in *Poems*, I, 25.

58. *Critical Essays* (1785, repr. 1969), pp. 41, 64; *Milton's Poems on Several Occasions* (1785), p. 35.

59. But he praises Milton for renewing those fictions: "what writer, of the same period, has made these obsolete fictions the vehicle of so much fancy and poetical description?" (p. 34).

60. "Life of Milton," in *Lives of the Poets*, I, 163.

61. *Critical Essays*, pp. 48, 54.

62. *Paradise Regained, Samson Agonistes, Poems upon Several Occasions*, ed. Thomas Newton, 2nd edn (London, 1753), II, 209.

63. *Poems on Several Occasions*, p. 35; *Critical Essays*, p. 40. Johnson of course found no "real passion." "Where there is leisure for fiction there is little grief." "Life of Milton," in *Lives of the Poets*, I, 163.

64. Johnson's elegy "On the Death of Dr. Levet," stanzaic in form, sober and contemplative in mood, is likewise modeled on the Horatian ode. See my "Johnson's Funeral Writings," *ELH*, 41 (1974), 192–211.

65. Of Tickell's elegy Johnson wrote "nor is a more sublime or more elegant funeral poem to be found in the whole compass of English literature." Of Smith's, "one of the best elegies which our language can show, an elegant mixture of fondness and admiration, of dignity and softness." *Lives of the Poets*, II, 16–17, 310.

66. See R. D. Havens on the minor "monody movement" beginning about mid-century and peaking c. 1770. *The Influence of Milton on English Poetry* (Cambridge, Mass., 1922), p. 554.

67. *Lives of the Poets*, I, 164.

68. Shawcross, *Critical Heritage*, I, 104, 121.
69. Newton paraphrases Fenton, without attribution, in his notes to the play.
70. Shawcross, *Critical Heritage*, II, 268.
71. *Works*, 6 vols. (1811, repr. 1969), I, 74.
72. J. H. Todd (ed.), *Poetical Works of Milton* (1803, 5th edn, 4 vols., 1852), III, 327.
73. *Ibid.*, III, 326.
74. See below, ch. 3.
75. *A Short View of Tragedy* (1692), in *Critical Works*, ed. Curt Zimansky (New Haven, 1956), p. 84.
76. *Lectures on Rhetoric and Belles Lettres*, "Tragedy," II, 477ff.
77. Hurd, in *Works*, 6 vols. (1811, repr. 1969), I, 145–46.
78. Todd (ed.), *Poetical Works*, III, 219.
79. *Works*, 4 vols., (London, 1811), II, 177.
80. Olivier Lutaud sees a political link, by way of *Killing No Murder* (see ch. 1), between Racine's play (about the killing of a wicked tyrant) and Milton's discussion of Old Testament tyrannicide in *Tenure of Kings and Magistrates* and the *Defenses. Des Révolutions d'Angleterre à la Révolution Française*, pp. 151–97. Milton (in the Trinity MS.) has projected a play on Athaliah.
81. See the Trinity MS., first printed in Birch's 1738 edition of Milton's prose.
82. Lines 38, 41: "we have sent gifts to Phoebus... and choirs chosen from the Druid race." See Mason, *Works*, II, 78. The Chorus in *Caractacus* consists of "Druids and Bards."
83. But *Athalie* and *Esther* were later played on the public stage without the chorus. As Milton noted, in the preface to *Samson Agonistes*, Renaissance Italian drama sometimes used a chorus, e.g., Tasso's *Aminta* and Guarini's *Il Pastor Fido*.
84. "A Parallel Betwixt Painting and Poetry" (1695), in Watson (ed.), *Of Dramatic Poesy*, II, 200.
85. See George Steiner, *The Death of Tragedy* (New York, 1961), esp. ch. 2.
86. Mason, *Works*, II, 181.
87. See below, ch. 5.
88. *Lives and Characters of the English Dramatic Poets* (1699), cited in Sherburn, "The Early Popularity of Milton's Minor Poems," p. 271.
89. See Anne Davidson Ferry, *Milton and the Miltonic Dryden* (Cambridge, Mass., 1968), pp. 127–218.
90. "Ben Jonson," in *Selected Essays*, 2nd edn (London, 1934), p. 160.
91. T. Warton, Milton's *Poems on Several Occasions*, p. 159n.
92. See the several studies by Stephen Orgel, including *The Jonsonian Masque* (Cambridge, Mass., 1965) and *The Illusion of Power: Political Theatre in the English Renaissance* (Berkeley, 1975).
93. Orgel makes the point that the masque scenic machine becomes the "normal dramatic stage" in the Restoration for all stageplays. See *English Drama to 1710*, Sphere History of Literature in the English Language, ed. C. Ricks (London, 1971), p. 367.
94. Davenant's *Salmacida Spolia*, presented on January 21, 1640, has been called the "last real court masque in England." See Orgel, in Ricks (ed.), *English Drama to 1710*, p. 366; and C. V. Wedgwood, "The Last Masque," in *Truth and Opinion: Historical Essays* (London, 1960), pp. 139–56.

95. *The London Stage, 1660–1800*, Part I: 1660–1700, ed. William Van Lennep *et al.* (Carbondale, Ill., 1965), p. 337.

96. Cf. Gilbert West's "Institution of the Order of the Garter. A Dramatic Poem" (1742), celebrating the Black Prince (a hero of the Oppositon to Walpole) as a "PATRIOT-KING" (p. 64). Printed with complete stage directions, set in Windsor Park and Castle, it recalls *Comus* in the iambic tetrameter spoken by the descending Genius of England. Lillo's *Britannia and Batavia. A Masque* was written to celebrate the marriage of the Princess Anne to Prince William IV of Orange. It combines the Jacobean elements of formal spectacle (a marriage procession) and political tendency (the struggle between Protestant Liberty and Papist Tyranny and Superstition). See *The Plays of Lillo*, ed. Trudy Drucker (New York, 1979), II, 207–19.

97. *The London Stage*, Part IV, vol. 1. Often, indeed, stage plays were adorned with inset "masques." *Timon of Athens* was frequently performed in the period with the "Masque of Bacchus and Cupid," as originally set by Purcell. See *The London Stage*, for details of performances in 1703, 1704, 1715, 1716. Shakespeare had provided for a "Mask of Ladies", with Cupid, in Act I.

98. Warton, *Poems on Several Occasions*, pp. 155, 265.

99. *Ibid.*, p. 127.

100. William Mason's *Sappho* was designed as a masque, "in which a part only … was meant to be set to Music," and later completed as a "lyrical drama" or "opera" in 1778, with continuous accompaniment to the recitative, duets, and airs. *Works*, II, 319–61. It is manifestly indebted to *Comus* in its prologue between Venus and Cupid and a scene in which the nymph Arethusa rises from her "translucent bed." Another non-political "masque" tradition thrives in the eighteenth century. Essentially short Italianate operas in English on a classical subject, these masques (also called "pastorals," "operas," "entertainments," or "serenatas") included sung recitative, airs and choruses, and some dancing. The best of these works is the Gay–Handel *Acis and Galatea* (1718), but other serious writers worked in the form. See, for example, Congreve's *The Judgment of Paris* (1701) and *Semele* (1707), and John Hughes' *Calypso and Telemachus* (1712) – similar in plot to *Comus* – and *Apollo and Daphne* (1716). For further details on the masque from Purcell to Handel, see Winton Dean, *Handel's Dramatic Oratorios and Masques* (London, 1959), pp. 153–59.

101. There is little evidence that Milton deterred poets from writing sonnets in the century after 1650. Indeed, his sonnets were relatively unavailable and unknown in the late seventeenth century. When the form was revived after 1750, the Miltonic sonnet was a common model for rhyme scheme and content. See Havens, *The Influence of Milton*, pp. 478–548.

5 Adaptations: re-making Milton

1. *Plays of Garrick*, ed. H. W. Pedicord and F. L. Bergman (Carbondale, Ill., 1981), III, p. xiii. Playwrights and theatre managers also altered Jacobean and Restoration plays for the eighteenth-century playhouse and audience.

2. The aesthetics of eighteenth-century adaptation have not been much studied. For one discussion, see Stephen Behrendt, "The Polished

Artifact: Some Observations on Imitative Criticism," *Genre*, 10 (1977), 47-62.

3. *Milton and English Art* (Manchester, 1970).

4. *Handel, Dryden, and Milton* (London, 1956, repr. 1970).

5. For articles prior to 1970 see Pointon's bibliography. See also Suzanne Boorsch, "The 1688 *Paradise Lost* and Dr. Aldrich," *Metropolitan Museum Journal*, 6 (1972), p. 149; John Dixon Hunt, "Milton's Illustrators," in *John Milton: Introductions*, ed. J. B. Broadbent (Cambridge, 1973), pp. 208-25; Judith Hodgson, "Satan Humanized: 18th-Century Illustrations of *Paradise Lost*," *Eighteenth-Century Life*, 1 (1974), 41-44; J. A. Wittreich, "Milton's 'First' Illustrator," *Seventeenth Century News*, 32 (1974), 70-71; Wittreich, *Angel of Apocalypse: Blake's Idea of Milton* (Madison, 1975), ch. 2; John Shawcross, "The First Illustrations for *Paradise Lost*," *Milton Quarterly*, 9 (1975), 43-46; M. D. Ravenhall, "Illustrations of *Paradise Lost* in England, 1688-1802," *DAI*, 41 (1980), 442A; Pamela Dunbar (ed.), *William Blake's Illustrations to the Poetry of Milton* (Oxford, 1980); M. D. Ravenhall, "Sources and Meanings in Dr. Aldrich's 1688 Illustrations of *Paradise Lost*," *ELN*, 19 (1982), 208-18; Stephen Behrendt, *The Moment of Explosion: Blake and the Illustrations of Milton* (Nebraska, 1983).

6. For a complete list of eighteenth-century performances, see the Index volume of *The London Stage*, ed. William Van Lennep *et al.* (Carbondale, Ill., 1965).

7. By J. C., William Hog, T. P., Charles Blake, Michael [not Matthew] Bold. John Shawcross, *Milton: The Critical Heritage* (London, 1972), II, 4-5. Shawcross also lists a number of translations of *Paradise Regained*, *Samson Agonistes*, and the minor poems. But he does not mention the translation of three passages from *Paradise Lost*, Bks. III, IV, and V in the *Gentleman's Journal* for May, June, and July 1694, by "Mr. Powers," apparently the same "T. P." or "Thomas Power" who translated Bk. I in 1691.

8. William Tilley, Robert Pitt, Samuel Say, Joseph Trapp, John Theobald, and William Dobson. Dobson's translation (1750) was commissioned by the Milton enthusiast William Benson. See Spence, *Observations, Anecdotes, and Characters of Books and Men*, ed. James D. Osborn, 2 vols. (Oxford, 1966), I, 137.

9. Shawcross omits versions by Ludovicus de Bonneval and "Miltonides" in *Gentleman's Magazine*, 16 (1746), 548-49, 20 (1750), 564-65, a 1768 abridgement of *Paradise Lost* into *Lapsum Protoparentum* in six books, and a 1740 translation of *Paradise Regained* by A. Jackson.

10. "Qui e libris Miltoni popularis nostri illum tibi exhibeo, erudite lector, Latine factum." *Paradissi Amissi Liber Primus* (Cambridge, 1691).

11. "Sed quia a Miltono Anglice scriptum fuit, ante hac exteris regionibus latuit incognitum." *Paraphrasis Poetica in Tria Johanni Miltoni Poemata* (London, 1690), p. vii.

12. Translation might also be a kind of grammatical interpretation. See Newton's citation of Trapp's translation of *Paradise Lost*, X. 569 to clarify an antithesis in the original.

13. Both Bentley and John Hawkey, whose edition of *Paradise Lost* appeared in 1747, were editors of Latin classics. One other motive might be noted: teaching Latin to schoolboys. Lauder had proposed a scheme "for making

a Latin School-book from *Paradise Lost.''* It was to be an abridgement, purged of all pagan mythology, put into Latin verse, and would serve as better moral instruction for Christian youth than traditional Latin classics. See *Gentleman's Magazine*, 17 (1747), 530–31.

14. Goldwin Smith, *Lectures and Essays* (Toronto, 1881), p. 324.

15. Johnson proposed an edition of the late-fifteenth-century poet Politian; Sarbiewski, "the Christian Horace," was commonly cited as a great lyric poet.

16. *Gentleman's Magazine*, 16 (1746), 548–49; 661; 18 (1750), 530–31.

17. *Milton's Paradise Lost Imitated in Rhyme. In the Fourth, Sixth, and Ninth Books, Containing Primitive Love. The Battel of the Angels. The Fall of Man* (London, 1699), "Preface." In 1708 appeared a paraphrase of *Paradise Lost*, II. 1–225, entitled *The Speeches of the Devils from Milton in Reflections Moral, Comical, Satyrical on the Vices and Follies of the Age, Pt. 6*. See M. M. Shudofsky, "An Early Eighteenth-Century Rhymed Paraphrase of *Paradise Lost*, II, 1–225," *MLN*, 56 (1941), 133–34.

18. *A Paraphrase in verse, on part of the first book of Milton's Paradise Lost* (1738), by W. Howard, and *Paradise Lost: A poem Attempted in rhime. Bk. I* (London, 1740), by A. Jackson.

19. This edition is described in Ants Oras, *Milton's Editors and Commentators from Patrick Hume to Henry John Todd* (Tartu, 1931, repr. 1964), pp. 173–83. It went through at least three further editions by 1770. *Paradise Regained* was done into prose as *The Recovery of Man* (1771).

20. Readers two hundred years later apparently still have such difficulties. A "Prose Rendition" of *Paradise Lost by John Milton* was published in 1983 by Seabury Press for the "contemporary reader who might be confused by Milton's syntax and vocabulary."

21. For a modern account of Wesley's popularization, see Oscar Sherwin, "Milton for the Masses: John Wesley's Edition of *Paradise Lost*," *MLQ*, 12 (1951), 267–85. Wesley seems also to have removed some passages – e.g., on eating and love in Eden and on the doctrine of election – for ideological reasons.

22. This edition, sometimes attributed to G. S. Green, is described in Oras, *Milton's Editors*, p. 183.

23. Preface to *Works of Shakespeare* (1732), pp. xxxix–xl.

24. E.g., V. 122, 765. For rejoinders by Pearce and Richardson to Bentley's emendations, arguing that he had misunderstood the passages, see Newton's edition.

25. *Correspondence of Pope*, ed. G. Sherburn (Oxford, 1956), II, 124.

26. One writer in 1715 thought *Paradise Lost* might "admit a second cultivation, and perhaps receive new beauties from another dress, at least be generally read with more pleasure and, which is no small benefit of rhyme, be retained with more ease." *Royal Grammar* (1715), in J. H. Todd (ed.), *Milton's Poetical Works*, 5th edn (1852), I, 396.

27. See *Milton Restor'd and Bentley Depos'd* (1732), in which a letter, allegedly addressed from "Dean Swift" to "Dr. Bentley" mockingly recommends that rhyme would make *Paradise Lost*, "in that only *defective*, more heroic and sonorous than it has hitherto been." See Todd, *Poetical Works*, 5th edn (1852), I, 396. Swift in fact had scorned the idea of "bestowing rhyme" on *Paradise Lost* in his "Letter of Advice to a Young Poet."

28. "Life of Milton," in *Lives of the Poets*, ed. G. B. Hill, 3 vols. (London, 1905), I, 194.

29. Dalton's was neither the first nor the last adaptation of *Comus* in the period. In 1737 Paul Rolli presented a masque entitled *Sabrina* at Covent Garden. Loosely "founded on the Comus of Milton," as its title page reads, it concerns two gentlemen and two ladies who set out for London and lose themselves in a wood along the way.

30. Ann Gossman and G. W. Whiting, "Comus, Once More, 1761," *RES*, 11 (1960), 56–60. See also *TLS*, September 17, 1954, p. 591.

31. "The Masque of Comus, with all its poetical beauties, not only maintained its place on the theatre chiefly by the assistance of Musick, but the Musick itself, as if overwhelmed by the weight of the Drama, almost sunk with it" ("Advertisement").

32. J. W. Good, *Studies in the Milton Tradition* (Urbana, 1915, repr. 1971), pp. 36–37.

33. George Sherburn, "The Early Popularity of Milton's Minor Poems," *MP*, 17 (1919–20), 259–78, 515–40.

34. Myers, *Handel, Dryden, and Milton*, p. 60.

35. William Hayes, *Remarks on Mr. Avison's Essay on Musical Expression* (1753), in Myers, *Handel, Dryden, and Milton*, p. 60.

36. For further comments on Jennens' text and an extended musical analysis of the Handel setting, see Michael O'Connell and John Powell, "Music and Sense in Handel's Setting of Milton's *L'Allegro* and *Il Penseroso*," *ECS*, 12 (1978), 16–46. I leave out of consideration a topic they deal with in detail – the way music can interpret and even "advance" Milton's meaning.

37. See Johnson's remark that "I always meet some melancholy in his mirth." "Life of Milton," in *Lives of the Poets*, I, 167.

38. In later performances, beginning in 1743, Handel omitted *Il Moderato*. O'Connell and Powell speculate that he sensed that the addition was not fully in keeping with the spirit of the original (p. 24).

39. Good lists editions in 1740 (twice), 1750, 1754, and 1779.

40. In 1715 John Hughes had added an 8-line "Supplement and Conclusion" to "Il Penseroso." See *Chalmers' English Poets* (1810), X, 56.

41. Milton's note "Of that Sort of Dramatic Poem Which is Called Tragedy."

42. Newton reported that Atterbury "had an intention of getting Mr. Pope to divide it into acts and scenes, and of having it acted by the King's Scholars at Westminster." 1773 edn, I, xxxix.

43. "Preliminary Observations," in *Critical, Poetical, and Dramatic Works* (1798), II, 213–14, repr. in Shawcross, *Critical Heritage*, II, 400.

44. Preface to the libretto, in Winton Dean, *Handel's Dramatic Oratorios and Masques* (London, 1959), p. 328.

45. *Ibid.*, p. 329. Hamilton also drew on "At a Solemn Music," "The Passion," and the epitaph on the Marchioness of Winchester. See *ibid.*, p. 330.

46. *Ibid.*, pp. 351–53.

47. Good, *Studies in the Milton Tradition*, p. 34.

48. Dean, *Handel's Dramatic Oratorios*, pp. 360–61.

49. As she wrote to a friend, "I begin with Satan's threatenings to seduce the woman, her being seduced follows, and it ends with the man's yielding

to the temptation.'' *The Autobiography and Correspondence of Mary Granville, Mrs. Delany*, ed. Lady Llanover, 3 vols. (London, 1861), II, 278. The "Morning Hymn" of Adam and Eve (V. 153–208) had been set, verbatim, by John Ernest Galliard in 1728. For a musical analysis, see Brian Morris, " 'Not Without Song': Milton and the Composers,'' in *Approaches to Paradise Lost*, ed. C. A. Patrides (Toronto, 1968), pp. 141–49.

50. *Paradise Lost. An Oratorio* (2nd edn, 1760), with a dedication by Stillingfleet to Mrs. Montagu in which he modestly notes the "hazardous" comparison he has exposed himself to by drawing on a "great original.'' The text follows Milton closely (though the 25 songs are newly composed from Miltonic "Sentiment").

51. Morris provides some musical analysis (pp. 151–55).

52. Published posthumously but prepared by Jago before his death in 1781.

53. A possible exception is Haydn's *The Creation*, based on a German adaptation of *Paradise Lost*, Bks. IV, V, and VII, that was subsequently translated back into English. It was first performed in Vienna in 1799 and printed in 1800.

54. Even the Milton Gallery project originated in plans for an elaborate edition of the poems.

6 New genres

1. R. D. Havens, *The Influence of Milton on English Poetry* (Cambridge, Mass., 1922), notes a number of contemporary parodies.

2. *Revaluation* (London, 1936), ch. 4, p. 108.

3. *Meditations and Contemplations* (Edinburgh, 1786), p. 263.

4. Cf. Virgil, *Eclogues* 1, 6, 10; Spenser, *Shepherd's Calendar*, "March,'' "April''; Phineas Fletcher, *The Purple Island*; Pope, *Pastorals*, "Autumn''; Dyer, "Country Walk.''

5. *Paradise Lost*, I. 743, 598; IV. 647, 654; IX. 1088; X. 95; III. 42.

6. Thomas Warton borrows "grateful evening mild'' in his *Pastoral Eclogues* (II. 14).

7. I have commented on the passage in "Milton's Evening,'' *Milton Studies*, 9 (1976), 151–67.

8. *Paradise Lost*, ed. Thomas Newton (1773 edn), I, 299–300.

9. *Explanatory Notes on Paradise Lost* (1734), p. 169.

10. For Dennis the lines produced "the Enthusiasm of Admiration'' by leading "the soul to its Maker'' so as to "shew... his Eternal Power and Godhead'' (*Critical Works of John Dennis*, ed. E. N. Hooker [Baltimore, 1939], I, 348–49). In his friend Thomson's opinion, "this equals any Image ever Milton gave us of the Evening.'' *James Thomson (1700–48): Letters and Prose Documents*, ed. A. D. McKillop (Lawrence, Kansas, 1958), p. 44. Richard Jago included it among the "particular beauties'' of *Paradise Lost* that he wove into his *Adam: An Oratorio* (see above, p. 70).

11. *Art of English Poetry* (1702), pp. 127, 263. When James Hervey describes the "gradual approaches of night,'' he quotes the first two lines of Milton's passage (*Meditations and Contemplations*, p. 272).

12. For these lines the faithful Lattimore gives simply "for by this time darkness had descended on the land.'' Cf. Pope's translation of *Odyssey* 3. 422 (in Pope's numbering): "And twilight gray her evening shade

extends.'' Fitzgerald gives ''the sun went down the sky and gloom came on the land.''

13. Cf. the anonymous ''An Evening Prospect'' (1786): ''Scarce onward steals the loitering stream, / And eve o'er all her mantle throws'' (*Gentleman's Magazine*, 56 [1786], p. 513).

14. *Poems on Several Subjects* (1769), I, 136.

15. Gray, ''Elegy Wrote in a Country Churchyard,'' line 1; anon., ''Ode to Night'', in Dodsley's *Collection*, vol. IV (1765); T. Warton, ''Summer,'' line 5; John Ogilvie, ''Ode to Evening,'' in *Poems on Several Subjects*, I, 100. Cf. also pp. 98, 99; John Brown, ''Fragment of a Rhapsody, Written at the Lakes in Westmoreland,'' in Anderson's *British Poets* (1765), X, 887.

16. In Dodsley's *Collection*, vol. IV.

17. *Oxford Book of Eighteenth-Century Verse*, ed. D. Nichol Smith (1926), p. 504.

18. ''The solitude that all around becalms / The peaceful air conspires to wrap my soul / In musings mild,'' T. Warton, *Five Pastoral Eclogues*, II. 28 – 30; ''the still, the mild, the melancholy hour,'' Mallet, *The Excursion*, I, 244; ''the slow, solemn, musing hour,'' Ogilvie, ''Ode to Evening.''

19. John Gilbert Cooper, *The Power of Harmony* (1745), II. 43 – 44; cf. Richard Jago, ''In purple vestments clad, the temper'd sky / Invites us from our hospitable roof, / To taste her influence mild,'' *Edge-Hill*, Bk. IV, ''The Evening''; T. Warton, ''Then let me walk the twilight meadows green, / Or breezy uplands, near thick-branching elms,'' *Five Pastoral Eclogues*, II. 20 – 21; Akenside, ''amid the calm / That soothes this vernal evening into smiles, / I steal impatient... / ...to attend / Thy sacred presence in the sylvan shade,'' *Pleasures of Imagination*, I. 574 – 78; Wordsworth, ''eve's mild hour invites my steps abroad,'' ''An Evening Walk'' (1793), line 88.

20. Cf. Spenser, who calls Hesperus ''the glorious lamp of love'' (''Epithalamium,'' line 288), and Milton, who calls the evening star ''Love's Harbinger'' (*Paradise Lost*, XI. 589). Earlier in the poem Hesperus lights ''the bridal Lamp'' (VIII. 520). For eighteenth-century examples, see also Robert Lloyd's ''To the Moon,'' ''An Evening Ode. To Stella,'' sometimes attributed to Johnson, and ''An Evening Ode to Delia,'' *Gentleman's Magazine*, 24 (1754), p. 428. For the distinction between the evening star poem and the evening poem, I am indebted to Prof. Charles Frey, who first prompted my thinking about evening poems more than fifteen years ago.

21. Cf. the ''dim misty orb'' and the ''cheerful radiance'' in John Scott's ''Tempestuous Evening,'' ''Melancholy Evening,'' and ''Pleasant Evening''; Robert Lloyd's ''To the Moon'' (set at evening); Langhorne's ''Evening Primrose,'' which celebrates ''the modest mien / Of gentle evening fair, and her star-train'd queen''; and T. Warton's *Pleasures of Melancholy*, where ''at twilight hour of Eve'' the pale moon ''Pours her long-levell'd rule of streaming light'' through a western window. Warton probably recalls the ''levelled'' evening rays of the setting sun in *Paradise Lost*, IV. 543.

22. *Meditations and Contemplations*, p. 321. Though a devout Miltonist, Hervey does not acknowledge his source. Both Fielding and Sterne remember Milton in their parodies of ''moon-pieces'' in *Tom Jones*, Bk. VIII, ch. 9, and *Tristram Shandy*, vol. VI, ch. 35.

23. "Fragment of a Rhapsody," in Anderson's *British Poets*, X, 887.
24. Pope's passage was singled out for admiration by James Ralph (Preface to *Night*, 2nd. edn, 1729, p. vii) and James Hervey (*Meditations and Contemplations*, p. 323n). Wordsworth as late as 1815 complained that "there is not a passage of descriptive poetry, which at this day finds so many and such ardent admirers" ("Essay Supplementary to the Preface," in the 1815 *Poems*, *Poetical Works*, ed. Hutchinson, rev. E. De Selincourt, Oxford, 1967, p. 747). John Brown's moonlight night, in his "Fragment of a Rhapsody," draws equally on Milton and Pope.
25. Cf. Mickle's "Pollio" (1765): "How bright, emerging o'er yon broom-clad height, / The silver empress of the night appears!"
26. Evening becomes a favorite setting for late-eighteenth-century aestheticians and Romantic poets. For a useful survey, see Mary Robbins Duncan, "'That Uncertain Heaven': Twilight Settings in 18th-century and Romantic Literature," unpubl. Ph. D. dissertation (Kentucky, 1983). For a characteristically suggestive discussion of Romantic developments, see Geoffrey Hartman, "Reflections on the Evening Star: Akenside to Coleridge," in *New Perspectives on Coleridge and Wordsworth*, ed. Hartman (New York, 1972), 85–132.
27. See the notes in R. Lonsdale (ed.), *The Poems of Gray, Collins, and Goldsmith* (London, 1969).
28. E. G. Ainsworth, *Poor Collins* (Ithaca, 1937), p. 145. See also Lonsdale's notes.
29. I quote Collins' poems from *The Works of Collins*, ed. Richard Wendorf and Charles Ryskamp (Oxford, 1979). "Ye genii" appears on pp. 76–77.
30. *Works of Collins*, p. 73.
31. Lonsdale notes that the latter poem imitates Pope's "Elegy to the Memory of an Unfortunate Lady." In the fourth *Oriental Eclogue*, set at midnight, "the Moon had hung her Lamp on high, / And past in Radiance thro' the cloudless sky" (lines 5–6).
32. *Works of Collins*, p. 9.
33. Compare the "Ode to Simplicity," where the nightingale "In Evening musings slow" soothes the "ear" of Sophocles (lines 17–18).
34. Paul Sherwin overstates the "submerged sexual element" and "prothalamic effect." In his view the "Ode" is a virtual love poem to Evening (*Precious Bane: Collins and the Miltonic Legacy* [Austin, Texas, 1977], p. 121).
35. *The Sister Arts* (Chicago, 1958), p. 286.
36. Patrick Hume, *Annotations on Paradise Lost* (1695, repr. 1971), p. 154.
37. Marshall Brown, "The Urbane Sublime," *ELH*, 45 (1978), p. 247; Richard Wendorf, *William Collins and Eighteenth-Century English Poetry* (Minneapolis, 1981), p. 133.
38. Sherwin, *Precious Bane*, pp. 121–22.
39. *The Pleasures of Imagination*, II. 504–06.
40. Sherwin, *Precious Bane*, p. 118.
41. Thomas Maresca notes briefly in his *Epic to Novel* (Columbus, 1974) that "*Paradise Lost* already contains the seeds of mock-epic" (p. 8).
42. *The Logical Epic* (Cambridge, 1967), p. 143.
43. See Barbara Lewalski's remarks on the "large component of satire in Milton's epics," in "Upon Looking into Pope's Milton," *Etudes anglaises*,

27 (1974), p. 499. Ronald Paulson, *The Fictions of Satire* (Baltimore, 1967), pp. 115–19, suggests that *Paradise Lost* opened up some opportunities for religious satire.

44. Sin later tells Satan that God "sits above and laughs the while / At thee ordained his drudge" (*Paradise Lost*, II. 190–91).

45. *Spectator* papers on *Paradise Lost*, repr. in Shawcross, *Critical Heritage*, I, 171. Addison quotes here from *Paradise Lost*, I. 529.

46. *Voltaire's Essay on Epic Poetry*, ed. F. D. White (Albany, 1915), p. 132.

47. John Clarke, *An Essay upon Study* (1731), repr. in Shawcross, *Critical Heritage*, I, 261.

48. *Critical Heritage*, I, 174.

49. *Voltaire's Essay on Epic Poetry*, pp. 141–42.

50. Kames, *Elements of Criticism* (London, 1762), I, 378.

51. Notes to the *Iliad*, in *Poems*, VII, 293.

52. See further, ch. 9 below.

53. "A Poem to the Memory of Mr. John Philips," in Philips' *Poems Attempted in the Style of Milton* (London, 1762), p. 29.

54. Cf. *Paradise Lost*, X. 540ff, where the devils eat fruit that turns in their mouths to dust and bitter ashes.

55. *Georgics* II. 246–47, cited by Newton.

56. George Sewell, "Life of Philips," in Philips' *Poems on Several Occasions* (1720), p. 15.

57. Preface to Parnell's *Life of Zoilus*, prefixed to his translation of the *Batrachomyomachia* (1717). See George Sherburn, *The Early Career of Alexander Pope* (Oxford, 1934), pp. 191–92.

58. *Lives of the Poets*, I, 317.

59. For a recent example, see Maresca, *From Epic to Novel*.

60. Henry Knight Miller, *Henry Fielding's Tom Jones and the Romance Tradition* (Victoria, 1976); J. Paul Hunter, *The Reluctant Pilgrim* (Baltimore, 1966); Walter Reed, *An Exemplary History of the Novel* (Chicago, 1981).

61. Melvyn New, "'The Grease of God': The Form of Eighteenth-Century English Fiction," *PMLA*, 91 (1976), 235–43.

62. See below, pp. 102–03.

63. Clarissa recognizes Lovelace as "Satan himself" (Everyman edition, III, 210). When Lovelace throws off his disguise at Hampstead he remembers Ithuriel's spear (III, 41). After Clarissa has run off with Lovelace she quarrels with him: "But here, sir, like the first pair (I, at least, driven out of my paradise), are we recriminating" (I, 502).

64. *Spectator* No. 240, 248, in *The Spectator*, ed. D. F. Bond, 5 vols. (London, 1965), II, 433, 463.

65. Miller, *Tom Jones and the Romance Tradition*, pp. 57, 58.

66. Milton's own description of the "progressive steps in repentance" in *De Doctrina Christiana*. See Fowler's note to *Paradise Lost*, X. 828.

67. This is Miller's example. *Tom Jones and the Romance Tradition*, p. 32.

68. J. Paul Hunter, *Henry Fielding and the Chains of Circumstance* (Baltimore, 1975), p. 149.

69. Patricia M. Spacks, *Imagining a Self* (Cambridge, 1976), p. 8.

70. *Critical Works of John Dennis*, ed. E. N. Hooker (Baltimore, 1939), I, 278.

71. *Critical Works*, I, 372.

72. "Life of Philips," in Philips' *Poems on Several Occasions* (1720), p. 26.
73. Sewell, in *Poems on Several Occasions* (1720), pp. 26–27.
74. For a full list, see Havens, *The Influence of Milton*.
75. *The Religious Sublime: Christian Poetry and Critical Tradition in 18th-Century England* (Lexington, 1972).
76. Boswell, *Life of Johnson*, ed. G. B. Hill, rev. L. F. Powell, 6 vols. (Oxford, 1934–50), IV, 278, 299.
77. See his *A Gathered Church* (1978) and *Dissentient Voice* (1982).
78. Lily B. Cambell, "The Christian Muse," *Huntington Library Bulletin*, 8 (1935), 29–70. See also Hooker's notes to Dennis's *Critical Works*.
79. *Critical Works*, I, 330, quoting Milton's *Reason of Church Government*.
80. *Critical Works*, I, 286, 335, 389.
81. Dennis also thought that religion in *Paradise Regained* hindered "the violence of the ordinary Passions" as well as the "Violence of Action, which is always attended by the Violence of ordinary Passion" (*Critical Works*, I, 369).
82. *Critical Works*, II, 114.
83. *Tracts and Pamphlets*, ed. Rae Blanchard (Baltimore, 1944), p. 36.
84. Charles Wesley alludes frequently to *Paradise Lost*. For Cowper's admiration of Milton, see below, ch. 12.
85. Watts apparently means either *The Grounds of Criticism in Poetry* or *The Advancement and Reformation of Poetry*. As P. Steese notes, Watts cites in his Preface many of the same examples of biblical poetry also found in ch. 5 of *The Grounds of Criticism*. *PQ*, 42 (1963), pp. 275–77.
86. Preface to *Hymns and Spiritual Songs*.
87. "When I survey the wondrous cross."
88. Watts deeply admired the neo-Latin poems of the Polish Jesuit Casimir Sarbiewski.
89. After the Fall Adam and Eve are "the hapless Pair" (X. 342).
90. Johnson conceded the lines to be smooth and easy, but wished for more "spriteliness and vigour" (*Lives of the Poets*, III, 311). For Watts' concern for "the ease and rest of the ear" and his dislike of strong enjambment, see his essay "Of the Different Stops and Cadences in Blank Verse," in *Reliquiae Juveniles* (1734).

7 Regaining paradise

1. *A Collection of Miscellanies*, 5th edn (1710), pp. 89–90.
2. Cf. his poem "The Retirement": "Lord of my self, accountable to none, / Like the first Man in *Paradise*, alone." *A Collection*, p. 19.
3. *Poems on Various Occasions* (1737), pp. 40–41. Milton's eighteen lines (*Paradise Lost*, XI. 268–86) are expanded to twenty couplets.
4. See above, ch. 5, note 5.
5. *Essay on Epick Poetry*, p. 143.
6. *Milton's Paradise Lost. A New Edition* (1732, repr. 1974), p. 399.
7. *The Castle of Indolence*, xxii. 5; *The Excursion* (1728), I. 241.
8. "With pensive steps and slow" (*Odyssey*, X. 286); "with solemn pace and slow" (*Odyssey*, XI. 397); "by timid steps, and slow" (*Dunciad*, IV. 46).

9. "Epistle to Hanmer," line 67; "Ode for Music," line 36; "Deserted Village," line 115 ("careless steps and slow"); "Edwin and Angelina," line 6 ("fainting steps and slow").

10. "Descriptive Sketches" (1793), line 813, in *Poetical Works: Poems Written in Youth, Poems Referring to the Period of Childhood*, ed. E. de Selincourt (Oxford, 1940), p. 90. Cf. a 1795 translation of Petrarch: "ling'ring steps and slow," in *Sonnets, Triumphs, and other Poems of Petrarch* (London, 1883), p. 38.

11. Ed. J. Nichols (1818), I, 63. It is possible that Dunton was remembering Samuel Crossman's *The Young Mans Monitor* (1664), later reprinted as *The Young Man's Calling* (1678): "You have the world now before you, your own mercy or misery yet to choose" (1664 edn, p. 5). Cf. Defoe's *A General History of Discoveries and Improvements* (1726): "the World lay before them" (p. 13). A 1729 periodical, *The Knight Errant*, has as its motto, "The World is all before thee," an appropriate field for a wandering knight. I owe the last two references to Paula Backscheider.

12. *Correspondence of Pope*, ed. G. Sherburn (Oxford, 1956), II, 165. Newton reports that Atterbury quoted the same lines to a group of Westminster scholars (of whom Newton was one) visiting him in the Tower. See H. C. Beeching, *Francis Atterbury* (London, 1909), p. 304.

13. Elsewhere Johnson uses Milton's phrase as an image of unlimited possibility. Shakespeare, he says, "engaged in dramatick poetry with the world open before him" (*Preface to Shakespeare*, in *Works* [Yale edition], vol. VII, *Johnson on Shakespeare*, ed. A. Sherbo [New Haven, 1968], p. 69).

14. *Correspondence*, ed. T. W. Copeland *et al.* (Cambridge and Chicago, 1958–78), VI, 384. Of some displaced cousins, William Cowper writes: "the world being all before them, where to choose their place of rest, could settle here if it were possible." *Letters and Prose Writings*, ed. James King and Charles Ryskamp (Oxford, 1982), III, 528.

15. *The Duenna*, Act I, sc. iv, in *Sheridan's Plays*, ed. Cecil Price (Oxford, 1975), p. 124.

16. Gray's editor cites *Paradise Lost*, V. 3–4, where Adam's sleep was "aerie light, from pure digestion bred." *The Poems of Gray, Collins, and Goldsmith*, ed. R. Lonsdale (London, 1969), p. 59.

17. *Paradise Lost*, IV. 156.

18. *Paradise Lost*, IV. 155–56.

19. Cf. Goldsmith's wish to "bend to the grave with unperceived decay" (line 109) with Adam and Eve's hope, in Dryden's *State of Innocence*, to melt "by unperceiv'd decay," finding thus a "painless way / Of kindly mixing with our native clay" (V. i). Dryden's lines are based on Adam's hopes to end in Edenic dust, his "native home" (*Paradise Lost*, X. 1084–85).

20. "Spot more delicious than those Gardens feign'd" (*Paradise Lost*, IX. 439); cf. "That spot to which I point is Paradise" (III. 733). Goldsmith seems also to have Pope's *Essay on Man* in mind: "Fix'd to no spot is Happiness sincere" (IV. 15).

21. *Natural Supernaturalism: Tradition and Revolution in Romantic Literature* (New York, 1971), pp. 27–28 and passim.

22. See, for example, James Engell, *The Creative Imagination: Enlightenment to Romanticism* (Cambridge, Mass., 1981).

23. *Oroonoko*, intro. L. Metzger (New York, 1973), p. 3.

24. John Edwards, *A Compleat History or Survey of all the Dispensations and Methods of Religion, from the Beginning of the World to the Consummation of all Things; as Represented in the Old and New Testament* (1699), in E. Tuveson, *Millenium and Utopia* (Berkeley, 1949), p. 133.
25. Tuveson, *Millenium and Utopia*, p. 133.
26. *The Use and Intent of Prophecy*, in *ibid.*, p. 141.
27. *The Scripture Theory of the Earth*, in *ibid.*, p. 141.
28. See Michael Macklem, *The Anatomy of the World: Relations between Natural and Moral Law from Donne to Pope* (Minneapolis, 1958).
29. For the traditional distinction between a "natural" and a "constructed" paradise, and for the pronouncedly "architectural" quality of Milton's heavenly paradise, see William McClung, *The Architecture of Paradise* (Berkeley, 1983). See also John Knott, *Milton's Pastoral Vision* (Chicago, 1971), pp. 62–87, for the combination of urban magnificence and pastoral landscape in Milton's heaven. Despite the splendor of contemporary European capitals, for the eighteenth-century imagination, thanks in part no doubt to Milton's Eden, paradise meant a garden.
30. First printed in *Thalia Rediviva: The Pass-Times and Diversions of a Countrey-Muse* (1678).
31. "Numquam minus solus quam cum solus" (*De republica* I. xvii. 27, and *De Officiis* III. i. i). In the seventeenth century the idea was commonplace. See Cowley, "Of Solitude"; *Paradise Lost*, IX. 249.
32. "The Retirement," first printed in D. Lewis, *Miscellaneous Poems* (1730), repr. *Oxford Book of Eighteenth-Century Verse*, ed. D. Nichol Smith (1926), pp. 202–03. For a later example, in which retreat-as-Eden has become cliché, see "Solitude. An Allegorical Ode": "Where Nature all her charms resumes, / And *Eden* still unfaded blooms," in *Gentleman's Magazine*, 18 (1748), p. 278.
33. "A Hymn to Contentment" (1714), in *Oxford Book of Eighteenth Century Verse*, pp. 154–56.
34. I am indebted to Leon Guilhamet, *The Sincere Ideal* (Montreal, 1974), for drawing my attention to this poem. Cf. Samuel Boyse, "Retirement: A Poem Occasioned by seeing the Palace and Park of Yester" (1735), in which Serena presides, "A firmer EVE, amidst a safer Grove" (p. 16).
35. *The Poetical Works of Isaac Watts and Henry Kirke White* (Boston, n.d.), p. 189, repr. *Oxford Book of Eighteenth-Century Verse*, p. 51.
36. That Milton's Eden continued to provide a metaphor for a recovered paradise within can be seen in a poem "Occasioned by a young Lady weeping on hearing the Author read *Paradise Lost*," in the *London Magazine* in 1759: "Let conscious virtue o'er your heart preside, / Controul each thought, and ev'ry action guide; / Then, in your breast, shall Eden bloom anew, / And long last Paradise revive in you." I owe this example to G. W. Whiting, *Notes and Queries*, 202 (1957), 446–47. Cf. also a poem in the *London Spy* for May, 1698, p. 12, in which a youth who spends time on study rather than "the tempting Sex" will be rewarded: "To Adam's first perfections he'd attain; / And by degrees Lost Paradise Regain."
37. Chalmers' *Works of the English Poets* (1810), XVII, 338–39.
38. Cf. his ode "To Sleep," in which Akenside asks for visions like the prophetic visions that soothed Milton (perhaps the "inward prompting"

that he might "leave something so written to aftertimes, as they should not willingly let it die" (*Reason of Church Government*).

39. Cf. Milton's "Things unattempted, yet in Prose or Rhyme" and "to the Highth of this great Argument" (*Paradise Lost*, I. 16, 24). In the revised *Pleasures of the Imagination* (1757) Akenside made this allusion closer: "unattempted theme" (I. 696).

40. Cf. Milton's narrator, who draws "Empyreal Air" in his poetic flights to heaven (VII. 14). "Aethereal" is a particularly Miltonic word, occurring 20 times in *Paradise Lost*.

41. See William Riggs, *The Christian Poet in 'Paradise Lost'* (Berkeley and Los Angeles, 1972).

42. John Sitter links Akenside too readily with Satan, and does not attend sufficiently to the parallels with Milton's narrator. His essay "Theodicy at Midcentury: Young, Akenside, and Hume," *Eighteenth-Century Studies*, 12 (1978), 90–106, has been included in his recent book, *Literary Loneliness in Mid-Eighteenth-Century England* (Ithaca, 1982).

43. Like Michael, the Genius makes a "slow descent" from a "purple cloud" (222–23). Cf. Michael who "slow descends" in a "Western Cloud" (IX. 205–07). Michael raises Adam by the hand and bids him see; the Genius touches Harmodius' forehead, bidding him "raise his sight."

44. Cf. Milton's "Silvan Scene" and "woody Theatre" (*Paradise Lost*, IV. 140–41).

45. Akenside's own notes to the passage suggest that his creation account is based on Plato's *Laws*, the *Meditations* of Marcus Aurelius, Leibniz, and Shaftesbury's *Characteristics*. But the context, together with the "vital flame" (cf. Milton's "vital virtue" and "vital warmth" in *Paradise Lost*, VII. 236) suggest that Akenside is also indebted to Milton's own heavily Platonic account.

46. "Tract of time" is Miltonic (*Paradise Lost*, V. 498).

47. Akenside has been called a "Prophet of Evolution" for his vision of the gradual march of generations to "higher scenes of being" and the development of inborn mental powers. See G. R. Potter, *MP*, 24 (1926), 55–62. But Akenside's notions should perhaps be seen as an elaboration of traditional ideas found in Milton and elsewhere.

48. Milton calls her "heart-easing Mirth" ("L'Allegro," line 12).

49. Cf. "Her long with ardent look his Eye pursu'd / Delighted, but desiring more her stay. / Oft he to her his charge of quick return / Repeated" (*Paradise Lost*, IX. 397–99).

50. Cf. "immortal Fruits" (*Paradise Lost*, XI. 285).

51. *The Pleasures of the Imagination*, III. 9–11.

52. Cf. "O my adventurous song" (6), "soar'd among the worlds above" (13), "A curious, but an unpresuming guest," "A different task remains" (20); cf. Milton, "my advent'rous Song" (I. 13), "soar / Above th' *Aonian* Mount" (I. 14), "I have presum'd, / An Earthly Guest" (VII. 13–14), "Half yet remains unsung" (VII. 21). Later in Bk. I of the revised *Pleasures of the Imagination* Fancy dreams of "happy groves / Where Milton dwells" (167–68).

53. Cf. Young's *The Centaur Not Fabulous*, an attack on the fashionable "man of pleasure," where Eden is an unstable paradise, nodding toward its

inevitable fall: "There is no man of Pleasure without his Eve; no Eve without her Serpent; no Serpent without its Sting" (2nd edn, 1755), p. 112.

54. In his own garden at Welwyn an inscription read "Ambulantes in horto audierunt vocem Dei." See *The Life and Letters of Edward Young*, ed. H. C. Shelley (Boston, 1914), p. 282, corrected by Maynard Mack, *The Garden and the City*, (Toronto, 1969), p. 25n. It is significant that Young alludes to Eden after the Fall (Genesis 3. 8).

55. I quote from the Loeb Library edition and translation of II. 472.

56. See Anthony Low, "Milton, *Paradise Regained*, and Georgic," *PMLA*, 98 (1983), 152–69, and Low's *The Georgic Revolution* (Princeton, 1985), on the uses of georgic in seventeenth-century English writers, including Milton.

57. *Essay on the Georgics*, originally published as a preface to Dryden's translation of Virgil's *Georgics*, in *Works of Addison*, 5 vols. (New York, 1853), II, 380–81.

58. For a fuller treatment of *Cyder* as a Virgilian georgic, see J. Chalker, *The English Georgic* (London, 1969). Chalker comments briefly on the Miltonic aspects of the poem, noting both seriousness and exaggeration, saying simply, "The reference to the Garden of Eden [*Cyder*, I. 512–17] reveals at once both the limitations and the excellencies of country life in Augustan England" (p. 43).

59. Philips draws equally on the military and the pastoral parts of *Paradise Lost*, the former most commonly in mock-heroic passages, the latter in descriptions of cider and apples, e.g. *Cyder*, I. 31, 142, 305; II. 53, 59, 62, 215, 442.

60. *Milton's Sublimity Asserted: In a Poem Occasion'd by a Late Celebrated Piece, Entituled Cyder. A Poem*, by "Philo-Milton" (London, 1709), pp. 20–21.

61. Cf. XI. 718, "From Cups to civil Broils."

62. In another passage describing the wars among the Saxon Heptarchy, Philips again draws on *Paradise Lost*. Cf. especially *Cyder*, II. 543–44 and *Paradise Lost*, VI. 211–16.

63. Cf. Dryden's prologue to *The Unhappy Favourite* (1681): "Our Land's an Eden, and the Main's our Fence, / While we Preserve our State of Innocence" (lines 27–28), i.e. while we obey our king. Alan Roper, who notes the traditional political interpretation of Eden, says Dryden here implies that men can "lose and retain paradise as often as they rebel against and restore their king." *Dryden's Poetic Kingdoms* (New York, 1965), p. 107. Philips appears to take the same view.

64. "Indissolubly firm" is borrowed from Milton's description of the movement of the angelic army in *Paradise Lost*, VI. 69. Anther sign of Philips' secularizing parody is that Robert Harley, in the conduct of the war, like God the Father during the War in Heaven, weighs "the Sum of Things, with wise Forecast" (*Cyder*, I. 655, cf. *Paradise Lost*, VI. 673–74: "Consulting on the sum of things, foreseen / This tumult"). "Strait" is another Miltonism. Milton uses the word three times in *Paradise Lost* in contexts involving commands or obedience.

65. See *Cooper's Hill*, lines 181–88, and six lines added in holograph by Denham, in the edition by Brendan O Hehir, *Expans'd Hieroglyphicks* (Berkeley, 1969), p. 150; and *Annus Mirabilis*, stanzas 297–302.

66. *Georgics*, II. 136–76, 458–74; *Eclogue* IV. That England (Gaunt's "this other Eden") was an earthly paradise is an ancient idea still alive in the mid-seventeenth century. See J.W. Bennett, "Britain Among the Fortunate Isles," *SP*, 53 (1956), 114–40. The example of Philips shows that, perhaps strengthened by *Paradise Lost*, the idea persists into the eighteenth century.

67. *Georgics*, I. 145–46 (Loeb translation).

68. For Pope's Miltonic georgic, *Windsor Forest*, see below, ch. 9.

69. *Poems* (1761, repr. Scolar Press, 1971), p. 54. Siluria, as Dyer's note reads, denotes "the part of England which lies west of the Severn."

70. An early admirer of Milton, Dyer as a young poet filled half a notebook with quotations from *Paradise Lost*. See Ralph Williams, *Poet, Painter, and Parson: The Life of John Dyer* (New York, 1956), p. 35n.

71. The view from Breaden Hill (p. 82) – "Woods, tow'rs, vales, caves, dells, cliffs, & torrent floods; / And here and there … / The broad flat sea" – recalls *Paradise Lost*, IX. 117–18: "Now Land, now Sea, and Shores with Forest crown'd, / Rocks, Dens, and Caves." The description of Kashmire, "the paradise of Indus," likewise derives from Milton's panoramas. Cf. "Within a lofty mound of circling hills / Spreads her delicious stores; woods, rocks, caves, lakes / Hills, lawns, and winding streams" (p. 105), with "a rural mound … loftiest shade … circling row / Of goodliest trees" (*Paradise Lost*, IV. 134–47, IX. 116–18).

72. "English Plains / Blush with pomaceous Harvests, breathing Sweets," *Cyder*, II. 58. *OED* gives one earlier example from 1706. Johnson quotes only Philips' line.

73. Cf. "as the Vine curls her tendrils" (*Paradise Lost*, IV. 307).

74. Milton uses "delicious" nine times to describe Eden or its fruits.

75. "What by frugal storing firmness gains," "rough, or smooth rin'd, or bearded husk" (*Paradise Lost*, V. 324, 342); "She tempers dulcet creams" (V. 347).

76. Arab shepherds roam through a dry land, but English swains walk beside the "liquid lapse / Of river" (p. 76). Cf. *Paradise Lost*, VIII. 263, "the liquid Lapse of murmuring Streams."

77. In Eden "sweet Gard'ning labor" makes "wholesome thirst and appetite / More grateful" (*Paradise Lost*, IV. 328–31).

78. That land improvement was a "new creation" may have become a kind of cliché. See the praise of Capability Brown ("At his command a new Creation blooms") in *The Rise and Progress of the Present State of Planting* (1767), p. 19.

79. Compare Milton's creator on the first day, who rides "Far into *Chaos* … to circumscribe / This Universe" (VII. 219–27); and *Paradise Lost*, I. 9–10: "how the Heav'ns and Earth / Rose out of *Chaos*."

80. Bk. IV, p. 186. Cf. "man shall every-where be cloath'd" (p. 187).

81. "To shut sheep in the fold" is still the first meaning of "fold" (v.) in Johnson's exactly-contemporary *Dictionary*.

82. For modern surveys of eighteenth-century garden theory and practice, with some emphasis on Milton's importance, see J. Walter Good, *Studies in the Milton Tradition* (Urbana, 1915, rpt. 1971), pp. 268–73; Maren-Sofie Rostvig, *The Happy Man* (2nd edn, 1971), vol. II, ch. 2; Max Schultz, "The

Circuit Walk of the Eighteenth-Century Landscape Garden and the Pilgrim's Circuitous Progress," *ECS*, 15 (1981), 1–26; and John Dixon Hunt, "Milton and the Making of the English Landscape Garden," *Milton Studies*, 15 (1981), 81–106. For Walpole's important contribution, see I. W. U. Chase, *Horace Walpole: Gardenist* (Princeton, 1943).

83. *Campania Faelix, or, a Discourse of the Benefits and Improvements of Husbandry* (1700), p. 339. When cultivated, he says (p. 2), a spot of ground "seems restor'd to its Primitive Beauty in the State of Paradise."

84. *Ichnographia Rustica*, 2nd edn, 3 vols. (London, 1718), I, 98–99. Switzer frequently quoted from poets, including Milton, in support of his theories.

85. See *Eden: or, A Compleat Body of Gardening* (London, 1757). Hill's book is a technical and practical treatise; its title contains the only allusion to paradise.

86. *The Centaur Not Fabulous* (2nd edn, 1755), p. 83. His garden is more like the medieval *hortus conclusus* than the eighteenth-century landscape garden.

87. By Nicholas Zinzano, formerly attributed to John Laurence (see David Foxon ed., *English Verse, 1701–1750* [Cambridge, 1975], entry Z2). The poem closes with a wish that the poet might "Innocence regain where once 'twas lost."

88. See a letter from Henry Hoare to his nephew Richard, quoted in Schulz, "The Circuit Walk," p. 8, and Gilpin's *Dialogue Upon the Gardens at Stowe* (1748), quoted in Schulz, "The Circuit Walk," p. 10. Joseph Heely's *Letters on the Beauties of Hagley, Envil, and The Leasowes* (1777) quotes *Paradise Lost*, V. 294–96 (slightly adapted) on its title page, implying plainly that these modern gardens recreate Milton's Eden.

89. *Correspondence*, ed. Rae Blanchard (London, 1941), p. 191.

90. *The Censor*, 3, no. 86 (1717), pp. 171–72.

91. *James Thomson, 1700–48: Letters and Documents*, ed. A. D. McKillop (Lawrence, Kansas, 1958), p. 145. Douglas called it the "famous Panegyric on Marriage" (Shawcross, *Critical Heritage*, II, 186).

92. For the fullest discussion of Milton's ideas of marriage, see John Halkett, *Milton and the Idea of Matrimony: A Study of the Divorce Tracts and 'Paradise Lost'* (New Haven, 1970). See in particular p. 92: "For Milton, marriage seems to be a corrective to the Fall, a condition in which it is possible for man to recover some of the happiness and freshness of the primitive world. Certainly man seeks in marriage a kind of emotional fulfillment impossible in any other condition."

93. *Longinus on the Sublime* (London, 1739, repr. 1975), p. 136. Cf. Voltaire: Milton "removes with a chaste Hand the veil which covers everywhere the enjoyments of that Passion. There is Softness, Tenderness and Warmth without Lasciviousness, the Poet transports himself and us, into that State of innocent Happiness in which *Adam* and *Eve* continued for a short time." *Voltaire's Essay on Epic Poetry*, ed. F. D. White (Albany, 1915), p. 133.

94. *The Spectator*, ed. D. F. Bond, 3 vols. (Oxford, 1968), I, 379–80.

95. For a number of eighteenth-century citations of these Miltonic marriage texts, see Ann Gossman and G. W. Whiting, "Milton, Patron of Marriage," *Notes and Queries*, n.s. 8 (1961), 180–81; and Nancy Lee Riffe, "Milton in the 18th-Century Periodicals: 'Hail, Wedded Love'," *Notes and Queries*, n.s. 12 (1965), 18–19. Ms. Riffe counts twenty quotations of

"Hail, wedded love" between 1709 and 1775, and comments that "no other single passage" from *Paradise Lost* "was quoted so frequently." See also Winton Dean, *Handel's Dramatic Oratorios and Masques* (London, 1959), p. 484.

96. "Epistle to Delia," in Chalmers' *English Poets*, VIII, 324. Cf. Thomas Warton, "On the Marriage of the King. To Her Majesty," in Chalmers, XVIII, 93.

97. Shepherd's account (p. 8) of Adam's "Emotions wild" and "Transports of his Heart" when he first inspects Eve's "Charms" makes the prelapsarian marriage sound ironically like the first onset of Adamic lust at the Fall (*Paradise Lost*, IX. 1013–39).

98. *Letters of Mary Wollstonecraft*, ed. Ralph Wardle (Ithaca, 1979), p. 351.

99. *Love Letters of William and Mary Wordsworth*, ed. Beth Darlington (Ithaca, 1981), p. 148. Wordsworth alludes to *Paradise Lost*, IV. 445–47 (actually Eve's words to Adam).

100. See C. A. Moore, "Miltoniana (1679–1741)," *MP*, 24 (1927), 321–24.

101. (London, 1709). Sprint puts considerable emphasis on Eve's transgression: "Because of the Womans Occasion the Man was ruined and undone" (p. 6). Sprint does not cite *Paradise Lost*.

102. The epigraph consists of *Paradise Lost*, X. 888–92, 895–98.

103. *Sex and Sensibility: Ideal and Erotic Love from Milton to Mozart* (Chicago, 1980). For a spirited poetic defense of equality in marriage, see *Wedlock a Paradice* (London, 1701).

104. *Notes and Remarks*, pp. 153–55; Newton, *Life of Milton* (1773 edn), I, 275–76. The relevant scripture is I Cor. 11.

105. *The Family, Sex, and Marriage in England, 1500–1800* (London, 1977).

106. *The Ladies Library*, "written by a Lady," published by Steele, 3 vols. (7th edn, 1772), II, 37. See also the chapter on "Meekness," esp. I, 159.

107. *Some Reflections on Marriage* (3rd edn, 1706), p. 27. Astell did not share Milton's political views; she affirmed the doctrine of passive obedience to a king (but not to a husband).

108. *Universal Spectator*, No. 167 (December 18, 1731).

109. *Gentleman's Magazine*, 8 (June 1738), p. 298; see also *Universal Spectator*, No. 506 (June 1738); and *Gentleman's Magazine*, 1 (December 1731), p. 524.

110. Even Margaret Doody, a sympathetic and admiring reader of the novel, regrets that Grandison is "almost an unfallen Adam, in a world which is still near Paradise. By the discipline of the right will, man can achieve near-perfection, in a life of virtue which is directed to the well-being of society." *A Natural Passion: A Study of the Novels of Samuel Richardson* (Oxford, 1974), p. 272.

111. *The History of Sir Charles Grandison*, ed. Jocelyn Harris, 3 vols. (Oxford, 1972), I, 56–57.

112. See Harris's note.

113. Richardson was probably also remembering Dryden's version of Chaucer's *Knight's Tale*: "His auburn locks on either shoulder flow'd" (*Palamon and Arcite*, III. 924). Cf. also Adam's erected "Stature" and his "far nobler shape erect and tall" (*Paradise Lost*, IV. 288, VII. 509).

114. Adam and Eve are called "our Grand Parents" at *Paradise Lost*, I. 29.

115. *Samuel Richardson: Dramatic Novelist* (London and Ithaca, 1973), pp.

284–89. For Milton's "casuistical habit of mind," as evidenced in both prose and poems, see Camille Slights, *The Casuistical Tradition in Shakespeare, Donne, Herbert, and Milton* (Princeton, 1981), pp. 247–300.

116. Fielding recognized the casuistical importance of this moment by imitating it in *Amelia* (see above, ch. 6).

117. She worries that if Adam does not taste the apple a "different degree" will "Disjoin" them (IX. 883–84).

118. See Dennis Burden, *The Logical Epic* (Cambridge, 1967), pp. 168ff.

119. Both Doody and Kinkead-Weekes find it difficult to admire Grandison.

120. She also disapproved of Milton's divorce tracts, regarding them as self-serving. See Richardson's *Correspondence*, VI, 198.

121. *Correspondence*, VI, 214, 222.

122. Milton could easily have made Adam's choice more painful if Eve had come to Adam in tears, pleading her fear of death. Adam might then have gone to God, and asked that Eve be forgiven. That Milton had Eve return "with countenance blithe" (IX. 886) and a flushed distempered cheek suggests perhaps that Adam should have rejected her. Richardson, in any case, imagines that Sir Charles would leave the matter to God's "pleasure."

123. Kinkead-Weekes, *Richardson: Dramatic Novelist*, p. 289.

124. *Ibid.*, pp. 281–84.

8 Dryden

1. I omit Swift, who knew and occasionally alluded to or parodied Milton in his poems. Were it not for his radical Protestantism, Milton displays qualities – an unflinching personal rectitude, a principled devotion to a cause – that Swift would have admired. See above, pp. 12–13, 30.

2. Prologue to *Aureng-Zebe* (1676), lines 21–22, in *Poems of John Dryden*, ed. James Kinsley, 4 vols. (Oxford, 1958), I, 156.

3. *Works of John Dryden*, ed. E. N. Hooker, H. T. Swedenberg *et al.* (Berkeley, 1961), I, 187–89 (hereafter cited as *Works*). See the recent biographical work by Paul Hammond, "Dryden's Employment by Cromwell's Government," *Transactions of the Cambridge Bibliographical Society*, 8 (1981), 130–36; and the forthcoming biography by James Winn, *John Dryden: A Contextual Biography*, ch. 4.

4. *Works*, I, 209. For an apparent allusion to "Lycidas" in the last decade of his career, see Earl Miner, "Dryden's Admired Acquaintance, Mr. Milton," *Milton Studies*, 11 (1978), 15–16.

5. The remark was first reported by Richardson in *Explanatory Notes and Remarks on Milton's Paradise Lost* (1734, repr. 1973), p. cxx. I quote from Richardson's MS. note in his own annotated copy, as reported by James Winn in his forthcoming biography of Dryden. In the printed text Richardson's phrase reads: "this Man...cuts us All Out, and the Ancients too." For "cut out" Johnson gives "To excel, to outdo" (*Dictionary*).

6. Aubrey is the source for this anecdote. See *Brief Lives*, repr. in *The Early Lives of Milton*, ed. Helen Darbishire (London, 1932), p. 7. H. F. Fletcher dates Dryden's visit to Milton no earlier than June 1673. See *Milton's Complete Poetical Works* (Urbana, 1945), III, 12. W. R.

Parker dates it in February 1674. See *Milton: A Biography* (Oxford, 1968), I, 634.

7. *Works*, XI, 10.
8. "For we have our lineal descents and clans as well as other families." Preface to *Fables*, in *Of Dramatic Poesy and Other Critical Essays*, ed. George Watson, 2 vols. (London, 1962), II, 270 (hereafter cited as Watson).
9. Watson, II, 270–71, 280.
10. Watson, II, 271.
11. *Works*, IV, 84.
12. Watson, II, 281.
13. *Works*, IV, 366; XVII, 73.
14. *Works*, I, 22.
15. *Works*, VIII, 5. Cf. Achitophel, who has bankrupted the family line but will "leave" a wealthy estate to a "shapeless Lump" of a son (*Absalom and Achitophel*, lines 165–70).
16. *Works*, XVII, 16. Dryden quotes from the *Historia Romana*, I. 17.
17. *Works*, IV, 12.
18. Watson, I, 242–43. Dryden quotes from *On the Sublime*, xiii. 4.
19. *Works*, IV, 366; cf. XVII, 72: Jonson, Fletcher, and Shakespeare are "honour'd, and almost ador'd by us, as they deserve; neither do I know any so presumptuous of themselves as to contend with them."
20. Watson, II, 237.
21. *Works*, XVII, 44, 377. Dryden quotes Velleius' Latin from *Historia Romana*, I. 17 (the translation is from the Loeb Library edition). Bate notes that Hume resurrected the long-forgotten remarks of Velleius Paterculus, who had "touched home to very few people before Hume" (*The Burden of the Past and the English Poet* [Cambridge, Mass., 1970], p. 83). Dryden in fact quoted the same passage.
22. *Works*, XVII, 73 (Dryden slightly misquotes from *Georgics*, III. 8–9).
23. *Works*, XVII, 73.
24. *Works*, XVII, 73.
25. "To My Dear Friend Mr. Congreve," *Works*, IV, 432.
26. Miner finds "no evidence at all to suggest that Dryden felt anxiety toward a poetic father," "no Romantic angst over a great predecessor" ("Dryden's Admired Acquaintance, Mr. Milton," pp. 3, 14).
27. In *Early Lives*, p. 7.
28. Watson, I, 196. Note that Dryden's qualifier – "*one* of the greatest poems" – would be dropped by most of Milton's eighteenth-century admirers.
29. *Works*, IV, 14.
30. *Works*, IV, 15; cf. Watson, II, 233.
31. Watson, II, 233.
32. Watson, II, 233; *Works*, IV, 15.
33. *Works*, III, 17.
34. *Works*, III, 17; cf. IV, 15.
35. *Works*, IV, 63.
36. Watson, II, 284.
37. *Works*, XVII, 55.
38. *Works*, IV, 14.

39. *Works*, III, 208. As Dennis pointed out, Dryden's epigram is "nothing but a Paraphrase" of Selvaggi's epigram written while Milton was in Italy. *Critical Works of John Dennis*, ed. E. N. Hooker (Baltimore, 1939–43), II, 170.

40. *Works*, IV, 12.

41. *Works*, IV, 374.

42. "There have been but one great Ilias and one Aeneis in so many ages. The next, but the next with a long interval betwixt, was the Jerusalem: I mean not so much distance in time, as in excellency" (Watson, II, 232).

43. Watson, II, 242.

44. Dryden claims personal knowledge on this point: "Milton has acknowledged to me that Spenser was his original" (Watson, II, 271).

45. Watson, II, 281.

46. Christopher Ricks' suggestion in "Allusion: The Poet as Heir," in *Studies in the Eighteenth Century*, III, ed. R. F. Brissenden and J. C. Eade (Canberra, 1976), p. 233.

47. Watson, I, 191.

48. In five manuscripts the opera carries this title. See M. H. Hamilton, "The Manuscripts of Dryden's *The State of Innocence* and the relation of the Harvard MS to the First Quarto," *Studies in Bibliography*, ed. F. Bowers (1953), 237–46. In the preface to the published play Dryden says that "many hundred [manuscript] copies" were dispersed without his knowledge or consent.

49. Watson, I, 196.

50. It is true that he also refers to it as a "poem" (Watson, I, 195, 196).

51. See Hamilton, "The Manuscripts of *The State of Innocence*," p. 244.

52. It has been suggested that the opera was originally commissioned to celebrate the marriage of James Duke of York to Mary of Modena (to whom Dryden later dedicated the play); and that plans for a court performance were dropped when public festivities were curtailed by opposition to the unpopular Catholic marriage. See W. J. Lawrence, *TLS*, August 6, 1931, p. 606; Milton's *Complete Poetical Works*, ed. H. F. Fletcher (Urbana, 1945), III. 12–13. Robert Hume has suggested to me that *The State of Innocence* might well have been commissioned to inaugurate the new Drury Lane theatre, which opened in March 1674. Costs of mounting a spectacular new opera may finally have required the King's Company – chronically short of money – to open with a cheaper imported French opera, Perin's *Ariane*.

53. *The Life of John Dryden*, by Sir Walter Scott (1834, repr. 1963), p. 163.

54. Dryden's *ad hominem* attack on Milton – the real reason Milton preferred blank verse, he says, is plainly "that rhyme was not his talent" (Watson, II, 85) – is an answer to Milton's own contentious note on the verse of *Paradise Lost*. Morris Freedman has considered *The State of Innocence* in the context of the rhyme-blank verse controversy. See "Dryden's 'Memorable Visit' to Milton," *HLQ*, 18 (1955), 99–108, and "Milton and Dryden on Rhyme," *HLQ*, 24 (1961), 337–44. George McFadden has argued that "interweaving and internal reinforcement of sound, more than concern to justify rhyme, was Dryden's main interest in what proved to be a technical experiment of the first importance for the development of his

poetic style." See "Dryden's 'Most Barren Period' – and Milton," *HLQ,* 24 (1961), 283–96.

55. Saintsbury noticed that by no means all of *The State of Innocence* is in couplets (V, 126). The contrast of Dryden's own blank verse with Milton's "is not such an unequal contrast as prejudice may suggest" (V, 136).

56. Watson, II, 233.

57. D. W. Jefferson has recently suggested that Dryden, mixing "the absurd and the grandiose," characteristically displays "his own imaginative flourishes and favourite sallies of wit" in apparently serious contexts. "Dryden's Style in *The State of Innocence*," *Essays in Criticism*, 32 (1982), 366–67.

58. Critics have noticed this aspect of *The State of Innocence*, from A. W. Verrall, *Lectures on Dryden* (Cambridge, 1914), p. 225, to K. W. Grandsen, "Milton, Dryden, and the Comedy of the Fall," *Essays in Criticism*, 26 (1976), 116–33.

59. It might be noted that in *Religio Laici* Dryden makes very little of the mystery of Christ's sacrifice, but treats it fairly drily in economic terms.

60. The increasing reputation of *Paradise Lost* did not obscure its fame. In 1699 Edward Ecclestone published an opera (never performed) on *Noah's Flood, or, The Destruction of the World*, imitating both *Paradise Lost* and *The State of Innocence. Noah's Flood* was reprinted in 1714 as "The Sequel to Mr. Dryden's Fall of Man." See G. B. Evans, "Edward Ecclestone: His Relationship to Dryden and Milton," *MLR*, 44 (1949), 550–52, and J. R. Baird, "Milton and Edward Ecclestone's *Noah's Flood*," *MLN*, 55 (1940), 183–87.

61. See Anne D. Ferry, *Milton and the Miltonic Dryden* (Cambridge, 1968), p. 24.

62. "Dryden's Charles: The Ending of *Absalom and Achitophel*," *PQ,* 57 (1978), 359–82.

63. See L. L. Brodwin, "Miltonic Allusion in *Absalom and Achitophel*," *JECP*, 68 (1969), p. 28.

64. *Works*, II, 235.

65. *Spectator* 315, repr. in John Shawcross, *Milton: The Critical Heritage* (London, 1970), I, 178–79.

66. "A Character of Charles II," in *The Complete Works of George Savile, First Marquess of Halifax*, ed. Walter Raleigh (Oxford, 1912), p. 198.

67. Cf. *Shamela* (1741), letter X, where "hinder part" is plainly a euphemism for arse.

68. *Milton and the Miltonic Dryden*, p. 116.

69. "David's mildness manag'd it so well, / The Bad found no occasion to Rebell" (lines 77–78). Cf. *OED*, "manage", vb. 5, 6b, 7, 8, 10. Another contemporary, Thomas Burnet, noted Charles's skill at managing: "he thought the great art of living and of governing was to manage all things and all persons with a depth of craft and dissimulation." *History of My Own Time*, ed. Osmund Airy (Oxford, 1897–1900), II, 468.

70. *Works*, IV, 84.

71. *Works*, III, 122. Sanford Budick suggests that "the major heroic constituent" of the poem may be Dryden's use of materials from the Book of Daniel that he later drew on for his sketch of a Christian epic. *Dryden and the Abyss of Light* (New Haven, 1970), p. 192.

72. The similarity between Dryden's "thy throne is darkness in th'abyss of light" (*The Hind and the Panther*, I. 66) and Milton's conception of God as "Fountain of light, thy self invisible / Amidst the glorious brightness where thou sit'st / Throned inaccessible" (*Paradise Lost*, III. 375–77) might lead one to notice that Dryden's several confessional passages in the poem correspond to the personal digressions in *Paradise Lost*. But such correspondences are not specific.

73. See above, ch. 2.

74. *Works*, IV, 16.

75. *Works*, IV, 17.

76. *Works*, IV, 20.

77. *Works*, IV, 23. The accession of William of Orange in 1688 may have helped dissuade Dryden from writing this projected epic.

78. Age, he says, has overtaken him, and "the Change of the Times" (i.e. the Revolution) "has wholly disenabl'd me" (*Works*, IV, 23).

79. Charles Ward, *Life of John Dryden* (Los Angeles and Berkeley, 1961), p. 272.

80. Watson, II, 274.

81. *Poems*, ed. J. Kinsley, 4 vols. (Oxford, 1958), III, 1006.

82. *Poems*, III, 1015. Robert Bell notices this point in passing: "For all the differences between Aeneas and Adam, they both learn that 'to obey is best,' achieving sovereignty over themselves through abnegation." "Dryden's 'Aeneid' as an Augustan Epic," *Criticism*, 19 (1977), p. 39.

83. Richardson, *Explanatory Notes and Remarks*, p. cxx. The remark was made, says Richardson, "when that Work [i.e. the *Aeneid* translation] was in Hand." I see no evidence that Dryden's words are ironic (see Morris Freedman, "Dryden's Reported Reaction to 'Paradise Lost'," *N & Q*, 203 [1958], 14–16). Dennis reported that Dryden at the end of his career (c. 1698–1700) confessed that when he wrote *The State of Innocence* he "knew not half the extent of his [i.e. Milton's] excellence." *Critical Works*, II, 169. The *Aeneis* may not be Dryden's final heroic poem. *Fables Ancient and Modern* (1700), with which Dryden ended his career, may be thought of as a many-paneled "Ovidian" epic. On this point, see the work of Earl Miner, as early as *Dryden's Poetry* (1967), and the more recent work of Judith Sloman.

9 Pope

1. *Correspondence of Pope*, ed. George Sherburn, 5 vols. (Oxford, 1956), I, 10.

2. *Correspondence*, I, 120. Into his copy of the 1645 *Poems* Pope made several transcriptions from the 1673 edition. He also owned two copies of Tonson's 1705 *Paradise Lost* (one of them a gift from Atterbury) and a 1705 edition of *Paradise Regained, Samson Agonistes*, and the minor poems. See Maynard Mack, "A Finding List of Books Surviving from Pope's Library, with a Few That May Not Have Survived," in *Collected in Himself* (Newark, Del., 1982), pp. 424–25.

3. Both the inventory and the will are reproduced in the appendices to Maynard Mack's *The Garden and the City* (Toronto, 1969).

4. See the preface to Newton's edition of *Paradise Lost* (1749).

5. *Correspondence*, III, 231, 240, 270, 327, 330–31.

6. This has been clear since R. D. Havens' *The Influence of Milton on English Poetry* (Cambridge, Mass., 1922).

7. Among the best of these general studies, I cite Reuben Brower, *Alexander Pope: The Poetry of Allusion* (Oxford, 1959); Barbara Lewalski, "On Looking into Pope's Milton," *Etudes anglaises*, 27 (1974), 481–500, repr. in *Milton Studies*, 11 (1978), 29–50; and Peter M. Briggs, "The Children of Light: A Comparative Reading of Milton and Pope," Diss. Yale 1974.

8. " 'Tis esay to mark out the General course of our poetry. Chaucer, Spenser, Milton, and Dryden are the great landmarks for it." Pope to Spence (1736), in *Observations, Anecdotes, and Characters of Books and Men*, ed. James D. Osborn, 2 vols. (Oxford, 1966), I, 178 (No. 410). Elsewhere Pope assigned Milton's "Juvenilia" to "The School of Spenser" (*Correspondence*, IV, 428).

9. Dryden's *Works* (California edition), IV, 14–15.

10. Preface to the *Iliad*, in *Poems of Alexander Pope* (Twickenham edition), VII, 23.

11. He recalled them to Spence in 1743. See *Observations, Anecdotes*, I, 32 (No. 73).

12. *The Grounds of Criticism in Poetry* (1704), in *Critical Works of John Dennis*, ed. E. N. Hooker (Baltimore, 1939), I, 333.

13. *Correspondence*, I, 10–11.

14. *Correspondence*, I, 39.

15. *Correspondence*, IV, 78.

16. W. K. Wimsatt, *The Portraits of Alexander Pope* (New Haven, 1965), p. 180.

17. See a forthcoming study of eighteenth-century portraiture and poetry by Richard Wendorf.

18. Wimsatt, *Portraits of Pope*, p. 182; Wendorf, the forthcoming study cited in the previous note.

19. See Mack, *The Garden and the City*, p. 214, and Wimsatt, *Portraits of Pope*, pp. 365–66.

20. See Mack, *The Garden and the City*, p. 227, and Wimsatt, *Portraits of Pope*, pp. 163–64.

21. Other Drydenian genres which Pope attempted include the dramatic prologue, the Ovidian epistle, the greater ode, and the lesser ode.

22. "A Receipt to Make an Epic Poem," first printed in *Guardian* No. 78 (June 1713), less than three months after Pope contracted with Lintot to produce an English *Iliad*. Reprinted in Pope's *Prose Works*, ed. N. Ault (Oxford, 1936), p. 118.

23. *Prose Works*, p. 120.

24. Postscript to the *Odyssey*, in Twickenham edition, X, 390.

25. Spence, *Observations, Anecdotes*, I, 173 (No. 395).

26. Spence, *Observations, Anecdotes*, I, 197 (No. 459).

27. Postscript to the *Odyssey*, in *Poems*, X, 391.

28. *Peri Bathous, or The Art of Sinking in Poetry*, ed. E. L. Steeves (New York, 1952), p. 41.

29. *Peri Bathous*, ch. 9, in Steeves, p. 39.

30. Preface to the *Iliad*, in *Poems*, VII, 19. Cf. Postscript to the *Odyssey*, *Poems*, X, 390.

31. Postscript to the *Odyssey*, *Poems*, X, 390.

32. Although the context suggests that Pope deplores the violence done to the

Miltonic original, the remark in *Peri Bathous* about the kind of imitation in which "we force to our own Purposes the Thought of others" in fact points toward the practice that Pope commends and adopts. See *Peri Bathous*, ch. 9, in Steeves, p. 41.

33. Spence, *Observations, Anecdotes*, I, 18 (No. 40). *Alcander* was burned on advice of Atterbury c. 1716–17. Of the eleven brief fragments that survive, printed in *Poems* (Twickenham edition), VI, 20–23, none is Miltonic. Throughout this chapter Pope's poems are cited from the Twickenham edition.

34. Spence, *Observations, Anecdotes*, I, 18 (No. 39).

35. Printed in Twickenham edition, VI, 373.

36. Jessides is David, the son of Jesse, who killed Uriah the Hittite in order to marry his wife Bathsheba. To punish him God demanded that the child by David would die (I Samuel 11–12). God later punishes David's sins (of "numbering the people") by sending plague and famine (II Samuel 21, 24).

37. Birch's edition of Milton's prose appeared in 1738, as did *Areopagitica*, with the preface by Thomson. The impending hostilities with Spain – and Walpole's reluctance to go to war – prompted Andrew Millar (the publisher of *Areopagitica*) to publish a new translation of the 1655 *Manifesto of the Lord Protector*, justifying Cromwell's war with Spain. This tract, attributed to Milton by Birch in his 1738 edition, was published along with Thomson's patriotic *Britannia*. (The *Manifesto* may not be by Milton; see *Complete Prose Works*, V, 711–12.) In the same year appeared Akenside's *The Voice of Liberty; or, a British Philippic: A Poem, in MILTONIC Verse Occasion'd by the insults of the Spaniards, and the Preparations for War*. The allusion to Milton serves to invoke both British "liberty" (in prosody and in politics) and British might (the bold and successful England of Cromwell's day). Walpole's corruption at home also came under "Miltonic" attack in 1738. *Miltonis Epistola ad Pollionem*, published in English in 1740 as *Milton's Epistle to Pollio* (attributed to William King), attacks Walpole (as Caesar) from the familiar Opposition point of view. It ends with a tribute to Pope's Horatian satires. Milton's name is apparently borrowed as a symbol of political rectitude.

38. Cf. Pope's earlier use of the mirror figure in the imitation of Horace's *Satire* II. i: "In this impartial Glass, my Muse intends / Fair to expose myself, my Foes, my Friends; / Publish the present Age" (lines 57–59).

39. Cf. *Comus*, lines 12–14: "Some there be that by due Steps aspire / To lay their hands on that golden key / That opes the palace of eternity."

40. *The Readie and Easie Way to Establish a Commonwealth*, in *Complete Prose Works*, VII (rev. edn), 463.

41. Richardson's translation, in *The Early Lives of Milton*, ed. Helen Darbishire (London, 1932), p. 223.

42. Twickenham edition, VI. 376.

43. Though a Roman Catholic Pope would not have been excluded from the Abbey (Dryden was buried there). But he made clear in his will (1744) that he wished to be buried with his parents in Twickenham Church. A monument in the Abbey was also to be scorned since it often reflected only the donor's vanity. Pope thought William Benson, who erected the monument to Milton, was primarily interested in procuring fame for

himself. See *Dunciad*, III. 325, IV. 110n, and the couplet designed for Shakespeare's epitaph, Twickenham edition, VI. 395.

44. Twickenham edition, VI. 404.
45. *Paradise Lost*, IX. 39–43.
46. *Elegia Prima*, lines 73–74.
47. *Epitaphium Damonis*, lines 162–63: "Ipse ego Dardanias Rutupina per aequora puppes / Dicam."
48. See chapter 3, above.
49. They are listed as portraits 62. 1 and 62. 2 in Wimsatt, *Portraits of Pope*, pp. 270–72.
50. Spence, *Observations, Anecdotes*, I, 15 (No. 34).
51. "There is scarce any work of mine in which the versification was more laboured than in my *Pastorals*." Pope to Spence, *Observations, Anecdotes*, I, 175 (No. 400).
52. Pope changed the name from Meliboeus (in the MS.) to Lycidas (in the printed version) perhaps, as the Twickenham editor suggests (p. 46), to recall Milton's elegy.
53. Cf. also *Spring*, line 23 and "Lycidas," line 145. Pope alludes to "Lycidas" at least eight times in his other poems.
54. Cf. "And Seas but join the Regions they divide" (line 400).
55. See Sanford Budick, *The Poetry of Civilization* (New Haven, 1974), p. 121.
56. Twickenham edition, I. 181n. Pope's revision alludes more fully to an earlier and more appropriate divine command (found in Milton but not in Genesis): "Silence, ye troubled waves, and thou deep, peace, / Said then th'omnific Word, your discord end" (*Paradise Lost*, VII. 216–17).
57. Michael Wilding, "Allusion and Innuendo in *Mac Flecknoe*," *Essays in Criticism*, 19 (1969), 355–70; William Kinsley, "Milton, Parody, and Pope: Some Observations on the Poetry of Multiple Allusion," a paper delivered at the 1978 meeting of the American Society for 18th-Century Studies, Chicago.
58. *Paradise Lost*, IX. 928, 980; XI. 457. See also *Samson Agonistes*, lines 493, 736. "Accurst" appears nine times in *Paradise Lost* alone.
59. Cf. *Windsor Forest*, 239 and *Comus*, 262, *Windsor Forest*, 253–54 and "Il Penseroso", 165–66. For a somewhat fuller discussion of Pope's use of Philips, see Dustin Griffin, "The Bard of Cyder-Land: John Philips and Miltonic Imitation," *SEL*, 24 (Summer 1984), 457–60.
60. Spence, *Observations, Anecdotes*, I, 197.
61. Pope's note reads: "*See* Milton, *lib.* 6." In 1717 he added "*of* Satan *cut asunder by the Angel* Michael," Twickenham edition, II. 179n.
62. Cf. *Rape of the Lock*, I. 41–43 and *Paradise Lost*, IV. 677; *Rape of the Lock*, II. 31 and *Paradise Lost*, I. 646–47; *Rape of the Lock*, IV. 88 and *Paradise Lost*, II. 1046.
63. "The Case of Miss Arabella Fermor," in *The Well-Wrought Urn* (New York, 1947), pp. 80–104.
64. Cf. *Rape of the Lock*, I. 107 and *Paradise Lost*, IV. 561–75.
65. For one well-known discussion of the Miltonic parallels, see Aubrey Williams, "The 'Fall' of China and *The Rape of the Lock*,' *PQ*, 41 (1962), 412–25. William Freedman recently suggests that Ariel is a Satanic tempter, urging Belinda not to embrace her humanity. But Pope inverts Milton. In Eden the message not to yield to the tempting bait would have

been angelic admonition. But "what is admirable in the perfect world before the fall is infantine in this fallen world we live in." See "The Garden of Eden in *The Rape of the Lock*," *Renascence*, 34 (1981), p. 36.

66. See Williams, "The 'Fall' of China," p. 419.

67. Twickenham edition, III-i, esp. pp. liii, lxiv, lxxii–lxxiv.

68. This idea is found earlier in Leslie Stephen, *Alexander Pope* (New York, 1880), p. 161.

69. Twickenham edition, III-i, p. lxxiii, and Mack's note to *Essay on Man*, I. 281–84.

70. He wrote "an address to our Saviour, imitated from Lucretius' compliment to Epicurus," but omitted it on the advice of Berkeley. See Spence, *Observations, Anecdotes*, I, 135 (No. 305).

71. Spence, *Observations, Anecdotes*, I, 136 (No. 306).

72. *An Essay on the Genius and Writings of Pope*, 2 vols. (4th edn, 1782, repr. 1969), II, 63–64.

73. Note to I. 70, in his edition of Pope's *Works*, 9 vols. (1797), III. 19–20.

74. *Works*, III. 33n.

75. Lewalski, "On Looking into Pope's Milton," p. 491.

76. *Ibid.*, p. 491.

77. Douglas Canfield, "The Fate of the Fall in Pope's *Essay on Man*," *The Eighteenth Century*, 23 (1982), p. 142.

78. *Ibid.*, p. 148.

79. Pope does not take literally the idea that aspiration to climb the chain of being (*Essay on Man*, I. 241–50) will cause it to break and the whole system to "fall" (Canfield, "The Fate of the Fall," p. 146).

80. I take some phrases in this paragraph from my account of the *Essay on Man* in *Alexander Pope: The Poet in the Poems* (Princeton, 1978), pp. 144–47.

81. *OED*, 3; Johnson's *Dictionary*, 4. Ironically, Johnson misquotes Milton: "I may assert eternal Providence, / And vindicate the ways of God to man.")

82. *Samson Agonistes*, line 475. In *Paradise Regained* the disciples call on God to "arise and vindicate thy glory" (II. 47). The word is not found in the Bible.

83. *Correspondence*, III, 354, referring perhaps to *Essay on Man*, I. 73–76. Cf. *Essay on Man*, IV. 341–46.

84. *Correspondence*, III, 354.

85. On the ultimate need for faith, see Canfield, "The Fate of the Fall," pp. 148–50.

86. Cf. Thomas Edwards, who writes of Pope's inability to "resolve... ideas into coherent unity," and of Pope's awareness of that inability. "Visible Poetry: Pope and Modern Criticism," in *Twentieth Century Literature in Retrospect*, ed. Reuben Brower, Harvard Studies in Literature, vol. 2 (Cambridge, Mass., 1971), pp. 316–17.

87. I have explored this deliberate juxtaposition more fully in *Pope: The Poet in the Poems*, pp. 141–64.

88. *Pope's Dunciad: A Study of its Meaning* (Baton Rouge, 1955).

89. "On Looking into Pope's Milton," p. 494.

90. See especially Donald T. Siebert, Jr., "Cibber and Satan: The *Dunciad* and Civilization," *ECS*, 10 (1976–77), 203–21; and my *Pope: The Poet in the Poems*, pp. 217–78.

91. See Maynard Mack, "'Wit and Poetry and Pope': Some Observations on his Imagery," *Pope and His Contemporaries*, ed. J. L. Clifford and L. Landa (Oxford, 1949), p. 39.
92. Cf. *Dunciad*, III. 54, 59, and *Paradise Lost*, XI. 366, 411–13.
93. Cf. *Dunciad*, III. 73, 79, 101–02, and *Paradise Regained*, III. 265, IV. 365.
94. For the Deist, cf. *Dunciad*, IV. 477 and *Paradise Lost*, IV. 181.
95. Cf. *Dunciad*, II. 63–65, and *Paradise Lost*, II. 947–50. Pope himself points the parody.
96. Cf. *Dunciad*, II. 67 and *Paradise Lost*, VII. 440–41. Again Pope points the parody: "Milton, of the motion of the Swan."
97. Cf. *Dunciad*, IV. 204 and *Paradise Lost*, I. 600–01, II. 302–03.
98. Cf. *Dunciad*, IV. 207 and *Paradise Lost*, XI. 249–50.
99. Cf. *Dunciad*, IV. 200 and *Paradise Lost*, VII. 411–14, II. 201–03.
100. For a fuller treatment of the *Dunciad* as the Triumph of Wit, see my *Pope: The Poet in the Poems*, pp. 269–77.

10 Thomson

1. *James Thomson (1700–1748): Letters and Documents*, ed. A. D. McKillop (Lawrence, Kansas, 1958), p. 74.
2. R. D. Havens, *The Influence of Milton on English Poetry* (Cambridge, Mass., 1922), pp. 123–48.
3. *The Seasons* is quoted from the edition by James Sambrook (Oxford, 1981).
4. Milton says that *Paradise Lost* is "the first" example "in English" of "ancient liberty recovered to heroic poem from the troublesome and modern bondage of rhyming" (the prefatory note to *Paradise Lost* on "The Verse").
5. Saintsbury comments on Thomson's frequent mid-line caesura: "There is nothing more characteristic of Thomson's blank verse than its peculiar broken character." Thomson's lines, he wrote, are "conjoined" rather than (as with Milton) "interfluent" ("the sense variously drawn out from one verse into another," as Milton put it). *The History of English Prosody* (London, 1908), II, 480.
6. "Life of Thomson," in *Lives of the Poets*, ed. G. B. Hill, 3 vols. (Oxford, 1905), III, 298.
7. "Life of Pope," in *Lives of the Poets*, III, 230–32.
8. Milton's paragraph breaks tend to be mere pauses in the dialogue. But what Saintsbury called Thomson's habit of marking the end of his paragraphs with "end catchlines" (*History of English Prosody*, II, 479) perhaps derives from Milton, who occasionally likes to close a verse paragraph with an unbroken line (e.g., I. 26, IV. 609, VII. 242). Thomson also provided visual breaks between his paragraphs. See *The Seasons* (1730, facs. repr. 1970).
9. Even "froze" can be taken as a participle, leaving the sentence with no active verb.
10. Cf. "he with his horrid crew" (*Paradise Lost*, I. 51), "hapless crew" (V. 879), "thou and thy wicked crew" (VI. 277), "he with a crew" (XII. 38), "thou with thy lusty Crew" (*Paradise Regained*, II. 178), "he and his cursed crew" (*Comus*, line 653).

11. Cf. "Heard in Oreb since," (*Paradise Lost*, XI. 74), "though faulty since" (XI. 509), "since called" (III. 495), "fabled since" (*Paradise Regained*, II. 358).

12. In 1750 Lyttelton removed the lines from *Autumn* and printed them separately as "The Return from the Fox-Chace, a Burlesque Poem, in the Manner of Mr. Philips." See Sambrook's edition, pp. lxxv, 321–22.

13. The line between mock-heroic loftiness and the occasional elevation in georgic language (e.g., *Georgics*, Bk. II on the sexual drive in animals) is sometimes a fine one.

14. I borrow the terms from W. K. Wimsatt, "The Augustan Mode in English Poetry," *Hateful Contraries* (Lexington, Ky., 1965), pp. 155, 158. Sambrook has recently drawn salutary attention to the mock-heroic element in Thomson. See the introduction to his edition, p. xxv.

15. Thomson himself told Collins that "the first hint and idea" for *The Seasons* came from Pope's *Pastorals* (Joseph Warton, *Works of Pope* [1797], I, 61 n). But it is difficult to see what else Thomson found in Pope besides the concept of four connected seasonal poems. See note 45, below.

16. A. D. McKillop, *The Background of Thomson's "Seasons"* (Minneapolis, 1942), p. 2.

17. The one clear borrowing from "Il Penseroso" is line 11, "Now wrapt in some mysterious dream." But Thomson probably also took from Milton the figures of Contemplation and the Hermit.

18. See Sambrook, p. xxxv.

19. *Letters and Documents*, p. 18; Sambrook, p. xxviii.

20. *Letters and Documents*, p. 16.

21. Compare L'Allegro and Il Penseroso who listen to the song of Orpheus that would have set Eurydice free. Cf. *Winter*, lines 33–39, with its allusions to *Comus*, lines 6–7, 376–79.

22. *Letters and Documents*, p. 45.

23. In a 1726 letter to Mallet, enclosing a draft of lines 183–306 of the 1727 version, Thomson says he "raises the Sun to nine, or ten, o'clock" (*Letters and Documents*, p. 40).

24. Almost all these lines are retained in the later editions of *Summer*. See also lines 331ff, 451ff, 467ff, and 494ff in the 1727 edition.

25. There is a minor allusion to "L'Allegro," lines 139–40 ("Such sights as youthful poets dream / On summer eves by haunted stream") at line 12.

26. Sambrook recently claims a strong subjective element in Thomson's descriptions: "He is concerned less with natural objects 'themselves' than with the emotional, intellectual, and devotional experience of a consciousness responding to those objects" (p. xxxii). I agree, but would note first that that consciousness is by no means an idiosyncratic or private one, and that it responds not consistently but variously. When Sambrook goes on to claim that "the poet is his own subject" (p. xxxiv) he goes too far.

27. It is perhaps not surprising that Thomson became a dramatist in the 1730s.

28. Lines 970–73 of *Autumn* first appeared in *Winter* (1726), lines 40–43.

29. For a full catalogue of Thomson's "Models and Sources," see the critical edition by Otto Zippel, in *Palaestra*, 66 (1908), pp. xxxii–xl. See also the "parallels" cited in Havens, *The Influence of Milton*, pp. 583–90.

30. First noted by James Beattie, *Dissertations Moral and Critical* (1783), p. 626.

31. Cf. the "common Hymn" sent up by all Earth's tribes in *Summer*, line 120,

and the "Hymn" from the "Chorus of this lower World" in *Summer*, line 1238.

32. The gales that "Breathe soft" derive from Milton's winds that "Breathe soft or loud" (VII. 193). God, "Riding sublime" on the "Whirlwind's Wing" (lines 18–19) derives from Christ who "rode sublime" on the "wings of cherub" (*Paradise Lost*, VI. 771).

33. See also the end of *Summer* in which Thomson expresses the faith that despite "this dark State," our end will be formed by God's "boundless LOVE and perfect WISDOM" (lines 1800–04).

34. For the strongest account of *The Seasons* as an Augustan devotional poem, see Ralph Cohen, *The Unfolding of The Seasons* (London, 1970).

35. *Winter*, line 1067; "A Hymn [on the Seasons]," line 114.

36. *Letters and Documents*, p. 170.

37. 1727 edition. In 1744 Thomson blurred the allusion. Cf. also *Autumn*, line 1030 and *Paradise Lost*, I. 303–04; *Autumn*, lines 783–84 and *Paradise Lost*, III. 431–32.

38. "Full-orbed" also recalls Satan's dream-temptation of Eve, when he speaks to her of the "full-orbed...moon" (V. 42).

39. Eighteenth-century editors regularly comment on these similes.

40. Thomson elsewhere quotes from the same speech (I. 254): "The Mind is it's own Place" (*Letters and Documents*, p. 166).

41. Cf. a letter of condolence in which Thomson alludes to *Lycidas*: "true Happiness is not the Growth of this mortal Soil, but of those blessed Regions where [the deceased] now is" (*Letters and Documents*, p. 170). Cf. *Lycidas*, lines 78, 81: "Fame is no plant that grows on mortal soil, / ... But lives and spreads aloft."

42. Cf. "decrepit winter" and "Solstitial summer's heat ... scarce tolerable," which begin at the Fall (*Paradise Lost*, X. 654–56).

43. See Sambrook's note.

44. They are "new-form'd Hills" in one manuscript version.

45. Cf. *Spring*, lines 902–03, "We feel the present DEITY, and taste the Joy of GOD to see a happy World!"

46. An intermediary text might have been *Spectator* No. 425 (July 8, 1712), attributed to Pope by Norman Ault (*Prose Works* [Oxford, 1936], pp. xlix–l, 49–55). After reciting lines from "Il Penseroso" the writer reflects on "the sweet Vicissitudes of Night and Day, on the charming Disposition of the Seasons, and their Return again in a perpetual Circle" (p. 51). Cf. *Guardian* No. 169 (September 24, 1713), also attributed to Pope (Ault, *Prose Works*, pp. lxviii–lxx): "the Vicissitudes of Night and Day, Winter and Summer, Spring and Autumn, the returning Faces of the several Parts of Nature" (p. 139).

47. Shaftesburian benevolism and a faith in material and moral progress are prominent themes in *The Seasons*, but as Sambrook and Cohen note they are often carefully qualified. See Sambrook, pp. xxvi–xxvii.

48. Thomson's use of Milton's Eden as metaphor naturally involves some generalizing of particulars but it also entails some loss of power: Thomson's lovers, unlike Milton's, would startle nobody's (false) sense of propriety, and his language sometimes blurs into cliché.

49. *Paradise Lost*, IX. 1087, IV. 246, XI. 741; *Comus*, line 127. Thomson's lines first appeared in *Winter* and were transferred to *Autumn* in 1730.

50. "Stooping through a fleecy cloud" (line 72).
51. "A Flood of Glory burst from all the Skies" (VIII. 696). Milton too had written of "liquid Light" (*Paradise Lost*, VII. 362).
52. Cohen comments on the evening passage in *Autumn* (*Unfolding of The Seasons*, pp. 219, 229–31) but he does not note the allusions to Milton.
53. Reproduced in Jean Hagstrum, *The Sister Arts* (Chicago, 1958), Plate XXIII.
54. Hagstrum makes this point (*ibid.*, p. 253).
55. The "Hymn to Solitude" and the poem "To the Memory of Newton" are cited from *The Seasons* (1730, repr. 1970, Menston, Yorkshire), pp. 246–47.
56. Cf. the evening in *Autumn* when rolling fogs "swim along / The dusky-mantled Lawn" (1087–88).
57. Cf. the flood that turns a plain into a "brown Deluge," or the spring thaw that produces "one slimy Waste" (*Winter*, lines 77, 997). What is of concern to Thomson charmed some mid-century poets. Cf. Gray's familiar "Now fades the glimmering landscape on the sight" ("Elegy," line 5), derived perhaps, as Roger Lonsdale thinks (*The Poems of Gray, Collins, and Goldsmith* [London, 1969], p. 119), from Mallet: "th'aerial landscape fades. / Distinction fails: and in the darkening west, / The last light quivering, dimly dies away" (*The Excursion*, I. 235–37).
58. "Life of Thomson," in *Lives of the Poets*, III, 299.

11 Johnson

1. *Remarks on Johnson's Life of Milton* (1780, repr. 1974), p. 131.
2. In a letter to William Unwin, in Cowper's *Letters and Prose Writings*, ed. James King and Charles Ryskamp, vol. I (Oxford, 1979), p. 307.
3. *Life of Milton* (2nd edn, 1796, repr. Gainesville, Fla., 1970), p. 103.
4. J. P. Hardy (ed.), *Johnson's Lives of the Poets* (Oxford, 1971), p. xiii.
5. "Life of Milton," in *Lives of the Poets*, ed. G. B. Hill, 3 vols. (Oxford, 1905), I, 172.
6. *An Introduction to the Political State of Great Britain* (1756), in *Political Writings*, ed. Donald Greene (New Haven, 1977), p. 134. Cf. *The False Alarm*, p. 342. Johnson may have honored the Stuart family, but as Greene notes his Toryism "included little idolatry of King Charles the Martyr" (p. 69n). Johnson would have equally condemned the murder of any English king.
7. See Chapter 1, pp. 16–17.
8. *Life of Blake*, in *Works*, 12 vols. (London, 1810), XII, 42–43.
9. *Life of Cheynel*, in *Works* (1810), XII, 194.
10. Nichols reports Johnson as saying: "This Mr. Hollis…was a bigotted Whig, or Republican; one who mis-spent an ample fortune in paving the way for sedition and revolt in this and the neighboring kingdoms, by dispensing democratical works." J. Nichols, *Illustrations of the Literary History of the 18th Century* (London, 1831), VI, 157.
11. In the fifth volume (1771) of her *History of England*, Mrs. Macaulay wrote of Milton's "deep sagacity of political science." In a debate over copyright laws, she praised Milton for his "attempt of fixing the ideas of good government and true virtue in the minds of a wavering people." *A Modest Plea*

for the Property of Copy Right, in the *Critical Review*, 37 (1774), 214–21. Milton makes only a brief appearance in Wilkes' 1768 Introduction to his proposed *History of England from the Revolution to the Accession of the Brunswick Line*. William Harris, nonconformist clergyman and friend of Birch and Hollis, published *An Historical and Critical Account of the Life and Writings of Charles I* (1758, repr. 1772), sharply critical of the Stuarts, and glowing in praise of Milton, "a name at all times to be mentioned with honour" (II, 45), whose works "greatly contributed" to the struggle for "natural equality" and "freedom."

12. *Remarks on Johnson's Life of Milton* (1780, repr. 1974), p. 3.

13. And yet in the paragraph immediately following the account of Milton's republicanism, Johnson notes in Milton's domestic relations and in his books "something like a Turkish contempt of females, as subordinate and inferior beings" (I, 157).

14. In an essay on Milton's versification (*Rambler* 86) Johnson notes that "there are in every age new errors to be rectify'd, and new prejudices to be opposed. False taste is always busy to mislead those that are entering upon the regions of learning." *Works* (Yale edn), IV, 88.

15. The point has been made before that Johnson in the *Lives* was writing a "critique of the critics." See Benjamin Boyce, "Samuel Johnson's Criticism of Pope," *RES*, 5 (1954), 37–46; F. W. Hilles, "The Making of the *Life of Pope*," in *New Light on Dr. Johnson*, ed. Hilles (New Haven, 1959), 257–84; M. W. Booth, "Johnson's Critical Judgments in *The Lives of the Poets*," *SEL*, 16 (1976), 505–16. V. M. Bell has noted that Johnson is sometimes "responsive less to Milton's poetry than to his critics" ("Johnson's Milton Criticism in Context," *English Studies* 49 [1968], 127–32).

16. There were of course other reasons why Johnson disapproved of *Lycidas*: pastoral elegy seemed to him an exhausted and inherently improbable genre; the mixing of "trifling fictions" and "sacred truths" offended his religious principles. See above, p. 54.

17. As Bell has noted, *Ramblers* 86, 90, and 95 were probably written in reaction to Newton's praise of Milton's prosody in his 1749 edition.

18. *Life of Samuel Johnson* (London, 1787), pp. 275–76.

19. Printed in Johnson's *Works* (1810), VIII, 9–22.

20. *Johnsonian Miscellanies*, ed. G. B. Hill (Oxford, 1897), I, 398.

21. There remain some unanswered questions in the episode. It is not clear when Johnson turned against Lauder. It is not clear what part, if any, he had in suppressing an early anti-Lauder letter to the *Gentleman's Magazine*. See James Clifford, "Johnson and Lauder," *PQ*, 54 (1975), 343–56, and the series of articles by Michael Marcuse (see above, ch. 2, note 8).

22. Newton was perhaps mistranslating Milton's Latin. Milton in the *Second Defense* had written "Paterno rure...evolvendis Graecis Latinisque scriptoribus summum per otium totus vacavi" (i.e., *totus per otium* = entirely at ease, or entirely devoted to my leisure).

23. Cf. *Lives of the Poets*, I, 85, 146, 147.

24. Cowper is in fact remarking on the following sentence in the *Life*, where Johnson mockingly says of Milton, "There are hours, he knows not why, when 'his hand is out'." See J. Copley, "Cowper on Johnson's *Life of Milton*," *N & Q*, 24 (1977), p. 314.

25. Joseph Ivemey, "Animadversions upon Dr. Johnson's Life of Milton," in *John Milton, His Life and Times, Religious and Political Opinions* (London, 1833, repr. 1970): "Did he not *envy* him on account of the superiority of his learning, talents, and fame? Not, it should seem, from any consciousness of his inferiority to him either, but from knowing that if his own name should happen to be mentioned at the same time with MILTON, it would only be for the purpose of its being used as a foil to set off his rival's pre-eminent knowledge and benevolence" (p. 350). Hayley, with higher regard for Johnson, would "rather ascribe to any causes than to mere envious malignity, his outrages against the poetical glory of Milton" (p. 223). But in the end he offers no other explanation.

26. *The Burden of the Past and the English Poet* (Cambridge, Mass., 1970), p. 24.

27. See ch. 2, pp. 13, 23.

28. After briefly describing Milton's "art of education," Johnson offers a long "digression" on educational schemes, including an outline of one of his own. While a schoolmaster, Johnson composed his own "Scheme for the Classes of a Grammar School." It is reprinted in Boswell's *Life of Johnson*, ed. G. B. Hill, rev. L. F. Powell, 6 vols. (Oxford, 1934–50), I, 99–100.

29. In dismissing Milton's sonnets Johnson said, "Milton, Madam, was a Genius that could cut a Colossus from a rock; but could not carve heads upon cherry-stones." Boswell's *Life of Johnson*, IV, 305.

30. Johnson's own ironic *Compleat Vindication of the Licensers of the Stage* (1739) is in Donald Greene's words "not unworthy to be mentioned in the same breath as its archetype, Milton's *Areopagitica*" (*Political Writings*, p. 55).

31. *Life of Johnson*, IV, 427–28.

32. *Life of Johnson*, II, 239.

33. *An Apology for Smectymnuus*, in *Complete Prose Works*, I, 890.

34. See chapter 2, pp. 27–32, above.

35. Johnson also remarks on self-confidence in Dryden (*Lives of the Poets*, I, 395), Addison (II, 120), and Pope (III, 89).

36. *Life of Johnson*, I, 185–86.

37. George Irwin, *Samuel Johnson: A Personality in Conflict* (Auckland, 1971), p. 44.

38. Later in the same tract Milton speaks of "those few talents which God at present lent me."

39. On wonder as a "pause of reason," see the "Life of Yalden," in *Lives of the Poets*, II, 302–03.

40. See the "Life of Cowley," in *Lives of the Poets*, I, 20–21.

41. This is common in the *Rambler* essays. D. M. Hill suggests that in the discussion of *Paradise Lost* Johnson is engaged in "scholastic disputation, arguing at one point wholeheartedly in favor of [the poem], and at another point wholeheartedly against it" ("Johnson as Moderator," *N & Q*, 201 [1956], 518).

42. In the *Dictionary* Johnson mentions "interesting" only as a derivative of the verb *interest*, "To affect; to move … as, this is an *interesting* story." As a noun ("human interest") the term means, he says, "share; part in any thing; participation; as, this is a matter in which we have *interest*." J. R. Brink ("Johnson and Milton," *SEL*, 20 [1980], 493–504) finds Johnson's remarks "only superficially contradictory" (p. 498), and finds the *Life* a balanced assessment of Milton's strengths and weaknesses.

43. *Samuel Johnson, Biographer* (Ithaca, 1978), p. 178. Folkenflik's two perspectives are derived from Johnson's own famous discussion of wit in the "Life of Cowley."

44. Cf. Joseph Towers' *Essay on the Life, Character, and Writings of Dr. Samuel Johnson* (1786): "There is something curious in tracing the conduct of Johnson with respect to Milton, and in observing the struggle there was in his mind concerning him" (p. 57). Towers goes on to attribute the "struggle," however, to Johnson's "reverence" for the poet as opposed to his "rooted dislike" for the political writer.

45. Robert Folkenflik, in an essay on "Johnson's Heroes," has recently noted how Milton is for Johnson "the poet as hero." See *The English Hero, 1660–1800*, ed. Folkenflik (Newark, Del., 1982), p. 164.

46. Even here, though, we may find a defensive countermovement in Johnson's mind. If Milton is to be admired rather than imitated, Johnson is let off the hook. If he is a hero, he is after all "like other heroes" (I, 194), and can thus be pigeon-holed. Johnson is condemned to succeed Milton, but Milton himself is in the end a successor to Homer: "his work is not the greatest of heroick poems, only because it is not the first" (I, 194).

12 Cowper

1. *Letters and Prose Writings*, ed. James King and Charles Ryskamp (Oxford, 1979), I, 308. Where possible, I quote Cowper's letters from this edition, now in progress.

2. *Correspondence*, ed. Thomas Wright, 4 vols. (London, 1904), IV, 305.

3. *The Late Augustans* (London, 1958), p. xxvii.

4. *Letters and Prose Writings*, III, 579. Cf. also III, 362, 597.

5. In his early "Dissertation on the Modern Ode" (1763) Cowper satirized the vogue for imitation of Milton's shorter poems.

6. *Letters and Prose Writings*, I, 307.

7. Preface to the first edition of Cowper's translation of the *Iliad*, in *Iliad*, 2 vols. (1810), I, xxv; see also pp. xxiv, xxvii, and the Preface to the second edition, *ibid.*, pp. xxxvi–xxxvii; letters to Bagot (August 31, 1786) and Lady Hesketh (March 6, 1786), in *Correspondence*, III, 92, and II, 480.

8. *Correspondence*, II, 280.

9. The epithets are Havens', in *The Influence of Milton on English Poetry* (Cambridge, Mass., 1922), pp. 165, 169.

10. See *Letters and Prose Writings*, III, 570, 572, 577–79, 588, 591–92, 594. The *Proposals* for the edition were published in London on September 1, 1791.

11. Cowper had earlier (c. 1780) translated Dryden's epigram on Milton into Latin. See *Poems*, ed. John Baird and Charles Ryskamp (Oxford, 1980), I, 223. About 1790 he wrote "Stanzas protesting the late indecent liberties taken with the remains of the great Milton," denouncing the disinterment of Milton's coffin.

12. It ultimately appeared in the *Latin and Italian Poems of Milton*, ed. Hayley (London, 1808), from which I quote, and, with Hayley's *Life*, in *Cowper's Milton*, 4 vols. (Chichester, 1810), II, 425–69.

13. *Correspondence*, IV, 373.

14. The image of Milton in the dream may also reflect the presentation of Milton's character in Hayley's apologetic *Life*, published in 1794 but no doubt discussed with Cowper during the years of composition.

15. Not published until 1816, when it appeared as *A Memoir of the Early Life of William Cowper*, it has recently been reprinted from an early manuscript source as *Adelphi*, in *Letters and Prose Writings*, ed. King and Ryskamp, I, 1–61.

16. *Adelphi*, in *Letters and Prose Writings*, I, 18, 28, 37.

17. Despair was Cowper's own hellish prison. Even a description of the Bastille's "cages of despair," where men languish "Immured though unaccused, condemned untried, / Cruelly spared, and hopeless of escape" (*The Task*, V. 383–445), suggests the despairing sinner's condition. Even more Miltonic is an account of the fallen state of "revolted man," who, like Satan, plunges "in the fathomless abyss... in heav'n-renouncing exile," suffering an "unrepealable enduring death" (*The Task*, V. 593–610).

18. Cf. the gypsies in *The Task*, Bk. I: "Strange! that a creature rational, and cast / In human mould, should brutalize by choice / His nature" (574–76). The guilt expressed in Cowper's letters in October 1792 concerning the uncompleted Commentary seems disproportionate to the failing, and suggests his dread of judgment: "the consciousness that there is much to do, and nothing done, is a burthen I am not able to bear. Milton especially is my grievance; and I might almost as well be haunted by his ghost, as goaded with continual reproaches for neglecting him." The letter is quoted by Hayley in the *Latin and Italian Poems of Milton*, pp. xxiv–xxv.

19. "In the year when I wrote The Task, I was very often most supremely unhappy, and am under God indebted in good part to that work for not having been much worse." *Correspondence*, II, 444.

20. Not all of Cowper's poems have yet appeared in the Oxford English Texts edition by John Baird and Charles Ryskamp. Accordingly I have adopted the following policy: poems from the period 1748–82 are quoted from the Baird/Ryskamp *Poems*, vol. I. *The Task* and all post-1785 poems are quoted from Cowper's *Poetical Works*, ed. H. S. Milford, 4th edn (London, 1934, rev. 1967).

21. For other allusions to Eden and the Fall, see *Conversation*, line 751, *The Progress of Error*, line 468, *Table Talk*, line 584, *Charity*, line 24, and *The Task*, V. 619–23.

22. In his Commentary (at II. 496) Cowper notes that Milton's intrusive reflections have been censured by critics, but he defends them as valuable.

23. Cf. the Miltonic beginning to Bk. I, "I who lately sang / Truth... / Escap'd with pain from that advent'rous flight," alluding to *Paradise Regained*, I, and *Paradise Lost*, I.

24. Two other details in the passage are Miltonic. The linking of "pleasure" and "ease" recalls *Paradise Lost*, XI. 794, "pleasure, ease, and sloth" (the life of Noah's contemporaries) and *Paradise Regained*, IV. 299, "In Corporal pleasure he, and careless ease" (a description of the Epicurean). "Devious course uncertain," though not found in Milton, is an invented Satanism. It might well describe Satan's motion through chaos or in the garden.

25. Richard Feingold notes briefly that we "can glean suggestions in his

gardening of the prelapsarian magic of Adam's work in Eden." *Nature and Society: Later Eighteenth-Century Uses of the Pastoral and Georgic* (New Brunswick, N.J., 1978), p. 168. I find the Miltonic allusions more pervasive and more ambiguous than does Feingold.

26. Cowper's study at Weston, where he composed his poems, was an old converted greenhouse.

27. Cf. *The Task*, VI. 348–458, where Cowper traces cruelty to animals back to man's original sin. Other allusions tie Cowper's garden to Milton's. Cf. *The Task*, III. 443, "vernal airs breathe mild," and *Paradise Lost*, IV. 264–65, "vernal airs, / Breathing the smell of field and grove"; *The Task*, III. 490, "the voluble and restless earth," and *Paradise Lost*, IV. 594, "this less voluble earth."

28. "Love Abused," in a letter to Unwin, July 27, 1780, in *Poems*, ed. Baird and Ryskamp, I, 231, and *Letters and Prose Writings*, ed. King and Ryskamp, I, 371.

29. Cf. also a minor evening piece in which Night, "from the east, in majesty sedate / And slow progression comes, with shade o'er shade / Of growing darkness." "Evening and Night," *Gentleman's Magazine*, 30 (1760), p. 586.

30. For a more naturalized evening scene, see the description of the "fleecy shower" of snow (*The Task*, IV. 322–32) which silently, slowly, and softly alights as a gladly received "thickening mantle." Milton's moonlight paradoxically offers a protective cloak, Cowper's snow a "warm...veil."

31. Cf. the poems by Langhorne and the Wartons quoted earlier, ch. 6, p. 77.

32. The Calvinist God may stand behind another pastoral figure in *The Task*, "Benevolus", identified in Cowper's note as John Courtney Throckmorton, a local landowner near Weston, who provided Cowper access to his park:

> The folded gates would bar my progress now,
> But that the Lord of this inclosed demesne,
> Communicative of the good he owns,
> Admits me to a share: the guiltless eye
> Commits no wrong, nor wastes what it enjoys.
>
> (I. 331–35)

The "gates," "inclosed demesne," and communicated "good" all suggest that Cowper projects onto "Benevolus" his own hopes to find a benevolent God.

33. Christopher Ricks comments on the passage from Milton in *Milton's Grand Style* (Oxford, 1963), pp. 69–72.

Afterword: notes toward an eighteenth-century theory of literary influence

1. "Imitation as Freedom: 1717–1798," in *Day of the Leopards* (New Haven, 1976), pp. 117–39. The essay was written in 1968.

2. "Tradition and the Individual Talent," in *Selected Essays*, 2nd edn (London, 1934), p. 14. The essay was written in 1919.

3. In *Milton's Poetry of Choice and its Romantic Heirs* (Ithaca, 1973), Leslie

Brisman notes how Wordsworth "shows his relationship with Milton to be a matter of conscious choice, not unconscious influence with its attendant anxieties about discovery and inadequacy" (p. 235).

4. John Paul Russo, *Alexander Pope: Tradition and Identity* (Cambridge, Mass., 1972).

5. For a fuller discussion of the "seeming diffidence" in Pope's early poems, see Dustin Griffin, *Alexander Pope: The Poet in the Poems* (Princeton, 1978), pp. 71-99.

6. Pope to Spence, March 1743, in *Observations, Anecdotes and Characters of Books and Men*, ed. James D. Osborn, 2 vols. (Oxford, 1966),I, 24 (No. 55).

7. Howard Weinbrot, *Alexander Pope and the Traditions of Formal Verse Satire* (Princeton, 1982). Cf. Dryden, who speaks in the Preface to *All for Love* of the "differences in style" between Shakespeare and Fletcher, "and wherein, and how far, they are both to be imitated." *Of Dramatic Poesy and other Critical Essays*, ed. George Watson, 2 vols. (Oxford, 1962), I, 231.

8. Spence, *Observations, Anecdotes*, I, 21 (No. 47).

9. Brower's phrase in *The Poetry of Allusion* (Oxford, 1959), p. 165.

10. See *The Dunciad*, Twickenham edition, pp. 230-35.

11. *Lectures on Rhetoric and Belles Lettres*, quoted in Bate, *The Burden of the Past and the English Poet* (Cambridge, Mass., 1970), p. 62.

12. From the title of the last chapter of his *Essay on Original Genius* (1767), slightly misquoted in Bate, *The Burden of the Past*, p. 50.

13. *The Works of John Dryden* (California edition), IV, 432.

14. Johnson, "Life of Denham," in *Lives of the Poets*, ed. G. B. Hill, 3 vols. (Oxford, 1905), I, 75, misquoting Prior, who had credited Davenant and Waller.

15. Johnson, "Life of Pope," in *Lives of the Poets*, III, 238.

16. Dubos's *Réflexions critiques sur la poésie et sur la peinture* (1719), tr. into English by Thomas Nugent (1748). For a recent discussion, see W. C. Edinger, "The Background of *Adventurer* 95," *MP*, 78 (1980), 14-37.

17. *Adventurer* 95, *Works* (Yale edition), vol. II, *The Idler and The Adventurer*, ed. W. J. Bate *et al.* (New Haven, 1963), pp. 428-29.

18. *Rambler* 121 (Yale edition), IV, 282. The inexhaustible variety of nature and "the combinations of the powers of art yet untried" are recurrent Johnsonian themes. See *Ramblers* 23, 124, 129.

19. William Duff, *An Essay on Original Genius* (1767, repr. 1964), p. 266.

20. *Ibid.*, pp. 277, 289-90.

21. Dryden's Preface to *All for Love*, in Watson, I, 221.

22. If we remember the fate of the suitors, we might wonder if Dryden's allusion also contains his own suppressed doubt about the success of any contender.

23. Dryden endeavors, he says, to be "an upright Judge betwixt the Parties in Competition." Chaucer, he notes with pride, "carries Weight" in his contest against Boccaccio, "and yet wins the Race at disadvantage" ("Preface to *Fables*," in *Poems*, ed. J. Kinsley, 4 vols. [Oxford, 1958], IV, 1452, 1460. Cf. "To Oldham," lines 9-10, the footrace in which Nisus falls and Euryalus wins, an analogue to Dryden's own race with Oldham).

24. See Bate, *The Burden of the Past*, p. 83.

25. *Longinus on the Sublime*, tr. William Smith (1739, repr. 1975), pp. 37-38.

26. *Observations on Pope* (London, 1796), p. 248.
27. Bate, *The Burden of the Past*, pp. 82–83. See also Young: "Let not the blaze of even Homer's muse darken us to the discernment of our own powers." *Conjectures on Original Composition*, ed. F. J. Morley (Manchester, 1918), p. 53.
28. Hurd, *Discourse on Poetical Imitation*, in *Works*, 8 vols. (1811), II, 240.
29. *Conjectures on Original Composition*, p. 48.
30. Trapp, *Lectures on Poetry* (1742, repr. 1969), p. 351. Trapp's lectures first appeared in Latin in 1711.
31. Hurd, *Works*, II, 229.
32. Dryden, Preface to *The Mock Astrologer*, in Watson, I, 147.
33. Warton, *Observations on the Faerie Queene*, II, 150.
34. Felton, *A Dissertation on Reading the Classics* (1713, repr. 1971), p. 44.
35. *Ibid.*, p. 45.
36. Richardson, *Works* (1792), p. 88.
37. Hurd, *Works*, II, 232–33.
38. "Preface to *Fables*," in *Poems*, IV, 1450.
39. Hurd, *Works*, II, 230.
40. *Correspondence*, ed. G. Sherburn, 5 vols. (Oxford, 1956), I. 20. Pope probably had in mind Dryden's earlier remark that "mutual borrowing, and commerce, makes the common riches of learning" (Watson, II, 81). See above, ch. 8.
41. For a contrary view, see Roger Lonsdale, who argues that beginning about mid-century Gray and his contemporaries reflect an increasing concern about the need to be original, and to avoid borrowing or plagiarism. "Gray and 'Allusion': The Poet as Debtor," *Studies in the Eighteenth Century*, IV, ed. R. F. Brissenden and J. C. Eade (Canberra, 1979), pp. 31–55.
42. "Preface to *Fables*," in *Poems*, IV, 1450; *Essay of Dramatick Poesie*, in *Works*, XVII, 21.
43. "Preface to *Fables*," in *Poems*, IV, 1445, 1450, 1456.
44. *Complete Plays of William Congreve*, ed. Herbert Davis (Chicago, 1967), p. 391.
45. Philips, *Poems on Several Occassions*, 3rd edn (London, 1720), p. 5.

INDEX

Note: This index is limited to substantive references, primarily to proper names, titles of Milton's works, and selected topics of critical or historical interest. Brief or passing references (without substantive interest) are omitted. I have not attempted to index each reference to "Milton" or to "*Paradise Lost*," or to the topics of imitation and influence.